TEACHER'S RESOURCE

Global Studies

GLOBE FEARON EDUCATIONAL PUBLISHER
A Division of Simon & Schuster
Upper Saddle River, New Jersey

Director of Editorial and Marketing, Secondary Supplementary: Nancy Surridge
Executive Editor: Jean Liccione
Senior Editor: Karen Bernhaut
Project Editor: Lynn Kloss
Assistant Editor: Brian Hawkes
Editorial Assistants: Ryan Jones and Kathleen Kennedy
Market Manager: Rhonda Anderson
Production Director: Kurt Scherwatzky
Production Editor: Alan Dalgleish
Art Directors: Pat Smythe and Mimi Raihl
Interior Design: Mimi Raihl
Cover Design: Marsha Cohen
Cover Art: Friedrich Fischbach, Owen James, N. Simakoff
Editorial Development: WestEd, Ink
Electronic Page Production: Jan Ewing

Printed in the United States of America 2 3 4 5 6 7 8 9 10   00 99 98 97

ISBN 0-835-92218-9

GLOBE FEARON EDUCATIONAL PUBLISHER
A Division of Simon & Schuster
Upper Saddle River, New Jersey

CONTENTS

REPRODUCIBLE MASTERS

UNIT 2: FOCUS ON SOUTH AND SOUTHEAST ASIA

UNIT 3: FOCUS ON EAST ASIA

UNIT 4: FOCUS ON LATIN AMERICA AND CANADA

UNIT 5: FOCUS ON THE MIDDLE EAST

UNIT 6: FOCUS ON EUROPE AND EURASIA

OUTLINE MAPS

ACKNOWLEDGMENTS

Grateful acknowledgment is made to the following publishers, authors, and copyright holders:

p. 126: *The Heritage Library of African People: Akamba* by Tiyambe Zeleza, Ph.D. © The Rosen Publishing Group. Proverbs reprinted by permission of the Rosen Publishing Group. **p. 127:** Illustration © by *World Press Review*. Reprinted by permission of *World Press Review*. **p. 128:** Poem "Daybreak" by Susan Lwanga © Heinemann Publishers (Oxford Limited). Globe Fearon has executed a reasonable and concerted effort to contact the copyright holder of the poem and eagerly invites that party to contact Globe Fearon to arrange for the customary publishing transactions. **p. 180:** Illustration by Arcadio, Costa Rica, Cartoonists and Writers Syndicate. **p. 201:** Illustration © by The Royal Academy of Denmark. Globe Fearon has executed a reasonable and concerted effort to contact the Royal Academy of Denmark to arrange for the customary publishing transactions and eagerly invites that party to contact Globe Fearon to arrange for the customary publishing transactions. **p. 204:** Excerpt from the Nobel lecture of García Márquez printed in *The New York Times*, February 6, 1983. Globe Fearon has executed a reasonable and concerted effort to contact the copyright holder of the speech and eagerly invites that party to contact Globe Fearon to arrange for the customary publishing transactions. **p. 228:** Poem "Drive" by Gersham Ben-Avraham. Globe Fearon has executed a reasonable and concerted effort to contact the author of the poem and eagerly invites that party to contact Globe Fearon to arrange for the customary publishing transactions; **p. 252:** Excerpt from *Open Letters* by Vaclav Havel. Copyright © 1991 by Vaclav Havel. Reprinted by permission of Alfred A. Knopf, Inc. **p. 253:** From *The Poems, Prose and Plays of Alexander Pushkin* by Alexander Pushkin. Copyright © 1936 and renewed 1964 by Random House, Inc. Reprinted by permission of Random House, Inc. **p. 255:** Illustration © The Buffalo Evening News. Reprinted by permission of The Buffalo Evening News.

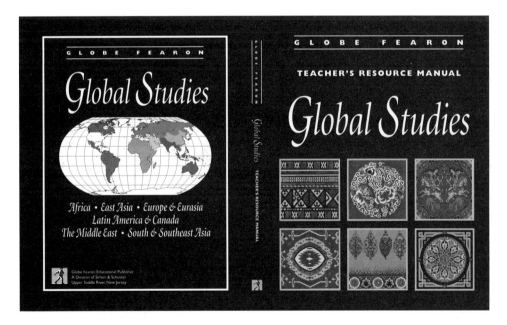

TEACHING THE COVER: Have students read "About the Cover" on page iii of the student text. Then, as students learn about the cultures of a particular region, encourage them to research the arts of those cultures. Have students compare the motifs on the cover of *Global Studies* to other artwork of the same region. Ask students to describe any similarities and differences that they see. Then ask them to think about the ways in which the arts reflect cultural beliefs and traditions.

OVERVIEW

Globe Fearon's Global Studies

The concept of the global village has existed for a number of years. In a global village, the people of the world recognize that although they live in sovereign nations, they are citizens of the world at large. Today, we are closer to living in a global village than ever before. Economically, politically, and geographically, the nations of the world are inextricably linked to one another. In addition, those of us who live in the United States live in a multicultural nation. Students in today's world need to develop an understanding and respect for people and cultures in their own nation and around the world. Globe Fearon's *Global Studies* hopes to contribute to building that understanding and respect.

Globe Fearon's *Global Studies* consists of one student book and one Teacher's Resource Manual. The student book introduces students to the geography, history, economics, and cultures of the following world regions:

- Africa
- South and Southeast Asia
- East Asia
- Latin America and Canada
- The Middle East
- Europe and Eurasia

THE STUDENT TEXT

Organization: The student text is organized into an Introduction and six units of study. The Introduction presents the general concept of culture and the basic principles of geography, including the five themes. Each unit presents the cultures, geography, politics, economics, and history of one of the world's major cultural and geographic regions: Africa, South and Southeast Asia, East Asia, Latin America and Canada, The Middle East, and Europe and Eurasia.

Units: Each unit opens with a three-page preview of the region. The first two pages provide a list of chapters in the unit; a three-tiered time line that presents key events in history, culture, and technology; and questions about the time line. The third page is called "Exploring Regional Issues." This page introduces students to one critical issue affecting the region and helps students build social studies skills, such as interpreting maps, graphs, and charts that relate to the issue.

Chapters: Each unit contains either six or seven chapters. Chapters open with a list of key terms and their definitions, as well as an ongoing "On Assignment" activity. Case Studies in each chapter provide a highly engaging inside look at a specific person, place, or event in the region. Section reviews, chapter reviews, and unit reviews check the understanding of concepts and critical thinking skills, offer closure to the ongoing assignment, and provide cooperative learning activities.

Features: Each unit contains two special features. The "Global Issues" feature emphasizes the interdependence of nations by addressing critical issues that impact more than just one region, such as environmental preservation, global urbanization, and enhanced telecommunications. This feature helps students to recognize that different regions of the world face common problems and often cooperate to find solutions. A "Taking Action" project further involves students in the issue through activities such as researching, conducting panel discussions and interviews, and writing political correspondence.

The "Literature Connection" introduces students to the poetry, fiction, and nonfiction of the world's cultures. Through the literature and primary source documents provided, students gain further insight into the values and beliefs of specific cultures. A short introduction provides background information about the selection and questions check students' understanding of the selection and its relevance to the culture.

An atlas of world, regional, and country maps; a glossary of key terms; and an index are provided at the back of the book.

THE TEACHER'S RESOURCE MANUAL

The Teacher's Resource Manual for each book provides you with NCSS correlations, lesson plans, reproducible worksheets, tests, outline maps, and a complete answer key.

NCSS correlations: The Teacher's Resource Manual contains a grid of the ten thematic strands for social studies as outlined by the National Council for the Social Studies. Specific page numbers for each chapter of *Global Studies* indicate where and how the chapter addresses each strand. Please note that the page references given are not exhaustive and are intended to highlight coverage of the strands in each chapter.

Unit lesson plans: A lesson plan for each unit contains a list of chapters in the unit, unit objectives, suggestions for teaching the time line and "Exploring Regional Issues" page, a checklist of worksheets, tests and maps that correspond to the unit, suggestions for enriching the "Literature Connection," and strategies for teaching the "Global Issues" feature.

Chapter lesson plans: Each lesson plan includes chapter objectives, a preview activity, an activity with which to develop each lesson, an ESL/LEP activity or a visual learning activity, an activity to close the lesson, support for the On Assignment and Working Together activities, and an extension activity.

Alternative Assessment: The On Assignment activity in each chapter and the Taking Action activity in each unit provide alternative assessment opportunities. Guidelines for scoring the On Assignment activity are included in the chapter lesson plans.

Reproducibles: There are three sets of reproducible worksheets. The first series of worksheets support the "Exploring Regional Issues" features in each unit opener. The second set supports the On Assignment activities in each chapter. The last set of worksheets are Critical Thinking Activity Worksheets. These worksheets reinforce and extend content through the application of critical thinking skills such as analyzing maps and charts and interpreting primary sources.

Outline maps of the world, regions, and countries provide opportunities for creative activities. Many of the lesson plans feature ideas that use these outline maps.

A one-page test for each chapter and a two-page test for each unit allow you to easily assess your students' understanding of the content.

CORRELATIONS TO NCSS STANDARDS*

	Culture	Time, Continuity, & Change	People, Places, & Environments	Individual Development & Identity	Individuals, Groups, & Institutions
UNIT 1: FOCUS ON AFRICA, PAGES 10-104					
CHAPTER 1 The Land and People of Africa, pp. 13-26	Identifying the people of Africa. Understanding that there are many cultures in Africa, pp. 21-24. Comparing East African culture to life in the United States, p. 26.	Acknowledging that people and cultures change through time because of a number of factors, pp. 13-26.	Identifying the regions of Africa and their physical and climatic characteristics, pp. 14-20. Recognizing how geography has influenced life in Africa, pp. 13-26.	Understanding that the peoples of Africa are influenced by their history, pp. 21-25. Explaining why English is spoken in Nigeria, p. 24.	Developing an awareness of the role of religion in Africa, p. 22-24.
CHAPTER 2 The Early History of Africa, pp. 27-38	Understanding how history affects culture in Africa, pp. 27-38.	Exploring the histories of the Nilotic kingdoms, the West African kingdoms, the East African city-states, pp. 28-34.	Explaining the importance of the Nile River in the development of Egyptian civilization, pp. 28-29. Recognizing the significance of the location of natural resources in the gold-salt trade, p. 31.	Identifying the causes and effects of the Atlantic slave trade on West Africans, pp. 35-37. Understanding how the slave trade affected a particular individual, p. 37.	
CHAPTER 3 Traditional Patterns of Life in Africa, pp. 39-47	Exploring the culture of the peoples of Africa, pp. 39-47.	Understanding how cultures change through time, pp. 39-47.	Explaining the way in which people's cultures are shaped by their environments and how people shape their environments, pp. 45-46.	Discussing the role of elders, children, and adults in traditional African societies, pp. 40-45. Explaining how an initiation ceremony establishes one's place in traditional African society, p. 43.	Understanding the role of the family in traditional African society, pp. 40-41. Describing how age sets influence society, p. 41. Exploring the importance of the Council of Elders, pp. 44-45.
CHAPTER 4 Modern History of Africa, pp. 48-61	Explaining the clash of European cultures and African cultures during the Age of Imperialism, pp. 49-55.	Discussing the history of Africa from European domination to the movement for independence, pp. 48-61.	Describing the physical features that delayed European exploration of Africa's interior until the mid-1800s, pp. 49-50.	Understanding what motivated European explorers such as David Livingstone to explore the African interior, pp. 49-51.	Exploring how Africans such as Shaka reacted to European domination, pp. 52-57. Explaining how European governments divided the African continent, pp. 52-54.
CHAPTER 5 Changing Patterns of Life in Africa, pp. 62-73	Explaining how African culture has changed in recent times, pp. 63-72.	Understanding how such movements as religious fundamentalism, urbanization, and population growth, have affected Africa, pp. 63-69.	Describing how urbanization affects culture in Africa, pp. 66-67.	Discussing how the role of women is changing in Africa today, pp. 64-65. Describing the changes in education in Africa today, p. 65.	
CHAPTER 6 Economic and Political Trends, pp. 78-91	Understanding how the physical boundaries drawn during the Age of Imperialism have affected African culture, pp. 79-82.	Explaining how history has affected politics and economics in Africa today, pp. 79-90.	Exploring the ways in which physical boundaries drawn by colonial powers have affected Africans, pp. 79-82.	Exploring the causes and effects of apartheid in South Africa, pp. 79, 89-90.	Explaining how the forces of culture shape the government and economy of the nations of Africa, pp. 79-90.

*The page numbers listed in this chart are not exhaustive and are intended to highlight coverage of the strands in each chapter.

Power, Authority, & Governance	Production, Distribution, & Consumption	Science, Technology, & Society	Global Connections	Civic Ideals & Practices
		Understanding how dams control flooding on the Nile and produce hydroelectricity, p. 17.	Explaining the effect of colonialism on languages spoken in Africa, p.24.	
Discussing the role of the pharaoh in ancient Egypt, p. 29. Recognizing the position of kings such as Mansa Musa, in West Africa, p. 31.	Explaining how the gold and salt trade brought great wealth to West African kingdoms, p. 31. Describing the trade of the city-states of East Africa, pp. 33-34. Understanding the effects of the Atlantic slave trade on West Africa's economy, p. 36.	Describing the pyramids of ancient Egypt, p. 28. Discussing how iron changed life in Africa, p. 30.	Explaining how Islam came to Africa, pp. 31-32. Understanding the effects of the movement of millions of Africans to the Americas during the Atlantic slave trade, pp. 35-37.	
Understanding the roles of chiefs, healers, councils of elders, and consensus in traditional African society, pp. 42, 44-45.	Describing how African villagers support themselves, pp. 45-46.	Discussing the technologies African villages use to farm and make a living, pp. 45-46.		Explaining the meaning of citizenship in terms of traditional African society, pp. 39-47.
Discussing the sources of power during the Age of Imperialism, pp. 51-55. Identifying the leaders of independence movements in Africa, pp. 55-60.	Explaining the effects of imperialism on Africa's economy, pp. 54-55, 60.	Understanding the causes and effects that European-built railroads, the telegraph, and telephones had on Africa, pp. 54-55.	Explaining how World War II and pan-Africanism contributed to nationalism and independence movements in Africa, pp. 55-57.	Describing how most European imperialists treated Africans during the colonial era, pp. 58-60.
Explaining how religious fundamentalism may affect government in Africa, pp. 63-64.	Discussing the economic causes of urbanization, pp. 66-67.	Describing the impact of the African film industry on culture, p. 71.	Understanding the global influence of African art, p. 71.	
Understanding the challenges many African nations have encountered in their struggles to create stable governments, pp. 79-83, 89-90.	Describing the impact of multinational corporations on Africa's economy, p. 84. Understanding why many African nations are saddled with heavy debt, p. 86.			Discussing how the status of blacks and other peoples of color in South Africa changed after the abolition of apartheid, pp. 79, 89-90.

11

	Culture	Time, Continuity, & Change	People, Places, & Environments	Individual Development & Identity	Individuals, Groups, & Institutions
CHAPTER 7 Africa in the World Today, pp. 92-102	Discussing the impact diversity has in Africa today, pp. 94-98.	Describing how historical conflicts have led to civil wars in such nations as Burundi and Rwanda, pp. 96-97.	Understanding how drought affects the people of Africa, pp. 97-98. Discussing how Africans are working to preserve their environments, pp. 98-101.	Explaining how civil wars, famine, drought, and other disasters affect individual Africans, pp. 96-98. Understanding the importance of education to Africans, pp. 95-96.	Discussing the concept of tribalism in determining authority in Africa, pp. 96-97.

UNIT 2: FOCUS ON SOUTH AND SOUTHEAST ASIA, PAGES 108-201

	Culture	Time, Continuity, & Change	People, Places, & Environments	Individual Development & Identity	Individuals, Groups, & Institutions
CHAPTER 8 The Land and People of South and Southeast Asia, pp. 111-122	Identifying the people of South and Southeast Asia and understanding the many cultures in this region, pp. 118-121.	Acknowledging that people and cultures change through time due to a number of factors, pp. 112-121.	Identifying the main physical and climatic regions of South and Southeast Asia, pp. 112-117.	Understanding that the people of South and Southeast Asia are influenced by their history, pp. 119-121.	Understanding that people have brought different governments, economies, and religions to the region, p. 121.
CHAPTER 9 The History of South Asia, pp. 123-134	Understanding how the forces of history affect culture in South Asia, pp. 124-133.	Understanding how culture in South Asia has changed through time, pp. 124-133.	Explaining how invaders have come through the mountains in the north and how the seas have allowed for contact with other cultures, p. 124-127.	Discussing how religion has affected South Asians, pp. 124-129, 130. Describing the effects of colonialism on people such as Mohandas Gandhi, pp. 131-132.	Explaining how the British affected the government, economy, and culture of the Indian subcontinent, pp. 129-132.
CHAPTER 10 Changing Patterns of Life in South Asia, pp. 135-142	Explaining how culture in South Asia has changed over-time, pp. 136-141. Describing traditional and modern trends in art and literature in South Asia, 139-141.	Describing the challenges India will face in the future, pp. 137-139.	Identifying major environmental problems facing South Asia, p. 138.	Describing how and why women's roles have changed, pp. 136-137.	Explaining why education is a key to success in South Asia, p. 139.
CHAPTER 11 South Asia in the World Today, pp. 147-158	Understanding how culture influences governments and economies in South Asia, pp. 148-154.	Explaining how South Asia's history has affected politics, economics, and foreign relations today, pp. 148-157.	Understanding that most farmers use traditional farming methods in South Asia today, p. 150. Describing the effects of floods and cyclones on Bangladesh, p. 153.	Explaining how Benazir Bhutto became the first woman to lead Pakistan, p. 157.	Describing the role of the National Congress Party in India, p. 148.
CHAPTER 12 The Heritage of Southeast Asia, pp. 159-168	Explaining how ancient kingdoms and European colonization of the region affected culture, pp. 160-167.	Identifying the effects of history on the cultures of Southeast Asia, pp. 160-167.	Discussing how Southeast Asia's natural resources and location made it attractive to Europeans, pp. 162-165.		Explaining how colonization affected the government, economy, and culture of the countries of Southeast Asia, pp. 164-165.
CHAPTER 13 Changing Patterns of Life in Southeast Asia, pp. 169-176.	Explaining how culture in Southeast Asia has changed through the years, pp. 169-175. Describing traditional and modern trends in art and literature in the region, pp. 173-175.	Identifying the elements of Southeast Asian culture that have changed and that have remained the same, pp. 170-175.	Explaining that most people farm the land in traditional ways in Southeast Asia, pp. 170-171.	Describing how some women's lives have changed in Southeast Asia, p. 172.	Explaining the role of the family in Southeast Asia, pp. 170-172. Discussing the role of education in Southeast Asia, p. 172.

Power, Authority, & Governance	Production, Distribution, & Consumption	Science, Technology, & Society	Global Connections	Civic Ideals & Practices
	Explaining how civil war, drought, and famine affect Africa's economy, pp. 96-98. Understanding the potential of ecotourism for some African nations, pp. 99-101.	Explaining the technologies Africans are employing to ease health problems, pp. 94-95.	Identifying the international organizations African nations belong to, pp. 93-94. Discussing why nations in other parts of the world are concerned with Africa's condition, pp. 93-94, 96-97, 100.	
Recognizing the role that religion plays in the governance of the region, p. 121.				
Describing the Maurya empire under Asoka, p. 128. Describing how the British gained power in India, pp. 129-131. Explaining how Mohandas Gandhi became a leader in India's drive for independence, pp. 131-133.	Understanding that Europeans wished to control trade in South Asia, pp. 129-130.		Explaining how World War II contributed to feelings of nationalism and independence in India, pp. 131-132.	Discussing Gandhi's strategy of using non-violent methods to gain independence for India, pp. 131-133.
	Recognizing that most people who move to the cities do so to find work and educational opportunities, p. 138-139.	Describing the effects of the chemical leak in Bhopal, India, in 1984, p. 138.		
Discussing the structure of government and major leaders in India, pp. 148-149. Describing power and government in Pakistan, Bangladesh, Sri Lanka, Bhutan, and Nepal, pp. 151-154.	Describing the economic challenges India faces, pp. 149-151.	Explaining the need for new technology to improve agricultural output in India, p. 150.	Describing how the countries of South Asia relate to other countries of the world, pp. 154-156.	
Describing the push for independence after World War II in Southeast Asia, pp. 165-167.	Understanding that the reason European countries colonized in Southeast Asia was to extract the region's natural resources, p. 164.	Explaining how the introduction of factory-made goods in Southeast Asia changed the region, p. 164.	Describing how the United States got involved in Vietnam after World War II, pp. 166-167.	
Describing the role of consensus in local government, p. 171.	Recognizing that most people farm for a living in Southeast Asia, pp. 170-172.			

	Culture	Time, Continuity & Change	People, Places & Environments	Individual Development & Indentity	Individuals, Groups, & Institutions
CHAPTER 14 Southeast Asia in the World Today, pp. 177-186	Describing how urbanization is changing culture in Southeast Asia, pp. 180-181.		Explaining the effects of the Green Revolution in Southeast Asia, pp. 180.	Discussing how the repression of democracy in some countries has led to the rise of political leaders who are fighting for democracy, pp. 181-182.	
CHAPTER 15 Australia, New Zealand, and Oceania, pp. 187-199	Describing the indigenous cultures of Australia, New Zealand and Oceania, pp. 191-192, 196-197. Explaining the effect of Europeans on indigenous cultures, pp. 191-193.	Understanding how cultures in the regions have changed through time, pp. 191-197.	Identifying the main physical and climatic regions of Australia, New Zealand, and Oceania, pp. 188-191.	Understanding that the peoples of the regions are influenced by their history, pp. 191-197.	Describing Australia and New Zealand's relationship to Great Britain, pp. 194-195.

UNIT 3: FOCUS ON EAST ASIA, PAGES 204-297

	Culture	Time, Continuity & Change	People, Places & Environments	Individual Development & Indentity	Individuals, Groups, & Institutions
CHAPTER 16 The Land and People of East Asia, pp. 207-220	Identifying who the people of East Asia are, pp. 214-219. Understanding that there are many cultures in East Asia, pp. 214-215.	Understanding that people and cultures change through time due to a number of factors, pp. 214-217	Identifying the regions of East Asia and their physical and climatic characteristics, pp. 208-214. Recognizing how geography has influenced the way in which the people of East Asia live, pp. 207-214.	Understanding that the peoples of China, Japan, and Korea have long interacted, pp. 214-215.	Developing an awareness of the role of language as a unifying factor in China, p. 215.
CHAPTER 17 China: The Longest History, pp. 222-234	Understanding how Chinese cultural development grew out of its long history, pp. 223-233. Understanding how the meeting of Europeans and Chinese involved a clash of cultures, pp. 227-228.	Exploring the histories of the Chinese dynasties, pp. 223-233.	Explaining the importance of the Yellow and other river valleys in the development of Chinese civilization, pp. 222-223.	Identifying the importance of Confucian ideas in the development of Chinese traditional values, pp. 223-225. Understanding how the Boxer Rebellion was caused by Western domination of China, p. 228.	
CHAPTER 18 The History of Japan and Korea, pp. 235-246	Exploring the cultural development of Japan and Korea, pp. 236-238, 242-243. Explaining why so many Koreans have the family name Kim or Lee, p. 245.	Exploring the histories of Japan and Korea, pp. 236-245.	Explaining the way in which the cultures of Japan and Korea were shaped by their proximity to China, pp. 236-242.	Discussing the role of samurai, shoguns, and daimyo in Japan, p. 237.	Understanding the role of feudalism in medieval Japan, p. 237. Describing the role of the military in Japanese expansion in the 1930s, p. 241. Exploring the role of Confusianism in Korea, p. 243.

Power, Authority, & Governance	Production, Distribution, & Consumption	Science, Technology, & Society	Global Connections	Civic Ideals & Practices
Understanding that there are many types of governments in Southeast Asia, pp. 181-182.	Identifying the main natural resources of Southeast Asia, p. 182.	Understanding the effects of the Green Revolution on agriculture in Southeast Asia, p. 180.	Describing the relationships of the countries of Southeast Asia with one another and with countries outside the region, pp. 183-184.	Understanding why gaining a voice in government is important to the people of Southeast Asia, pp. 181-182.
Explaining how the British took control of Australia and New Zealand, pp. 191-194.	Understanding how the Great Depression of the 1930s affected Australia and New Zealand, p. 194. Explaining why Australia and New Zealand's economic relationship with Great Britain changed in the 1970s, pp. 194-195.		Describing Australia, New Zealand, and Oceania's relationship with the nations of the world, pp. 194-195, 197.	
Understanding the role of the Dalai Lama as the spiritual leader of the Tibetan people, pp. 218-219.		Understanding how dams control flooding on China's rivers and provide hydroelectricity, p. 212.	Explaining why the Dalai Lama was awarded the Nobel Peace Prize in 1989, pp. 218-219.	
Discussing the role of the "mandate of heaven" in supporting rule by the emperors, p. 223. Recognizing the reasons why the power of the central government declined, pp. 226-228.	Discussing how the European division of China into colonial spheres was prompted by the desire to control China's resources and markets, pp. 227-228.	Describing how early governmental authority grew out of the effort to build dikes to keep the Yellow River from flooding, p. 222.	Explaining how European penetration of China reduced the country to powerlessness, pp. 227-228.	Recognizing the conflict of philosophies and ideals among participants in the Chinese civil war of the 1930s and 1940s, pp. 230-233.
Examining the ways that shoguns gained power in Japan, p. 238. Understanding the impact of Commodore Perry's visit to Japan, p. 239. Explaining how the Meiji Restoration modernized Japan, pp. 239-240. Explaining the reasons why Korea was divided into two nations after World War II, p. 244.	Describing how the Japanese economy was strengthened during the Meiji Restoration, p. 240.	Discussing why Japan imported technology from the West beginning in the late 19th century, pp. 239-240.		Weighing whether nuclear weapons should have been used to defeat Japan in World War II, p. 241.

	Culture	Time, Continuity, & Change	People, Places, & Environments	Individual Development & Identity	Individuals, Groups, & Institutions
CHAPTER 19 Changing Patterns of Life in East Asia, pp. 247-256	Exploring the way tradition and change mix in the different cultures of East Asia, pp. 248-254.	Understanding the historical role of Confucianism, Daoism, and Buddhism in Chinese life, p. 248. Understanding the historical role of Shintoism in Japan, p. 251.		Understanding the role of the martial arts in contemporary Japanese society, p. 249. Understanding the progress that women have made in Japanese society, p. 252.	Explaining how communism has transformed China in the past half century, pp. 249-250. Discussing the importance of the family in the cultures of China, Japan, and Korea today, pp. 249, 252, 254.
CHAPTER 20 China Today, pp. 257-266	Explaining how a Communist value system has replaced the traditional culture of China, pp. 258-262.	Understanding how the Great Leap Forward and the Cultural Revolution changed China, pp. 258-261.	Describing Mao's rule in China, pp. 259-260. Describing the assault in Tienanmen Square in 1989, p. 263.	Discussing how the role of women is changing in China, p. 261. Describing changes in education in China today, pp. 261-262.	Explaining how the Communists clamped down on dissent and reduced political freedoms in China, p. 260.
CHAPTER 21 Japan and Korea Today, pp. 271-282	Exploring the cultural traits that played a key role in Japan's "economic miracle," pp. 274-275. Recognizing how the lives of Tomoko and Hiroshi Matsuko are similar to and different from that of American youths, p. 278.	Explaining why the American occupation of Japan was able to help build a world-class economy and a thriving democracy, pp. 272-273. Explaining why Korea was split in two parts after the end of World War II and why it has remained split, pp. 279-281.	Recognizing how the environment of Tokyo has had a major impact on the lives of a family that lives in the Tokyo metropolitan area, p. 278. Explaining how Kim Il Sung's rule had a long-term effect on the political environment in North Korea, pp. 280-281.	Exploring how Tomoko Matsuko is working to achieve her personal goals within the framework of her environment and her family's means, p. 278.	Understanding how the Constitution of Japan reflects the values of postwar Japan, p. 272.
CHAPTER 22 East Asia and the World Today, pp. 283-295	Describing how the cultures of Hong Kong blend Chinese and British ways, pp. 288-289.	Identifying the major stages in China's foreign relations, 284-286. Identifying the major stages in Japan's foreign relations, pp. 291-294.	Identifying the major turn in the Cold War when President Richard Nixon journeyed to China in 1972, p. 286. Understanding the crucial nature of relations between China and Taiwan, p. 290.		

UNIT 4: FOCUS ON LATIN AMERICA AND CANADA, PAGES 300-398

	Culture	Time, Continuity, & Change	People, Places, & Environments	Individual Development & Identity	Individuals, Groups, & Institutions
CHAPTER 23 The Land and People of Latin America, pp. 303-316	Identifying who the people of Latin America are and understanding that there are many cultures in Latin America, pp. 309-311, 314-315.	Acknowledging that people and cultures change through time due to a number of factors, pp. 303-316.	Identifying the regions of Latin America and their physical and climatic characteristics, pp. 304-309, 312-313. Recognizing how geography has influenced the way in which people in Latin America live, pp. 303-316.	Understanding how the Aymará are shaped by their culture and environment, pp. 314-315.	

Power, Authority, & Governance	Production, Distribution, & Consumption	Science, Technology, & Society	Global Connections	Civic Ideals & Practices
Describing how communism consolidated its power in China after 1948, pp. 249-250.	Explaining how the Chinese attempted to break the power of the landlords in the years after their seizure of power, p. 251. Explaining changes in industry instituted by the Communists, p. 252.	Understanding how Japanese educational practices built a strong sense of group loyalty and how in business, workers are expected to share ideas and cooperate, p. 252.	Describing how Japanese concepts of business organization and quality control are achieving worldwide prominence, p. 252.	
Describing how Communist rule in China has caused much turmoil, p. 258. Describing how Mao's Cultural Revolution created a radical environment that left China and the Communist party deeply divided, pp. 258-259.	Discussing the farms established by the Communists during the Great Leap Forward, p. 258. Discussing how moderates have attempted to reform the Chinese economy since 1977, pp. 259-260. Discussing how a prosperous free market economy has developed off shore from China on the island of Taiwan, pp. 260-261.	Describing the impact of Communist rule on the arts and literature in China, p. 262.	Understanding how Taiwan's status has become a major international issue, pp. 264-265. Understanding how the outside world recoiled in shock at the repression of Chinese dissenters in the 1980s and 1990s, pp. 260-261, 263.	Understanding how Chinese dissenters fighting for more democracy have been punished severely for asserting their rights, pp. 260-261, 263.
Understanding why the rule of the Liberal Democratic party satisfied the needs of the Japanese people for almost 40 years, pp. 273-274. Understanding the differences between the government of North Korea and South Korea, pp. 279-281.	Recognizing that Japan's "economic miracle" grew out of a concerted national effort to transform the country from a feudal economy, pp. 274-277. Describing the nature and scope of South Korea's "economic miracle," p. 280. Explaining how North Korea has imposed strict controls on economic activity in a desire to gain self-sufficiency, pp. 280-281.	Explaining how Japan has gained world leadership in the exploration of new technologies to meet the challenges of international competition, p. 275.	Understanding the global impact of Japan's economic transformation, p. 275. Recognizing that the division of Korea into two parts is a major problem that threatens international peace, pp. 279-281.	Recognizing the similarities and differences between Japan's system of parliamentary democracy and the system in the United States, p. 273.
Understanding the transitional status of the present-day British colony of Hong Kong and its prospects when sovereignty is transferred to China, pp. 288-289. Recognizing the complexity of the relationship between Taiwan and China, p. 290.	Understanding how Japan's transformation into an economic powerhouse has affected the world balance of trade, pp. 291-292.	Explaining how Japan's technological superiority has made it both a valued ally and a potential threat to other nations of East Asia, pp. 292-294.	Identifying the major issues involved in China's relations with the United States, Russia, and the nations of Asia, pp.285-290. Identifying the issues involved in Japan's relations with the United States, China, Russia, and Southeast Asia, pp. 291-294.	Debating how the United States can maintain its friendship with Japan and improve its relations with China and still maintain its security and keep its economy strong, pp. 286-287, 291-294.
	Identifying some of Latin America's natural resources, pp. 305.		Exploring the impact of recent immigration to Latin America from Asia, p. 309.	Discussing what the term *American* means within the context of North and South America, p. 309.

	Culture	Time, Continuity & Change	People, Places & Environments	Individual Development & Identity	Individuals, Groups, & Institutions
CHAPTER 24 The Early Civilizations of Latin America, pp. 317-327	Describing the effects of Latin America's early civilizations on the cultures of the region today, pp. 318-323.	Exploring the affects of ancient kingdoms such as the Maya, Aztec, and Inca on Latin American society today, pp. 319-322.	Explaining how the Aztecs altered their environment to create the city of Tenochtitlán, pp. 320-321.		
CHAPTER 25 Breaking the Grip of the Crown, pp. 328-339	Explaining how domination of much of Latin America by Spain created a blend of cultures in the region, pp. 329-332	Discussing the history of Latin America and how it affects the region today, pp. 329-338.	Describing how Spain, Portugal and other European countries divided Latin America, pp. 329-331. Understanding the role of geography in preventing the formation of federations in Central and South America after independence, pp. 335-336.	Explaining how the Roman Catholic Church affected individuals such as Sor Juana, p. 332. Describing how slavery affected people such as Toussaint L'Ouverture, p. 333.	Describing the role of Spain in establishing social and political order in its American colonies, pp. 330-331. Understanding the role of the church in converting Native Americans, p. 330.
CHAPTER 26 Changing Patterns of Life in Latin America, pp. 340-350	Exploring the roots of culture in Latin America and how culture has changed in modern times, pp. 341-345.	Describing how urbanization has changed Latin America, pp. 345-347.		Exploring the influence of the Roman Catholic Church on everyday life, pp. 342-433. Understanding the importance of the family in the development of individuals in Latin America, pp. 343-344.	Understanding the role of the Roman Catholic Church in Latin America, pp. 342-343.
CHAPTER 27 The Changing Face of Latin America, pp. 351-363	Understanding how economics and politics in Latin America have affected culture, pp. 352-359.	Explaining how history has affected politics and economics in Latin America, pp. 352-359.	Discussing land reform in Latin America in recent times, pp. 352-354. Understanding the issues regarding the natural resources of Latin America, pp. 355-356.	Explaining how efforts to institute land reform affect farmers, pp. 352-354 . Discussing how poverty affects individuals, pp. 354-355.	Discussing how political changes have affected individuals in Latin America, pp. 357-359.
CHAPTER 28 Latin America and the World, pp. 364-375	Describing art and literature in Latin America, pp. 370-371.	Discussing U.S. relations with Latin America through time, pp. 365-367. Describing how and why Latin America's role in the world is changing, pp. 367-369.	Understanding how Latin America's location near the United States has affected the region's history, economy, and culture, pp. 365-370.		Explaining how commonwealth status has affected Puerto Rico, pp. 365, 372-373.

Power, Authority, & Governance	Production, Distribution, & Consumption	Science, Technology, & Society	Global Connections	Civic Ideals & Practices
Understanding the power of emperors in Aztec and Incan society, pp. 320-321, 322-323. Discussing how Hernan Cortés and other European explorers established authority over the Aztecs, pp. 323-325.	Describing the trade that took place in an ancient Mayan marketplace, p, 319. Explaining how tribute helped make the Aztec empire wealthy, p. 321.	Identifying the scientific achievements of the Mayas, Aztecs, and Incas, pp. 319-323.	Describe the impact of European exploration in the Americas on the Mayas, Aztecs, and Incas, p. 323-325.	
Explaining the authority of Spain and other colonial powers in the Americas, pp. 330-331. Describing how leaders such as Simón Bolívar and Toussaint L'Ouverture gained power in the struggle for independence pp. 333-335. Describing how power changed hands in Mexico during the revolution, pp. 336-338.			Explaining the relationship between the United States and Mexico during the 1800s, p. 336.	Comparing the meaning of citizenship in colonial America and in post-independence America, pp. 329-338.
Describing the authority of the father and of god-parents in Latin American culture, pp. 343-344.	Understanding that most Latin Americans move to cities in search of economic opportunities, pp. 345-348.			
Describing how caudillos and dictators have gained control in some Latin American countries, pp. 357-359. Understanding the causes of the rise of democracy in Latin America, pp. 357-359.	Understanding why many Latin American nations are trying to diversify their economies, pp. 355-356. Describing how debt affects Latin America's economy, p. 359. Understanding how trade agreements such as NAFTA affect Latin America's economy, p. 359.		Explaining why rain forest development is a global concern, pp. 353-354. Identifying the reasons why the United States and other countries set up factories in Latin American countries such as Mexico, p. 359.	Exploring how democracy and communism affect citizenship in Latin America, pp. 357-359, 360-361.
Discussing the role of power and government in such Latin American countries as Nicaragua, Puerto Rico, Cuba, Haiti, and Panama, 367-369. Describing the role of the Organization of American States, p. 369.	Discussing the effectiveness of the Alliance for Progress, p. 368. Explaining how Latin American nations are encouraging trade, pp. 369-370. Explaining how Puerto Rico modernized its economy, pp. 372-373.	Describing the technological changes Puerto Rican businesses employed in the 1950s, 1960s, and 1970s, pp. 372-373.	Discussing the relationship between the United States and the countries of Latin America, pp. 365-367. Explaining how Latin America's role in the world has changed, pp. 367-369.	Discussing the status of Puerto Ricans, pp. 365, 372-373.

	Culture	Time, Continuity, & Change	People, Places, & Environments	Individual Development, & Identity	Individuals, Groups, & Institutions
CHAPTER 29 Canada: Building the Mosiac, pp. 378-396	Identifying the main Native American cultures in Canada, pp. 383-384. Describing how European arrival in Canada altered culture, pp. 384-386. Discussing the conflict between British and French culture in Canada, pp. 390, 394-395. Describing how immigration has made Canada into a mosaic of cultures, p. 394.	Explaining how history has affected culture in Canada, pp. 384-389.	Identifying the main geographic and climatic regions of Canada and explaining how they affect the way of life, pp. 379-382. Describing the debate between Cree and Inuit Native Americans and the Canadian government over how to use the James Bay region, pp. 387-389.	Describing how Native Americans are affected by decisions made by the Canadian government and how Native Americans have gained more power in recent years, pp. 383-389. Explaining how the conflict between French and British Canadians affects individuals, pp. 394-395.	Explaining the significance of Canada's membership in the Commonwealth of Nations, p. 395.

UNIT 5: FOCUS ON THE MIDDLE EAST, PAGES 402-495

	Culture	Time, Continuity, & Change	People, Places, & Environments	Individual Development, & Identity	Individuals, Groups, & Institutions
CHAPTER 30 The Land and People of the Middle East, pp. 405-418	Identifying the people who live in the Middle East, pp. 411-412 Understanding the differences between Arabs and Muslims, pp. 411-412. Understanding the relationship between the Hebrew and Arabic languages, p. 411.	Describing how tradition remains strong in the Middle East, pp. 415. Exploring the way oil has changed traditional ways of life, p. 409. Describing how traditional ways of the Bedouin have changed in recent years, p. 416-417	Identifying the major physical and climatic characteristics of the Middle East, pp. 408-410. Recognizing how geography has influenced the way in which the people of the Middle East live, pp. 405-418.	Understanding that "Arab" and "Muslim" are different concepts, p. 411. Understanding how the Bedouin have preserved their individual identity, pp. 416-417.	
CHAPTER 31 The Rich Heritage of the Middle East, pp. 419-432	Understanding how the development of three great religions has affected the variety of cultures in the Middle East, pp. 425-431.	Exploring the development of civilizations along the Tigris/Euphrates and Nile river systems, pp. 420-425. Exploring the development of Islamic cultures throughout the Middle East, pp. 428-431	Explaining the importance of Middle Eastern river systems in the development of civilizations, pp. 420-425.	Identifying the Middle East as the source of three of the world's great religions, pp. 425-428. Understanding how the *hajj* is one of the pillars of Islamic belief pp. 428-429.	Developing an awareness of the role of religion in Middle Eastern life, pp. 425-428. Understanding the teachings of Muhammand and the main tenets of Islam, p. 428.
CHAPTER 32 From Empire to Independence, pp. 433-442	Exploring how the Ottoman empire was culturally diverse, p. 437 Describing how the Arab world felt culturally alienated from Western colonialists, pp. 438-439.	Identifying how Mustafa Kemal tried to westernize Turkey. pp. 438 Describing the reaction against "westernizers" in the Arab world, pp. 438-439.	Describing how oil in the Middle East increased the interest of the Western powers in the Middle East, pp. 437-438.	Understanding the growth of Arab nationalism in the 20th century, pp. 436-439. Understanding how the Holocaust helped develop the idea of a Jewish state in the Middle East, p. 440.	Explaining how the founding of the state of Israel fulfilled an historic dream of many Jewish people, pp. 440-441.
CHAPTER 33 Traditional Patterns of Life, pp. 447-458	Explaining the traditional patterns of life in the Middle East, pp. 447-458.	Discussing the continuity of traditional Middle Eastern life in villages and cities, pp. 448-451.	Describing environments of villages and the environmental changes that are speeding the movement of people into the cities, pp. 448-449.	Discussing the role of hospitality in Middle Eastern culture, p. 451 Discussing the role of the individual in marriage and divorce in the Middle East, pp. 452-453.	Understanding the role of the family in traditional Middle Eastern life, 452-454. Describing how religion is a key part of everyday life in the Middle East, p. 456.

Power, Authority, & Governance	Production, Distribution, & Consumption	Science, Technology, & Society	Global Connections	Civic Ideals & Practices
Explaining that power in Canada divided between the government and the ten provinces, p. 395.	Describing how the fur trade changed Canada, pp. 384-385. Discussing trade between Canada and the world, pp. 395.		Understanding Canada's relationship to the rest of the world, p. 395.	Explaining why Canada is considered a mosaic, pp. 379-395.
	Recognizing the role that environmental conditions have played in the development of agriculture and industry in the Middle East, pp. 409-410.	Understanding how development of the oil industry has changed ways of life, pp. 409-410, pp. 416-417.	Recognizing that urbanization is a global trend that has had a profound impact on the Middle East, pp. 414-415.	
Discussing the role of the pharaoh in ancient Egypt, p. 423. Recognizing how conquest spread Sumerian culture, p. 421.	Understanding how the switch from hunting and gathering to a settled farming life allowed specialization and the development of civilizations along the river valleys of the Middle East, pp. 420, 423.	Describing the development of writing in Sumeria and Egypt, pp. 420, 424. Describing how the Egyptians built pyramids, p. 424.	Explaining how Judaism and Christianity grew and spread from their founding in the Middle East, pp. 427. Understanding how Islam grew from the Arabian peninsula to influence people in Europe, Africa, and Asia, pp. 430-431.	Understanding how religion is a basic part of the heritage of all cultures, pp. 425-430
Understanding the reasons why the Ottoman Empire gained territory and power and why it declined and collapsed, pp. 434-437.	Describing how the spread of the Industrial Revolution weakened the Ottoman Empire and led to the growth of nationalism among the Empire's ethnic groups, pp. 435-436.	Discussing the role of the Industrial Revolution in altering the power balance between Europe and the Middle East, p. 435.	Seeing that Europe's interest in the Middle East increased in the 20th century as oil played an increasing role in global industrialization, pp. 434-439.	Explaining the impact of imperialism on the growth of nationalism, pp. 437-439.
Understanding the role of village elders in traditional life, pp. 448-449. Explaining family leadership patterns in the traditional family, pp. 452-453.	Describing the role of the *suq,* or marketplace in city life, pp. 450-451. Describing how oil-rich states have been transformed by the infusion of wealth, pp. 460-461.	Discussing how technology is changing Bakhtiari and other nomadic life, p. 451.		Explaining the meaning of citizenship in terms of traditional Middle Eastern societies, pp. 448-452.

	Culture	Time, Continuity, & Change	People, Places, & Environments	Individual Development & Identity	Individuals, Groups, & Institutions
CHAPTER 34 Changing Patterns of Life, pp. 459-468	Explaining how Middle Eastern culture has changed in recent times, pp. 459-468.	Understanding how such movements as industrialization, urbanization, and religious fundamentalism, have affected the Middle East in recent years, pp. 459-465.	Describing how the oil industry has transformed the environments of Middle Eastern states, pp. 460-461. Describing the growth of Middle Eastern cities in the past half-century, pp. 461-463.	Discussing how the role of women is changing in the Middle East, pp. 463-465. Describing how wealth has changed lifestyles in Saudi Arabia today, pp. 466-467.	Understanding how religious fundamentalism has affected the lives of individual Middle Easterners, pp. 464-465.
CHAPTER 35 Economic and Political Trends, pp. 469-481	Explaining how Israel has managed to blend differing cultures into a unified nation, pp. 473-475.	Understanding how changing patterns of culture have affected economic and political trends in the Middle East, pp. 476-480.	Describing how major personalities such as the Ayatollah Khomeini personify sweeping fundamental changes, pp. 477-478. Describing how Israelis have improved an unproductive environment, p. 474.	Understanding how Israelis have built a sense of identity in their society, p. 475.	Understanding how nationalism overwhelmed the forces of colonialism in the Middle East, pp. 476-477.
CHAPTER 36 The Middle East in the World Today, pp. 482-493	Describing the components of the Middle East's rich heritage in the arts, pp. 489-491. Describing Middle Eastern accomplishments in architecture, poetry, and fiction, pp. 490-491.	Explaining progress and obstacles in the search for progress in the Middle East, pp. 487-488. Describing how cooperation between nations is helping change the region, pp 488-489.	Describing how Middle Eastern nations are making efforts to share resources and investments, p. 488.	Describing how arts and culture are an expression of individual values and heritage, pp. 489-490.	Understanding why the Kurds seek independence from other countries, pp. 491-492.

UNIT 6: FOCUS ON EUROPE AND EURASIA, PAGES 498-589

	Culture	Time, Continuity, & Change	People, Places, & Environments	Individual Development & Identity	Individuals, Groups, & Institutions
CHAPTER 37 The Land and People of Europe and Eurasia, p. 501-512	Understanding that Europe is a place of great cultural diversity, pp. 507-509. Understanding the relationship between few geographic barriers and cultural diversity, p. 504.	Discussing how Europe and Eurasia are heir to a proud tradition that includes the civilization of the Greeks, p. 508.	Understanding the major physical regions of Europe and Eurasia, pp. 504-506. Recognizing how geography has influenced the way in which the people of Europe and Eurasia live, pp. 504-507.	Understanding how multilingualism and multiculturalism are an important part of today's Europe and Eurasia, p. 509.	Developing an awareness of the role of ethnic nationalism in Europe and Eurasia, p. 509.
CHAPTER 38 The Roots of European Civilization, pp. 513-525	Understanding how the traditions and values of European civilization have helped shape our world today, pp. 519-524.	Exploring the development of European civilizations from the ancient Greeks to the Industrial Revolution, pp. 519-524.	Explaining how major economic developments led Europe to explore and dominate new environments, pp. 519-520.	Discussing the questioning spirit and the worth of the individual in ancient Greek civilization, p. 515. Understanding how these values were transmitted to us through Renaissance thinkers, p. 518.	Understanding the role of the Roman Catholic Church in Medieval life, p. 517. Describing the reasons for nationalism in Europe , p. 521.

Power, Authority, & Governance	Production, Distribution, & Consumption	Science, Technology, & Society	Global Connections	Civic Ideals & Practices
Explaining how oil wealth has strengthened Middle Eastern governments and led them to massive spending on public works, pp. 460-461.	Discussing the economic reasons for urbanization, pp. 462-463.	Describing how technology has produced a greater demand for labor and allowed many Middle Eastern women to enter the job market, pp. 464-465.	Understanding how oil wealth has attracted foreign workers to the oil-rich states and how they are treated, p. 461.	Recognizing that the values of a society are a function of its history and environment, pp. 463-465.
Explaining how nationalism and fundamentalism have affected power and authority in the Middle East, pp. 476-478.	Describing changing economic patterns in the Middle East, pp. 478-480.	Describing how new ways of farming have improved agricultural productivity in the Middle East, p. 480.	Understanding how the Arab-Israeli conflict has affected relations far beyond the Middle East, pp. 470-472.	Explaining how building a sense of common identity has helped unify Israel, a nation of differing cultures, pp. 473-475.
Describing how the OPEC cartel has become a power on the world scene, pp. 483-484. Describing how the quest for power over oil resources led Saddam Hussein of Iraq into a disastrous war with an alliance of nations, pp. 485-486.	Describing how OPEC has gained a monopoly over the production and distribution of oil., pp. 483-484. Explaining how Middle Eastern nations are discussing sharing of resources, p. 488.	Discussing the ways that Arabsat and other advanced telecommunications are helping to bring together people throughout the Arab world, p 489.	Understanding the global impact of Arab oil embargoes and OPEC price setting, pp. 484. Explaining how conflicts between Iran and Iraq have global implications, pp. 484-485.	Recognizing that the search for peace in the Middle East has importance for people in the United States, pp. 487-488.
	Recognizing the role that environmental conditions have played in the production and distribution of raw materials and finished goods in Europe and Eurasia, pp. 504-506.		Recognizing that much of the world is heir to Europe's traditions of democracy, p. 507.	Understanding that democracy is fragile in Eastern Europe and must be nurtured, p. 507.
Discussing the impact of the development of the nation-state in Europe, pp. 519-520. Recognizing how the French Revolution spawned new ideals that spread across Europe, p. 522.	Understanding how capitalism developed a commercial revolution, p. 520. Understanding how the Industrial Revolution changed the way people worked, pp. 522-524.	Describing the technological innovations which led to the Industrial Revolution, pp. 522-524.	Explaining the global impact of such eras and events as the age of exploration and the Industrial Revolution, pp. 520-524.	Understanding how the idea of democracy developed and changed throughout Europe's history, pp. 514-522. Understanding how the Industrial Revolution brought injustices as well as progress, pp. 523-524.

	Culture	Time, Continuity, & Change	People, Places, & Environments	Individual Development, & Identity	Individuals, Groups, & Institutions
CHAPTER 39 Europe in the 20th Century, pp. 526-534		Exploring the development of Europe in the 20th century, pp. 527-533.	Describing how virtually all parts of Europe and Eurasia were affected by two world wars in the 20th century, 527-531.	Understanding the impact of the Holocaust on millions of innocent people, pp. 530-531.	Understanding how the German and Italian people allowed brutal dictatorships to come to power, pp. 529-531.
CHAPTER 40 Patterns of Life in Europe, pp. 535-547	Explaining patterns of life in Northern Europe, Western Europe, Central Europe, and Southern Europe, pp. 536-546.	Discussing the continuity of life in the various regions of Europe, pp. 536-546.	Describing impact of differing environments on different cultures and lifestyles in Europe, pp. 536-546.	Discussing the role of individual value and worth in European cultures, pp. 538-539.	Understanding the role of the welfare state in Swedish life, pp. 537. Describing British reactions to their constitutional monarchy, pp. 539-540.
CHAPTER 41 Europe in the World Today, pp. 550--558	Explaining how disagreements between ethnic groups has troubled Europe in recent years, pp. 552, 556-557.	Understanding how the end of Europe's empires affected its role in the world, p. 551. Describing the reasons why the Soviet Union crumbled, 552-554. Describing the breakup of Czechoslovakia, pp. 556-557.	Explaining how European empires crumbled throughout the world after World War II, pp. 551-552. Identifying Vaclav Havel and describing his role in affairs in the Czech republic in recent years, pp. 556-557.	Describing how Mohandas Gandhi led the successful struggle to oust the British from India, p. 551. Describing how a writer/intellectual such as Vaclav Havel can gain political leadership in his country, pp. 556-557.	Understanding the forces of nationalism in shattering Europe's empires, pp. 551-552. Understanding the forces of nationalism and economic resentment in toppling communism in the Soviet Union and Eastern Europe, pp. 552-555.
CHAPTER 42 The Heritage of Russia and the Eurasian Heartland, pp. 560-569	Understanding how the traditions and values of Russia and the Eurasian Heartland are a product of its history, pp. 561-568.	Understanding how the historical development of Russia and the Heartland affect present-day events, pp. 561-565.	Describing how Peter the Great, Catherine the Great, and Lenin made a long-standing impact on the history of the Heartland, pp. 563-566.		Discussing the role of individuals such as Mikhail Gorbachev and Boris Yeltsin in the fall of communism in the Soviet Union, p. 568.
CHAPTER 43 Changing Patterns of Life in Russia and the Heartland, pp. 570-578	Describing how cultural patterns are changing in Russia and the Eurasian Heartland since the fall of the Soviet Union, pp. 571-577.	Understanding that problems Russians face today stem from a Communist past, pp. 571-572. Understanding the historical development of the new republics of the Heartland, pp. 573-576.	Describing how each of the new nations of the Heartland has a distinctive history and different problems, pp. 573-576.		Understanding how hard economic times have added to the burden of Russian women, p. 572. Understanding how the Russian Orthodox Church is gaining new influence after the fall of communism, p. 572.
CHAPTER 44 Russia and the Heartland in the	Understanding the cultural differences between the Russians and the Chechens, p. 584	Explaining the goal of Soviet foreign policy before the outbreak of World War II, pp. 580-581. Explaining the reasons for the Cold War, pp. 582-583.	Explaining the impact of environmental pollution on individuals such as Berik, a teenage boy in Kazakstan, pp. 580-581.		

Power, Authority, & Governance	Production, Distribution, & Consumption	Science, Technology, & Society	Global Connections	Civic Ideals & Practices
Describing how totalitarian dictatorships challenged European democracies, pp. 529-533.		Discussing how technological change made total war possible in the 20th century, pp. 527-528.	Recognizing the global implications of conflicts such as two world wars and the Cold War, pp. 527-532.	Understanding why Germans did nothing to stop the Holocaust, pp. 530-531.
Understanding how countries can be both monarchies and democracies, pp. 539-540. Explaining the role Britain had in spreading ideas of democracy throughout the world, pp. 539-540.	Describing how a welfare state makes decisions about how goods and services are going to be produced and distributed, pp. 536-537. Describing the impact of industrialization on Central Europe, pp. 542-543.	Discussing how technology transformed Germany into an economic powerhouse, p. 543.	Understanding the implications of European traditions of economic development and democracy on the rest of the world, pp. 541-543.	Explaining the responsibility of people in affluent areas of a country to improve life in poorer areas, pp. 545-546.
Developing an understanding of the weaknesses in communism that led to its fall in Eastern Europe and the Soviet Union, pp. 552-555.	Recognizing the role that European unification has had in strengthening the economies of European nations, p. 555.	Describing the role of technology in helping to unify Europe, including the building of the 'chunnel" linking Britain and the European mainland, p. 555.	Understanding how the removal of tariffs between members of the European Union has made Western Europe an economic power on the world scene, p. 555.	Recognizing the need to understand and value different perspectives to overcome ethnic hostility, p. 552.
Understanding how serfdom helped guarantee the continued rule of the wealthy over Russia, p. 563. Explaining the role of terror in helping install communism in the Soviet Union, p. 567.	Discussing how communism changed traditional economic patterns in the Soviet Union, p. 566. Discussing how the failure to meet economic expectations led to the demise of communism in the Soviet Union, pp. 567-568.	Describing how the Soviet Union managed to industrialize in the 1930s, pp. 566-567.	Understanding the impact of the Mongol conquest on people throughout Central Asia, p. 561. Describing how the fall of the Soviet Union affected power balances far beyond the Heartland, p. 568	Understanding how Stalin's ambition and power affected millions of innocent Russian citizens, p. 567.
Describing how the transfer of political power to independent republics in the Heartland has led to increasing tensions between ethnic groups, pp. 575-577.	Describing how the end of communism in Russia and the Heartland has caused economic upheaval over the area, pp. 571-576.	Discussing the status of Russian science and technology as the nation seeks to rebound from the troubles of the early 1990s, p. 572.	Recognizing the global importance of ethnic hostilities, such as that besetting Russia and the Heartland, pp. 574-575, 577.	
Recognizing how stability and leadership in the new republics is dependent on resolving major points of tension in the Heartland, pp. 584-585.	Understanding the difficulties that moving from a Communist economic system to free enterprise has caused, p. 585.	Recognizing that in times of economic instability, technological advances are slowed, p. 585.	Describing global implications of Soviet foreign policy before World War II, pp. 581-583. Understanding how nuclear weapons in the new nations of the Heartland may threaten world peace, 583-584.	Understanding how rampant crime is a threat to democracy, p. 585.

The World and Its Cultures

OBJECTIVES

After reading this chapter, students will be able to

- define and discuss the meaning of culture.
- identify and explain the five themes of geography.

PREVIEW

Write the word *culture* on the chalkboard. Ask students to look at the definition of *culture* in the list of key terms on page 1. Then have students brainstorm and list words and phrases they associate with the term *culture*.

DEVELOPING THE CHAPTER

List the five themes of geography—place, location, interaction, movement, and region—on the board. Have students work in groups to relate each of the themes to their city or town, metropolitan area, county, and state. For example, to relate absolute location to their city, have students find its latitude and longitude.

ALTERNATIVE ASSESSMENT: ON ASSIGNMENT

To help your students complete the On Assignment activity, you may wish to

1. copy and distribute the reproducible On Assignment Activity Sheet on page 113.
2. divide students into small groups to work on the project.
3. share with students the standards by which you will evaluate their projects. You may wish to use the following scoring rubric.

0 **Fail/Unacceptable** The project is not attempted.

1 **Limited/Acceptable** There are fewer than five questions. Questions do not focus on the content and contain serious grammatical and structural errors.

2 **Commendable** There are at least five questions that focus on the content. Questions contain minor grammatical and structural errors.

3 **Outstanding** There are more than five questions that are focused, thoughtful, and grammatically correct.

ESL/LEP ACTIVITY

If students are comfortable doing so, have them discuss differences between U.S. culture and the culture of their native country. Suggest that they consider differences in food, types of greetings, government, religion, housing, and education.

CLOSING THE LESSON

In closing, ask students to answer the preview questions that appear at the beginning of the chapter and each section. Instruct them to write the answers in their notebooks and refer to them when reviewing this chapter.

MORE TO DO

Creating a World Data Resource Have interested students create a world data resource for the classroom. The data resource could focus on one specific region covered in this book, or if you are planning to study other regions, students could work in groups to create resources for all the regions that you plan to cover.

The resource could take the form of a poster and contain such information as population, type of government, type of economy, major cities, percentage of population living in urban and rural areas, and age distribution.

Focus on Africa

UNIT OBJECTIVES

After completing this unit, students will be able to

- discuss how the geography of Africa affects its culture and has affected its history.
- compare traditional ways of life and modern ways of life in Africa.
- identify economic and political trends in Africa.
- describe the role of Africa in the world today.

PREVIEW

Use the unit time line and Exploring Regional Issues on pages 10–12. Have students study the time line and answer the questions. Then assign Population in Africa: Reading Population Pyramids on page 12. After students have completed work on their population pyramids, use the worksheet on page 116 in this Teacher's Resource Manual to reinforce the concepts and skills.

After they have completed the worksheet, discuss with students the differences and similarities in the age distribution of the population of various countries of Africa. Lead a discussion about how age distribution affects a country's economy, system of education, and social structure.

You may wish to have volunteers transfer population pyramids to poster board for a class display.

DEVELOPING THE UNIT

Use the section, chapter, and unit reviews in the student text and the following resources in this Teacher's Resource Manual to develop the chapters in this unit.

- Lesson Plans, pp. 26–34
- On Assignment Worksheets, pp. 117–123
- Critical Thinking Activity Worksheets, pp. 124–130
- Chapter Tests, pp. 131–137
- Unit Test, pp. 138–139
- Outline Maps, pp. 267–271

LITERATURE CONNECTIONS

Assign students the three African poems on pages 74–77. Before students read the poems, have them study the painting on page 74 and the photo on page 77. Ask students to provide answers to the following questions in their journals: What do I see? What does each work show me about African culture? After students have read the poems, have a class discussion about how the poems and the art reflect the themes of pride in African heritage and the influence of Western culture.

CLOSING THE UNIT

- Assign the Unit Review on pages 103–104 in the student text.
- Assign the Unit Test on pages 138–139 in the Teacher's Resource Manual.

LINKING THE UNITS: GLOBAL ISSUES

You may wish to use the Taking Action activity on page 107 as a performance assessment opportunity or portfolio entry.

To complete the activity, divide the class into three groups. Assign each group a form of government to present in the panel discussion. Students might choose a specific country to show that form of government at work. Library research may be needed.

The Land and People of Africa

OBJECTIVES

After reading this chapter, students will be able to

- describe how geography has influenced life in Africa.
- describe the different regions of Africa.
- discuss the diversity of Africa's people.

PREVIEW

Before students begin reading, display a physical map of Africa. Lead a discussion about different geographical features of Africa. Ask students to predict which physical features limit travel and contact between regions of Africa.

DEVELOPING THE CHAPTER

Divide the class into pairs. Provide each pair with one copy of the outline map of Africa and some colored pencils.

Ask the pairs of students to label the following elements on their maps: major rivers, major lakes, mountains, deserts, the Great Rift Valley, Africa's five geographic regions, climate regions, and major cities. You may wish to provide students with atlases to help them locate these elements.

When students are finished with their maps, lead a discussion about how geography has affected the lives of the people of Africa.

ALTERNATIVE ASSESSMENT: ON ASSIGNMENT

To help your students complete the On Assignment activity, you may wish to

1. copy and distribute the reproducible On Assignment Activity Sheet on page 117.
2. model the creation of a display poster. Ask a student to describe a travel and tourism poster or a social issues poster he or she has seen and sketch it for the class.
3. divide students into small groups to work on the project.
4. provide materials such as poster board or construction paper, as well as colored markers or pencils.
5. share with students the standards by which you will evaluate their projects. You may wish to use the following scoring rubric.

0 Fail/Unacceptable The project is not attempted.

1 Limited/Acceptable The poster artwork and text contain limited information. The text contains many grammatical and structural errors.

2 Commendable The poster artwork and text are well coordinated. The presentation is informative and accurate. The text contains minor grammatical and structural errors.

3 Outstanding The poster artwork and text are carefully organized, clearly written, and contain a great deal of information. The text is grammatically and structurally correct.

COOPERATIVE LEARNING

Working Together: Writing a Letter For this project, you may wish to pair students of different ability levels. Tell students to create a list of the major characteristics of Africa's geography and people. For each of the characteristics they list, have pairs identify the similarities or differences between Africa and the United States. Students should use this list to write their letters.

USING THE VISUALS TO TEACH...

Geography Have students study the photo of Mt. Kilimanjaro on page 15. Ask them if they are surprised to learn that there is snow on a mountain in Africa. Discuss with them the effect of elevation on climate. Have students who have gone on camping or hiking trips in the mountains to describe how the weather changed as they climbed to higher altitudes.

CLOSING THE LESSON

In closing, ask students to answer the preview questions that appear at the beginning of the chapter and each section. Instruct them to write the answers in their notebooks and refer to them when reviewing this chapter.

MORE TO DO

Interviewing Divide the class into small groups. Tell them to review Chapter 1 and choose one region mentioned in the chapter. Have students create a series of questions and answers on what life is like in that region. Then have them role-play and perform an interview for the class.

The Early History of Africa

OBJECTIVES

After reading this chapter, students will be able to

- describe the ancient civilizations of Africa.
- discuss the rise and fall of the great empires of Africa.
- discuss the impact of the slave trade on African history.

PREVIEW

Before students begin reading, display photographs of paintings or other artwork that depict each of the major civilizations or empires covered in Chapter 2. Based on these photographs, lead a discussion of what life might have been like in each of these civilizations.

DEVELOPING THE CHAPTER

Break the class into three groups. Assign to each group one of the following periods of African history: (1) ancient civilizations of Egypt, Axum, and Kush; (2) sub-Saharan kingdoms of Ghana, Mali, Songhai, Benin, and Zimbabwe; (3) the slave trade of Europeans and Arabs. Have each group prepare a description of the major empires and significant events to which they were assigned. Ask students to use this description to prepare a brief presentation. Have each group present its findings to the rest of the class.

ALTERNATIVE ASSESSMENT: ON ASSIGNMENT

To help your students complete the On Assignment activity, you may wish to

1. copy and distribute the reproducible On Assignment Activity Sheet on page 118.

2. model the creation of a storyboard. Ask a student to describe a movie or television show he or she has seen and to sketch a storyboard based on its plot.

3. divide the class into small groups to work on the project.

4. provide materials such as poster board or construction paper, as well as colored markers or pencils.

5. share with students the standards by which you will evaluate their projects. You may wish to use the following scoring rubric.

0   **Fail/Unacceptable**   The project is not attempted.

1   **Limited/Acceptable**   The storyboards and narration contain limited information and contain serious grammatical and structural errors.

2   **Commendable**   The storyboards and narration are well coordinated. The presentation is informative and accurate and contains minor grammatical and structural errors.

3   **Outstanding**   The storyboards and narration are carefully organized, clearly written, contain a great deal of information, and are grammatically and structurally correct.

COOPERATIVE LEARNING

Working Together: Writing a Report For this project, you may wish to pair students of different ability levels. Tell students to review the section of the chapter related to a kingdom of their choice and create a list of important facts about that kingdom. Students should use this list to help them write their report.

ESL/LEP STRATEGY

Have pairs of students review the terms listed on page 27 in the student text. Have students write a sentence for each term that explains its significance in African history.

CLOSING THE LESSON

In closing, ask students to answer the preview questions that appear at the beginning of the chapter and each section. Instruct them to write the answers in their notebooks and refer to them when reviewing this chapter.

MORE TO DO

Making a Diagram Divide the class into small groups. Ask groups to gather information on the Atlantic slave trade. Have groups make a poster-sized diagram of the triangular trade route involving Europe, Africa, and the Americas. Have them show the information they gather on their diagrams.

Traditional Patterns of Life in Africa

OBJECTIVES

After reading this chapter, students will be able to

- describe the traditional ways of life of people in Africa.
- explain the economic and political systems of traditional African societies.

PREVIEW

Before students begin reading, lead a discussion about the difference between a nuclear family and an extended family. Review the definitions of these terms. (See page 1 in the Introduction.) Ask which type of family is most commonly found in the United States. Discuss the benefits and drawbacks of each.

DEVELOPING THE CHAPTER

Break the class into groups of six to eight. Have students prepare a skit about traditional life in Africa. Students in each group should choose one of the following roles from an extended family: parent, child, aunt or uncle, cousin, grandparent.

Have each group review the information in Chapter 3 and prepare a description of life in traditional Africa from which to prepare their skits. Skits should describe the role of each person in the family, the family's religious beliefs, how the family earns its living, and life in this family's village. Have each group perform its skit for the rest of the class.

ALTERNATIVE ASSESSMENT: ON ASSIGNMENT

To help your students complete the On Assignment activity, you may wish to

1. copy and distribute the reproducible On Assignment Activity Sheet on page 119.
2. model the creation of a collage. Ask a student to describe a collage he or she has seen and sketch its layout for the class.
3. divide the class into small groups to work on the project.
4. provide materials such as poster board or construction paper, colored markers or pencils, old magazines, scissors, and glue.

5. share with students the standards by which you will evaluate their projects. You may wish to use the following scoring rubric.

0 Fail/Unacceptable The project is not attempted.

1 Limited/Acceptable The artwork and pictures contain limited information. Words in the collage contain serious grammatical and spelling errors.

2 Commendable The artwork, pictures, and words are well coordinated. The presentation is informative and accurate and contains minor grammatical and spelling errors.

3 Outstanding The collage contains a great deal of information and is especially attractive. It contains no grammatical or spelling errors.

COOPERATIVE LEARNING

Working Together: Making a Chart For this project, you may wish to pair students of different ability levels. Tell students to review the chapter and create a list of aspects of traditional African life. Have them use this list to compare traditional African life with their own.

USING THE VISUALS TO TEACH...

Government Point out to students the picture of the tribal leader on page 44. Ask them to describe how traditional African tribal government compares with government in the United States. Ask: What are the advantages and disadvantages of each system?

CLOSING THE LESSON

In closing, ask students to answer the preview questions that appear at the beginning of the chapter and each section. Instruct them to write the answers in their notebooks and refer to them when reviewing this chapter.

MORE TO DO

Literature Have students read one of the selections in Unit 1, Chapter 1 of Globe Fearon's *World Tapestries* that deals with traditional life. Ask students to write a brief essay on the elements of traditional African culture that they identify in that selection.

Modern History of Africa

OBJECTIVES

After reading this chapter, students will be able to

- discuss the effects of imperialism on Africa.
- describe how African nations gained their independence from imperial powers.
- discuss the challenges newly independent nations in Africa faced.

PREVIEW

Before students begin reading, tell them that in the 1800s, Europeans considered Africa to be primitive and inferior. Europeans believed it was their responsibility to bring Christianity and Western culture to Africa. Lead a discussion on the concept of ethnocentricity. Ask students if they think this sentiment prevails today.

DEVELOPING THE CHAPTER

Ask students to imagine they are native Africans living in one of the following situations: a resident of Ujiji during Stanley and Livingstone's explorations, an Egyptian during the building of the Suez Canal, a South African Zulu during the time of the Great Trek, or a native of Ghana during the fight for independence.

Ask students to write a letter to a friend or relative telling them of events that have been occurring. The letters should include a description of events, the reasons they are happening, and the writer's feelings about what is going on around him or her. When the letters are completed, have students read them aloud to the class.

ALTERNATIVE ASSESSMENT: ON ASSIGNMENT

To help your students complete the On Assignment activity, you may wish to

1. copy and distribute the reproducible On Assignment Activity Sheet on page 120.

2. describe the components of a diary entry.

3. organize students into pairs to work on the project.

4. provide materials such as paper and pencils and resources such as almanacs and encyclopedias.

5. share with students the standards by which you will evaluate their projects. You may wish to use the following scoring rubric.

0 Fail/Unacceptable The project is not attempted.

1 Limited/Acceptable The diary entries provide limited information and contain serious grammatical and structural errors.

2 Commendable The diary entries are well coordinated and written. They contain minor grammatical and structural errors. The presentation is informative and accurate.

3 Outstanding The diary entries are carefully organized and clearly written. They contain a great deal of information and are grammatically and structurally correct.

COOPERATIVE LEARNING

Working Together: Completing a Study Chart For this project, you may wish to pair students of different ability levels. Show students a sample study chart. Tell them to review the chapter and other resources to find specific information on three or four nations. Have them fill in the chart with information on each country they choose. Encourage students to write a short report describing one of the countries in their chart.

ESL/LEP STRATEGY

Have pairs of students choose one of the sections from Chapter 4. Have students look up any unfamiliar words. Then, have them write a summary of the section.

CLOSING THE LESSON

In closing, ask students to answer the preview questions that appear at the beginning of the chapter and each section. Instruct them to write the answers in their notebooks and refer to them when reviewing this chapter.

MORE TO DO

Drawing Maps Divide students into pairs. Provide each pair with two copies of the Africa outline map. Ask students to create two maps showing African boundaries: colonial boundaries of 1900 and the current independent nations of Africa.

Changing Patterns of Life in Africa

OBJECTIVES

After reading this chapter, students will be able to

- discuss changes in cultural traditions in modern Africa.
- discuss the growth of cities in Africa and the effects of urbanization on African life.
- describe the role of literature, art, and music in African life.

PREVIEW

Before students begin reading, play for them a recording of Western music that has been influenced by traditional African music. One example is Paul Simon's "Graceland." Lead a discussion on how African literature, art, and music have influenced Western arts in recent years.

DEVELOPING THE CHAPTER

Divide students into pairs. Tell them that they will be role-playing an interview between an African citizen and a Western journalist. Have pairs choose one of the following roles: an Islamic fundamentalist, a modern African woman, an African teenager going to school, a recent migrant to a large African city.

Direct each pair of students to decide who will be the African and who will be the journalist. Have students create a series of questions and answers on what life is like in the role they chose. Then have them perform their interview for the class.

ALTERNATIVE ASSESSMENT: ON ASSIGNMENT

To help your students complete the On Assignment activity, you may wish to

1. copy and distribute the reproducible On Assignment Activity Sheet on page 121.
2. model the creation of a fact sheet. Draw a sample chart on the board showing different countries and five categories of information.
3. divide students into small groups to work on the project.
4. provide materials such as poster board or construction paper, colored markers or pencils, rulers, and information sources.

5. share with students the standards by which you will evaluate their projects. You may wish to use the following scoring rubric.

0 Fail/Unacceptable The project is not attempted.

1 Limited/Acceptable Fact sheets contain limited information and have serious grammatical and structural errors.

2 Commendable Information in the fact sheets is accurate. Fact sheets contain minor grammatical and structural errors.

3 Outstanding The information in the fact sheets is carefully organized and accurate. Fact sheets are grammatically and structurally correct.

COOPERATIVE LEARNING

Working Together: Creating a Museum Exhibit Pamphlet For this project, you may wish to pair students of different ability levels. Show students sample museum pamphlets. Have them describe the major works of the writers and artists they have chosen. Encourage students to use drawings and pictures in their pamphlets.

USING THE VISUALS TO TEACH...

Sociology Ask students to look at the picture of the woman doctor in Uganda on page 64. Ask them to describe how the role of African women is changing.

CLOSING THE LESSON

In closing, ask students to answer the preview questions that appear at the beginning of the chapter and each section. Instruct them to write the answers in their notebooks and refer to them when reviewing this chapter.

MORE TO DO

Writing an Art Review Ask students to find an example of African literature, film, art, or music. Tell students to imagine they are art critics for the local newspaper and prepare a review for the next edition. Have students present these reviews to the rest of the class.

Economic and Political Trends

OBJECTIVES

After reading this chapter, students will be able to

- describe the political and economic challenges facing African nations today.
- discuss apartheid in South Africa.

PREVIEW

Before students begin reading, ask a volunteer to define apartheid. Tell students that before 1990, black South Africans had no rights in their own country. Lead a discussion about the causes and effects of racial discrimination.

DEVELOPING THE CHAPTER

Divide the class into four groups. Assign each group one of the following issues discussed in the chapter: the challenge of building democracy, apartheid in Africa, socialism vs. free enterprise, and current economic challenges in African nations.

Have groups create a television or radio news report on their issue. In the report, students should describe the challenge their issue poses in South Africa today and what, if anything, is being done to meet the challenge. Have each group role-play its report for the rest of the class.

ALTERNATIVE ASSESSMENT: ON ASSIGNMENT

To help your students complete the On Assignment activity, you may wish to

1. copy and distribute the reproducible On Assignment Activity Sheet on page 122.
2. show the class photographs of murals. Ask a student to describe a mural or collage he or she has seen and to sketch it for the class.
3. divide students into pairs or groups to work on the project.
4. provide materials such as poster board or construction paper, colored markers or pencils, magazines, scissors, and glue.
5. share with students the standards by which you will evaluate their projects. You may wish to use the following scoring rubric.

0 **Fail/Unacceptable** The project is not attempted.

1 **Limited/Acceptable** The artwork and pictures contain limited information.

2 **Commendable** The artwork and pictures are well coordinated. The presentation is informative and accurate.

3 **Outstanding** The artwork and pictures are carefully organized and presented in an especially attractive way.

COOPERATIVE LEARNING

Working Together: Finding Solutions to Problems For this project, you may wish to pair students of different ability levels. Tell students to review the chapter and to create a list of problems facing African nations. Have them choose five problems and brainstorm possible solutions to use in their reports. Encourage students to create a chart that summarizes the problems they find and their solutions.

ESL/LEP STRATEGY

Discuss using a concept map as a means of organizing ideas visually. Write the topic of the chapter on the board. Ask students to pick three main ideas from the chapter. Put them in circles around the topic. Put the supporting details in "spokes" around each main idea circle.

CLOSING THE LESSON

In closing, ask students to answer the preview questions that appear at the beginning of the chapter and each section. Instruct them to write the answers in their notebooks and refer to them when reviewing this chapter.

MORE TO DO

Summarizing Current Events Ask students to find articles in a current newspaper or news magazine about economic or political issues facing Africa. Based on the articles they find, tell students to prepare a summary describing a current issue in Africa. Have students present their summaries to the rest of the class.

Africa in the World Today

OBJECTIVES

After reading this chapter, students will be able to

- discuss the challenges facing African nations in the world today.
- describe the actions Africans are taking to meet these challenges.

PREVIEW

Before students begin reading, ask whether they have read or heard of any issues facing Africa recently. Have students brainstorm all the issues they can think of that people in Africa are currently confronting. In addition, you may wish to distribute newspapers or magazines and have students scan them for articles about Africa.

DEVELOPING THE CHAPTER

Ask students to imagine they live in Africa. Have them select a policy or issue about which they feel strongly and write a letter to the editor of a local newspaper about that issue. Possible suggestions include, but are not limited to, the following: refugees, health, education, drought and famine, desertification, endangered species, and regional unity. The letter should include a description of the issue and explain the writer's feelings about the issue. When the letters are complete, have students read them aloud to the class.

ALTERNATIVE ASSESSMENT: ON ASSIGNMENT

To help your students complete the On Assignment activity, you may wish to

1. copy and distribute the reproducible On Assignment Activity Sheet on page 123.
2. distribute copies of African fables and myths. Ask a student to describe a story they have read, seen, or heard and act it out for the class.
3. divide students into small groups to work on the project.
4. share with students the standards by which you will evaluate their projects. You may wish to use the following scoring rubric.

0 Fail/Unacceptable The project is not attempted.

1 Limited/Acceptable The story's plot and narrative contain limited information. The story contains serious grammatical and structural errors.

2 Commendable The story's plot and narrative are well coordinated. The presentation is informative and accurate. The story contains minor grammatical and structural errors.

3 Outstanding The story's plot and narrative are carefully organized and particularly well coordinated. The story contains a great deal of information and no grammatical or structural errors.

COOPERATIVE LEARNING

Working Together: Writing a Public Service Campaign For this project, you may wish to pair students of different ability levels. Show or describe a sample public service campaign. Tell students to review the chapter and create a list of problems facing Africans today. Have them choose one problem and draft a campaign to address the problem. Encourage students to write a paragraph describing their solution.

ESL/LEP STRATEGY

Have students find the term *refugee* in the dictionary and define it in their own words. Ask students to review the chapter and make a list of all the examples of refugees in Africa and of what situation each group is fleeing.

CLOSING THE LESSON

In closing, ask students to answer the preview questions that appear at the beginning of the chapter and each section. Instruct them to write the answers in their notebooks and refer to them when reviewing this chapter.

MORE TO DO

Researching Divide students into small groups. Ask groups to choose one animal species native to Africa that has been placed on the Endangered Species list. Provide library time for groups to do research. Have each group give a five-minute presentation on why the species is endangered and what is being done to save it.

Focus on South and Southeast Asia

UNIT OBJECTIVES

After completing this unit, students will be able to

- describe the key geographic features of South and Southeast Asia.
- discuss important events in the history of South and Southeast Asia.
- explain the role of the region in the world today.
- identify the key geographic and historical features of Australia, New Zealand, and Oceania.

PREVIEW

Use the unit time line and Exploring Regional Issues on pages 108–110 of the student text. Have students study the time line and answer the questions. Then assign Trade in South and Southeast Asia: Analyzing a Chart on page 110. After students have completed work on the chart, use the worksheet on page 140 in this Teacher's Resource Manual to reinforce the concepts and skills.

After they have completed the worksheet, lead a discussion on the importance of trade in a nation's economy. You might have students examine the labels in their clothing or on other items they own to see where they were made. Have a student volunteer write on the chalkboard all the countries mentioned. You might ask volunteers to look up in an almanac the major trading partners of the United States.

DEVELOPING THE UNIT

Use the section, chapter, and unit reviews in the student text and the following resources in this Teacher's Resource Manual to develop the chapters in this unit.

- Lesson Plans, pp. 35–43
- On Assignment Worksheets, pp. 141–148
- Critical Thinking Activity Worksheets, pp. 149–156
- Chapter Tests, pp. 157–164
- Unit Test, pp. 165–166
- Outline Maps, pp. 272–273

LITERATURE CONNECTIONS

Assign students "The Tiger," on pages 143–146. After they have read the story, have students study the painting of the tiger on page 144. Ask students to imagine that they are Fatima as she comes face to face with a tiger such as the one in the painting. What does she see? What does she think? Next, have students study the photo on page 146. Lead a discussion about why villagers might react to a tiger as they do in the story.

CLOSING THE UNIT

- Assign the Unit Review on pages 200–201 in the student text.
- Assign the Unit Test on pages 165–166 in this Teacher's Resource Manual.

LINKING THE UNITS: GLOBAL ISSUES

You may wish to use the Taking Action activity on page 203 as a performance assessment opportunity or portfolio entry.

To complete the activity, have students use such library resources as *The Readers' Guide to Periodical Literature* or an on-line periodical research system to choose a subject to interview and to decide the questions they will ask. Ask pairs of students to conduct their interviews for the class.

The Land and People of South and Southeast Asia

OBJECTIVES

After reading this chapter, students will be able to

- describe the physical features and climate of South and Southeast Asia.
- discuss the characteristics of the people of South and Southeast Asia.

PREVIEW

Before students begin reading, show them a physical map of South and Southeast Asia. Lead a discussion about the different geographical features in this region. Point out to students the many islands that are part of Southeast Asia. Ask students to discuss how life on an island might be different from life on the mainland.

DEVELOPING THE CHAPTER

Divide the class into pairs of students. Provide each pair with a copy of the outline maps of South Asia and Southeast Asia and some colored pencils.

Ask the pairs of students to use the maps in their text to help them label the following features on the outline maps: major rivers, the Himalayas and other mountain ranges, deserts, and countries.

When students are finished with their maps, lead a discussion about the geography of the region. Ask students to explain how the mountains of South Asia isolated the region. Ask how the proximity of mainland Southeast Asia to China might have affected the region.

ALTERNATIVE ASSESSMENT: ON ASSIGNMENT

To help your students complete the On Assignment activity, you may wish to

1. copy and distribute the reproducible On Assignment Activity Sheet on page 141.
2. bring to class and show students examples of travel brochures.
3. divide the class into small groups to work on the project.
4. provide materials such as construction paper, colored markers or pencils, and resources such as travel posters.
5. share with students the standards by which

you will evaluate their projects. You may wish to use the following scoring rubric.

0 Fail/Unacceptable The project is not attempted.

1 Limited/Acceptable The brochure artwork and text contain limited information and serious grammatical and structural errors.

2 Commendable The brochure artwork and text are well coordinated; the presentation is informative and accurate. The project contains minor grammatical and structural errors.

3 Outstanding The brochure artwork and text are carefully organized, clearly written, and contain a great deal of information.

COOPERATIVE LEARNING

Working Together: Creating Quiz Questions For this project, you may wish to pair students of similar ability levels. Provide students with sample quiz questions and describe the quiz format. Tell students to review the chapter and create a list of main ideas. Have them draft at least ten questions from the chapter. Encourage students to write the answers to their questions on a separate sheet of paper.

USING THE VISUALS TO TEACH . . .

Economics Ask students to scan the pictures in Chapter 8, including those in the photo essays on pages 112–113 and 118–119. Lead a discussion about how geography affects the way in which people make a living.

CLOSING THE LESSON

In closing, ask students to answer the preview questions that appear at the beginning of the chapter and each section. Instruct them to write the answers in their notebooks and refer to them when reviewing this chapter.

MORE TO DO

Interviewing Divide students into small groups. Tell them to review Chapter 8 and choose one of the regions discussed. Have students create a series of questions and answers on what life is like in that region. Then have them prepare and perform an interview for the class.

The History of South Asia

OBJECTIVES

After reading this chapter, students will be able to

- describe the major religions of South Asia.
- describe the ancient empires and civilizations of South Asia.
- discuss European colonization of South Asia and the independence movement.

PREVIEW

Before students begin to read the chapter, display photographs of paintings or other artwork that depict each of the major religions in South Asia. Have students use the information in the pictures to discuss what life is like for members of each religion.

DEVELOPING THE CHAPTER

Break students into seven small groups. Assign to each group one of the following topics covered in Chapter 9: Hinduism, Buddhism, Islam, the Maurya and Gupta empires, the Delhi sultanate and Mogul Empire, European colonization, and the independence movements.

First, have each group brainstorm a list of key people and events related to their topic. Then have students use these lists to create a one-scene skit based on their topic. Have each group perform its skit for the class.

ALTERNATIVE ASSESSMENT: ON ASSIGNMENT

To help your students complete the On Assignment activity, you may wish to

1. copy and distribute the reproducible On Assignment Activity on page 142.
2. show students pictures of murals. Ask them to point out the theme of each mural and to note how the artists depicted events and people.
3. divide students into pairs or groups to work on the project.
4. provide materials such as poster board or construction paper, colored markers or pencils, magazines, scissors, and glue.
5. share with students the standards by which you will evaluate their projects. You may wish

to use the following scoring rubric.

0 **Fail/Unacceptable** The project is not attempted.

1 **Limited/Acceptable** The mural artwork and pictures contain limited information and serious structural errors.

2 **Commendable** The mural artwork and pictures are well organized; the presentation is informative and accurate. The project contains minor structural errors.

3 **Outstanding** The mural artwork and pictures are carefully organized and presented. They contain a great deal of information.

COOPERATIVE LEARNING

Working Together: Making a Time Line For this project, you may wish to pair students of different ability levels. Draw a sample time line for students. Tell them to review the chapter and create a list of main events and their dates. Have them draw a time line and place the events on it. Encourage students to illustrate their time lines, using original drawings or pictures cut from old magazines or newspapers.

ESL/LEP STRATEGY

Have pairs of students create flash cards for each term listed on page 123 in the Student Text. Ask students to use the flash cards to practice each term and its meaning. Have students write a sentence for each term that explains its significance in South Asian history.

CLOSING THE LESSON

In closing, ask students to answer the preview questions that appear at the beginning of the chapter and each section. Instruct them to write the answers in their notebooks and refer to them when reviewing this chapter.

MORE TO DO

Researching Divide students into small groups. Ask groups to choose one significant event from South Asian history. Provide library time for groups to research the event they chose. Have each group give a five-minute presentation on the historical event that it researched.

Changing Patterns of Life in South Asia

OBJECTIVES

After reading this chapter, students will be able to

- discuss the changes that have occurred in India since independence.
- discuss the challenges that will face India in the future.
- describe the role of religion in the arts and literature of South Asia.

PREVIEW

Before students begin to read, play for them a recording of Indian music or Indian-influenced Western music. (A good example might be late 1960s Beatles music.) Lead a discussion on the differences between Western music and South Asian music.

DEVELOPING THE CHAPTER

Divide students into pairs. Tell them that they will be creating an interview between a person from South Asia and a journalist from the United States. Have pairs choose one of the following roles: a village dweller, a city dweller, a South Asian woman, or a teenager who attends high school.

Tell each pair to decide who will be the South Asian and who will be the journalist. Have students create a series of questions and answers on what life is like in the role they chose. Then have them perform their interview for the class.

ALTERNATIVE ASSESSMENT: ON ASSIGNMENT

To help your students complete the On Assignment activity, you may wish to

1. copy and distribute the reproducible On Assignment Activity Sheet on page 143.
2. review the components of a letter. Ask a student to describe for the class a letter that he or she has written or received.
3. divide students into pairs to work on the project.
4. provide almanacs and travel guides.

5. share with students the standards by which you will evaluate their projects. You may wish to use the following scoring rubric.

0 **Fail/Unacceptable** The project is not attempted.

1 **Limited/Acceptable** The letters contain limited information and serious grammatical and structural errors.

2 **Commendable** The letters are well organized and well written; the information is accurate. They contain minor grammatical and structural errors.

3 **Outstanding** The letters are carefully organized and clearly written. They contain a great deal of information.

COOPERATIVE LEARNING

Working Together: Writing and Performing a Skit Before they begin to write their skits, have students review the chapter and create a list of main ideas. Then have them choose a scenario and describe characters that would appear in that scenario. Finally, ask them to write and perform the skit.

USING THE VISUALS TO TEACH...

Art and Music Tell students to study the picture on page 140 that shows an Indian dancer. Ask them to point out similarities and differences between Indian dance and Western-style dance.

CLOSING THE LESSON

In closing, ask students to answer the preview questions that appear at the beginning of the chapter and each section. Instruct them to write the answers in their notebooks and refer to them when reviewing this chapter.

MORE TO DO

Literature Have students read the Tamil poems in Unit 2, Chapter 2, of Globe Fearon's *World Tapestries*. Ask students to write a brief essay on the elements of Tamil culture that they identify in the selections.

South Asia in the World Today

OBJECTIVES

After reading this chapter, students will be able to

- describe the political and economic challenges that the nations of South Asia have faced since independence.
- discuss the role that the nations of South Asia play in world politics.

PREVIEW

Provide students with newspapers and news magazines. Ask them to scan the material for articles about the countries of South Asia. Have students create a list of issues that these countries face and refer to this list while they read.

DEVELOPING THE CHAPTER

Tell students to choose one issue that they read about in the chapter and to write a letter to the editor of a local newspaper stating their opinions on this issue. Possible suggestions include, but are not limited to, the following: independence for Punjab; India's economic challenges; the independence of Pakistan; the division of East Pakistan and West Pakistan; Benazir Bhutto's rule; and relations between India and China, India and the United States, or India and the Soviet Union. When the letters are complete, have volunteers read them aloud to the class.

ALTERNATIVE ASSESSMENT: ON ASSIGNMENT

To help your students complete the On Assignment activity, you may wish to

1. copy and distribute the reproducible On Assignment Activity Sheet on page 144.

2. divide students into small groups to work on the project.

3. provide materials such as poster board or construction paper and colored markers, as well as information sources such as almanacs.

4. share with students the standards by which you will evaluate their projects. You may wish to use the following scoring rubric.

0 **Fail/Unacceptable** The project is not attempted.

1 **Limited/Acceptable** The time line artwork and text contain limited information and serious grammatical and structural errors.

2 **Commendable** The time line artwork and text are well coordinated; the information presented is accurate. The project contains minor grammatical and structural errors.

3 **Outstanding** The time line artwork and text are carefully organized and clearly written. The project contains a great deal of accurate information.

COOPERATIVE LEARNING

Working Together: Writing Quiz Questions Tell students to review the chapter and to create a list of facts about each country. Have them choose a country and draft at least five questions about that country along with answers to the questions. Provide students with a "quiz show" format and have students play the game using their questions and answers.

ESL/LEP STRATEGY

Have students find the terms *non-alignment* and *non-aligned* in a dictionary. Ask them to rewrite the definitions in their own words. Ask students to review the chapter and make a list of the ways in which India implemented its policy of non-alignment. Ask students why they think India chose non-alignment. Ask them how the United States felt about India's policy.

CLOSING THE LESSON

In closing, ask students to answer the preview questions that appear at the beginning of the chapter and each section. Instruct them to write the answers in their notebooks and refer to them when reviewing this chapter.

MORE TO DO

Analyzing Current Events Ask students to use the articles they identified in the Preview activity to prepare a summary describing a current issue in the region. Have students present their summaries to the rest of the class.

The Heritage of Southeast Asia

OBJECTIVES

After reading this chapter, students will be able to

- describe the ancient empires and civilizations of Southeast Asia.
- discuss European colonization of Southeast Asia and the independence movement.

PREVIEW

Write *Southeast Asia* on the chalkboard and draw a large circle around it. Have students use their text or a classroom map to identify the countries in the region. Write each country around the circle and have students brainstorm at least one fact about each country they have listed.

DEVELOPING THE CHAPTER

Tell students that they will make a time line of significant events in Southeast Asian history. Draw a sample time line on the board and point out the difference between dates labeled B.C. and A.D.

Have students create a time line that begins in 100 B.C. and ends in the present. Tell students to list significant events and rulers from Southeast Asian history along with the dates on which events occurred. The list of events should be in chronological order. Instruct students to use their lists to place the historical events on the time line. Encourage students to illustrate their time lines with original drawings or pictures from magazines and newspapers. Students may work in pairs or individually on this assignment.

ALTERNATIVE ASSESSMENT: ON ASSIGNMENT

To help your students complete the On Assignment activity, you may wish to

1. copy and distribute the reproducible On Assignment Activity Sheet on page 145.
2. bring to class history books for third graders to give students a sense of how a third-grade book looks.
3. divide students into small groups to work on the project.
4. provide materials such as reference books, pencils and markers, and sheets of paper.

5. share with students the standards by which you will evaluate their projects. You may wish to use the following scoring rubric.

0 Fail/Unacceptable The project is not attempted.

1 Limited/Acceptable The mini-history contains limited information and factual errors; few, or inappropriate, illustrations; and serious grammatical and structural errors.

2 Commendable The mini-history is at least ten pages long, is illustrated, and is factually correct. The project contains minor grammatical and structural errors.

3 Outstanding The mini-history is 10 to 12 pages long, is richly illustrated, and is appropriate for third graders.

COOPERATIVE LEARNING

Working Together: Creating a Newspaper Show students samples of local or school newspapers. Tell them to review the chapter and to create a list of main ideas. Have them draft at least two news stories and two features. Encourage students to find or draw pictures to include in their newspapers.

ESL/LEP STRATEGY

Have pairs of students choose one of the sections from Chapter 12. Ask students to review the section, looking up unfamiliar words. Then have them summarize the information, rewriting the section in their own words.

CLOSING THE LESSON

In closing, ask students to answer the preview questions that appear at the beginning of the chapter and each section. Instruct them to write the answers in their notebooks and refer to them when reviewing this chapter.

MORE TO DO

Drawing Maps Provide pairs of students with two copies of the outline map for Southeast Asia. Ask students to create one map that shows Southeast Asia under colonial rule in about 1900. A second map should show the present-day boundaries of these countries.

Changing Patterns of Life in Southeast Asia

OBJECTIVES

After reading this chapter, students will be able to

- describe the cultures of the people of Southeast Asia.
- discuss the art and literature of Southeast Asia.

PREVIEW

Before students begin to read, play a recording of Indonesian music or show students a sample of Southeast Asian art or architecture. Lead a discussion on the differences between the arts in Western and Southeast Asian cultures.

DEVELOPING THE CHAPTER

Ask students to imagine that they live in Southeast Asia. Have students choose one of the following roles: a rice farmer living in a kampung, a recent migrant to Jakarta, a resident of Singapore, a Southeast Asian woman, or a school-age child.

Ask students to write a letter to a friend or relative describing their life. Letters should include a description of what their house looks like, how they make a living or what school is like, and what their neighbors are like. When the letters are completed, have volunteers read them aloud to the class.

ALTERNATIVE ASSESSMENT: ON ASSIGNMENT

To help your students complete the On Assignment activity, you may wish to

1. copy and distribute the reproducible On Assignment Activity Sheet on page 146.

2. model the creation of a travel presentation. Describe to students the text and pictorial information that would be included in a travel presentation.

3. divide students into small groups to work on the project.

4. provide art materials such as poster board or construction paper, colored markers or pencils, as well as reference material.

5. share with students the standards by which you will evaluate their projects. You may wish to use the following scoring rubric.

0 **Fail/Unacceptable** The project is not attempted.

1 **Limited/Acceptable** The presentation text and pictures contain limited information and serious grammatical and structural errors.

2 **Commendable** The presentation text and pictures are well coordinated. The presentation is informative and accurate, but contains minor grammatical and structural errors.

3 **Outstanding** The presentation text and pictures are carefully organized and clearly written. They contain a great deal of information.

COOPERATIVE LEARNING

Working Together: Defining Vocabulary For this project, you may wish to pair students of different ability levels. Tell students to review the chapter and to create a list of words that are new to them. Have each group select five words and write the words and definitions on separate sheets of paper. Provide students with a "game show" format and have students play the game using the words and definitions they created.

USING THE VISUALS TO TEACH...

Economics Have students compare the photograph of the rice farmer on page 170 with the photographs of modern Southeast Asia in Chapter 14. Lead a discussion based on these photographs about the differences in the economies of the rural and urban areas of Southeast Asia.

CLOSING THE LESSON

In closing, ask students to answer the preview questions that appear at the beginning of the chapter and each section. Instruct them to write the answers in their notebooks and refer to them when reviewing this chapter.

MORE TO DO

Writing an Art Review Ask students to find an example of Southeast Asian literature, film, art, or music. Tell students to imagine that they are art critics for the local radio station and to prepare art reviews for the next broadcast. Have students present their reviews to the class.

Southeast Asia in the World Today

OBJECTIVES

After reading this chapter, students will be able to

- discuss recent political and economic trends in Southeast Asia.
- describe Southeast Asia's changing role in world politics and economics.

PREVIEW

Before students begin reading, ask volunteers to define communism and democracy. Tell them that before 1990, the world's power was balanced between these two political ideologies. Lead a discussion in which students make inferences about the effects of such an ideological struggle.

DEVELOPING THE CHAPTER

Divide the class into six groups. Assign to each group one of the following economic or political issues discussed in the chapter: the move toward privately owned businesses, the Green Revolution, communism vs. democracy, events in the Philippines, foreign investment, and events in Cambodia.

Ask students to review the information in the chapter. When they have finished, have groups create a news report on the issue. In their report, students should describe the challenge their issue poses in Southeast Asia today and what, if anything, is being done to meet the challenge. When the news reports are complete, have each group present its report to the class.

ALTERNATIVE ASSESSMENT: ON ASSIGNMENT

To help your students complete the On Assignment activity, you may wish to

1. copy and distribute the reproducible On Assignment Activity Sheet on page 147.
2. ask students to describe board games they have played.
3. divide students into small groups to work on the project.
4. provide materials such as poster board or construction paper, colored markers or pencils, and information sources.
5. share with students the standards by which

you will evaluate their projects. You may wish to use the following scoring rubric.

0 Fail/Unacceptable The project is not attempted.

1 Limited/Acceptable The board game and questions contain limited information; rules are confusing; questions contain serious grammatical and structural errors.

2 Commendable The board game design and questions are well coordinated and the rules are easy to follow. The questions contain minor grammatical and structural errors.

3 Outstanding The board game design and questions are carefully organized and clearly written. The rules are concise and easy to follow.

COOPERATIVE LEARNING

Working Together: Conducting an Interview Model or describe an interview for students. Tell them to review the chapter and choose a Southeast Asian leader to "interview." Have them draft at least six questions and answers for their interview. Encourage students to write a short biography of the leader to accompany their interview.

ESL/LEP STRATEGY

Use a concept map to discuss the process of organizing ideas visually. Write the topic of the chapter on the board. Ask students to choose three main ideas from the chapter. Arrange these ideas in circles around the topic. Write the details that support each of the main ideas in "spokes."

CLOSING THE LESSON

In closing, ask students to answer the preview questions that appear at the beginning of the chapter and each section. Instruct them to write the answers in their notebooks and refer to them when reviewing this chapter.

MORE TO DO

Current Events Ask students to find articles about a Southeast Asian nation in a newspaper or news magazine. Tell students to use these articles to prepare a summary that describes a current issue in the region. Have students present their summaries to the class.

Australia, New Zealand, and Oceania

OBJECTIVES

After reading this chapter, students will be able to

- describe the geography and people of Australia, New Zealand, and Oceania.
- discuss European colonization of Australia and New Zealand and the subsequent independence movements.

PREVIEW

Before students read, ask them what they know about Australia, New Zealand, and Oceania (the South Pacific). Locate these regions on a world map.

DEVELOPING THE CHAPTER

Ask pairs of students to label the following elements on outline maps: deserts and semi-dry areas, mountains, rivers, major physical regions, and features of Australia and New Zealand; major islands and the three main groups of Oceania; and the natural resources of each region.

When students are finished, lead a discussion of how the lives of the people have been affected by the geography of the different regions.

ALTERNATIVE ASSESSMENT: ON ASSIGNMENT

To help your students complete the On Assignment activity, you may wish to

1. copy and distribute the reproducible On Assignment Activity Sheet on page 148.
2. show students copies of travel posters.
3. divide students into pairs to work on the project.
4. provide materials such as poster board or construction paper, as well as colored markers or pencils.
5. share with students the standards by which you will evaluate their projects. You may wish to use the following scoring rubric.

0   Fail/Unacceptable The project is not attempted.

1   Limited/Acceptable The posters present limited information or are incomplete and contain serious errors in language and structure.

2   Commendable The posters are well executed.

The presentation is informative and accurate, but contains minor flaws in language and structure.

3   Outstanding The posters are carefully executed and clearly written and show an excellent understanding of the subject. They contain a great deal of information and are virtually error free.

COOPERATIVE LEARNING

Working Together: Creating a Talk Show For this project, you may wish to create heterogeneous groupings. Describe or model a sample TV or radio talk-show format. Have students select a role. Tell students to review the chapter and library resources and to create a list of characteristics for their roles. Have them draft their dialogue using these characteristics. Make sure that each group selects a moderator. Students may wish to videotape or audiotape their talk show, or they may present it live to the class.

USING THE VISUALS TO TEACH...

Geography Ask students to compare the photographs of Australia, New Zealand, and Oceania. Ask them how the geography of the regions differ. Then ask them how the geography compares to the region in which they live.

CLOSING THE LESSON

In closing, ask students to answer the preview questions that appear at the beginning of the chapter and each section. Instruct them to write the answers in their notebooks and refer to them when reviewing this chapter.

MORE TO DO

Literature Have students read a folk tale or short story in Unit 2, Chapter 3, of Globe Fearon's *World Tapestries*. Ask students to prepare an oral report on the culture presented in that selection. For the students who choose a folk tale, suggest that they discuss the meaning of that folk tale to the culture. For the students who choose a short story, suggest that they highlight the culture's attitudes toward women and the family, or cultural differences between native and Western-influenced cultures.

Focus on East Asia

UNIT OBJECTIVES

After completing this unit, students will be able to

- describe the key geographic features of East Asia.
- discuss the history of China, Japan, and Korea.
- describe how culture has evolved in the countries of East Asia.
- explain how East Asia relates to the world today.

PREVIEW

Use the unit time line and Exploring Regional Issues on pages 204–206 of the student text. Have students study the time line and answer the questions. Then assign Population Density and Landforms of East Asia: Analyzing Maps on page 206. After students have completed work on the maps, use the worksheet on page 167 in this Teacher's Resource Manual to reinforce the concepts and skills.

After they have completed the worksheet, have students study a physical map of the United States. Ask them to use what they have learned about population density and landforms to guess which parts of the United States are most populated and which are least populated. Present students with a population density map of the United States and have them check the accuracy of their guesses.

DEVELOPING THE UNIT

Use the section, chapter, and unit reviews in the student text and the following resources in this Teacher's Resource Manual to develop the chapters in this unit.

- Lesson Plans, pp. 44–51
- On Assignment Worksheets, pp. 168–174
- Critical Thinking Activity Worksheets, pp. 175–181
- Chapter Tests, pp. 182–188
- Unit Test, pp. 189–190
- Outline Maps, pp. 274–277

LITERATURE CONNECTIONS

Assign students "No Way Out" on pages 267–270. Before students read the selection, have them use a dictionary to define the following words: *proceeding, reform, expel, warrant, scrawl, perch,* and *agile.* After they read "No Way Out," ask them to write a letter to Harry Wu expressing their feelings about his arrest and conviction. In the letter, ask students to compare Wu's trial with the way in which someone in the United States is usually tried for a crime.

CLOSING THE UNIT

- Assign the Unit Review on pages 296–297 in the student text.
- Assign the Unit Test on pages 189–190 in the Teacher's Resource Manual.

LINKING THE UNITS: GLOBAL ISSUES

You may wish to use the Taking Action activity on page 299 as a performance assessment opportunity or portfolio entry.

To complete the activity, ask students to find a partner who shares their opinion. Have pairs discuss their opinions and generate arguments to use in their e-mail messages to the President. Students should work collaboratively to develop strong arguments to support their opinions.

The Land and People of East Asia

OBJECTIVES

After reading this chapter, students will be able to

- describe the landforms, climate, and vegetation of East Asia.
- explain the common elements of culture in East Asia.

PREVIEW

Review the explanation of the geographic theme of place. (See pages 6–7 of the Student Edition.) Ask students to study the photographs and map in Chapter 16. Then have them list the characteristics of place for East Asia. Record students' observations on the chalkboard or on an overhead transparency.

DEVELOPING THE CHAPTER

Instruct students to make an informal outline of the chapter as they read. Review outlining techniques before they begin. Explain that an informal outline does not have the strict format of a formal outline, but contains the same information. After each section, allow students in small groups to review their outlines.

ALTERNATIVE ASSESSMENT: ON ASSIGNMENT

To help your students complete the On Assignment activity, you may wish to

1. copy and distribute the reproducible On Assignment Activity Sheet on page 168.

2. supply students with paper and chalk, paint, or felt-tipped markers.

3. require groups to write captions for their murals.

4. have each group present its mural and then display the murals in the classroom.

5. share with students the standards by which you will evaluate their projects. You may wish to use the following scoring rubric.

0 Fail/Unacceptable The mural is not attempted.

1 Limited/Acceptable The mural and captions are sketchy or present inaccurate information. The captions contain serious grammatical errors and the art is sloppy or inappropriate.

2 Commendable The mural and captions are informative and accurate. The art is complete and shows effort; the captions contain minor flaws.

3 Outstanding The mural is carefully drawn, thorough, and clear. It presents a great deal of information; captions are well written and interesting.

COOPERATIVE LEARNING

Working Together: Writing Letters
Review letter-writing techniques. (This will also be useful for students who do the More To Do activity.) For the first draft, have group members pass the letter around the group and have each one add a paragraph. After the letter has been revised, have groups exchange letters for editing and proofreading. Include an evaluation form that asks:

- What did we like about the letter?
- What needs improvement?
- What would we like to know more about?
- What other suggestions can we make?

Have students complete this form for each letter.

USING THE VISUALS TO TEACH . . .

Economics Ask students to study the pictures and map on pages 208–209 in the photo essay on the land. Then have them name one industry that is important to Japan. Discuss with them the role of China's rivers in the economy of China.

CLOSING THE LESSON

In closing, ask students to answer the preview questions that appear at the beginning of the chapter and each section. Instruct them to write the answers in their notebooks and refer to them when reviewing this chapter.

MORE TO DO

Writing Letters Suggest that students write letters to the embassies or consulates or to the UN delegations of the lands they will study: China, Taiwan, Japan, North Korea, and South Korea. Have them request such material as maps and statistical information. The materials received will be useful for other chapters as well as Chapter 16.

China: The Longest History

OBJECTIVES

After reading this chapter, students will be able to

- summarize Chinese history.
- explain how the Communists came to power in China.

PREVIEW

Write on the board or read to students the quotation at the beginning of Section 1. Have students give their interpretations of its meaning. Ask for historical examples from other places that support these interpretations. Suggest that as they read the chapter, students evaluate whether the statement is valid for China's history.

DEVELOPING THE CHAPTER

Explain that this chapter presents a long period of history. Students may find it helpful to create a chart to organize information. Distribute a chart with the following columns:

Rulers	Time Period	Significant Events	Important People	Reasons for Decline

Instruct students to fill in the chart as they read. Explain that the chart will be useful in completing the On Assignment skit and the Working Together activity. Students might work in small groups to check one another's charts.

ALTERNATIVE ASSESSMENT: ON ASSIGNMENT

To help your students complete the On Assignment activity, you may wish to

1. copy and distribute the reproducible On Assignment Activity Sheet on page 169.

2. assign students with a variety of talents and ability levels to small groups so that the skits can be performed more easily.

3. arrange for research time in the library so that students can find information about costumes, appropriate scenery, and other details to make their skits more authentic.

4. provide class time for students to rehearse.

5. share with students the standards by which you will evaluate their projects. You may wish to use the following scoring rubric.

0 Fail/Unacceptable The skit is not attempted.

1 Limited/Acceptable The skit presents limited information; the performance shows little practice or polish. The skit contains serious errors in facts, in language use, and in structure.

2 Commendable The skit is informative and accurate. The performance is well organized and rehearsed, but contains minor flaws in language use and in structure.

3 Outstanding The skit is carefully organized and clearly written and the performance is polished. Extra effort has gone into the details.

COOPERATIVE LEARNING

Working Together: Preparing a Group Report Organize groups in which ability levels are evenly distributed. Suggest that the groups begin by sharing information that the members collected on their charts. Arrange for research time and materials so that each group can examine the dynasties in depth. After the presentations, provide a forum such as a read-around or a discussion for the groups to exchange information.

ESL/LEP ACTIVITY

As students read the text, have them create an illustrated dictionary with definitions in English and in their native language. Explain that words can be key terms or other new words. Suggest that they also include words from Chapter 16. Collect the dictionaries when the study of East Asia is complete.

CLOSING THE LESSON

In closing, ask students to answer the preview questions that appear at the beginning of the chapter and each section. Instruct them to write the answers in their notebooks and refer to them when reviewing this chapter.

MORE TO DO

Writing Letters Have students imagine that they participated in the Long March. Have them write several letters to friends about events, difficulties, and triumphs along the way.

The History of Japan and Korea

OBJECTIVES

After reading this chapter, students will be able to

- chronicle highlights of Japanese and Korean history.
- explain why Korea is a divided country.

PREVIEW

Write *Korea* and *Japan* on the chalkboard or on an overhead transparency. Ask students to create a word web to show their previous knowledge of these two countries. Discuss issues of fact versus opinion that may surface in the activity. Explain that students will learn about the history of both countries in Chapter 18.

DEVELOPING THE CHAPTER

Students will create parallel time boxes as graphic organizers for Japan and Korea. Have students fold sheets of notebook paper in half lengthwise and label one column *Japan* and the other *Korea*. Instruct students to list important events and dates in Japanese history in chronological order. As they read about Korea, have them place important dates and events in the time box next to similar dates in Japanese history. Suggest that students skip two lines after each entry to make it easier to place corresponding Korean events. Add that the parallel time box will help with the On Assignment and Working Together activities.

ALTERNATIVE ASSESSMENT: ON ASSIGNMENT

To help your students complete the On Assignment activity, you may wish to

1. copy and distribute the reproducible On Assignment Activity Sheet on page 170.
2. present a lesson on proofreading marks.
3. establish read-around groups or pairs for peer evaluation and proofreading.
4. provide time for students to make corrections in their journals.
5. share with students the standards by which you will evaluate their projects. You may wish to use the following scoring rubric.

0 **Fail/Unacceptable** The journal is not attempted.

1 **Limited/Acceptable** The journal is incomplete or presents limited information. It contains serious errors in language use and in structure.

2 **Commendable** The journal is well organized, informative, and accurate. It contains minor flaws in language use and in structure.

3 **Outstanding** The journal is carefully organized and clearly written. It contains a great deal of information and insightful comments and is virtually error free.

COOPERATIVE LEARNING

Working Together: Creating a Historical Poster Provide time for groups to choose an event to portray on their posters. Ensure that there is no duplication. Bring to class poster board and other art supplies. Have a spokesperson from each group explain its poster to the class.

ESL/LEP ACTIVITY

Have students continue the illustrated dictionary that they began in Chapter 17. Also, pair ESL/LEP students with native English speakers to create impromptu dialogues based on the visuals in the chapter. Ask pairs to write a brief evaluation of their experiences with this activity.

CLOSING THE LESSON

In closing, ask students to answer the preview questions that appear at the beginning of the chapter and each section. Instruct them to write the answers in their notebooks and refer to them when reviewing this chapter.

MORE TO DO

Making a Presentation Ask interested students to research Japanese heraldry and present their findings to the class. Encourage students to include visuals such as drawings or photographs in their presentations. If possible, have students draw parallels to European heraldry. Students might speculate on why particular symbols were chosen.

Changing Patterns of Life in East Asia

OBJECTIVES

After reading this chapter, students will be able to

- explain how life in China changed under Communist rule.
- discuss how traditions affect modern Japanese life.
- contrast life in North and South Korea.

PREVIEW

Have students examine the photographs in the chapter. After they have studied the visuals, ask them what conclusions they can draw about life in China, Japan, and the two Koreas. Have them interpret and discuss their observations. Encourage students to compare what they discover about life in East Asia to life in the United States or in their native countries.

DEVELOPING THE CHAPTER

After students have read each section, give them a few minutes to brainstorm the ten most important ideas from the section. After the brainstorming activity, have them meet in small groups to compare their ideas. Allow students to add or delete ideas from their individual clusters as part of the group activity.

ALTERNATIVE ASSESSMENT: ON ASSIGNMENT

To help your students complete the On Assignment activity, you may wish to

1. copy and distribute the reproducible On Assignment Activity Sheet on page 171.

2. present a lesson on interviewing.

3. collect and review students' interview questions and show the class some exemplary ones.

4. arrange for the interviews to be videotaped or recorded and then made into a television or radio show.

5. share with students the standards by which you will evaluate their interviews. You may wish to use the following scoring rubric.

0 **Fail/Unacceptable** The interview is not attempted.

1 **Limited/Acceptable** The interview is incomplete or presents limited or inaccurate information. It contains irrelevant or frivolous accounts and possesses serious errors in language use and in interviewing techniques.

2 **Commendable** The interview is thoughtful, informative, and accurate. Partners have shared equally in the effort. The interview contains minor flaws in language use and in interviewing techniques.

3 **Outstandin**g The interview contains a great deal of interesting information. The interviewing techniques are perceptive and bring out exceptional answers; the presentation is virtually flawless.

COOPERATIVE LEARNING

Working Together: Planning a Chinese New Year Celebration Arrange for research time in the library or bring pertinent materials to the classroom. If possible, show a video of an actual Chinese New Year celebration or invite someone from the Chinese community to serve as a resource for the class. If time allows, have groups perform the celebration they planned.

ESL/LEP ACTIVITY

Have students add to the illustrated dictionaries they began in Chapter 17. In addition, ask small groups of ESL/LEP students to prepare crossword puzzles of important words and terms from the chapter. Give classmates the puzzles to solve.

CLOSING THE LESSON

In closing, ask students to answer the preview questions that appear at the beginning of the chapter and each section. Instruct them to write the answers in their notebooks and refer to them when reviewing this chapter.

MORE TO DO

Literature Have students read the selections written by Chinese writers from Unit 2, Chapter 1, of Globe Fearon's *World Tapestries*. Ask students to compare and contrast the culture of China before and after the Communist takeover.

China Today

OBJECTIVES

After reading this chapter, students will be able to

- discuss changes in China since the 1960s.
- explain how Chinese values changed under communism.
- present the story of Taiwan.

PREVIEW

Write these lines from a Red Guard poster on the board: "We are the critics of the old world; we are the builders of the new world." Ask students to interpret these lines. Explain their authorship. Ask students to identify other people who could have made similar statements.

DEVELOPING THE CHAPTER

Ask students to imagine that they are newspaper reporters who have worked in China since the 1960s. Explain that, as reporters, they are to send short dispatches similar to telegrams to their home office after important events. Have them create dispatches for the important events that they read about in Chapter 20. At the end of each section, collect these dispatches and read two or three of them aloud.

ALTERNATIVE ASSESSMENT: ON ASSIGNMENT

To help your students complete the On Assignment activity, you may wish to

1. copy and distribute the reproducible On Assignment Activity Sheet on page 172.
2. show students examples of Chinese posters and encourage them to adopt the Chinese style.
3. supply poster board and other materials.
4. consider having students work in small groups to produce a series of posters.
5. share with students the standards by which you will evaluate their projects. You may wish to use the following scoring rubric.

0 **Fail/Unacceptable** The poster is not attempted.

1 **Limited/Acceptable** The poster presents limited information or is incomplete; workmanship is poor. The poster contains serious errors in language use and in structure.

2 **Commendable** The poster is well executed. The presentation is informative and accurate and contains minor flaws in language use and in structure.

3 **Outstanding** The poster is carefully executed and clearly written. It shows excellent understanding of the subject, uses the Chinese model, and is virtually error free.

COOPERATIVE LEARNING

Working Together: Writing a Petition For this project, you may wish to form groups so that ability levels are evenly distributed. Show the groups examples of petitions and have students identify some common elements. If necessary, give groups time to research causes and proposed solutions. Have class members vote to grant or deny the petitions.

USING THE VISUALS TO TEACH . . .

Government Have students study the picture of a student protest on page 264. Ask students to think of times in U.S. history during which people protested for civil rights. Have students create a Venn diagram that shows similarities and differences between civil rights protests in the United States and China.

CLOSING THE LESSON

In closing, ask students to answer the preview questions that appear at the beginning of the chapter and each section. Instruct them to write the answers in their notebooks and refer to them when reviewing this chapter.

MORE TO DO

Creating a Persuasive Speech Reread the lines from the Preview activity. Again, ask students to identify other people who could have expressed similar ideas. Have the students assume the identity of an appropriate individual or group and add to the lines to create a persuasive speech.

Japan and Korea Today

OBJECTIVES

After reading this chapter, students will be able to

- describe Japan's democratic government.
- explain why Japan's economy thrives.
- contrast life in South Korea and North Korea.

PREVIEW

Read aloud with students the first four paragraphs of the case study on page 278. As a class, create a Venn diagram that shows the similarities and differences between student life in Japan and in the United States. As they study the chapter, ask students to look for other similarities and differences in how they live and in how people in Japan and Korea live.

DEVELOPING THE CHAPTER

Students will probably be familiar with the success of Japanese businesses. Ask students to name several of these businesses. They may suggest Toyota, Sony, and other companies. Tell students that this economic success is recent. Japanese factories were largely destroyed in World War II. Suggest that students take notes as they read of ideas and practices that may have led to Japan's good business climate today. Students should pay attention to economic practices as well as to employee-relations activities.

ALTERNATIVE ASSESSMENT: ON ASSIGNMENT

To help your students complete the On Assignment activity, you may wish to

1. copy and distribute the reproducible On Assignment Activity Sheet on page 173.
2. review the proper form for letters.
3. provide time for peer evaluation.
4. share with students the standards by which you will evaluate their projects. You may wish to use the following scoring rubric.

0 Fail/Unacceptable The letter is not attempted.

1 Limited/Acceptable The letter presents limited information and contains serious errors in language use and structure.

2 Commendable The letter is thorough, interesting, informative, and accurate, but contains minor flaws in language use and structure.

3 Outstanding The letter is carefully organized, clearly written, and creative. It contains a great deal of information and provides a unique perspective.

COOPERATIVE LEARNING

Working Together: Creating a Mural
Consider creating groups in which talent and ability levels are evenly distributed. Provide materials such as butcher paper, felt-tipped pens, paint, and so forth. Have representatives from each group present information about its mural to the class.

ESL/LEP ACTIVITY

Continue the illustrated dictionary students began in Chapter 17. In addition, have small groups of ESL/LEP students ask and answer questions about the photographs in the chapter.

CLOSING THE LESSON

In closing, ask students to answer the preview questions that appear at the beginning of the chapter and each section. Instruct them to write the answers in their notebooks and refer to them when reviewing this chapter.

MORE TO DO

Literature Have students read a selection by a contemporary Japanese or Korean writer in Unit 2, Chapter 2, of Globe Fearon's *World Tapestries*. Ask students to write a brief essay on the elements of the Japanese or Korean culture that they identify in that selection.

East Asia and the World Today

OBJECTIVES

After reading this chapter, students will be able to

- explain the relationships that China and Japan have with the rest of the world.
- discuss the problems associated with Japan's economic success.
- describe Hong Kong's special situation.

PREVIEW

Ask students to turn to the East Asia map on pages 596–597 of the student book. Ask them to guess which countries are allies and trading partners, and which have problems with the four Asian countries that the students are studying. Have them support their choices with reasons. Tell students to support or reassess their choices as they read the chapter.

DEVELOPING THE CHAPTER

Inform students that they will make a documentary about one of the modern regions of East Asia. Create four groups—one each for China, Taiwan, Hong Kong, and Japan. Each group will prepare a "shooting script" with dialogue, locales, sound effects, and so forth. Have students videotape their documentaries or make live presentations.

ALTERNATIVE ASSESSMENT: ON ASSIGNMENT

To help your students complete the On Assignment activity, you may wish to

1. copy and distribute the reproducible On Assignment Activity Sheet on page 174.

2. reproduce editorials from school and local newspapers to use as models.

3. discuss techniques of persuasive writing.

4. create read-around groups for peer evaluation and proofreading.

5. share with students the standards by which you will evaluate their editorials. You may wish to use the following scoring rubric.

0 **Fail/Unacceptable** The editorial is not attempted.

1 **Limited/Acceptable** The editorial presents limited or inaccurate information and is not persuasive. It contains serious errors in language use and in structure.

2 **Commendable** The editorial is persuasive. The presentation is informative and accurate, but it contains minor flaws in language use and in structure.

3 **Outstanding** The editorial is carefully organized, persuasive, and clearly written. It contains a great deal of information and excellent arguments.

COOPERATIVE LEARNING

Working Together: Conducting a Debate When forming groups, ensure that ability levels and talents are distributed equally. Review procedures for a debate. Choose an impartial moderator for the debate. After voting, ask students to evaluate themselves by answering these questions:
- What did I do well?
- What could I have done better?

USING THE VISUALS TO TEACH . . .

International Politics Have students look at the picture of Stalin and Mao on page 285 and the picture of Nixon and high-ranking Chinese officials on page 286. Ask them to compare the two pictures. Discuss with them what the events portrayed in the pictures say about China's foreign policy.

CLOSING THE LESSON

In closing, ask students to answer the preview questions that appear at the beginning of the chapter and each section. Instruct them to write the answers in their notebooks and refer to them when reviewing this chapter.

MORE TO DO

Researching Have volunteers research North Korea and South Korea in the world today. Ask the researchers to present their information in a lecture complete with visual aids and to be prepared to answer questions. Require classmates to take notes.

Focus on Latin America and Canada

UNIT OBJECTIVES

After completing this unit, students will be able to

- describe the geography and people of Latin America.
- discuss the impact of colonialism on the cultures of Latin America.
- explain the role of Latin America in the world today.
- identify Canada's key geographic and cultural features and historical events.

PREVIEW

Use the unit time line and Exploring Regional Issues on pages 300–302 of the student text. Have students study the time line and answer the questions. Then assign Urbanization in Latin America: Reading a Line Graph on page 302. After students have completed work on the graph, use the worksheet on page 191 in this Teacher's Resource Manual to reinforce the concepts and skills.

After they have completed the worksheet, have students use the *Readers' Guide to Periodical Literature* or their library's on-line periodical search to find one or two articles about one of the cities on the graph. Ask students to write a one-paragraph summary of the articles and to report their findings to the class.

DEVELOPING THE UNIT

Use the section, chapter, and unit reviews in the student text and the following resources in this Teacher's Resource Manual to develop the chapters in this unit.

- Lesson Plans, pp. 52–59
- On Assignment Worksheets, pp. 192–198
- Critical Thinking Activity Worksheets, pp. 199–205
- Chapter Tests, pp. 206–212
- Unit Test, pp. 213–214
- Outline Maps, pp. 278–283

LITERATURE CONNECTION

Assign students "Chilean Earth" on pages 376–377. Before students read the selection, have them use a dictionary to define the following words: *orchards, vineyards,* and *exalt.* After they read "Chilean Earth," ask them to write a short poem about their town or any other place that is important to them.

CLOSING THE UNIT

- Assign the Unit Review on pages 397–398 in the student text.
- Assign the Unit Test on pages 213–214 in this Teacher's Resource Manual.

LINKING THE UNITS: GLOBAL ISSUES

You may wish to use the Taking Action activity on page 401 as a performance assessment opportunity or portfolio entry.

To complete the activity, students might work in groups to research the topic. Have students use such library resources as *The Readers' Guide to Periodical Literature* or an on-line periodical research system to find up-to-date information about the issue. Have groups write a 3–5 page report on their findings.

The Land and People of Latin America

OBJECTIVES

After reading this chapter, students will be able to

- describe the physical and climatic features, and the natural resources of Latin America.
- identify the major groups of people in Latin America.
- describe how Latin Americans interact with the environment.

PREVIEW

Write the words *Latin America* on the board and have students brainstorm words and phrases that they associate with the region. Then have students look at the photo essays on the land (pages 304–305) and the people (pages 310–311) and decide whether the visuals and captions confirm or refute their initial thoughts about the region.

DEVELOPING THE CHAPTER

Have students create a chart to organize information about Latin America. Tell them to draw a chart with four rows and three columns. Ask students to label the rows "Mexico," "Central America," "the Caribbean," and "South America." Have them label the columns "Physical Features," "Climates," and "People." Using the information in their texts, instruct students to work individually or in small groups to complete their charts.

ALTERNATIVE ASSESSMENT: ON ASSIGNMENT

To help your students complete the On Assignment activity, you may wish to

1. copy and distribute the reproducible On Assignment Activity Sheet on page 192.
2. show students examples of advertisements. Have students find examples of print advertisements and tell whether or not they think the ads are effective and why.
3. provide materials such as poster board or butcher paper, markers or pencils, and reference books with pictures of the region.
4. share with students the standards by which you will evaluate their projects. You may wish to use the following scoring rubric.

0   Fail/Unacceptable The project is not attempted.

1   Limited/Acceptable The poster does not have a clear message or visual image. The paragraphs are not written clearly and contain serious spelling and grammatical errors.

2   Commendable The poster has a good message and an appropriate visual image. The paragraphs are well written and contain minor spelling and grammatical errors.

3   Outstanding The poster has a very clear message and a well-coordinated visual image. The paragraphs clearly explain the intent of the poster and are free of spelling and grammatical errors.

COOPERATIVE LEARNING

Working Together: Writing a Script Provide students with copies of plays so they can see what a script with stage directions looks like. In addition, have them discuss a TV show or movie they recently watched. Tell them to think about how the script for the show or movie might read. When students have completed their work, encourage volunteers to act out a portion of their script.

USING THE VISUALS TO TEACH . . .

Geography Ask students to study the pictures and map on pages 304–305 in the photo essay on the land. Lead a discussion in which students talk about how rivers and mountains might affect communications in a region as large as Latin America.

CLOSING THE LESSON

In closing, ask students to answer the preview questions that appear at the beginning of the chapter and each section. Instruct them to write the answers in their notebooks and refer to them when reviewing this chapter.

MORE TO DO

Literature Have students read two poems in Unit 4, Chapter 2 of Globe Fearon's *World Tapestries*. Ask students to prepare a brief essay that compares how the two poets view the land of Latin America.

The Early Civilizations of Latin America

OBJECTIVES

After reading this chapter, students will be able to

- discuss and describe the cultures of the Mayas, Aztecs, and Incas.
- explain why and how Europeans came to the Americas.

PREVIEW

Distribute the outline map of the world included in this Teacher's Resource Manual. Have students locate Europe and Latin America on the map. As students read the chapter, have them locate the places they are learning about.

DEVELOPING THE CHAPTER

Distribute the Critical Thinking Activity Worksheet on page 200: Making a Time Line. Have students work in groups to complete the assignment and answer the questions. Then have groups transfer their time lines onto large sheets of paper. You may wish to have students use library resources to add more Latin American or world events to their time lines. Tell students to keep their time lines and add to them as they read Chapter 25: Breaking the Grip of the Crown.

ALTERNATIVE ASSESSMENT: ON ASSIGNMENT

To help your students complete the On Assignment activity, you may wish to

1. copy and distribute the reproducible On Assignment Activity Sheet on page 193.

2. show students samples of journal entries kept by such European explorers as Christopher Columbus or Bernal Díaz del Castillo who accompanied Cortés in Mexico.

3. model for students what a typical journal entry might look like. Write a sample journal entry on the board describing your day.

4. share with students the standards by which you will evaluate their projects. You may wish to use the following scoring rubric.

0 **Fail/Unacceptable** The project is not attempted.

1 **Limited/Acceptable** Fewer than three journal entries are submitted. Entries contain limited or incomplete information and contain serious grammatical and structural errors.

2 **Commendable** At least one journal entry on each culture is submitted. Entries are descriptive, but contain minor grammatical and structural errors.

3 **Outstanding** Three to five journal entries are submitted. Entries are descriptive, contain many facts about each culture, and are grammatically and structurally correct.

COOPERATIVE LEARNING

Working Together: Creating a Cartoon Book Have each group work on a different event from the chapter. When students are finished, compile their work into a loose-leaf binder or report folder that may be displayed in class. You may wish to provide students with books about early Latin American civilizations and European exploration for reference. Choose books with many pictures and drawings.

ESL/LEP ACTIVITY

Have pairs of students work together to write 10 to 15 lines of dialogue between Cortés and Montezuma. Then have students role play their dialogue for the class.

CLOSING THE LESSON

In closing, ask students to answer the preview questions that appear at the beginning of the chapter and each section. Instruct them to write the answers in their notebooks and refer to them when reviewing this chapter.

MORE TO DO

Preparing a Research Report Have interested students research and report to the class about one of the following: the ice age; Mayan, Aztec, or Incan civilization; early European explorations.

Breaking the Grip of the Crown

OBJECTIVES

After reading this chapter, students will be able to

- describe life in Latin America under Spanish and Portuguese rule.
- explain how Latin American nations won independence.

PREVIEW

Tell students to look at the maps on pages 333 and 335. Have them note the similarities and differences between the two maps.

DEVELOPING THE CHAPTER

Assign students one of the following roles: (a) a Latin American settler who had been born in Spain; (b) a Creole; (c) a mestizo; (d) a mulatto; (e) a Native American; (f) an African. Have students write one or two diary entries from the point of view of the person they have been assigned. Diary entries should describe the conditions under which the person lived in the early 1800s and how that person would feel about the region declaring its independence.

ALTERNATIVE ASSESSMENT: ON ASSIGNMENT

To help your students complete the On Assignment activity, you may wish to

1. copy and distribute the reproducible On Assignment Activity Sheet on page 194.
2. bring history books for third graders into class to give students a sense of how a third-grade book looks.
3. divide students into small groups to work on the project.
4. provide materials such as reference books, pencils and markers, and sheets of paper.
5. share with students the standards by which you will evaluate their projects. You may wish to use the following scoring rubric.

0 Fail/Unacceptable The project is not attempted.

1 Limited/Acceptable The mini-history contains limited information and factual errors.

Few illustrations are used or are used inappropriately. The mini-history contains serious grammatical and structural errors.

2 Commendable The mini-history is at least 10 pages long, is illustrated, and contains three chapters with useful information that is factually correct. The mini-history contains minor grammatical and structural errors.

3 Outstanding The mini-history is 10 to 12 pages long, is richly illustrated, and contains three chapters that cover content in a style appropriate for third graders. The mini-history is grammatically and structurally correct.

COOPERATIVE LEARNING

Working Together: Creating an Illustrated Time Line If students have completed the Critical Thinking Activity Worksheet: Making a Time Line on page 200 and have continued their time line to include events in Chapter 25 (see Developing the Chapter, Chapter 24, p. 54), have them use their notes and time lines to create illustrations. Display students' work in class.

USING THE VISUALS TO TEACH . . .

Science and Math Have students study the picture of Vera Cruz on page 330 of the text. Ask: What technology is the man using to raise the bucket to the roof of the building? (*pulley*) If the man did not have access to a pulley, how else might he move materials to the roof?

CLOSING THE LESSON

In closing, ask students to answer the preview questions that appear at the beginning of the chapter and each section. Instruct them to write the answers in their notebooks and refer to them when reviewing this chapter.

MORE TO DO

Completing a Map Distribute copies of the outline map of Latin America on page 278 of this Teacher's Resource Manual. Have students work in groups to find out the date each country gained independence. Ask them to put the dates on the map and to write captions for two or three countries describing their struggles for independence.

Changing Patterns of Life in Latin America

OBJECTIVES

After reading this chapter, students will be able to

- explain why Latin America is a culturally diverse region.
- discuss the challenges of city life in Latin America.

PREVIEW

Before students begin reading, ask them to look at the photographs in Chapter 26. Lead a discussion in which students make inferences about what Latin American cities are like based on the pictures.

DEVELOPING THE CHAPTER

Write the following generalizations on the chalkboard:

- Everyone in Latin America speaks Spanish and is Roman Catholic.
- People who live in Latin American cities are wealthy.

Explain to students that a generalization is a broad statement that simplifies complex information. Tell them that generalizations can be accurate or inaccurate. Accurate generalizations can be supported by facts.

Ask students to use facts from the chapter to challenge the generalizations on the chalkboard. Then ask them to formulate accurate generalizations about changing patterns of life in Latin America.

ALTERNATIVE ASSESSMENT: ON ASSIGNMENT

To help your students complete the On Assignment activity, you may wish to

1. copy and distribute the reproducible On Assignment Activity Sheet on page 195.
2. model the creation of a storyboard. Ask a student to describe a show he or she has seen and to sketch a storyboard based on its plot.
3. divide students into small groups to work on the project.
4. provide materials such as poster board or construction paper and colored markers or pencils.

5. share with students the standards by which you will evaluate their projects. You may wish to use the following scoring rubric.

0 **Fail/Unacceptable** The project is not attempted.

1 **Limited/Acceptable** The storyboards and narration contain limited information and serious grammatical and structural errors.

2 **Commendable** The storyboards and narration are well coordinated. The presentation is informative and accurate and contains minor grammatical and structural errors.

3 **Outstanding** The storyboards and narration are carefully organized and clearly written. They contain a great deal of information and no grammatical or structural errors.

COOPERATIVE LEARNING

Working Together: Writing Newspaper Headlines For this project, you may wish to pair students of different ability levels. Show students sample newspaper headlines. Then tell them to review the chapter and to create a list of main ideas. Finally, have them draft at least three headlines from those main ideas. Encourage students to write a lead paragraph to accompany one of their headlines.

USING THE VISUALS TO TEACH . . .

Economics Use the picture on pages 340 and 348 to ask students the following question: Why do people from rural areas move to cities?

CLOSING THE LESSON

In closing, ask students to answer the preview questions that appear at the beginning of the chapter and each section. Instruct them to write the answers in their notebooks and refer to them when reviewing this chapter.

MORE TO DO

Interviewing Divide students into small groups. Tell groups to review Case Study 26 and create at least five questions to ask Marcos, Juana, and Hector. Then have them role-play and perform an interview.

The Changing Face of Latin America

OBJECTIVES

After reading this chapter, students will be able to

- explain why land ownership has been a key issue in most Latin American countries.
- discuss factors that have contributed to poverty in Latin America.
- discuss the recent move toward democracy in a number of Latin American countries.

PREVIEW

Have students look at the chart of Latin American countries on page 356. Ask them to choose one of the following countries and to find out at least one fact about its economy and government as they read Chapter 27: Argentina, Bolivia, Brazil, Cuba, Guatemala, Mexico, Nicaragua, Venezuela.

DEVELOPING THE CHAPTER

Remind students of the importance of land reform issues in Latin America. Divide the class into two groups, unequal in number. Group one will represent Latin American landowners. This group should be comprised of perhaps 20 percent of the class. The other group will represent poor Latin American farmers. Tell students to prepare to role play a meeting between the landowners and the poor farmers. The poor farmers are pressing for land reform, while the landowners are resisting it. Have each group prepare their arguments and anticipate the arguments of the other group.

ALTERNATIVE ASSESSMENT: ON ASSIGNMENT

To help your students complete the On Assignment activity, you may wish to

1. copy and distribute the reproducible On Assignment Activity Sheet on page 196.
2. show students examples of resource maps in atlases.
3. divide students into small groups to work on the project.
4. provide materials such as copies of the outline maps included in this Teacher's Resource Manual, pencils and markers, and a resource atlas of Latin America.
5. share with students the standards by which you will evaluate their projects. You may wish to use the following scoring rubric.

0   **Fail/Unacceptable** The project is not attempted.

1   **Limited/Acceptable** The map is sloppy and contains limited or incorrect information.

2   **Commendable** The map is neatly drawn and contains accurate information.

3   **Outstanding** The map is well drawn and accurate information is presented in an especially attractive way.

COOPERATIVE LEARNING

Working Together: Writing an Editorial Show students examples of editorials from the local newspaper. Tell them to come to a consensus on their support or opposition to land reform. Then instruct them to brainstorm the arguments they will present in their editorial.

ESL/LEP ACTIVITY

If there are students from Latin America in your class, encourage them to prepare a brief oral report to give to the class explaining a bit about the political and economic situation in their home countries. Tell students that if they wish, they may prepare the report in their first language and translate it into English.

CLOSING THE LESSON

In closing, ask students to answer the preview questions that appear at the beginning of the chapter and each section. Instruct them to write the answers in their notebooks and refer to them when reviewing this chapter.

MORE TO DO

Writing a Research Report Have students review the information in Case Study 27 and write a report explaining Cuba's present-day economic and political situation.

Latin America and the World

OBJECTIVES

After reading this chapter, students will be able to

- explain Latin America's relations with the United States and the world.
- discuss the relationship of Latin American nations with one another.
- describe some of Latin America's achievements in literature and the arts.

PREVIEW

Read the following quote from Símon Bolívar to the class: "America is ungovernable. Those who have served the revolution have plowed the seas." Based on what they have already learned about Latin America, discuss with students whether they agree or disagree with Bolívar.

DEVELOPING THE CHAPTER

Tell students to write a letter to their representative in Congress expressing their opinion of U.S. policy in one Latin American nation. Possible choices include Haiti, Nicaragua, Panama, or Chile. Encourage students to use library resources to find out about recent U.S. involvement in the country they choose. Remind students that their letters should be no longer than one page and should state facts to support their opinions.

ALTERNATIVE ASSESSMENT: ON ASSIGNMENT

To help your students complete the On Assignment activity, you may wish to

1. copy and distribute the reproducible On Assignment Activity Sheet on page 197.

2. show students examples of time lines or model the construction of a portion of a time line.

3. divide students into small groups to work on the project.

4. provide materials such as poster board or butcher paper, markers and pencils, and magazines and newspapers from which students can cut pictures.

5. share with students the standards by which you will evaluate their projects. You may wish to use the following scoring rubric.

0   Fail/Unacceptable The project is not attempted.

1   Limited/Acceptable The time line contains fewer than ten events and fewer than three illustrations. Much of the information is inaccurate or incomplete.

2   Commendable The time line contains ten events and three illustrations. Most of the information is accurate and grammatically correct.

3   Outstanding The time line contains ten or more events and three or more illustrations. All information is accurate, clearly organized, and grammatically correct.

COOPERATIVE LEARNING

Working Together: Preparing an Oral Report For this project you may wish to organize heterogeneous groups, or groups that contain students of different ability levels. Have students decide which country they will choose and which students in the group will be responsible for researching, organizing, and presenting the material.

USING THE VISUALS TO TEACH . . .

Art Tell students to study the political cartoon on page 366. Then have them create a cartoon or a description of a cartoon they would draw to express their view of another issue in this chapter.

CLOSING THE LESSON

In closing, ask students to answer the preview questions that appear at the beginning of the chapter and each section. Instruct them to write the answers in their notebooks and refer to them when reviewing this chapter.

MORE TO DO

Creating a Brochure Have students find out more about the Organization of American States (OAS) and create a brochure explaining the history of the organization, its purpose, and some of its accomplishments.

Canada: Building the Mosaic

OBJECTIVES

After reading this chapter, students will be able to

- describe the physical and cultural geography of Canada.
- discuss the history of Canada.
- discuss some of the issues that divide Canadians today.

PREVIEW

Have students look at the photographs in this chapter. Then tell them to read the definition of *mosaic* on the first page of the chapter. Based on the photographs and the definition, ask them to discuss why Canada is considered a mosaic of people and cultures.

DEVELOPING THE CHAPTER

Tell students to choose one province or territory of Canada and create a four- to six-page pamphlet discussing the following information: (a) the geography and climate of the area; (b) the Native Americans who live or lived there; (c) when European settlers arrived; (d) the impact of European settlers on the area; (e) a profile of the people and the economy today. Encourage students to use library resources to complete their pamphlets.

ALTERNATIVE ASSESSMENT: ON ASSIGNMENT

To help your students complete the On Assignment activity, you may wish to

1. copy and distribute the reproducible On Assignment Activity Sheet on page 198.
2. show students videotapes of people making presentations.
3. divide students into small groups to work on the project.
4. provide materials such as resource and reference books.
5. share with students the standards by which you will evaluate their projects. You may wish to use the following scoring rubric.

0 Fail/Unacceptable The project is not attempted.

1 Limited/Acceptable The presentation is less than three minutes long and contains limited or inaccurate information.

2 Commendable The presentation is about three minutes long and focuses on an interesting topic. Most of the information is accurate.

3 Outstanding The presentation is about three minutes long and is given in a particularly lively way. The topic of the presentation is interesting and all information presented is accurate. The visuals selected are appropriate.

COOPERATIVE LEARNING

Working Together: Debating an Issue Divide the class into groups that will support or oppose independence for Quebec. Remind students to use newspaper accounts as well as reference books to gather support for their position. In addition, suggest that students brainstorm to come up with creative ways to argue for or against independence.

USING THE VISUALS TO TEACH...

Cultural History Have students look at the photographs on pages 384 and 386. Ask them the following question: Why is it important for people to preserve their cultural heritage?

CLOSING THE LESSON

In closing, ask students to answer the preview questions that appear at the beginning of the chapter and each section. Instruct them to write the answers in their notebooks and refer to them when reviewing this chapter.

MORE TO DO

Creating a Fact Sheet Have students find out more about the territory of Nunavut. Tell them to create a fact sheet explaining the agreement that created the territory, who lives in the territory, and how it will be governed.

Focus on the Middle East

UNIT OBJECTIVES

After completing this unit, students will be able to

- describe the geography and people of the Middle East.
- discuss important events in the history of the Middle East.
- explain how history has influenced culture in the Middle East.
- discuss the role of the Middle East in the world today.

PREVIEW

Use the unit time line and Exploring Regional Issues on pages 402–404 of the student text. Have students study the time line and answer the questions. Then assign Energy Production and Consumption in the Middle East: Comparing Circle Graphs on page 404. After students have completed work on the graph, use the worksheet on page 215 in this Teacher's Resource Manual to reinforce the concepts and skills.

After they have completed the worksheet, discuss with them the efforts people have made to conserve energy. Create a class list of the conservation efforts individuals can make (for example, shutting off the lights when leaving a room or using car pools to get to work or school).

DEVELOPING THE UNIT

Use the section, chapter, and unit reviews in the student text and the following resources in this Teacher's Resource Manual to develop the chapters in this unit.

- Lesson Plans, pp. 60–67
- On Assignment Worksheets, pp. 216–222
- Critical Thinking Activity Worksheets, pp. 223–229
- Chapter Tests, pp. 230–236
- Unit Test, pp. 237–238
- Outline Maps, pp. 284–286

LITERATURE CONNECTION

Assign students "The House on the Border" on pages 443–446. Then have students study the painting on page 444. Based on the story and the painting, ask students to identify some problems they might experience living on a border. For example, if they had a problem, to whom would they go for help? How would living on a border affect the way they viewed their community and their place in the community?

CLOSING THE UNIT

- Assign the Unit Review on pages 494–495 in the student text.
- Assign the Unit Test on pages 237–238 in this Teacher's Resource Manual.

LINKING THE UNITS: GLOBAL ISSUES

You may wish to use the Taking Action activity on page 497 as a perfomance assessment opportunity or portfolio entry.

Have students work in small groups to create a model of a city of the future. Encourage students to use library resources to find pictures of cities around the world. Tell them that they can use these photographs or drawings as springboards, but that they should use their own information and creativity in their drawings. After students have finished their drawings, ask volunteers to present them to the class.

The Land and People of the Middle East

OBJECTIVES

After reading this chapter, students will be able to

- describe the landforms, climate, and vegetation of the Middle East.
- explain the common elements of culture in the Middle East.

PREVIEW

Before students begin reading, show them a map of the region on an overhead projector or wall map. Brainstorm what they know about the region. Record their responses. You may choose to review the responses later and solicit comments about their accuracy.

DEVELOPING THE CHAPTER

Have students work in small groups to create one scene for a mural that depicts the major characteristics of the Middle East. Assign or let the groups choose their scene. Some possibilities are: deserts, river valleys, mountain regions, a city, a farming village, a Bedouin camp. Require each group to write a short caption that explains the relevance of the scene to the Middle East.

After students have completed the scenes, display the entire mural. You might choose to use the mural as a springboard to discuss the accuracy of student responses in the initial brainstorming session.

ALTERNATIVE ASSESSMENT: ON ASSIGNMENT

To help your students complete the On Assignment activity, you may wish to

1. copy and distribute the reproducible On Assignment Activity Sheet on page 216.

2. require students to outline their speeches so you or their peers can suggest improvements.

3. provide tape recorders for students to use as they rehearse their speeches.

4. suggest that students practice their speeches with partners or in small groups.

5. share with students the standards by which you will evaluate their projects. You may wish to use the following scoring rubric.

0 Fail/Unacceptable The speech is not attempted.

1 Limited/Acceptable The speech includes limited or inaccurate information, shows lack of preparation, and contains serious grammatical and structural errors.

2 Commendable The speech is informative and accurate. The delivery is poised and effective. The speech contains minor errors in English.

3 Outstanding The speech is carefully organized and clearly written. The presentation is especially lively and polished and contains a great deal of information.

COOPERATIVE LEARNING

Working Together: Creating Quiz Questions For this assignment, you may wish to create groups in which the ability levels are approximately equal. You might collect all the questions and act as a game show host for the contest. Consider adding a few questions of your own to help students prepare for their evaluation.

USING THE VISUALS TO TEACH . . .

Geography and Economics Have students study the map and pictures on pages 406–407 in the photo essay on the land. Tell students that the Middle East has been called the "crossroads of the world." Ask students the following: Based on the map, why do you think that was so? What role do you think the location of the region played in making it an early center of trade? What resource featured on the map do you think brings money to the region today?

CLOSING THE LESSON

In closing, ask students to answer the preview questions that appear at the beginning of the chapter and each section. Instruct them to write the answers in their notebooks and refer to them when reviewing this chapter.

MORE TO DO

Mapping Have students make both a political and a physical map of the Middle East. Have them include nations, capitals, major cities, important bodies of water, landforms, and resources.

The Rich Heritage of the Middle East

OBJECTIVES

After reading this chapter, students will be able to

- explain the roots of the ancient civilizations and religions that developed in the Middle East.
- describe the major achievements of each civilization and characteristics of each religion.

PREVIEW

Write on the chalkboard or on an overhead transparency, "An eye for an eye and a tooth for a tooth." Ask students to explain what the statement means. Then ask where the statement comes from. If they identify the law as Babylonian, explain that written law is only one of many contributions our civilization received from the ancient Middle East. If the students do not identify it correctly, explain that they will discover the many achievements of the ancient civilizations of the Middle East as they read the chapter.

DEVELOPING THE CHAPTER

Tell students that after reading the chapter, they will participate in a debate. Explain that students will assume the roles of citizens of ancient civilizations and try to convince judges that their civilization made the most important contributions to human kind. Assign students to each of the ancient civilizations covered in the chapter. As students read, suggest that they keep notes on the positive contributions their civilization made and any negative points to be made about other civilizations.

After completing the chapter, have students meet with those who were assigned to the same civilization to plan their arguments. Give each group three minutes to present the good points of their civilization. Then give each group two minutes to challenge other groups' arguments. Have an impartial panel of judges evaluate the presentations and choose the winner.

ALTERNATIVE ASSESSMENT: ON ASSIGNMENT

To help your students complete the On Assignment activity, you may wish to

1. copy and distribute the reproducible On Assignment Activity Sheet on page 217.

2. provide butcher paper or other materials
3. encourage students to illustrate the time lines.
4. share with students the standards by which you will evaluate their projects. You may wish to use the following scoring rubric.

0 Fail/Unacceptable The time line is not attempted.

1 Limited/Acceptable The time line has many chronological errors or unimportant events and contains serious spelling errors. Art, if any, is sloppy.

2 Commendable The time line is illustrated, informative, and accurate. It contains minor spelling or structural errors.

3 Outstanding The time line is carefully organized, well illustrated, and clearly written. It contains a great deal of information and is grammatically correct.

COOPERATIVE LEARNING

Working Together: Interviewing For this project, you may wish to allow students time for research. Consider allowing the students role-playing the religious experts in each group to work together to research their particular religion. Then have students return to the original groups to write the questions and answers for their interviews.

ESL/LEP ACTIVITY

Pair an ESL/LEP student with a native English speaker. Have the partners take turns asking and answering questions about the visuals in the chapter.

CLOSING THE LESSON

In closing, ask students to answer the preview questions that appear at the beginning of the chapter and each section. Instruct them to write the answers in their notebooks and refer to them when reviewing this chapter.

MORE TO DO

Visiting a Museum Arrange a field trip to a museum that has exhibits from ancient Middle Eastern civilizations or show a film or video, such as one about King Tut's treasures. Discuss how the artifacts support what students have learned in the chapter.

From Empire to Independence

OBJECTIVES

After reading this chapter, students will be able to

- explain the reasons for the rise and decline of the Ottoman Empire.
- describe the formation of new nations from Ottoman lands.
- discuss the founding of Israel.

PREVIEW

Ask students to give a brief account of how the United States became a country. If there are students from other countries in the class, ask them to explain how their native lands became nations. Tell students to keep these histories in mind as they read the chapter, so they can see similarities in nations' struggles for independence.

DEVELOPING THE CHAPTER

Explain to students that this chapter tells how the modern nations of the Middle East came into being. Have students create a chart to organize information about the countries discussed in the chapter. The headings for the columns should be: *Country, Dates, How Founded or Changed, Controlled By / Governed By, Important People, Important Events.* The headings for the rows will be the names of the countries. Have students add facts to their charts as they read the chapter. Explain that these charts will be useful in developing the murals and doing the Working Together assignment in the Chapter Review.

ALTERNATIVE ASSESSMENT: ON ASSIGNMENT

To help your students complete the On Assignment activity, you may wish to

1. copy and distribute the reproducible On Assignment Activity Sheet on page 218.
2. supply students with paper and chalk, paints, or felt-tipped markers.
3. divide the class into small groups to create a class mural.
4. require students or groups to write descriptions for the scenes as captions.
5. share with students the standards by which

you will evaluate their projects. You may wish to use the following scoring rubric.

0 **Fail/Unacceptable** The mural is not attempted.

1 **Limited/Acceptable** The mural and corresponding captions are very sketchy or present inaccurate information. The captions contain serious grammatical errors, and art is sloppy.

2 **Commendable** The mural and captions are informative and accurate. The art is complete and shows effort. The captions contain minor grammatical errors.

3 **Outstanding** The mural is carefully drawn, thorough, and clear. It presents a great deal of information. The captions are well written and grammatically correct.

COOPERATIVE LEARNING

Working Together: Ordering Events Give each group an equal number of index cards to complete. Organize the card swapping so that each group has a chance to arrange the cards from all the other groups. Have a recorder in the group keep a record of the time spent arranging each set of cards. When groups are finished, list all the times on the board. Ask students if they see a pattern. (Times should become shorter.)

ESL/LEP ACTIVITY

Pair ESL/LEP students with partners who are proficient in English. Have the pairs discuss the vocabulary words and use each word in a sentence or in a conversation to ensure understanding.

CLOSING THE LESSON

In closing, ask students to answer the preview questions that appear at the beginning of the chapter and each section. Instruct them to write the answers in their notebooks and refer to them when reviewing this chapter.

MORE TO DO

Performing Dialogues Have pairs of students choose one of the Middle Eastern countries and create a dialogue that compares its struggle for independence with that of the United States. Have students perform their dialogues for the class.

Traditional Patterns of Life

OBJECTIVES

After reading this chapter, students will be able to

- discuss the traditional life of villagers, city dwellers, and nomads.
- explain the importance of the family in the Middle East.
- describe daily life and religious practices.

PREVIEW

Before students begin reading, ask them to analyze the photographs in Chapter 33 to discover aspects of daily life in the Middle East. Have students point out similarities to and differences from life in the United States.

DEVELOPING THE CHAPTER

Extend the concept introduced in the Preview by having students create charts that compare and contrast ways of living in the Middle East and the United States. Tell students to divide a sheet of notebook paper in half lengthwise to create two large columns. Have students title their charts "Comparing the Middle East and the United States," the first column "Similarities," and the second column "Differences." Encourage students to add information as they read and explain that what they write will be helpful for the On Assignment and Working Together activities.

After students have completed the charts, ask if the two regions are more similar than different. Lead students to see that although there are many differences, people in both regions share some basic beliefs and traditions.

ALTERNATIVE ASSESSMENT: ON ASSIGNMENT

To help your students complete the On Assignment activity, you may wish to

1. copy and distribute the reproducible On Assignment Activity Sheet on page 219.
2. review the format for a friendly letter by showing a friendly letter on the overhead projector and discussing the elements.
3. use small groups for peer review to allow letters to be edited and proofread.

4. share with students the standards by which you will evaluate their projects. You may wish to use the following scoring rubric.

0 **Fail/Unacceptable** The letters are not attempted.

1 **Limited/Acceptable** The letters are incomplete or include faulty information. They contain serious grammatical and structural errors.

2 **Commendable** The letters are well organized, informative, and accurate. They contain minor grammatical and structural errors.

3 **Outstanding** The letters are carefully organized, lively, and clearly written. They contain a great deal of information and are grammatically correct.

COOPERATIVE LEARNING

Working Together: Creating a One-Act Play After students have completed their performances, have them evaluate their individual contributions to the group. Ask them to respond to these questions:

- What did I do well?
- What could I have done better?
- What did I learn from doing this assignment?

ESL/LEP ACTIVITY

Consider altering the comparison chart in Developing the Chapter for ESL/LEP students by allowing them to find the similarities and differences between the Middle East and their native countries. In the class discussion that follows completion of the charts, encourage ESL/LEP students to present their conclusions so classmates can better understand more groups of people.

CLOSING THE LESSON

In closing, ask students to answer the preview questions that appear at the beginning of the chapter and each section. Instruct them to write the answers in their notebooks and refer to them when reviewing this chapter.

MORE TO DO

Literature Have students read one selection from Unit 1, Chapter 2 of Globe Fearon's *World Tapestries*. Ask students to write a brief essay on the traditional patterns of life in a Middle Eastern culture that they identify in the selection.

Changing Patterns of Life

OBJECTIVES

After reading this chapter, students will be able to

- discuss how oil has changed life in the Middle East.
- explain how cities have changed.
- describe the changing roles of women.

PREVIEW

Write the word *oil* on the chalkboard. Explain that oil is sometimes called black gold. Elicit from students that the term means oil creates great wealth. Ask them to predict how the discovery of abundant supplies of oil changed life in the Middle East. Record student responses.

DEVELOPING THE CHAPTER

As students begin to study the chapter, tell them that after they have finished reading, they will be asked to assume the roles of people from the Middle East. Explain that as those people, they will discuss their thinking about such issues as women's place in society, the importance of Islam, rights of foreigners and citizens, how life changed because of oil, and so forth. Suggest that notes will help them prepare for the role-playing and will be useful for the On Assignment and Working Together activities.

On the day of the performances, have students draw from a hat the nation that they "live in" (Bahrain, Syria, Kuwait, Israel, Iran, Iraq, Saudi Arabia) and the type of person that they will play (citizen, foreign worker, wealthy, poor, fundamentalist). Then call on small groups of students to role-play the discussion of the issues listed above.

ALTERNATIVE ASSESSMENT: ON ASSIGNMENT

To help your students complete the On Assignment activity, you may wish to

1. copy and distribute the reproducible On Assignment Activity Sheet on page 220.
2. suggest that students tape record the broadcasts as practice.
3. allow students to rehearse and give peer evaluations in small groups.

4. have groups of students present their radio broadcasts as news magazines with individual students focusing on different aspects of change.
5. share with students the standards by which you will evaluate their projects. You may wish to use the following scoring rubric.

0 **Fail/Unacceptable** The broadcast is not attempted.

1 **Limited/Acceptable** The broadcast is incomplete or incorrect. Lack of preparation and structural errors are evident.

2 **Commendable** The broadcast is informative and accurate. It contains minor factual errors or mistakes in presentation.

3 **Outstanding** The broadcast is engaging and well presented. It contains a great deal of accurate information.

COOPERATIVE LEARNING

Working Together: Holding a Press Conference Assign sections of the chapter to the groups. Suggest that classmates take notes on each press conference. After all groups have finished their interviews, have classmates evaluate each presentation for factual accuracy.

USING THE VISUALS TO TEACH . . .

Economics Have students study the picture on page 460 of a Bahraini bank. Ask students how the discovery of oil in the Middle East has affected the economies of countries within the region and of countries outside the region.

CLOSING THE LESSON

In closing, ask students to answer the preview questions that appear at the beginning of the chapter and each section. Instruct them to write the answers in their notebooks and refer to them when reviewing this chapter.

MORE TO DO

Evaluating the Accuracy of Predictions Reproduce the student responses to the preview activity. Ask students individually or in small groups to evaluate the accuracy of their predictions. Encourage students to research information necessary to assess accuracy.

Economic and Political Trends

OBJECTIVES

After reading this chapter, students will be able to

- discuss Arab-Israeli relations.
- chronicle nations' struggles for independence and identity.
- explain the Middle East's economic challenges and achievements.

PREVIEW

Remind students that in Chapter 32 they explored similarities between the U.S. struggle for independence and the struggles of the nations of the Middle East. Explain that a cluster map can help organize and clarify that information. On the chalkboard or on an overhead transparency, write "American Revolution." Then have students cluster reasons why the colonists wanted independence. To sum up the activity, ask volunteers to give reasons why a group of people would want to control their own country. As they read the chapter, have students compare their ideas with actual events in the Middle East.

DEVELOPING THE CHAPTER

Have students make a cause and effect chart as they read the chapter. Use this graphic organizer to help them begin.

CAUSE	DATE	EFFECT
Meeting at Camp David	1978	Peace agreement between Israel and Egypt

Students with greater ability can include virtually all events on the chart. Consider limiting the number of entries per section or supplying more examples for students with average ability. For students with lesser ability, give specific dates and specific events to analyze.

ALTERNATIVE ASSESSMENT: ON ASSIGNMENT

To help your students complete the On Assignment activity, you may wish to

1. copy and distribute the reproducible On Assignment Activity Sheet on page 221.
2. supply materials for book and cover.
3. collect magazines and other sources for pictures.
4. share with students the standards by which you will evaluate their projects. You may wish to use the following scoring rubric.

0 Fail/Unacceptable The picture book is not attempted.

1 Limited/Acceptable The pictures are inappropriate, and the text is inaccurate. The book contains serious grammatical and structural errors.

2 Commendable The text and pictures are informative, accurate, and appropriate. The book contains minor errors.

3 Outstanding The book is creative, interesting, and clearly written. It contains a great deal of information and is grammatically correct.

COOPERATIVE LEARNING

Working Together: Summarizing Assign sections to the groups to ensure no repetition. Brainstorm for alternate ways to explain a section.

USING THE VISUALS TO TEACH . . .

Geography Have students study the map on page 471. Ask them to list the countries that border Israel. Then provide a map showing present-day boundaries of Israel and ask: How have Israel's borders changed from 1967 to today?

CLOSING THE LESSON

In closing, ask students to answer the preview questions that appear at the beginning of the chapter and each section. Instruct them to write the answers in their notebooks and refer to them when reviewing this chapter.

MORE TO DO

Comparing and Contrasting Have students write short reports that compare and contrast the struggles for independence of Middle Eastern countries with that of the United States. Invite them to use the cluster map from the preview activity as a prewriting tool.

The Middle East in the World Today

OBJECTIVES

After reading this chapter, students will be able to

- identify major issues in the Middle East today.
- discuss the Arab-Israeli peace process.
- describe Middle Eastern achievements in the arts.

PREVIEW

Ask students to scan newspapers and news magazines for articles that cover events in the Middle East. Have them read the first paragraph or two of at least one article. Then ask students to list issues the Middle East is facing today. This activity may also be used to prepare students for the On Assignment activity for this chapter.

DEVELOPING THE CHAPTER

Explain to students that after studying the chapter, they will participate in a UN meeting to establish a peace process in the Middle East. Assign roles. Have some students be ambassadors from Middle Eastern countries and others represent other world nations. Select a student to serve as Secretary General. Encourage note taking which will help in this activity as well as the On Assignment activity. After students have completed the chapter, proceed with the UN meeting.

ALTERNATIVE ASSESSMENT: ON ASSIGNMENT

To help your students complete the On Assignment activity, you may wish to

1. copy and distribute the reproducible On Assignment Activity Sheet on page 222.
2. review the format and elements of news articles by distributing models and examples.
3. compile the feature stories into a class book and reproduce them for the students.
4. share with students the standards by which you will evaluate their projects. You may wish to use the following scoring rubric.

0 **Fail/Unacceptable** The feature story is not attempted.

1 **Limited/Acceptable** The feature story is incomplete, off target, or inaccurate. It contains serious grammatical and structural errors.

2 **Commendable** The feature story is informative, well organized, and accurate. It contains minor grammatical and structural errors.

3 **Outstanding** The feature story is carefully organized, interesting, and clearly written. It contains a great deal of information and perceptive insights. It is gramatically and structurally correct.

COOPERATIVE LEARNING

Working Together: Creating a Poem or Song For this assignment, organize groups so talents and abilities are evenly distributed. Provide poems as models and play carefully selected rap music as motivation. Encourage students to think creatively and suggest that they use sound effects, choral readings, live music, and so forth.

ESL/LEP ACTIVITY

Have ESL/LEP students create an illustrated dictionary of the chapter's terms. Definitions may be in their native language as well as in English. Encourage them to share their dictionaries with classmates.

CLOSING THE LESSON

In closing, ask students to answer the preview questions that appear at the beginning of the chapter and each section. Instruct them to write the answers in their notebooks and refer to them when reviewing this chapter.

MORE TO DO

Giving Audiovisual Presentations Ask small groups of students to research the arts and literature of the Middle East. Suggest that students read several of the selections in Unit 1, Chapter 2 of Globe Fearon's *World Tapestries*. Have each group give an audiovisual presentation about the art and literature they researched.

Focus on Europe and Eurasia

UNIT OBJECTIVES

After completing this unit, students will be able to

- describe the geography of Europe and Eurasia.
- discuss the history of Europe and Eurasia.
- describe the culture of Europe and Eurasia.
- explain the role of Europe and Eurasia in the world today.

PREVIEW

Use the unit time line and Exploring Regional Issues on pages 498–500 of the student text. Have students study the time line and answer the questions. Then assign Per Capita Income in Europe and Eurasia: Interpreting a Bar Graph on page 500. After students have completed work on the graph, use the worksheet on page 239 in this Teacher's Resource Manual to reinforce the concepts and skills.

After they have completed the worksheet, have students look up in an almanac the per capita income of the United States and add it to the graph on the worksheet. Discuss with students the meaning of *per capita income* and explain that it is not the only indicator of the wealth of a country. Ask students to brainstorm a list of other things that might indicate the wealth of a country.

DEVELOPING THE UNIT

Use the section, chapter, and unit reviews in the student text and the following resources in this Teacher's Resource Manual to develop the chapters in this unit.

- Lesson Plans, pp. 68–76
- On Assignment Worksheets, pp. 240–247
- Critical Thinking Activity Worksheets, pp. 248–255
- Chapter Tests, pp. 256–263
- Unit Test, pp. 264–265
- Outline Maps, pp. 287–288

LITERATURE CONNECTIONS

Assign students "Facing Hatred During Kristallnacht" on pages 548–549. Before students read the selection, have them work in small groups to create a word web based on the word *Holocaust*. After they read "Facing Hatred During Kristallnacht," ask them to write the first two paragraphs of a newspaper article on the events of Kristallnacht. You may wish to show students sample newspaper articles as a model.

CLOSING THE UNIT

- Assign the Unit Review on pages 588–589 in the student text.
- Assign the Unit Test on pages 264–265 in this Teacher's Resource Manual.

LINKING THE UNITS: GLOBAL ISSUES

You may wish to use the Taking Action activity on page 591 as a perfomance assessment opportunity or portfolio entry.

You might ask students to work in small groups to create the advertisement collage. You may wish to provide students with books and articles about the UN to help them conceptualize their collages. When students have completed their collages, have them present them to the class.

The Land and People of Europe and Eurasia

OBJECTIVES

After reading this chapter, students will be able to

- discuss the geographical features that influence life in Europe and the Eurasian Heartland.
- describe the ethnic differences among the people who live in Europe and the Heartland.

PREVIEW

Before students begin reading, have them study the photo essays on the land (pages 502–503) and the people (pages 508–509). Ask students to list one thing they already know about Europe and the Eurasian Heartland and one thing they would like to find out about this region.

DEVELOPING THE CHAPTER

Organize students into pairs. Provide each pair with outline maps of Europe and of Russia and the Independent Republics, and some colored pencils. Outline maps can be found in this teacher's manual.

Ask student pairs to label the following elements on their maps: major rivers, major ports, mountains, the four geographic regions, natural resources, and major cities.

When students have finished their maps, lead a discussion about the characteristics of the people of the region and how geography has affected the region's cultures and economies.

ALTERNATIVE ASSESSMENT: ON ASSIGNMENT

To help your students complete the On Assignment activity, you may wish to

1. copy and distribute the reproducible On Assignment Activity Sheet on page 240.
2. show students advertisements or ask them to describe billboards or posters they have seen.
3. divide students into small groups to work on the project.
4. provide materials such as poster board or construction paper, as well as colored markers or pencils.
5. share with students the standards by which

you will evaluate their projects. You may wish to use the following scoring rubric.

0 Fail/Unacceptable The project is not attempted.

1 Limited/Acceptable The poster artwork and text contain limited information. The text contains serious grammatical and structural errors.

2 Commendable The poster artwork and text are well coordinated. The presentation is informative and accurate, but the text contains minor grammatical and structural errors.

3 Outstanding The poster artwork and text are carefully organized and clearly written. They contain a great deal of accurate information.

COOPERATIVE LEARNING

Working Together: Writing Newspaper or Magazine Headlines You may wish to pair students of different ability levels. Show students sample newspaper headlines. Tell them to review the chapter and to create a list of main ideas. Have them draft at least three headlines from this list. Encourage students to write a lead paragraph to accompany one of their headlines.

USING THE VISUALS TO TEACH . . .

Geography and Economics Have students study the map and pictures in the two photo essays on pages 502–503 and 508–509. Ask: What geographic features have probably made trade easier between countries in the region? What effect do you think language and other elements of culture have on trade in Europe and the Heartland?

CLOSING THE LESSON

In closing, ask students to answer the preview questions that appear at the beginning of the chapter and each section. Instruct them to write the answers in their notebooks and refer to them when reviewing this chapter.

MORE TO DO

Interviewing Divide the class into small groups. Tell them to review Chapter 37 and choose one region mentioned in the chapter. Have students create a series of questions and answers on what life is like in their region. Then have them conduct interviews in class.

The Roots of European Civilization

OBJECTIVES

After reading this chapter, students will be able to

- describe the history of Europe through the time of the Industrial Revolution.
- discuss how the history of Europe has shaped events in Europe today.

PREVIEW

Before students begin reading, display photographs of paintings or other artwork depicting each of the major historical periods covered in Chapter 38. Use the photographs to lead a discussion on what life might have been like in Europe in each of these time periods.

DEVELOPING THE CHAPTER

Break the class into eight small groups. Assign each group one of the following historical periods covered in Chapter 38: ancient Greece, the Roman Empire, the Middle Ages, the Renaissance and Reformation, the Age of Exploration, European monarchies, the Enlightenment and the French Revolution, and the Industrial Revolution.

Have each group prepare a description of the important events and people in their historical period. Ask students to use this description to prepare a short skit that depicts their time period. Have each group perform their skit for the rest of the class.

ALTERNATIVE ASSESSMENT: ON ASSIGNMENT

To help your students complete the On Assignment activity, you may wish to

1. copy and distribute the reproducible On Assignment Activity Sheet on page 241.
2. model the creation of a storyboard. Ask a student to describe a television show that he or she has seen and to sketch a storyboard based on its plot.
3. divide the class into small groups to work on the project.
4. provide materials such as poster board or construction paper, as well as colored markers or pencils.

5. share with students the standards by which you will evaluate their projects. You may wish to use the following scoring rubric.

0 Fail/Unacceptable The project is not attempted.

1 Limited/Acceptable The storyboards and narration contain limited information and serious grammatical and structural errors.

2 Commendable The storyboards and narration are well coordinated. The presentation is informative and accurate, but contains minor grammatical and structural errors.

3 Outstanding The storyboards and narration are carefully organized and clearly written. They contain a great deal of information.

COOPERATIVE LEARNING

Working Together: Making a Time Line For this project, you may wish to pair students of different ability levels. Draw a sample time line for students. Tell them to review the chapter and create a list of main events and their dates. Have them draw a time line and place the events on it. Encourage students to use pictures as well as text on their time lines.

ESL/LEP STRATEGY

Have pairs of students create flash cards for each term listed on page 513 in the student text. Ask students to use the flash cards to review each term and its meaning. Have students write a sentence for each term that explains its significance in European history.

CLOSING THE LESSON

In closing, ask students to answer the preview questions that appear at the beginning of the chapter and each section. Instruct them to write the answers in their notebooks and refer to them when reviewing this chapter.

MORE TO DO

Researching Divide the class into small groups. Ask each group to choose one significant event in European history. Provide library time for groups to research the event they chose. Have each group give a five-minute presentation on the historical event they researched.

Europe in the 20th Century

OBJECTIVES

After reading this chapter, students will be able to

- describe key historical events in Europe in the 20th century.
- discuss the effect of two world wars and the Cold War on Europe.

PREVIEW

Before students begin reading, tell them that World War I was nicknamed "the war to end all wars." Ask students to guess why it was given that nickname. What does the name suggest about earlier wars? What does the name suggest about World War I?

DEVELOPING THE CHAPTER

Ask students to imagine they are one of the following: a European soldier in World War I, a German citizen before World War II, a European Jew during World War II, a Western European during the Cold War, or a resident of Berlin during the Cold War.

Ask students to write a letter to a friend or relative describing events that they have seen. The letters should include a description of events as well as the writer's feelings and opinions about these events. When they have completed this task, have students read their letters aloud.

ALTERNATIVE ASSESSMENT: ON ASSIGNMENT

To help your students complete the On Assignment activity, you may wish to

1. copy and distribute the reproducible On Assignment Activity Sheet on page 242.

2. model the process of writing a newspaper article. Ask a student to describe the "five Ws" of a newspaper story for the class.

3. divide the class into pairs to work on the project.

4. provide examples of news articles from your local paper. Have students identify the "five Ws" in one article.

5. share with students the standards by which you will evaluate their projects. You may wish to use the following scoring rubric.

0 **Fail/Unacceptable** The project is not attempted.

1 **Limited/Acceptable** The newspaper articles contain limited information and serious grammatical and structural errors.

2 **Commendable** The newspaper articles are well organized and headlines reflect content, but the articles contain minor grammatical and structural errors.

3 **Outstanding** The newspaper articles are carefully organized, clearly written, and accurate. The headlines reflect content.

COOPERATIVE LEARNING

Working Together: Prioritizing Events For this project, you may wish to pair students of different ability levels. Tell students to review the chapter and to create a list of all the events they consider to be important. Have them choose five events from this list to present to the rest of the class. Encourage students to explain why they have included each event in their list.

ESL/LEP STRATEGY

Have pairs of students choose one section from Chapter 39. Ask students to review the section and look up unfamiliar words. Then have students summarize the information by rewriting the section in their own words.

CLOSING THE LESSON

In closing, ask students to answer the preview questions that appear at the beginning of the chapter and each section. Instruct them to write the answers in their notebooks and refer to them when reviewing this chapter.

MORE TO DO

Drawing Maps Divide the class into groups of three. Provide each group with three copies of the outline map of Europe on page 287. Ask each group to create maps that show each country's borders: (1) before World War I, (2) after World War I, and (3) after World War II.

Patterns of Life in Europe

OBJECTIVES

After reading this chapter, students will be able to

- describe what life is like in different parts of Europe.
- discuss the problems that people face in different parts of Europe.

PREVIEW

Before students begin reading, ask them to look at the four charts in the chapter. Lead a class discussion on the differences among the four regions in Europe in terms of population, area, and per capita income.

Ask students to rank the four regions in each of these categories.

DEVELOPING THE CHAPTER

Divide the class into four groups. Assign each group to one of the four regions of Europe. Ask students to review the information in their section and to use library resources to create a travel brochure on their region. In their brochures, students should describe the people and the land of their region, as well as any problems the people of the region are experiencing. Brochures should also highlight or give a specific description of one country in the region. When its work is finished, have each group present its brochure to the rest of the class.

ALTERNATIVE ASSESSMENT: ON ASSIGNMENT

To help your students complete the On Assignment activity, you may wish to

1. copy and distribute the reproducible On Assignment Activity Sheet on page 243.
2. discuss the components of a personal letter. Ask a student to list the types of information that might be included in a letter describing the people or land of a region.
3. share with students the standards by which you will evaluate their projects. You may wish to use the following scoring rubric.

0 Fail/Unacceptable The project is not attempted.

1 Limited/Acceptable The letter contains limited information and serious grammatical and structural errors.

2 Commendable The letter is well organized and contains lively descriptions of people and places in Europe. It contains minor grammatical and structural errors.

3 Outstanding The letter is carefully organized and clearly written and contains a great deal of interesting information about people and places in Europe.

COOPERATIVE LEARNING

Working Together: Making a Chart For this project, you may wish to pair students of different ability levels. Draw a sample blank chart on the chalkboard. Tell students to review the chapter. Have them fill out the chart for four of the countries detailed in the chapter. Encourage students to choose one of the regions discussed in this chapter and to make a similar chart for all of the countries in that region.

USING THE VISUALS TO TEACH . . .

Government Have students look at the photo of the Houses of Parliament on page 540. Ask them what building in Washington, D.C., would be the U.S. equivalent of the Parliament building.

CLOSING THE LESSON

In closing, ask students to answer the preview questions that appear at the beginning of the chapter and each section. Instruct them to write the answers in their notebooks and refer to them when reviewing this chapter.

MORE TO DO

Literature Have students read one selection from Unit 3, Chapter 2, of Globe Fearon's *World Tapestries*. Ask students to prepare and present an oral report on the culture presented in that selection. Suggest that they highlight one aspect of the culture, such as its attitudes toward the role of women, the family, or work.

Europe in the World Today

OBJECTIVES

After reading this chapter, students will be able to

- explain why Europe's role in world events has changed in recent years.
- describe what factors led to the fall of communism in Europe.
- discuss the changing relationships among the nations of Europe.

PREVIEW

Before students begin reading, ask them to bring to class at least two articles about Europe from a newspaper or news magazine. Discuss with students the contents of their articles and list on the chalkboard some of the issues that face Europe today.

DEVELOPING THE CHAPTER

Divide the class into groups of three or four. Tell students that they will be writing a skit that dramatizes recent events in a European country or in a country that is affected by Europe. Ask each group to choose one country. Examples include: Britain, India, Ireland, Russia or the Soviet Union, Poland, Germany, Hungary, and Czechoslovakia.

Ask students to review the chapter and write a summary of the issues that face their country. Direct students to use this summary to write a short skit that depicts these issues. Have each group perform its skit for the class.

ALTERNATIVE ASSESSMENT: ON ASSIGNMENT

To help your students complete the On Assignment activity, you may wish to:

1. copy and distribute the reproducible On Assignment Activity Sheet on page 244.
2. describe the components of an interview. Ask two students to model a short interview for the class.
3. organize students into pairs to work on the project.
4. share with students the standards by which you will evaluate their projects. You may wish to use the following scoring rubric.

0 **Fail/Unacceptable** The project is not attempted.

1 **Limited/Acceptable** The interview contains limited information and serious grammatical and structural errors.

2 **Commendable** The interview is well written. The presentation is informative and accurate, but contains minor grammatical and structural errors.

3 **Outstanding** The interview is carefully organized and clearly written. It contains a great deal of information that indicates an understanding of the events discussed in this chapter.

COOPERATIVE LEARNING

Working Together: Making a Time Line
For this project, you may wish to pair students of different ability levels. Draw a sample time line for students. Tell them to review the chapter and to list at least seven main events and their dates. Have them draw a time line and place the events on it. Encourage students to use pictures as well as text on their time lines.

ESL/LEP STRATEGY

Discuss using a concept map to organize ideas visually. Write the topic of the chapter on the board. Ask students to choose three main ideas from the chapter. Put them in circles around the topic. Put the details that support each of the main ideas in "spokes" around each of the main idea circles.

CLOSING THE LESSON

In closing, ask students to answer the preview questions that appear at the beginning of the chapter and each section. Instruct them to write the answers in their notebooks and refer to them when reviewing this chapter.

MORE TO DO

Current Events Ask students to find articles about one or more European countries in a newspaper or news magazine. Tell students to use these articles to prepare a summary that describes a current issue in Europe. Have students present their summaries to the rest of the class.

The Heritage of Russia and the Eurasian Heartland

OBJECTIVES

After reading this chapter, students will be able to

- describe the history of Russia through the time of the Russian Revolution.
- discuss the rise of communism in the Soviet Union.

PREVIEW

Before students begin reading, tell them that before 1990, the Soviet Union was considered to be "public enemy number 1" to the United States. Ask students why they think one country might want its citizens to believe that another country is its enemy.

DEVELOPING THE CHAPTER

Tell students they will make a time line of the significant events in Russian and Soviet history from A.D. 800 to 1990. Draw a sample time line on the board. Tell students to make a list of significant events and rulers in Russian and Soviet history and the dates the events occurred and the rulers reigned. Have them arrange the events in chronological order.

Instruct students to use their lists to place these events on the time line. Encourage students to use drawings and pictures on their time lines as well as text. Students may work in pairs or individually on the assignment.

ALTERNATIVE ASSESSMENT: ON ASSIGNMENT

To help your students complete the On Assignment activity, you may wish to

1. copy and distribute the reproducible On Assignment Activity Sheet on page 245.
2. describe the components of a journal entry. Ask a student to describe the type of information that might be included in a journal.
3. share with students the standards by which you will evaluate their projects. You may wish to use the following scoring rubric.

0 **Fail/Unacceptable** The project is not attempted.

1 **Limited/Acceptable** The journal entries

contain limited information. The journal and pamphlets contain serious grammatical and structural errors.

2 **Commendable** The journal entries are well written and contain interesting information. The pamphlets are informative and accurate, but contain minor grammatical and structural errors.

3 **Outstanding** The journal entries are carefully organized and clearly written. The pamphlets contain a great deal of information about the daily lives of Russians.

COOPERATIVE LEARNING

Working Together: Making a Chronological List For this project, you may wish to pair students of different ability levels. Have a student define *chronology* for the class. Tell students to review the chapter and to create a list of rulers and the dates they ruled. Have them organize the list in chronological order. Schedule one class session in the school library to give students an opportunity to research and write the summaries of their lists.

USING THE VISUALS TO TEACH . . .

Economics Have students study the picture of Russian peasants on page 560 and the picture of Karl Marx on page 566. Discuss with students what Marx had to say about the contribution of peasants to a country's economy.

CLOSING THE LESSON

In closing, ask students to answer the preview questions that appear at the beginning of the chapter and each section. Instruct them to write the answers in their notebooks and refer to them when reviewing this chapter.

MORE TO DO

Researching Divide the class into small groups. Ask groups to choose one ruler from Russian or Soviet history. Provide library time for groups to research the ruler they choose. Have each group write at least five questions to ask that ruler. Then have students create answers to their questions and role-play an interview with the ruler.

Changing Patterns of Life in Russia and the Eurasian Heartland

OBJECTIVES

After reading this chapter, students will be able to

- describe what life is like in different parts of Russia and the Eurasian Heartland.
- describe how life has changed in Russia and the Heartland since the fall of the Soviet Union.

PREVIEW

Before students begin reading, display a map of Russia and the Eurasian Heartland. Lead a discussion about the physical size of this region. Have students make inferences about how life might be different in different areas of the region.

DEVELOPING THE CHAPTER

Divide the class into four groups. Assign one of the four regions of Russia and the Heartland discussed in the chapter to each group. Ask students to review the information in their section. When they have finished, have groups create a news report on issues and lifestyles of their region. In their report, students should describe the people and the land, as well as any problems or issues that the people of the region are experiencing. When the reports are complete, have each group present their news report for the rest of the class.

ALTERNATIVE ASSESSMENT: ON ASSIGNMENT

To help your students complete the On Assignment activity, you may wish to

1. copy and distribute the reproducible On Assignment Activity Sheet on page 246.

2. model the creation of a map. Show a sample map to students. Ask a student to describe the components of the map and sketch it for the class.

3. divide the class into small groups to work on the project.

4. provide a copy of the outline map of Russia and the Independent Republics and materials such as poster board or construction paper, as well as colored markers or pencils.

5. share with students the standards by which you will evaluate their projects. You may wish to use the following scoring rubric.

0 **Fail/Unacceptable** The project is not attempted.

1 **Limited/Acceptable** The maps in the atlas contain limited and inaccurate information.

2 **Commendable** The maps in the atlas are neat and easy to read, but contain a few misspellings and errors.

3 **Outstanding** The maps in the atlas are carefully organized and clearly drawn. They contain a great deal of accurate information.

COOPERATIVE LEARNING

Working Together: Discussing an Issue Tell groups of students to review the chapter and pick a country and issue they wish to discuss. (You might want students to study a different region from the one they studied in the Developing the Chapter activity described above.) Groups should assign roles (facilitator, timekeeper, recorder, reporter) to each member. Give students a time limit to discuss their issue and its possible solutions. Have each group report back to the class.

ESL/LEP STRATEGY

Have students find the term *nationalism* in the dictionary and define it in their own words. Ask students to review the chapter and list examples of nationalism in Russia and the Eurasian Heartland. Have them note the effects that nationalism has had in each region.

CLOSING THE LESSON

In closing, ask students to answer the preview questions that appear at the beginning of the chapter and each section. Instruct them to write the answers in their notebooks and refer to them when reviewing this chapter.

MORE TO DO

Current Events Ask students to find news articles about Russia or one of the independent republics. Tell students to prepare a summary of the articles describing a current issue in the region and some of the approaches that people are taking to try to resolve it.

Russia and the Heartland in the World Today

OBJECTIVES

After reading this chapter, students will be able to

- discuss the collapse of the Soviet Union and the fall of communism.
- describe how Russia and the republics are dealing with each other.
- describe how Russia and the republics are dealing with the outside world.

PREVIEW

Before students begin reading, ask whether they have read or heard of any issues facing Russia or the Heartland recently. Have students brainstorm issues that are currently facing people in this region.

DEVELOPING THE CHAPTER

Ask students to imagine that they live in the former Soviet Union. Have them select a policy or issue about which they feel strongly and write a letter to the editor of a local newspaper about that issue. Possible suggestions include, but are not limited to, nuclear testing, the Nazi-Soviet pact and World War II, the Cold War (nuclear arms race, Berlin Airlift, Cuban missile crisis), current ethnic problems, the economy, or environmental problems. The letter should include a description of the issue as well as the writer's feelings about the issue. When the letters are complete, have students read them aloud to the class.

ALTERNATIVE ASSESSMENT: ON ASSIGNMENT

To help your students complete the On Assignment activity, you may wish to

1. copy and distribute the reproducible On Assignment Activity Sheet on page 247.
2. describe the components of a newspaper editorial. Show students a copy of a typical editorial. Ask a student to describe its components for the class.
3. divide the class into pairs to work on the project.
4. provide materials such as poster board or construction paper, as well as colored markers or pencils.

5. share with students the standards by which you will evaluate their projects. You may wish to use the following scoring rubric.

0　**Fail/Unacceptable** The project is not attempted.

1　**Limited/Acceptable** The editorial contains limited information and does not clearly express the writer's point of view. It contains serious grammatical and structural errors.

2　**Commendable** The editorial is informative; the writer uses facts to support opinions. It contains minor grammatical and structural errors.

3　**Outstanding** The editorial is carefully organized and well written and clearly expresses a point of view supported by facts.

COOPERATIVE LEARNING

Working Together: Writing a Petition For this project, you may wish to pair students of different ability levels. Have the class brainstorm some possible uses for petitions. Tell students to review the chapter and to create a list of policies that they might like to change if they were Russian citizens. Have them draft a petition to persuade the government to change one of the policies on their lists.

USING THE VISUALS TO TEACH . . .

International Politics Have students study the photos on pages 584 and 586. Discuss with them why control over nuclear weapons and the environment are of worldwide concern.

CLOSING THE LESSON

In closing, ask students to answer the preview questions that appear at the beginning of the chapter and each section. Instruct them to write the answers in their notebooks and refer to them when reviewing this chapter.

MORE TO DO

Literature Organize the class into pairs and have students read one selection from Unit 3, Chapter 1, of Globe Fearon's *World Tapestries*. Ask students to draw conclusions about how the politics of modern-day Russia and the Heartland have influenced the writer of that selection.

Student Edition

Introduction

Section 1 Review

1. Culture is the way of life of a group of people, including their ideas, customs, skills, and arts.
2. Multicultural means many cultures. The United States is a multicultural society because many cultures live there.

Section 2 Review

1. The five themes are location, place, interaction, movement, and region. The themes classify information in ways that help people understand how people interact with the environment and how the environment affects the way in which people live.
2. Understanding where people live helps to create an understanding of who they are and why their culture developed as it did.

Section 3 Review

1. Possible answer: Fertilizers have had both good and bad effects. Fertilizers have helped farmers grow more food. However, they have sometimes damaged the environments of some birds and fish. 2. Answers will vary. Students' answers should reflect an awareness of environmental issues in their communities.

Reviewing the Introduction

I. 1. d 2. e 3. b 4. a 5. c
II. 1. They are referring to a world in which people are interdependent; where they communicate with one another and share experiences. 2. People begin learning about their culture the moment they are born. They learn it from family members, from friends, and from their communities. 3. Scarcity means "not enough." Scarcity of resources can happen because of natural disasters, poor planning, or unequal distribution of resources. 4. Possible answer: Refugees or immigrants coming into a country is an example of movement.
III. Location refers to exactly where a place is located; location can be absolute or relative. Place refers to the geographic or cultural features of a place. Examples students provide will vary.

UNIT 1

Previewing the Unit

1. 3000 B.C. 2. more than 500 years later 3. about 300 years 4. 46 years 5. about 300 years later

Exploring Regional Issues

1. (a) The numbers on the left show age ranges; the numbers on the bottom show percent of population. (b) the percentage of population of a specific age group, male or female 2. (a) Both have very young populations. (b) The population of the U.S. is more evenly distributed by age. 3. Possible answer: To

educate so many young, Nigeria and Kenya would have to spend a great deal of money on education and have many schools.

Chapter 1

Section 1 Review

1. Rapids along Africa's rivers prevent easy travel inland. Deltas and sandbars located at the mouths of many of the region's rivers make navigation difficult. The Sahara makes reaching Africa from the north a challenge. In addition, much of Africa's coastline is smooth without natural harbors.
2. The climate of the Sahara is hot and dry. The rain forest has a tropical wet climate. It is hot and humid in the rain forest all year long.

Section 2 Review

1. Artificial boundaries created by European nations in the 1800s sometimes divided people who belonged to a single ethnic group.
2. English is spoken in Nigeria today because in the past, Nigeria was a British colony.

Case Study Review

1. sleeping sickness
2. Disease has prevented economic development and slowed progress in equatorial Africa. Infected horses and oxen cannot be used for transportation or plowing. They also cannot be used for food.

Reviewing Chapter 1

I. Reviewing Vocabulary: 1. c 2. d 3. b 4. a
II. Understanding the Chapter: 1. Because without the Nile River, Egypt would be a desert and humans could not live there. 2. by movements in the earth's crust 3. The deserts and rain forests are very lightly populated. Most people live in the highlands and near river banks, lakes, and the coast. 4. Disease-carrying insects are responsible for spreading diseases which kill humans and animals.
III. Building Skills: 1. Morocco, Algeria, Tunisia, Libya, Egypt 2. Gabon, Congo, Zaire, Rwanda, Uganda, Kenya, Somalia 3. Tunisia is furthest north; South Africa is furthest south; Mauritius is furthest east; Senegal is furthest west. 4. Zaire

Chapter 2

Section 1 Review

1. Deserts protected the kingdom on the east and west. The Nile rapids prevented invaders from entering Egypt via the river.

2. There was a pharaoh at the top, his family and a tiny class of nobles just below him. The great majority of Egyptians made up the base of the pyramid.

Section 2 Review

1. gold and salt

2. New weapons—guns—caused the fall of Songhai.

Section 3 Review

1. The cheap goods Africans imported made it unnecessary for them to develop their own industries.

2. Possible answer: The slave trade piqued European's interest in Africa. West Africa, weakened economically and socially by the slave trade, could not resist colonization.

Case Study Review

1. Timbuktu

2. Their appearance was so different—they had long hair and red faces. They also spoke a foreign language.

Reviewing Chapter 2

I. Reviewing Vocabulary: **1.** b **2.** a **3.** c **4.** d

II. Understanding the Chapter: **1.** The Egyptians created mummies and tombs because they believed in an afterlife that required the human soul to have a resting place and riches to use. **2.** because the trade in gold and salt was so important to the economy of these kingdoms **3.** After their capture, African slaves were chained together, forced to march barefoot to the coast, and then thrown on boats. **4.** West Africa suffered a dramatic decline in population and was economically weakened through trade with Europe. This allowed the Europeans to easily colonize West Africa.

III. Building Skills: **1.** primary source **2.** primary source **3.** secondary source

Chapter 3

Section 1 Review

1. the idea of God as the creator; the belief in lesser gods; the belief in ancestral spirits; the belief that some people have special powers

2. The ideal African woman is obedient, a wife, and a mother. Answers will vary as to what the ideal woman is in U.S. society.

Case Study Review

1. Shaving the hair represents the shedding of childhood.

2. Answers will vary. Rites of passage in the United States might include confirmation, bar or bat mitzvah, or obtaining a driver's license.

Section 2 Review

1. The chief's subjects believed he had special connections to their ancestors, he usually controlled an army, and he was usually able to govern a large area effectively.

2. Possible answer: Discussion and debate allow everyone to voice an opinion. If decisions are

agreed to by all, it is more likely that they will be adhered to.

Section 3 Review

1. It means that people grow food on small farms mostly for their own families.

2. The Maasai want to remain nomadic cattle herders. The Kenyan government wants them to become farmers.

Reviewing Chapter 3

I. Reviewing Vocabulary: **1.** a **2.** d **3.** c **4.** b

II. Understanding the Chapter: **1.** In an extended family, several generations of a family live together. A nuclear family includes only parents and children. **2.** Women are responsible for maintaining the home, preparing the meals and feeding and caring for children. In some societies, they carry water from the local well, gather wood for fire, and help in the fields. **3.** The Yum is the person responsible for watching a younger child if the parents are busy and plays an important role in that child's initiation ceremony. **4.** Most are farmers and herders.

III. Building Skills: **1.** Possible answer: The officials of African governments do not want to save memories of traditional culture. **2.** Governments may want to encourage their citizens to be more modern or they may wish to foster feelings of national unity in place of tribal unity. **3.** Answers will vary. Check students' responses for sensitivity to the subject.

Chapter 4

Section 1 Review

1. The desert made it hard to travel by land. It was hard to travel by water because many of the rivers had rapids and waterfalls and there were relatively few large harbors.

2. Possible answer: The European powers did not consider the opinions of Africans important enough to include them.

Section 2 Review

1. Answers will vary, but should reflect that European rule weakened the traditional political systems, the traditional system of subsistence farming, and traditional family and village life.

2. a. cause **b.** effect **c.** effect **d.** effect

Section 3 Review

1. a belief that people of African descent have common interests and should work together for freedom

2. because so many African countries gained their independence that year

Case Study Review

1. He was jailed for fighting against British colonial rule in Kenya.

2. Answers will vary. Students' answers should show a sensitivity to the situation in Kenya during the fight for independence.

Section 4 Review

1. They were not given a chance to participate in colonial government.

2. Legacies include: the creation of national boundaries, the destruction of traditional African culture, and the destruction of the traditional African legal system.

Reviewing Chapter 4

I. Reviewing Vocabulary: **1.** d **2.** b **3.** a **4.** c

II. Understanding the Chapter: **1.** Answers may include: the Industrial Revolution; desire for natural resources; desire for new markets; nationalism; desire to control other lands because of their location; "white man's burden." **2.** Britain, France, Belgium, Germany, Portugal, Spain **3.** Answers may include the following: promotion of the idea of African inferiority; exploitation of Africans; weakening of traditional African culture; loss of respect for African kings and chiefs **4.** Students might suggest that imperialism weakened family and tribal ties and the African system of land ownership.

III. Building Skills: **1.** He believed the British purposely emphasized the differences among the peoples of Kenya to divide them and make ruling them easier. **2.** as a government that provides freedom and promotes unity, equality, and respect among the people of Kenya **3.** Possible answer: Kenya's government will be one that emphasizes unity and nationalism.

Chapter 5

Section 1 Review

1. Possible answer: Many young people believe that Western ideas are destroying the traditional values of their society. Fundamentalism seems like a way to preserve those traditional values.

2. Similarities include primary responsibility for caring for the home and family. Differences include clothing and the type of work they do in the communities.

Section 2 Review

1. Answers may include: the lack of opportunity in the countryside; the desire for money; the desire to break the strict bonds of traditional rural society; the excitement of the city in comparison to village life.

2. Educated Africans are more likely to be westernized. They tend to enjoy the comforts of modern life and would feel restricted by the confines of traditional village life.

Case Study Review

1. Lagos lacks adequate public transportation and has few bridges.

2. Lagos offers exciting entertainment and other diversions, an opportunity to break away from the constraints of traditional village life, and a chance to acquire wealth.

Section 3 Review

1. the family, the clash between old and new values, and the problems of young people

2. Answers will vary, but should reflect the idea that art and music are a part of everyday life. Art is not produced as an object to be sold, but as an expression of beauty and culture.

Reviewing Chapter 5

I. Reviewing Vocabulary: **1.** c **2.** b **3.** d **4.** a

II. Understanding the Chapter: **1.** They believe that the Koran contains God's words and that it is the absolute truth. **2.** Generally, urbanization has meant fewer farmers and less food production. **3.** In the West, most stories are written, while Africa has a strong oral tradition. **4.** Answers may include: shortage of housing; high unemployment rate; massive slums; widespread corruption; traffic congestion.

III. Building Skills: **1. a.** effect **b.** cause **2. a.** cause **b.** effect **3. a.** effect **b.** cause

Literature Connections

1. Kanié and Senghor celebrate their African identity in the poems by writing of the historical and cultural legacy of Africa: "sparkling soft carpets from Timbuktu," "dark, heavy furniture from Guinea and the Congo," "mats thick with silence," and other metaphorical allusions. **2.** Possible answers: Senghor suggests that the lamp ("knowledge," perhaps) helps soften his constant thoughts of the African freedom movement. The colors black, brown, and red seem to refer to the black African struggle, the land of Africa, and the blood that has been shed in the service of colonialism.

Chapter 6

Section 1 Review

1. Military officers often believed that civilian rule had failed as a number of civilian rulers and their governments were corrupt.

2. a large educated class; a tradition of a free press to inform people of public issues; trained opposition leaders to take turns holding power

Section 2 Review

1. selling state-owned industries to private buyers; keeping taxes low to encourage private investment; setting low tariffs on foreign trade; having few regulations for businesses to follow; leaving prices free to rise or fall; encouraging investments by multinationals and other foreign investors

2. to avoid "putting all their eggs in one basket"; a one-crop or one-mineral economy can be severely hurt if the price of the crop or mineral suddenly drops. Also, drought or other problems may destroy the crop and wipe out a year's income.

Case Study Review

1. By limiting the powers of the central government and leaving significant powers at a lower level, it was hoped that each ethnic group would be able to run its own affairs. That way, the groups could live together peacefully.

2. Possible answer: Nigerian leaders wanted to keep the country unified. Biafra also had valuable oil fields.

Section 3 Review

1. It deprived them of most rights, such as the right to vote for the national government, the right to choose where to live, the right to move freely within the country, and so on.

2. Students' questions should reflect an understanding of apartheid and the role Mandela played in putting a stop to it in South Africa.

Reviewing Chapter 6

I. Reviewing Vocabulary: **1.** b **2.** d **3.** a **4.** c

II. Understanding the Chapter: **1.** Colonial borders lumped people of various ethnic groups together within African colonies. At the same time, they divided some groups whose people lived both within and outside a colony. **2.** One-party rule was based on African techniques of consensus. Advocates of one-party rule felt that it would promote unity by preventing the establishment of ethnic political parties and that it would get people to work together to build up their country. **3.** Free enterprise encourages large companies to invest in a country's industry, bringing money into a country's treasury.

III. Building Skills: **1.** In African nations that lean toward socialism, governments exert a strong influence over economic decisions. Governments often own all or part of major industries. They give subsidies to industries and consumers. Often that means high taxes. In African nations that lean toward capitalism, governments take a more "hands-off" approach. They are less likely to own industries. They try to encourage private investment by keeping taxes and tariffs low. They have few regulations for businesses to follow. They generally leave prices free to rise or fall. **2.** Under apartheid, white South Africans had far more rights than South Africans of other races. The whites were a privileged group that got to choose the government, received the best educations, and lived in the best areas. In contrast, nonwhite South Africans had few rights. They had no role in choosing the government. They could not move freely about the country. They were considered to be citizens of ethnic "homelands." They were treated badly and had an extremely limited choice of jobs. Nowadays, white and nonwhite South Africans live in a multiracial democracy. At least in theory, they have equal rights. They share in choosing and running the government. They can move about freely and live where they wish. **3.** Similarities include: Both are very large, have multicultural populations, experienced civil wars that began with the secession of a part of the country, are producers of oil, have strong university systems and energetic newspapers, started out with constitutions that provided for democratic rule. Differences include: Nigeria has had many periods of military rule; in the United States, only elected civilian governments have ruled. The United States has a stronger economy and higher standard of living. Corruption seems to be a greater problem in Nigeria than in the United States.

Chapter 7

Section 1 Review

1. African nations have created regional organizations such as the OAU to promote development and they have joined international organizations such as the UN and OPEC.

2. Possible answer: Self-help programs can concentrate on problems that are regional or local. For example, a program in Tanzania allowed villagers to build a school and clinic that addressed local needs.

Section 2 Review

1. Any four of the following: tropical disease control, AIDS, health care, refugees, tribalism, drought, famine

2. Answers will differ. Students should support their choices with logical arguments and appropriate facts.

Section 3 Review

1. Any three of the following: reversing desertification by planting trees and limiting grazing, environmental education such as Roots & Shoots, protecting rain forests, saving mountain gorillas and their habitats, reclaiming park land, protecting elephants, saving orphan chimpanzees, preserving primate habitats, licensing forest use

2. Answers will differ. Responses should acknowledge that preserving the environment is good for the entire world, saves endangered species that would otherwise become extinct, and has financial advantages because it brings in tourist dollars.

Case Study Review

1. Tourists bring money to spend when they come to Zaire to see the gorillas.

2. Answers will differ. Students should support their opinions with logical arguments and appropriate facts.

Reviewing Chapter 7

I. Reviewing Vocabulary: **1.** a **2.** c **3.** d **4.** b.

II. Understanding the Chapter: **1.** OAU created a program calling for self-sufficient food production, industrial development, construction of highways and railroads, increased trade, and regional economic organizations. OAU stopped wars and encouraged international economic cooperation. **2.** All African nations joined the UN when they became independent. African countries are the largest voting block in the UN. They work for policies favorable to developing nations. African nations receive UN help in new technology, agriculture, education and the environment. Africa has also received famine relief, help with disease outbreaks, and assistance with refugees. **3.** African people are making progress in health care and disease control, education, and controlling drought. Students also might mention preserving the environment and saving endangered species. **4.** Desertification is turning agricultural land into desert. It reduces the food supply and forces people off their farms. Experts fear that desertified land will not return to productivity for years.

III. Building Skills: **1.** desertification, loss of agricultural land, and reduction of the food supply **2.** tribal wars between the Hutu and Tutsi in Rwanda and Burundi **3.** universal primary education, increased higher education, public health programs

UNIT 1 REVIEW

I. 1. (a) Plateaus, mountains, valleys, lakes, and rivers are among Africa's main physical features. (b) Dense jungles made exploration difficult. In addition, high plateaus created waterfalls along rivers. **2.** Possible answer: Due to trade and travel along the Nile, the Kushites learned Egyptian forms of writing and pyramid building, and learned to make iron weapons. In West Africa, Arab traders spread Islam throughout the region. In East Africa, the Swahili language developed as a result of trade between Arabs and Bantu peoples. **3.** Manufactured products traded during the Atlantic slave trade led to the decline of local crafts; also Africans did not develop their own manufacturing centers. **4.** (a) Students should recognize that children, women, and elders had defined roles in traditional African society. For example, children had jobs to do and became adults through initiation ceremonies. Women were subservient to men. Elders were respected for their knowledge. (b) When Africans move to cities, these traditional roles break down. Children may attend modern schools, women often work outside the home, and elders lose the status they held in their villages. **5.** (a) They built railroads, telephone wires, schools, and hospitals. (b) These improvements allowed them to rule more efficiently. (c) They were used as a base on which to build new facilities. **6.** Possible answer: Theater uses traditional audience participation formats, films focus on the real lives of Africans, and sculpture and paintings often feature traditional subjects. **7.** (a) Diversity in Nigeria nearly tore the country apart. (b) In Tanzania, a strong central government called for *ujamaa* and most people cooperated. (c) In Rwanda, diversity has led to civil war. (d) In Burundi, civil war has also broken out among different ethnic groups. **8.** The economies of many African nations rely on the export of one or two resources. To reduce this reliance many are trying to diversify. For example, Zambia gets 80 percent of its income from exporting copper. If copper prices drop, Zambia's economy suffers.

II. 1. Nationalism caused European nations to compete for colonies in Africa and in other parts of the world. Each nation wanted to increase its standing in the world. Nationalism also caused the people in Africa to rise up against the colonial powers and

fight for independence. **2.** Lesotho, Swaziland, Botswana, Zimbabwe, Zambia, and Malawi are landlocked. They would have to cooperate with South Africa, Namibia, Mozambique, and perhaps Angola to export or import goods.

III. Students' essays should show an understanding that life in African villages is different than in the cities.

IV. 1. (a) 1 per 12 (b) Kenya **2.** (a) South Africa (b) Nigeria **3.** If the amount of newspapers circulated is directly related to the literacy rate of a country, then Algeria and South Africa probably have the highest literacy rates.

Global Issues: The Many Forms of Government

1. Majority rule is when the government responds to the wishes of most of the people it rules. **2.** Possible answer: In a monarchy, leaders are chosen based on the family ties, not on ability to rule. In a dictatorship, a ruler has complete control over the people of a country, the people have no say in government; often there is a struggle for power when a ruler leaves office. In a democracy, leaders need to respond to the wishes of the people. At times, this can be difficult to manage.

UNIT 2

Previewing the Unit

1. Hinduism **2.** in about A.D. 750 **3.** 35 years **4.** It became capitalist. **5.** to encourage economic growth and regional peace

Exploring Regional Issues

1. amount earned in exports and the products exported; products imported and amount spent on imports; main trading **2.** (a) Australia earns $22.7 billion more than India. (b) Singapore earns $23.3 billion more than Indonesia. **3.** (a) Students should recognize that a trade surplus would help bring money to a country. (b) A deficit would mean that a country is spending more than it earns and may go into debt.

Chapter 8

Section 1 Review

1. The spring monsoons bring the rain the country needs to grow crops. The fall monsoons bring cooler air. **2.** The volcanic eruptions have made the soil rich, allowing productive farming.

Case Study Review

1. The monsoons provide water for drinking, growing crops, and developing electric power. **2.** If the monsoon is late, it may cause problems with the crops and with hydroelectricity. If it does not come at all, there will be crop failures and people may starve.

Section 2 Review

1. People from many different countries have migrated to the region and geographic features have acted as barriers. **2.** Answers will vary.

Students may say that having different languages makes it difficult for people to communicate and to resolve their differences. It may also make people feel that they are separate from one another.

Reviewing Chapter 8
I. Reviewing Vocabulary: **1.** c **2.** d **3.** a **4.** b

II. Understanding the Chapter: **1.** The mountains stop the rain and cause it to fall in the lowland plains and not in the Deccan Plateau. **2.** The Indus, Brahmaputra, and Ganges Rivers all rise in the Himalayas. **3.** Island Southeast Asia is located on a major trade route. That means that many people have come to the region from many different places. **4.** Immigrants from China and India have brought their cultures to Malaysia. They are sometimes resented because Malaysians think that they are taking jobs from the native people.

III. Building Skills: **1.** It is difficult for rain clouds to get over the Ghat Mountains. **2.** It is hard to develop the resources of Southeast Asia. **3.** There are many different cultures and languages in South Asia.

Chapter 9

Section 1 Review
1. The Five Pillars of Islam are the five main duties of Muslims. They are the belief in one God, prayer, giving charity, fasting during Ramadan, and a pilgrimage to Mecca. **2.** Answers will vary, but may mention that because a significant number of people in Akbar's empire were Hindus, his tolerance won their support.

Section 2 Review
1. The British won control of India by defeating the French and then encouraging division among the Indians. **2.** Answers will vary. Students may mention the different perspectives of the participants. The British considered the uprising a rebellion against legal authority and the Indians considered it a war to win self-rule.

Section 3 Review
1. India was split into two countries because Muslims wanted their own country. **2.** Students may write that Gandhi was successful because he showed that ordinary people could achieve their goals.

Case Study Review
1. Gandhi intended to show that the Indians did not need the British. **2.** People followed Gandhi to the sea because they believed in the cause, and they believed in him.

Reviewing Chapter 9
I. Reviewing Vocabulary: **1.** b **2.** c **3.** d **4.** a

II. Understanding the Chapter: **1.** The Hindu religion developed out of Aryan religious writings known as the Vedas. **2.** The major religions of South Asia are Hinduism, Buddhism, and Islam. **3.** The sepoy uprising occurred because Hindu soldiers believed

that their culture, language, and religious beliefs were threatened. **4.** The INC's first goal was to fight for Indians' rights. Later, its goal was to win independence from Britain.

III. Building Skills: **1.** c **2.** a **3.** d **4.** b

Chapter 10

Section 1 Review
1. People move from the villages to the cities to become educated, because there is not enough land to farm in the villages, and because there are more opportunities in the cities. **2.** The village now has a hospital and electricity. More people go to the cities, there is less reliance on caste, and women have the vote. Some women go on to higher education.

Section 2 Review
1. A bustee is a shantytown outside a big city. **2.** In India, many young people in rural villages do not go to school because they are too important as workers. In addition, many fewer girls than boys go to school.

Section 3 Review
1. Early Indian literature was poetry written in Sanskrit that was based on religious themes. Later works were based on themes such as love and war and were written in other languages. **2.** Much art, literature, music, and drama is based on religion. This includes literature and art of both Muslims and Hindus.

Case Study Review
1. *Masala* means "spicy mixture." A masala movie has a little bit of everything—singing, dancing, drama, comedy, action, and adventure. **2.** Ray's movies provide a look at the real way people live, while masala movies are fantasy and meant to be pure entertainment.

Reviewing Chapter 10
I. Reviewing Vocabulary: **1.** a **2.** d **3.** b **4.** c

II. Understanding the Chapter: **1.** Women are winning more freedom to get educations, jobs, and careers. **2.** The population growth has led to a shortage of land and to overcrowded cities. The government has tried to punish couples with large families. Now, the government is trying to convince families to have fewer children. **3.** Many Indians don't learn to read and write because there is no school in their village and because they are needed by their families to work. Girls may not go to school because their families think it is not necessary. **4.** It is difficult to become an Indian dancer because it takes 10 years to learn the art and because dancers need to learn 140 poses, as well as complete control over the muscles in their neck, face, and hands.

III. Building Skills: **1.** Life in the cities is crowded. People who live in the poor parts of the city often lack fresh water and sanitation. Life in the villages, in contrast, is less crowded. People farm. Caste matters more in the villages than in the city and life is more traditional. **2.** There are more than

10 times as many people per square mile in India as in the United States. **3.** Educational opportunities for poor children in India are limited. There are extensive educational opportunities for wealthy children in India.

Literature Connections

1. Fatima's feelings for the tiger change from fear to sympathy or empathy. **2.** Possible answers include: the habit of bathing in the river; living within an extended family; the division of responsibilities between men and women; and using a midwife during births.

Chapter 11

Section 1 Review

1. Farmers face the problems of small farms, old-fashioned tools, rats, little storage, and insufficient water or fertilizer. They also often owe large debts. **2.** Answers will vary. Students may decide that they would deal with the problem of poverty by helping farmers grow more food.

Section 2 Review

1. East and West Pakistan, although both Muslim, were very different. East Pakistan was poorer than West Pakistan. The army was mostly in West Pakistan, leaving East Pakistan unprotected. The army then put down a riot, killing tens of thousands of East Pakistanis. **2.** Both Bhutan and Nepal lie in the mountains north of India, both are ruled by kings, and most people in both countries are illiterate and very poor. Nepal welcomes tourists and elects some of its leaders. Bhutan's king has kept his country isolated and has complete control over its people.

Section 3 Review

1. Both the United States and the Soviet Union wanted India to support them. **2.** India and the Soviet Union had close ties because the two countries were close geographically, they had some problems in common, their leaders were friendly, and the Soviet Union gave $1 billion in aid to India.

Case Study Review

1. Bhutto restored democracy, released political prisoners, and allowed a free press. **2.** Answers will vary. Students may say it was a combination of her education and leadership, and of following in her father's footsteps.

Reviewing Chapter 11

I. Reviewing Vocabulary: **1.** c **2.** d **3.** b **4.** a

II. Understanding the Chapter: **1.** Most Indians make their living through farming. The second most frequent occupation is working in a cottage industry. **2.** East Pakistan became Bangladesh because East and West Pakistan were a thousand miles apart and did not get along. As a result, East Pakistan fought a war to break away. The newly independent country took the name Bangladesh.

3. Neutrality is not taking sides; non-alignment means looking at situations case by case and deciding whether to back anyone. **4.** Bhutto was accused of corruption and forced from office.

III. Building Skills: **1.** Bangladesh **2.** Sri Lanka **3.** Nepal **4.** India **5.** Bangladesh

Chapter 12

Section 1 Review

1. India and China influenced the early kingdoms of Southeast Asia by conquering them. **2.** Answers may vary. Some may say that the water system broke down, causing malaria and plague.

Case Study Review

1. The viewer can tell that Rangda is evil because her tongue is a flame, her face is set in a terrible sneer, and she wears a necklace of human parts. **2.** Myths probably come from many sources because Indonesia has been visited by people of many cultures, many of whom have stayed to add their influence to the island nation.

Section 2 Review

1. The positive effects of foreign rule were the building of roads, school, hospitals, and factories. The foreign powers also sometimes kept local leaders from fighting. The negative effects were that the foreign powers took the best land and paid little or nothing for it, that local craftspeople could not compete and so they stopped making goods, and that the foreigners ran things, not the people who lived there. **2.** The European powers wanted the riches of Southeast Asia, the markets for their goods, and the control of as much of the world as possible.

Section 3 Review

1. The United States thought that if Vietnam became Communist, the rest of Southeast Asia would, too. **2.** Education helped train the people of the colonial world. It also taught them about democracy and self-government.

Reviewing Chapter 12

I. Reviewing Vocabulary: **1.** b **2.** a **3.** d **4.** c

II. Understanding the Chapter: **1.** The Angkor kingdom in Cambodia was a Hindu kingdom that built canals and beautiful temples. There were two Thai kingdoms. The Ayutthaya kingdom flourished for 400 years. The second kingdom dates from the revolt of General Pya Taksin in 1767. **2.** European powers were able to control Southeast Asia because they had superior weapons and trained soldiers, and they were well organized. **3.** Southeast Asian colonies wanted to throw off foreigners in the early 20th century because colonies around the world were beginning to gain their independence, education had taught the colonized peoples to value freedom, and archaeological digs had shown the Southeast Asians that they had a long history of self-government. **4.** Southeast Asians first welcomed the Japanese because it meant the hated

European powers would leave. They changed their minds when it became clear that the Japanese also wanted to colonize them.

III. Building Skills: The correct order is 2, 4, 5, 1, 3.

Chapter 13

Section 1 Review

1. Most villages are governed by a leader who makes decisions by consensus. **2.** Answers will vary. Students may suggest that farm people are too poor to be able to spare a child for school and that job opportunities in the city are more dependent on education.

Section 2 Review

1. Religion is the basis for many of the arts, from music to architecture, to dance, to traditional epics. **2.** Many of the dances are based on Hindu epics. The women who do these dances often use tiny, graceful movements, and wear clothing of silk and gold.

Case Study Review

1. Answers will vary. Students might mention the splendor of the buildings or how well they have been restored. **2.** Answers will vary. Students may say that other nations want to learn about the past and to preserve the region's rich heritage.

Reviewing Chapter 13

I. Reviewing Vocabulary: **1.** b **2.** d **3.** a **4.** c

II. Understanding the Chapter: **1.** Land is running out in the villages, so more people, especially young ones, are leaving. **2.** For most Southeast Asians, the family is central. Most Southeast Asians would not think of living alone or making decisions alone. **3.** Life for women in Southeast Asia is freer than for many women in some Muslim countries. More women work outside their homes. **4.** China and India brought the religions of Hinduism and Buddhism to Southeast Asia, which today play a major role in the arts of the country.

III. Building Skills: **1.** fact—This can be proved. **2.** opinion—People may argue that women have a better life in other countries. **3.** opinion—This is a judgment. **4.** fact—This can be proved.

Chapter 14

Section 1 Review

1. The Green Revolution meant that there was more food for people; the bad effects were that families lost their farms when they could not pay their loans and that pesticides began showing up in the water supply. Also, there was less crop diversification, which meant that a single pest could wipe out a crop. **2.** Charts should describe differences in how economic decisions are made and in how property is owned.

Section 2 Review

1. The main types are Communist governments, military governments, and democracies. **2.** The

Filipinos may have been able to force Marcos out because the people and the military were angered by his corruption.

Section 3 Review

1. ASEAN is the Association of Southeast Asian Nations, which was formed to provide help and cooperation among the countries of Southeast Asia. **2.** The Communist countries may become more capitalistic. If this happens, they may increase their profits and compete with other countries in the region.

Case Study Review

1. Sarat began in Cambodia, watching her husband being beaten to death by Pol Pot's men. Then she was marched to a farm, where she worked for four years before escaping. She finally came to the border of Thailand to a refugee camp. **2.** They were called the *killing fields* because so many lost their lives there.

Reviewing Chapter 14

I. Reviewing Vocabulary: **1.** c **2.** b **3.** a **4.** d

II. Understanding the Chapter: **1.** In market economies, as in Singapore, factories make what people want to buy. In Communist economies, as in Vietnam, the government tells factories what goods to make. **2.** There is little unused land in the villages and people think that there might be a better life in the city. **3.** The end of the Soviet Union and the Cold War meant that Communist countries, such as Vietnam, no longer would receive large amounts of aid. **4.** Cambodian refugees began returning when Pol Pot's regime was overthrown.

III. Building Skills: **1.** In the 1950s, the Green Revolution began, bringing more rice production, less hunger, and larger farms, but introducing environmental problems. **2.** Since World War II, there have been many kinds of governments in Southeast Asia, but since the fall of communism, more of the countries that had Communist regimes are developing representative governments. **3.** ASEAN allows Southeast Asia to form political, cultural, and trade bonds that help all the countries in the region succeed.

Chapter 15

Section 1 Review

1. Australia and New Zealand are both island nations. While most of Australia is flat and dry, New Zealand is mountainous and green. **2.** They left the gifts on the beach. Cook describes the differences between a culture that was acquisitive versus one that was not.

Section 2 Review

1. Because the European Union helped trading within Europe, Australia and New Zealand were forced to develop new markets for their goods. **2.** Many Aborigines and Maoris were killed by wars and disease and they lost much of their land to the settlers.

Section 3 Review

1. The remoteness of the different islands and the mistrust among groups led to many separate cultures. **2.** The high islands are the tops of mountains. They contain more fertile land and support more people. The low islands are usually coral reefs or atolls. Many barely reach above the surface of the water. Life on the low islands is much harder because there is little drinking water and the soil is thin.

Case Study Review

1. The Dreamtime was the time thousands of years ago during which, the Aborigines believe, nature and people became one and life began. **2.** The 1993 ruling may allow Aborigines to claim land that belonged to their ancestors thousands of years ago.

Reviewing Chapter 15

I. Reviewing Vocabulary: **1.** b **2.** c **3.** a **4.** d

II. Understanding the Chapter: **1.** The Great Western Plateau takes up more than half the country. To the east lies the east-central lowlands. On the eastern edge is the Great Dividing Range. This range drops to the eastern coastal plains. **2.** Two effects of European settlement on the Aborigines and Maoris were the loss of land and the spread of disease. **3.** The three main divisions are Polynesia, Micronesia, and Melanesia. **4.** The Aborigines marched to protest the 200th anniversary of the European settlement of Australia.

III. Building Skills: **1.** Australia is south of the equator. **2.** Polynesia takes up the most area. **3.** The Tasman Sea lies between Australia and New Zealand. **4.** About 2,500 miles separate Australia and the Samoas.

UNIT 2 REVIEW

I. 1. (a) Monsoons are seasonal winds that bring moisture and rain. (b) Monsoons bring about 80 percent of the region's annual rainfall; without the rains, drought would cause crop failure. However, too much rain can cause flooding. **2.** (a) A caste system is a rigid social class system that became part of the Hindu religion. (b) The Indian government has outlawed discrimination and has set aside jobs for Untouchables. **3.** (a) Europeans wanted to trade with India and Southeast Asia for spices, tea, jewels, silk, and cotton. (b) Trade with Asia increased after 1488, when Portuguese explorers discovered an all-sea route from Europe to India. **4.** Students may describe any three of the following: overpopulation, environmental problems, rapid growth of cities, lack of educational opportunities for villagers, economic challenges, agricultural problems. **5.** (a) After India won its independence, Muslims in the north, who were afraid of the power of the majority Hindus, wanted their own country. (b) People in East Pakistan, who were divided geographically from West Pakistan, resented the economic power of the West and feared they would not get enough protection if needed. **6.** Students may

describe any two of the following civilizations: the Maurya empire, the Delhi Sultinate, the Mogul empire, the kingdoms of Vietnam, the Pagan kingdom, the Angkor kingdom, the Thai kingdoms, the kingdoms of Indonesia. **7.** (a) Australia was first settled as a penal colony. The first settlers were convicts. (b) The discovery of gold led people from all over the world to come to Australia in hopes of making their fortune.

II. 1. Hinduism, Buddhism, and Islam are the most prevalent religions in the region. Hinduism practices a strict system of class division, believes in reincarnation and in following the rules of class. Buddhism was developed by Siddhartha Gautama as a reaction to Hinduism. Buddhists believe that people can find happiness by losing desire for possessions, and nirvana by doing good deeds and living a good life. Islam was developed in the Middle East and teaches belief in one God and that all people are equal before him. **2.** Non-alignment was a policy of not taking sides during the Cold War. India would decide how to act in each foreign policy situation. India hoped this policy would allow it to remain friendly with all nations during the Cold War, and avoid making enemies with anyone. While India did have friendly relations with both the U.S. and the Soviet Union at various times during the Cold War, it was never at the same time; and at various times, it did offend both due to its relationship with the other.

III. Answers will vary. Students should discuss the issues common to both, including overpopulation, rapid urbanization, economic problems, environmental problems, access to education, and opportunities for women. Issues specific to particular areas include the caste system in India, ethnic difficulties in South Asia, and the move toward a free market economy in Southeast Asia.

IV. 1. Indonesia **2.** Thailand **3.** Brunei appears to be the most diverse. Indonesia and Thailand have very little religious diversity, while Brunei has Muslims, Christians, and Buddhists, as well as 10 percent of other religious persuasions.

Global Issues: How Economic Systems Compare

1. They recognize the fact that it results in more efficient business and greater income. **2.** Possible answer: In a dictatorship, a ruler wishes to control all aspects of a country including its economy.

UNIT 3

Previewing the Unit

1. 422 years **2.** 1215 **3.** 1889 **4.** 1950-1953 **5.** 1997

Exploring Regional Issues

1. (a) how many people live per square mile (b) plains, mountains, hills, and plateaus **2.** (a) in western and northern China (b) It is difficult for people to live in mountainous regions. **3.** (a) pollution, inadequate services, high crime rate, unemployment (b) Students might suggest that governments build more housing; attract people to less crowded areas by creating jobs there, etc.

Chapter 16

Section 1 Review

1. The monsoon system gives East Asia a long rainy season during the summer and a dry period in winter. **2.** Winds that blow over land are generally dry because they have not been able to pick up moisture from a large body of water.

Section 2 Review

1. The Chinese system of writing was borrowed by Korea and Japan. **2.** Answers will vary. One possibility is that the ethnic compositions of China, Korea, and Japan are relatively homogeneous.

Case Study Review

1. The Dalai Lama is both a political and spiritual leader in Tibetan Buddhism. **2.** The Dalai Lama went into exile in 1959 when Communist Chinese soldiers crushed a revolt in Lhasa, Tibet's capital.

Reviewing Chapter 16

I. Reviewing Vocabulary: **1.** b **2.** c **3.** a **4.** d

II. Understanding the Chapter: **1.** The eastern part of China has both level land and sufficient rain for growing crops. Much of western China is mountainous, and parts of the north are so dry that there are deserts. **2.** Both are island nations near a large continent. Because they are surrounded by seas, they have been sheltered from outside attack. Also, both are trading nations. **3.** Mountains block movements of moist air masses from ocean areas, cutting inland areas off from rain. **4.** At stake in the dispute is the right of Tibetans to govern themselves. China claims the Tibetans already have self-government.

III. Building Skills: **1.** Dalai Lama: implies that Tibetans and Chinese should be kept separate **2.** Chinese government: stresses centralized control **3.** Dalai Lama: highly critical of Chinese actions in Tibet

Chapter 17

Section 1 Review

1. In theory, it meant that the ruler no longer had Heaven's permission to rule. In practice, it meant that the ruler had been overthrown. **2.** Answers will vary. Here is one possibility: Under the Qin dynasty, China became unified under its first emperor. There was a network of roads and a system of common weights and measure. The Great Wall was built.

Section 2 Review

1. The Boxer Rebellion was a protest against foreign influence in China and was secretly backed by the rulers. **2.** The cause of the Opium War was British anger at Chinese efforts to cut off British sales of opium in China. The effect of the war was to reveal China's weakness.

Section 3 Review

1. The Nationalists led the Revolution of 1911 that overthrew the Qing dynasty. Communists like Mao Zedong followed the ideas of Marxism. They wanted China to adopt a Communist system. **2.** Students may infer that the Soviet Union wanted to promote Marxism and communism in China. They may infer that the Nationalists wanted any help they could get in their struggle against the warlords.

Case Study Review

1. Soldiers of the Red Army and their families went on the Long March. **2.** Answers will vary. Students should realize that the shared experience of the Long March was likely to enhance the Communists' unity.

Reviewing Chapter 17

I. Reviewing Vocabulary: **1.** c **2.** d **3.** a **4.** b

II. Understanding the Chapter: **1.** Answers may include language, reverence for ancestors, ideas of Confucius, building of the Great Wall. **2.** The Manchus adopted Chinese ways and became like the Chinese. The Mongols brought in other outsiders to run the government. **3.** After the Opium War, Britain and other foreign powers imposed "unequal treaties" on China. **4.** Sun Yat-sen helped stir up the revolution. He led the Nationalist party.

III. Building Skills: Students should identify 1, 2, and 3 as primary sources.

Chapter 18

Section 1 Review

1. The Japanese learned about Buddhism from China. They adopted the Chinese system of writing. They also borrowed Chinese methods of organizing the government. **2.** Because local leaders like the daimyo were powerful, the imperial government had only limited authority.

Section 2 Review

1. The Meiji reforms put an end to the rule of the shoguns and made the emperor and the central government more powerful. **2.** Japan's goal was to expand its empire and gain access to more raw materials. When the United States stopped the sale of military goods and cut off oil sales, Japan responded by attacking Pearl Harbor.

Section 3 Review

1. Korea reacted to the coming of the Europeans by trying to preserve its isolation. It expelled Catholic missionaries and killed Korean Catholics. **2.** China ruled over parts of Korea at various times, and Koreans absorbed many elements of China's civilization. Those included Confucianism, Buddhism, a government bureaucracy, and Chinese writing.

Section 4 Review

1. Korea became divided when Soviet troops invaded the north in 1945 to expel the Japanese. **2.** Questions and answers will vary. Here are some possibilities: *Q:* Who started the Korean War? *A:* North Korea, by attacking South Korea.

Case Study Review

1. In the United States, the given name comes first; in Korea, it comes after the family name. **2.** Women in Korea had an inferior status.

Reviewing Chapter 18

I. Reviewing Vocabulary: **1.** b **2.** d **3.** a **4.** c
II. Understanding the Chapter: **1.** The visit of the "black ships" led to Japan's being forced to accept unequal treaties with more modern nations. **2.** Japan had only limited natural resources and looked to nearby nations to provide them. In the late 1800s and early 1900s, Japan copied the style of the leading powers in creating an empire by conquering other nations or forcing them to accept its demands. **3.** Korea had been a "Hermit Kingdom" and had few contacts with the outside world. Like China and Japan, Korea had not yet adopted modern ways. Therefore, it was weaker than the European powers (and weaker than Japan, once Japan began to modernize). **4.** South Korea is an industrialized country with a free enterprise system and democratic government. North Korea is a more agricultural country with a Communist government.
III. Building Skills: **1.** Seoul; **2.** Pyongyang; **3.** Yalu River; **4.** Sea of Japan

Chapter 19

Section 1 Review

1. Confucian ideas taught a great respect for authority. Within the nation, the chief authority was the ruler. Within the family, it was the father, whose word was law. Sons and daughters were taught to show him respect. **2.** Answers will vary. However, poorer farmers will benefit by being able to pool their resources to purchase expensive farm machinery. More prosperous farmers might resent them because they are forced to use their resources to help the poorer farmers.

Section 2 Review

1. Shinto is Japan's national religion. It teaches that there are many gods or spirits. These spirits are a part of nature. **2.** Answers will vary. An appreciation of beauty and simplicity is deeply rooted in Japanese culture.

Section 3 Review

1. Korean women had an important role to play in shamanism, where they often held the position of shaman. Under Confucianism, on the other hand, they were kept in a position of subservience to men. **2.** Students should recognize that the quote indicates that Korea borrowed heavily from Chinese culture, but that it nonetheless developed its own unique Korean culture.

Case Study Review

1. Buddha summoned all the world's animals. However, only 12 animals showed up. They were the ones chosen. **2.** They could express the year's name in Chinese chronology, such as 4696; in Western chronology, 1998; or as the Year of the Tiger.

Reviewing Chapter 19

I. Reviewing Vocabulary: **1.** d **2.** a **3.** c **4.** b
II. Understanding the Chapter: **1.** The Chinese Communists have tried to substitute the authority of the Communist party for that of the father and emperor. The Communist value system opposes religion and many of China's traditional ways. Among the new values are equality for women. **2.** In all three countries, women have been emerging from second-class status. Changes in the law have sought to give women new rights and opportunities. Many now have jobs outside the home, although barriers to full equality remain. **3.** Nowadays the absolute authority of men has declined, families have grown smaller, and women have gained higher status. **4.** *Haiku* poetry and *Noh* plays are two performing arts that are distinctively East Asian and sumo wrestling is a sport that is distinctive to East Asia.

Chapter 20

Section 1 Review

1. Radicals wanted to increase the pace of collectivization; moderates wanted to slow it. **2.** Answers will vary, but should reflect the impact that increasing dissent would have on the Chinese political process.

Section 2 Review

1. The Communists attempted to break down the tradition of respect for one's elders and build a greater sense of independence among children. **2.** Answers will vary but should reflect an understanding of the issues discussed in the chapter.

Case Study Review

1. China's government responded to the democracy movement by sending soldiers and tanks to crush it. The attack killed hundreds and perhaps thousands of the protesters. **2.** The causes of the 1989 democracy movement included a desire on the part of many Chinese citizens for greater democracy and anger at corruption among Communist party officials. The effects included increased awareness among China's people of the desire for democratic change but also large numbers of deaths and a hardening of government policies against those who opposed the party's policies.

Section 3 Review

1. When the United States began exploring ways of improving relations with Communist China, Taiwan began losing support among the world's countries. The UN voted in 1971 to let the Beijing government assume China's seat in the world body. **2.** Answers will vary. Similarities might include being populated largely by people of Chinese ancestry, having a government that claims to represent all of China (mainland plus Taiwan), and having carried out land reform policies to boost farm production. Differences might include Taiwan's more vibrant economy, its system of free enterprise, its more democratic political system, and its much smaller population.

Reviewing Chapter 20

I. Reviewing Vocabulary: **1.** d **2.** b **3.** a **4.** c

II. Understanding the Chapter: **1.** The Communist party won the war, taking control of the government on the mainland. The Nationalist party and its army fled to Taiwan, still claiming to represent all of China. **2.** Answers may vary. Students could mention such events as Mao's 1956 campaign to "let a hundred flowers bloom" (ending in a crackdown against dissent), the Great Leap Forward of 1958 (featuring creation of communes and disruption of the economy), the Great Proletarian Cultural Revolution that started in 1966 (whereby Mao caused chaos and deepened divisions within the Communist party), the economic reforms promoted by Deng Xiaoping from 1977 onwards (putting an end to the communes, opening the economy up to individual enterprise), and the democracy movement of 1989 (expressing a desire for greater democracy but ending in political repression). **3.** Mao was leader of the Communist party and head of state from 1949 until his death in 1976. He pushed China toward radical policies that promoted the Communist dream of equality. **4.** Taiwan claims to be the rightful government of all of China.

III. Building Skills: **1.** opinion **2.** fact **3.** fact **4.** opinion

Literature Connections

1. The title reflects Harry Wu's situation–he had no way to escape from Communist China. **2.** Possible answer: In modern China, freedom of expression and individualism is not fully accepted. Those who try to change the system are often punished.

Chapter 21

Section 1 Review

1. Article Nine of the constitution requires Japan to give up war as a national right. Therefore, Japan maintains only small "self-defense forces." **2.** Both the United States and Japan have democratic political systems. Both have free elections at which women and men have the vote. The top leader in the United States is the president; in Japan, the prime minister. U.S. voters elect a president directly, while Japanese voters elect the members of the Diet (parliament), who then elect the prime minister.

Section 2 Review

1. Japan's "economic miracle" was the rapid growth of its economy after the devastation and defeat of World War II. By the 1980s, Japan's economy ranked second only to that of the United States. **2.** Answers will vary, but should reflect the fact that Japan's industrial infrastructure is relatively new because so much was destroyed during World War II.

Case Study Review

1. Japanese homes are only about half as large as U.S. homes. Also, they are very expensive, as are all living costs in Japan. **2.** Answers will vary. Students should address issues that are raised in the case study, such as living in close quarters, sleeping on a mat on the floor, going to cram school, collecting CDs or comic books, and so on. Students' answers should be consistent with information in the case study.

Section 3 Review

1. South Korea's government allows businesses to be privately owned. The South Korean government's role has been to promote these privately owned businesses. On the other hand, the North Korean government maintains strict control over its industries. The government owns and runs its factories and farms. **2.** Answers will vary, but some details that could be cited are the establishment of a secret police, the portrayal of Kim Il Sung as almost a superhuman figure, and the stamping out of all opposition.

Reviewing Chapter 21

I. Reviewing Vocabulary: **1.** b **2.** a **3.** d **4.** c

II. Understanding the Chapter: **1.** The U.S. occupation had political, military, and economic effects. It led to limitations on the power of the emperor, a revised system of parliamentary democracy, and constitutional restrictions on maintaining a military force. Efforts of the occupation authorities to break up the *zaibatsu* had only limited success. **2.** Japan's military was limited in size, and the use of military force was restricted to "self defense." **3.** Business and government are much more closely linked in Japan than in the United States. In Japan, business and government work closely to plan for the future. **4.** Elements that contributed to Japan's "economic miracle" included a strong Japanese work ethic, careful planning through business-government links, teamwork on the job, strong loyalty of workers to large companies, and a high rate of savings by Japanese citizens.

Chapter 22

Case Study Review

1. That was the date when British colonial rule would end and China would resume possession of Hong Kong. **2.** Answers may vary. One possible answer: Colonial rule involves the control of a powerful nation over a distant territory, allowing people of the territory little say in how they are governed. Colonial rule does not necessarily prevent people in the territory from making economic advances.

Section 1 Review

1. Mao meant that the United States was not really as powerful as it seemed to be. The Chinese could support "people's wars" in Third World countries without serious risk. **2.** China has tried to improve relations with Japan, although the Chinese view the Japanese with suspicion. China's relations with Vietnam have improved, although China was upset that Vietnam sided with the Soviet Union during the Soviet-Chinese split. China has built closer economic relations with Taiwan, but has maintained its insistence that Taiwan is an integral part of China.

Section 2 Review

1. Japan sells more to the United States than it buys in return. The United States claims that unfair Japanese practices are responsible for the resulting U.S. trade deficit. **2.** Answers may vary. Japan could continue the policy of maintaining only token military forces and depending on the United States "nuclear umbrella." Or it could be represented in the UN peacekeeping forces that serve abroad. Or it could build up larger military forces and put less dependence on the United States, while continuing as a U.S. ally. Or it could end its alliance with the United States and "go it alone," trying to become a major military power itself.

Chapter 22 Review

I. Reviewing Vocabulary: **1.** c **2.** a **3.** d **4.** b

II. Understanding the Chapter: **1.** The United States wanted to widen the Soviet-Chinese split, gain China's help in ending the war in Vietnam, and benefit from trade with China. China's leaders wanted to end the Beijing government's isolation, take over China's seat in the United Nations, and promote China's economic growth through increased trade. **2.** U.S. leaders want the Japanese to change ways of doing business that favor Japanese over outsiders. For example, the U.S. wants Japan's companies to stop dealing mainly with other Japanese companies. It wants U.S. companies to be able to bid on government contracts in Japan. It wants Japan to quit favoring Japanese food products over imported ones. The United States seeks such changes because it wants to reduce or eliminate the U.S. trade deficit with Japan. **3.** Japan and Russia have never signed a formal peace treaty because they cannot agree on which of them should have ownership over the Kurile Islands. The Soviet Union took the Kuriles from Japan in the last days of World War II. **4.** China promised that it would allow the territory to keep its way of life "essentially" unchanged until 2047. Under an agreement between China and Britain, Hong Kong was to be allowed to maintain its economic, political, and social systems.

UNIT 3 REVIEW

I. 1. (a) Japan is an island nation with many mountains. (b) The seas have traditionally protected it from attack, allowing it to develop its own unique culture. The seas have also provided a path for trade and contacts from other cultures. The mountains isolated parts of the country from the rest of Japan. **2.** (a) The Great Wall was built by the First Emperor, ruler of the Qin Dynasty. (b) The Great Wall of China was built to keep nomadic tribes from the north from invading China. **3.** (a) Feudalism in Japan was based on ties of loyalty and service. Lords granted protection and favors to vassals, who in return, fought on behalf of lords. Rival lords fought for lands. (b) A warrior class known as samurai fought for the lord as part of the feudal system. The leader of the winning group of lords became the military leader, or shogun, of Japan. The shoguns and the warrior class ran Japan for many centuries. **4.** (a) Japan wanted to expand its empire in the first half of the 1900s. It looked to nearby lands for supplies of the raw materials it needed for its growing industry and began to attain colonies. (b) Japan's increasing imperialism resulted in seizure of Indochina from France. The U.S. cut off shipments of oil in response. Japanese leaders saw this as a threat to their expansion and attacked Pearl Harbor. **5.** (a) The Soviet Union attacked Japanese forces in Korea at the end of World War II and occupied the northern half of the country. The U.S. occupied the southern half shortly thereafter. (b) During the Cold War, Korea was formally divided into Communist North Korea and non-communist South Korea. **6.** Students should identify and describe any three of the following: Confucianism, Daoism, Buddhism, Shintoism, and the native Korean religion. **7.** (a) Japan became a leading producer and exporter of automobiles and electronic equipment and computer chips (b) Students should discuss any three of the following: the strong Japanese work ethic, careful planning and coordination between industry and government, focus on teamwork and quality, strong worker loyalty to one company, and a great emphasis on education. **8.** (a) The trade imbalance is a major source of conflict. The U.S. buys much more from Japan than it sells to them. (b) The U.S. has accused Japan of unfair trade policies, preventing U.S. firms from having fair access to Japanese markets. They claim that Japan has put a limit on U.S. imports. The U.S. has asked Japan to open government contracts to U.S. bidders and to end laws that favor Japanese food products over imported ones.

II. 1. The Communist vision of a "new China" included: changing traditional family life by turning family loyalty into party loyalty; changing farming methods to make them more productive; giving women more rights and responsibilities; taking government control over industry; providing greater access to education; and reducing overpopulation. **2.** Lifestyle similarities include cultural heritage, such as language and traditional religion. However, the people of North Korea are not allowed to practice their cultural heritage. Economically and politically, North and South Korea are very different. Economic differences include the success of South Korea's economy, its high standard of living, and successful trade relationships, in contrast to North Korea's isolationist policies and its desire for self sufficiency. The political difference between North Korea and South Korea is that North Korea is a Communist nation, while South Korea has a Western-styled democracy.

III. Answers will vary. Students should discuss the relationship between Nationalists, led by Chiang Kaishek, and Communists, led by Mao Zedong, before the revolution. Students may also mention the Long March in this discussion. Students should discuss Mao's goals for China once he came to power. Finally, students should discuss the Nationalists' retreat to the island of Taiwan and the uneasy relationship Taiwan has had with Communist China.

IV. 1. (a) 5.7 billion people (b) 97.5 people per square mile **2.** (a) Asia (b) Oceania **3.** Students should suggest the affect geography and climate have on population density.

Global Issues: The Information Age

1. Communication has gone wireless over the last 100 years. For example, people can communicate quickly and easily over vast distances using radio waves and lasers. **2.** Possible answer: More people may work from home and families will be able to communicate over long distances.

UNIT 4

Previewing the Unit

1. 1325; 196 years later **2.** superior weapons **3.** L'Ouverture **4.** it crippled economies around the world **5.** by reducing trade barriers

Exploring Regional Issues

1. (a) the percentage of population that lives in cities (b) years **2.** (a) about 30 percent (b) In 1960, it was almost 7 percent of the population. The percentage rose to a little over 10 percent by 1970, but then declined to about 8.5 percent in 1980 and to 7 percent in 1990. 3. (a) Possible answer: The populations in these cities will continue to grow at rapid rates. (b) Possible answer: Since there are very few people living in the countryside, services such as transportation are probably inadequate.

Chapter 23

Section 1 Review

1. Mexico, Central America, the Caribbean, and South America **2.** Vast mountains and dense tropical forests have isolated people from each other. Because they are so rugged, the Andes have made it hard to travel by land from one part of South America to another.

Section 2 Review

1. Possible answer: Tropical wet-and-dry climate areas have warm temperatures and rain throughout the year. The humid-subtropical climate has mild winters and warm summers. **2.** While it is winter in Chicago, it is summer in the Southern Hemisphere.

Section 3 Review

1. The four main groups of Latin Americans are Native Americans, Europeans, Africans, and people of mixed parentage. **2.** Latin America is also part of the Americas.

Section 4 Review

1. wood and chicle **2.** Oil has brought Venezuela a great deal of wealth.

Case Study Review

1. *Altiplano* is Spanish for high plain. It refers to the high plains between ranges of the Andes in South America. **2.** Answers will vary. Students might compare the foods they eat and the job opportunities they have.

Reviewing Chapter 23

I. Reviewing Vocabulary: **1.** b **2.** a **3.** d **4.** c

II. Understanding the Chapter: **1.** Mexico is a narrow land with mountains running down the center and a coastal plain on either side. Central America is a volcanic, mountainous ribbon of land. The islands of the Caribbean stretch between North and South America in the shape of a half moon. South America is by far the largest land area in Latin America. South America has almost every type of known landform. **2.** Vertical climate occurs in mountainous areas and determines the kinds of crops that can be grown in the area. **3.** Most Latin Americans live in two general areas. One is on the east and west coasts of South America. The other is on a broad strip of land from central Mexico into Central America. These areas have the best farmland. **4.** Many Aymará are leaving their traditional villages for the cities because of the hardships of living on the altiplano. Aymará life is difficult; food is scarce because most crops will not grow at such an altitude, and jobs are in short supply.

III. Building Skills: **1.** The parts of Latin America north of the equator are the West Indies (Caribbean islands), Mexico, Central America, and the following South American countries: Venezuela, Guyana, Suriname, and French Guiana. Brazil, Colombia, and Ecuador straddle the equator. Peru, Bolivia, Paraguay, Uruguay, Argentina, and Chile are south of the equator. **2.** Brazil is the largest country in Latin America in terms of size. **3.** the Atlantic Ocean, the Pacific Ocean, and the Caribbean Sea **4.** Some of the nations in Latin America that are on islands are Cuba, the Dominican Republic, and Haiti.

Chapter 24

Section 1 Review

1. People first came to the Americas over a land bridge that had been created by the advent of glaciers during the ice age. They were following the game that was naturally migrating over the bridge from Asia to the Americas. **2.** Students should understand that farming was a critical stage in the development of civilization because it allowed people to settle down, build cities, and specialize in other tasks, such as education, governance, writing, and crafts.

Section 2 Review

1. Scientific theories include changes in climate, civil war, and foreign invasion as possible reasons for the decline of Mayan civilization. **2.** Answers will vary, but most students will probably ask questions related to the move from Guatemala to Yucatán or the decline of Mayan civilization.

Section 3 Review

1. News of the strangers in the east frightened Montezuma because there was an Aztec legend that fair-skinned gods would return to reward the Aztecs. The Aztecs were not sure if the Spanish were enemies or gods. **2.** Answers will vary. Students might suggest that the people didn't feel loyal because they had to pay taxes and were treated cruelly by the Aztecs.

Section 4 Review

1. Incan advances included terrace farming, crop rotation, use of fertilizers, and building a system of aqueducts that brought water from the Andes to the dry coastal area. **2.** The contrast was striking. The Incas pursued a relatively benign policy. Subject groups that accepted Incan rule received protection. By contrast, the Aztecs ruled harshly, levying heavy tribute and taking subject peoples for human sacrifice.

Section 5 Review

1. Columbus convinced Isabella to finance a voyage to reach Asia by sailing westward across the Atlantic. **2.** Spain was more interested than Portugal because the Portuguese had already pioneered a route to Asia by sailing around the southern tip of Africa. Knowing this route, they saw no need to finance a risky expedition.

Case Study Review

1. Cuauhtémoc was the last emperor of the Aztecs. **2.** Students should recognize that people tend to glamorize their own history. A triumph because of heroism is much more satisfactory than one that suggests that the spread of the disease was responsible.

Reviewing Chapter 24

I. Reviewing Vocabulary: **1.** d **2.** b **3.** a **4.** c
II. Understanding the Chapter: **1.** Some examples of advanced Mayan culture include the development of large cities, such as Tikal, the creation of a calendar that was very accurate, and the development of a system of mathematics. **2.** According to legend, an Aztec god told them to built a settlement at a place where an eagle was eating a snake. That place was the site of Tenochtitlán. **3.** The Incas built terraces on steep hillsides. They knew about crop rotation and how to use fertilizers to increase crops. They built large systems of aqueducts to bring water to dry regions. They constructed a vast system of roads over their empire. Some of the roads are so

well constructed that they are in use today. Incan builders also built attractive stone buildings. **4.** The Spanish brought horses, cattle, sheep, citrus fruits, and sugar cane to the Americas. They carried the potato, corn, and tobacco back to Europe.
III. Building Skills: Maya: 300 B.C.-A.D. 900; built pyramids, experts at mathematics and astronomy, developed an accurate calendar; Aztec: 1325-1521; built causeways, a system of aqueducts, a huge city with zoos and parks; Inca: 1200-1533; built irrigation systems, used fertilizer, crop rotation, and terrace farming, constructed great roads and buildings of stone

Chapter 25

Section 1 Review

1. The heart of every Spanish town was the main square. This square, or plaza, was the place where colonists met their friends. The most important building in the Spanish town was the church. **2.** Answers will vary. Possible answer: The Jesuits may have preserved Guaraní heritage by protecting the Guaraní from capture by people of other cultures, preserving their language and traditions. The Jesuits changed Guaraní culture by introducing them to Christianity.

Case Study Review

1. because she was a woman **2.** Sor Juana was interested in developing her mind and not in acquiring wealth.

Section 2 Review

1. Bolívar's dream of a unified South American nation did not come to pass because South Americans remained divided after independence. They were divided by geography as well as culture. **2.** Mexico's struggle was long and bloody. By contrast, Brazil's was peaceful, with the emperor declaring independence from Portugal that was not challenged.

Section 3 Review

1. Juárez tried to curb the power of the military and the Roman Catholic Church. He also tried to take lands from the church and redistribute them to the poor. **2.** Foreign money both helped and hurt the economies of Latin American countries. Money from Britain and Europe helped countries such as Argentina develop its industrial economy. On the other hand, the new development made Latin American countries dependent on good economic times in the economically developed lender countries. The lender countries also developed a strong economic and political influence in Latin American countries. American fruit companies exercised great influence in many of the countries of Central America, for example.

Reviewing Chapter 25

I. Reviewing Vocabulary: **1.** d **2.** a **3.** c **4.** b
II. Understanding the Chapter: **1.** Silver, foremost, and gold, to a lesser extent, were the resources that

allowed Spain to become the wealthiest nation in Europe during the 1500s. **2.** In general, Roman Catholic missionaries acted as protectors to the Native Americans. Native Americans were educated on missions; they were protected from slavers and from semi-slavery conditions. **3.** Haiti gained its independence after a long revolt. It was led by Toussaint L'Ouverture, a self-educated former slave. Although L'Ouverture was captured by the French, and eventually died in prison, the revolt continued until the French were finally driven out. **4.** Foreign investment in Latin America created an economy that was dependent on markets and economic conditions in industrial nations. In addition, large fruit companies owned by foreign entities came to have an enormous influence in Central America.

III. Building Skills: Check students' summaries for accuracy.

Chapter 26

Section 1 Review

1. (a) Diversity means *differences* and is sometimes used to refer to a mix of cultures in a society. **(b)** In Mexico and Brazil, Native American, African, and European influences have mixed to create diverse cultures. **2. (a)** Historical events include European settlement of Latin America beginning in the 1500s and the slave trade. **(b)** Lack of diversity in some countries was a result of strong European influence and diseases that killed off Native Americans.

Section 2 Review

1. Most Latin Americans speak Spanish, enabling people of different nations to communicate with each other. **2.** Answers will vary. Some students might say that the idea of a chaperon is old fashioned and indicates a distrust of young people. Others might feel that it is a good idea for young people to be chaperoned.

Section 3 Review

1. Latin American cities have experienced tremendous growth in recent times. About three fourths of the population in Latin America lives in cities. The region is also home to the "mega-city"—huge cities that contain a significant proportion of a country's population. **2.** Possible answer: Two problems facing Latin American cities are slums and terrible traffic. To remedy the terrible conditions in slums, cities might provide more basic services, such as garbage collection and electricity. To alleviate some of the problems caused by traffic, cities might improve public transportation.

Case Study Review

1. Marcos came to the city to find work and build a better life than he had in the village. **2.** Compared to the life he had in the village, the life he has in the city is much better. He is also optimistic about the future.

Reviewing Chapter 26

I. Reviewing Vocabulary: **1.** b **2.** c **3.** d **4.** a
II. Understanding the Chapter: **1.** Mexico and Brazil

have diverse cultures; Argentina and Uruguay do not. **2.** Many priests and nuns have begun working to help the poor. Some adhere to liberation theology, a philosophy that holds that poverty was created by the people who had power in society, and that the Catholic Church should help to change society, so that it treats people in a more just way. **3.** A mega-city is a city where a large portion of the people of a country live. Mega-cities are changing the face of Latin America as it becomes a region of city-dwellers. **4.** Like other cities in Latin America, Caracas has experienced tremendous growth. During the 1970s, money from oil discovered in Venezuela poured into Caracas. Huge skyscrapers and a subway system were built. At the same time, many poor people flocked to the city in search of jobs. With the influx of the poor came slums and shantytowns.

III. Building Skills: Recognizing Cause and Effect
1. a. cause **b.** effect **2. a.** effect **b.** cause
3. a. cause **b.** effect.

Chapter 27

Section 1 Review

1. The city of Brasília was built in order to encourage Brazilians to move to the largely undeveloped interior of the country. **2.** Most wealthy people in Latin America are landowners. There is a tremendous gap between the rich and the poor in Latin America. Land reform has been a major issue in Latin America and has caused violent uprisings.

Section 2 Review

1. They hope to find new jobs and new opportunities in the city. **2.** Latin American nations that are dependent on one crop or one natural resource can find themselves in a bad situation if world demand for that resource drops suddenly or if the price suddenly drops.

Section 3 Review

1. The skilled working class has protested against military rule. In many countries, democracy has prevailed. **2.** The debt crisis was caused by excess borrowing to finance industrial growth. Many Latin American countries expected to finance this debt with money earned from the sale of commodities such as coffee, oil, and tin. When the price of these products went down, Latin American countries were unable to repay their debts.

Case Study Review

1. Fulgencio Batista was the dictator of Cuba. He was overthrown in 1958. **2.** Cubans troubled by the conversion of the Cuban economy to communism left the island.

Reviewing Chapter 27

I. Reviewing Vocabulary: **1.** d **2.** a **3.** b **4.** c
II. Understanding the Chapter: **1.** Land reform efforts proceeded slowly in Latin America because the people who owned the land and resources were very powerful. They had strong allies in military leaders. **2.** The U.S. government felt threatened by the

Guatemalan reformers. It stepped in to protect the interests of U.S.-owned businesses, including the United Fruit Company. **3.** Latin American nations that are dependent on one crop find themselves in an economic crisis when world demand for, or the price of, that crop drops suddenly. **4.** Cuba was severely hurt by the collapse of the Soviet Union. Cuba had depended on massive aid from the Soviet Union, and the new government of Russia that emerged after the collapse did not continue the aid.

III. Building Skills: **1.** The Peters projection shows the Southern Hemisphere as larger. **2.** The Peters projection shows South America as larger. **3.** The Mercator view of the Northern Hemisphere can lead us to perceive that hemisphere as dominant. Peters represents the size and importance of the Southern Hemisphere more accurately.

Chapter 28

Section 1 Review

1. The Monroe Doctrine was issued by President James Monroe in 1823. It warned European nations not to interfere in Latin America's newly independent countries. **2.** Answers will vary. But if answered from the United States point of view, troops were sent in to protect U.S. interests and U.S. investments from harm during periods of upheaval.

Section 2 Review

1. The United States reacted to Castro's policies with hostility. The U.S. cut off relations with Castro, and supported anti-Castro campaigns, including the Bay of Pigs invasion. **2.** Answers will vary. Here is an acceptable sample: The United States seized the Canal Zone in 1903 by illegal dealings with Panamanian rebels. In 1978, the United States agreed to give up control of the Canal Zone in order to improve its relations with the rest of Latin America.

Section 3 Review

1. The Organization of American States, among other things, works to settle disputes between nations of the Americas without force. **2.** Answers will vary. Students' paragraphs should reflect an understanding of the two points of view of the issue.

Section 4 Review

1. Gabriel García Márquez is a Nobel Prize-winning Colombian writer who mixes dreams with reality. He writes of ghosts, fantasy, and history. **2.** The "big three" painted scenes of the Mexican Revolution and other significant events in Mexican history.

Case Study Review

1. Puerto Rico is a commonwealth of the United States. It is self-governing, but it does not have the full status of a state. Puerto Ricans serve in the armed forces. However, they pay no federal taxes. **2.** Answers will vary. Accept any reasonable answer if it is supported by reasonable facts.

Chapter 28 Review

I. Reviewing Vocabulary: **1.** b **2.** d **3.** a **4.** c

II. Understanding the Chapter: **1.** The "Good Neighbor Policy" attempted to soften Latin American fear and suspicion of the United States by renouncing the use of force and providing assistance to needy Latin American nations by the United States. **2.** Policy toward the two presidents was vastly different. The U.S. government supported the Chilean military in the overthrow of the Marxist president. It opposed the military takeover of the Haitian government and threatened the Haitian military with invasion if Aristide was not allowed to return and assume power. **3.** The goals of the Alliance for Progress were to provide substantial aid for worthy projects to improve living conditions in Latin America. **4.** "Operation Bootstrap" was the program devised by Luis Muñoz Marín and other supporters of Puerto Rican commonwealth status. It provided, among other things, substantial tax credits to factories that established plants in Puerto Rico.

III. Building Skills: **1.** Investments grew substantially in every region of Latin America during the period. **2.** They grew faster in the first period, 1897 to 1908.

Literature Connections

1. It reflects the author's love of the Chilean land and her desire for freedom in Chile. **2.** Students will learn that there are green orchards and grapevines, and that there are rivers.

Chapter 29

Section 1 Review

1. Canada's size and geographical barriers have tended to separate people. Canadians live in pockets of settlements scattered across the country. Between these pockets are huge geographical barriers such as the vast forests of the Canadian Shield or the high mountains of the Canadian Rockies. These barriers increase the sense of isolation and lead to the creation of regional loyalties. **2.** Students might point to such things as language, common heritage and history, religion, and similar values as things that unify a nation. Things that divide a nation might include differences in values, language, and heritage.

Section 2 Review

1. The six major culture regions are the Arctic, Subarctic, Eastern Woodlands, Great Plains, Plateau, and Northwest Pacific Coast. Possible answer: People in the Subarctic region were nomads who moved from place to place following herds of animals. The people of the Great Plains followed buffalo herds. They used the buffalo for food, clothing, and shelter. **2.** The Mohawks decided to use the incident to bring to the public's attention other grievances they held. Students opinions of the Mohawks' actions will vary.

Case Study Review

1. James Bay I was a project that dammed the La Grand River in order to harness hydroelectric power. The dam created a lake that submerged Cree land and destroyed ancient burial and hunting grounds. 2. Roads allowed outsiders to affect the Cree way of life. Dams caused many Cree to move and destroyed hunting grounds.

Section 3 Review

1. French is a national language and most people of French origin have remained Roman Catholic. 2. Students might point out that Canada is the second largest country in area, but has only a tenth of the United States' population.

Section 4 Review

1. Canada's cities have grown larger as job opportunities have expanded with the spread of commerce and industry. This has led Canadians to migrate from rural areas and has led to substantial immigration from Europe and Asia. 2. Answers will vary. Accept answers backed by thoughtful judgment and adequate detail.

Chapter 29 Review

I. Reviewing Vocabulary: 1. a 2. d 3. c 4. b
II. Understanding the Chapter: 1. Most of Canada's lakes are located in the Canadian Shield.
2. Ontario is most like Quebec in geography and economics. Both provinces are very large. Both border on the United States. Both reach far to the north. Both are heavily populated in the south and lightly populated in the north. Culturally, however, the two provinces are different. Quebec has the most French Canadians of any province.
3. Canada's "breadbasket" is the three prairie provinces: Alberta, Saskatchewan, and Manitoba. These provinces produce the most wheat and other grains. 4. Many French Canadians fear that their culture will be overwhelmed by the larger English Canadian culture.
III. Building Map Skills: 1. Newfoundland is located furthest east. The Yukon is located furthest west.
2. Ottawa 3. the Arctic, Pacific, and Atlantic oceans

UNIT 4 REVIEW

I. 1. (a) Some of the main physical features of Latin America are the Amazon River, the Andes mountains, Caribbean Sea, tropical rainforest, and plains in the south. The climate of Latin America varies by distance from equator and altitude. Among these are the tropical wet-and-dry climates near the equator and the humid subtropical north and south of the equator. (b) People settled on coastal plains and highlands. Few people live in mountains or rainforests. In addition, mountains and dense rainforests isolated people from one another. 2. The major ethnic groups in Latin America are Europeans, Native Americans, Africans, Mulattos (mixed African and European), and Mestizos (mixed Native American and European). 3. (a) The three major civilizations in ancient Latin America are the Mayas, Aztecs, and Incas. (b) Europeans had more and better weapons. They also brought with them diseases to which Native Americans had no immunity. Many Native Americans died from diseases brought from Europe. 4. (a) New countries faced the challenge of building new governments and economies. The army took control of many countries. Many farmers lost their land in the fighting and moved to cities. (b) Foreign investments provided assistance, but brought new dependence on industrial nations. 5. (a) European missionaries brought Christianity to Latin America in colonial times. (b) The Church grew in power and wealth until it became the wealthiest landowner in Latin America and the center of Latin American village life. 6. (a) Latin Americans are moving to cities to escape the poverty and unemployment of rural life. (b) Many cities are modern with highways, skyscrapers, parks, universities, theaters, restaurants, shopping districts, and a growing middle class. Rapid growth has made city living difficult however, with growing air pollution, traffic, and crime. City living is particularly difficult for the poor who often live in terrible slums. 7. (a) Possible answer: Poverty is Latin America's biggest problem. (b) Two causes of Latin America's poverty are the lack of educational opportunities and the dependence on one crop. Two effects of Latin Americas poverty are the rapid growth of cities and the lack of readily available resources to build industry. 8. Many Latin Americans see the relationship between themselves and the U.S. as an unequal one. Latin Americans resent the United States meddling in their affairs. 9. (a) French and English are the two official languages of Canada. (b) French Canadians resent the power and control of the English speaking Canadians and have tried to secede from the country in recent years.

II. 1. Roosevelt wanted the United States to maintain control over Latin America by being the police force of the Americas. Examples of U.S. involvement in Latin America include the Spanish-American War, the Mexican American War, the Panama Canal, and revolutions in Guatemala, Nicaragua, and other Central American countries. 2. Native Americans stress that the land is their ancestral homeland, that they were there before Europeans, that their ancestors are buried there, and that the Europeans took the land from them forcefully. Europeans stress that they have been on the land for over 400 years, that they have planted the land and made it more valuable, and that they have no where else to go. Two examples include the Maya in Guatemala and the Cree in Canada.

III. Answers will vary. Students should provide descriptions and issues for each year as follows: A.D. 1000—one of the ancient Latin American civilizations (Maya, Aztec, Inca); A.D 1500—Spanish conquest of the Native Americans and settlement of Latin America; A.D 1800—Latin America under Spanish colonial rule and the independence movement; A.D 1996—modern life in Latin America. The issues the students write about will vary.

IV. 1. (a) 43 percent (b) 5 percent 2. (a) Peru (b) Chile 3. Possible answer: A number of countries in

Latin America are ethnically diverse, but some, such as Honduras, are not.

Global Issues: Rain Forests Around the World

1. Rain forest resources may provide life-saving medicines and more than half of all the earth's plant and animal species live in rain forests. **2.** Students' answers will vary. Accept answers that are clear and logical.

UNIT 5

Previewing the Unit

1. Judaism, Christianity, Islam **2.** between 1095 and 1291 **3.** 592 years **4.** the Suez Canal **5.** about 40 years after

Exploring Regional Issues

1. (a) 32 percent (b) 5 percent **2.** (a) North America (b) more (c) 10 percent more **3.** (a) Oil brings income. (b) Possible answer: Supplies can be disrupted causing increases in gas and oil prices and problems for industry.

Chapter 30

Section 1 Review

1. Without rivers, settled life would not be possible in the Middle East. Because there is so little rainfall, people have depended on the rivers to provide life-sustaining water.

2. Answers will vary. Here is one example: Mountains are the sources of the river systems that provide the people of the Middle East with the water they need to survive.

Section 2 Review

1. The major cultural tie is language. Arabs, by definition, are people who speak the Arabic language. Most, but not all, are Muslims.

2. The Egyptian would find the Algerian newspaper easiest to read. Students should understand that the Algerian and the Egyptian speak the Arabic language, while the Iranian and the Israeli speak other languages.

Case Study Review

1. Bedouin tents are called "houses of hair" because they are made of long strips of goat or camel hair.

2. Answers will of course vary. Here some possibilities. "How has the discovery of oil changed your life?" "I thought all Bedouins rode on camels. Why don't you have a camel?" "Do you still lead a nomadic existence?"

Reviewing Chapter 30

I. Reviewing Vocabulary: **1.** d **2.** a **3.** b **4.** c

II. Understanding the Chapter: Rivers are important because the region is so dry that settled life would be impossible without the water provided by rivers. The river floods have made farming possi-

ble since ancient times. **2.** Language binds people in the Arab world. Arabic is the dominant language of most of the countries of the Middle East and North Africa. While the spoken language may vary from place to place, the written language is very similar. **3.** Cities of the Middle East are growing quickly as people from rural villages migrate to the cities in search of jobs. **4.** The number of nomadic Bedouins has declined because jobs in the oil industry are available and many Bedouins are choosing to give up the hard life as nomads in place of the settled life as refinery workers.

III. Building Skills: **1.** Cause: Great reserves of oil have been discovered in the Middle East. **2.** Effect: Middle Eastern population is growing. **3.** Cause: Most Syrians and Algerians speak Arabic, while Turks speak Turkish. The written form of the Arabic language is similar from place to place in the Middle East.

Chapter 31

Section 1 Review

1. Civilizations began in Mesopotamia when people gained the knowledge of agriculture. This allowed them to settle down and grow crops large enough for certain people in societies to specialize.

2. Answers will vary, but students should suggest that the affluence of the settled city-states attracted other peoples to invade. From the previous chapter, students should be aware that the lack of geographic barriers also encouraged the movement of peoples.

Section 2 Review

1. Among the accomplishments of the ancient Egyptians: the building of pyramids, developments in irrigation, development of a system of picture writing, accurate knowledge of calendars, study of the human body to mend broken bones and performance of brain surgery.

2. The yearly floods along both river systems brought silt down from the mountains and spread it along the banks of the rivers. This silt and the promise of water in a dry land helped farmers to plant their crops in a land otherwise unsuited to farming.

Section 3 Review

1. The major similarity is that both religions are monotheistic; they believe in one God.

2. Middle Eastern rulers feared that loyalty to Judaism and Christianity threatened their own positions and religions.

Section 4 Review

1. The hejira was the flight of Muhammad from Mecca to Medina in order to escape his enemies.

2. The five duties of Muslims are known as the "Five Pillars" because pillars hold up a building. These pillars support the major beliefs of Islam.

Case Study Review

1. The crowds were on pilgrimage.

2. Ibn Batuta was a devout Muslim. The Koran teaches that Muslims should make a pilgrimage to Mecca at least once in their lives.

Section 5 Review

1. The Seljuk Turks were nomads from Central Asia who brought Iraq, Egypt, and Syria under their control in the 1100s.

2. Answers will vary. Some students will say that the problems within the Islamic empire left the empire weak and susceptible to outside invaders such as the Seljuk Turks and the Mongols.

Reviewing Chapter 31

I. Reviewing Vocabulary: **1.** b **2.** d **3.** c **4.** a

II. Understanding the Chapter: **1.** These were ideal locations to encourage the growth of agriculture. Development of agriculture allowed specialization to occur. **2.** The ancient Egyptians believed that for the spirit to live, the body must be preserved. Therefore, the bodies of the pharaohs were preserved, along with much of their personal wealth. **3.** All three religions believe in one God. **4.** The Koran is the holy book of teachings of Islam. It contains the most important rules of life for Muslims.

III. Building Skills: **1.** a **2.** d **3.** b **4.** c

Chapter 32

Section 1 Review

1. The "Young Turks" were Turkish officers who were angered by the way Europe dominated the Ottoman Empire.

2. Answers will vary. Some may cite the domination of European powers. Some may cite the alliance between the Ottoman Empire and Germany during World War I. Others may identify ethnic groups in conflict as the main cause.

Section 2 Review

1. The British broke their promise to grant independence to nations formerly of the Ottoman Empire.

2. European colonial empires in the Middle East shrank after World War I. Nationalist movements led to the independence of such countries as Turkey and Iran after World War I. Nationalist movements also led to the end of the British protectorate in Egypt.

Case Study Review

1. The Balfour Declaration was an announcement by the British government that it would support "a national home for the Jewish people" in Palestine.

2. The Israeli will cite the historical presence of Jews; the Bible, the thousands-of-years-old quest for a Jewish homeland, the Balfour Declaration and the struggles and sacrifices that have taken place since the end of World War II. The Arab will cite the Koran, the continuous presence of

Arabs in Palestine, British promises for national self-determination, and the sacrifices that have taken place since the end of World War II.

Reviewing Chapter 32

I. Reviewing Vocabulary: **1.** b **2.** c **3.** a **4.** d

II. Understanding the Chapter: **1.** The Industrial Revolution and the rise of nationalism were two factors in Europe that led to the breakup of the Ottoman Empire. **2.** The Ottoman Empire's alliance with Germany put it on the losing side in World War I. After the war, the victorious Allies determined to break up the empire. **3.** Mustafa Kemal tried to make Turkey more modern by starting new industries and building schools. **4.** There was fighting in Israel after it became an independent state in 1948 because Arabs contested the founding of Israel.

III. Building Skills: **1.** the Balkan Peninsula **2.** the Danube River **3.** before 1566 **4.** Constantinople, Cairo, Vienna

Literature Connections

1. Most people would not expect a thief to have any right to sue in court. **2.** Possible answer: The author believes that government workers are apathetic or that they are so concerned with following the rules that they forget that their main job is to protect people from injustices.

Chapter 33

Section 1 Review

1. Nomadic people are moving to cities because jobs are available in the cities that allow the nomads to give up their difficult lifestyle.

2. Answers will vary, but students should express some anxiety or confidence about the dramatic changes that they would be forced to face.

Section 2 Review

1. Traditional marriage practices include selection of spouse by parents, matchmaking, couples not meeting before the wedding. Students should be aware that the idea of love does not play a big role in most Middle Eastern marriages.

2. Answers will, of course, vary. Look for a realistic presentation of the lives of Middle Eastern women.

Section 3 Review

1. Ramadan is the holiest month of the year, a time when Muslims do not eat or drink between sunrise and sunset.

2. Hospitality is an essential part of the coffee ritual. The ceremony proceeds at a slow pace, with much time for talk.

Case Study Review

1. The case study gives a number of examples of differences between Western and Middle Eastern ideas of privacy, including the space between people when they are talking, use of compliments, shaking hands, questions that might be considered invasive in Western cultures.

2. Answers will vary, but should reflect that the person could be insulted.

Reviewing Chapter 33

I. Reviewing Vocabulary: **1.** c **2.** d **3.** b **4.** a

II. Understanding the Chapter: **1.** Most village residents are from farm families. Most are poor. Villagers often believe in the old ways and work hard to preserve their traditions. **2.** Hospitality, loyalty, honor, and reverence for Islam are important nomadic values that are still important to Middle Easterners. **3.** Generally, divorce is easier for men than for women. In some parts, the man has only to say "I divorce you," three times. A wife usually needs approval from a religious leader. **4.** You should not say you like it because the host may feel compelled to give it to you.

III. Building Skills: **1.** Nomads move from place to place; village dwellers live settled lives. **2.** In general, men have greater rights and responsibilities than women do. **3.** For both men and women, traditional dress is long robes; traditionally, Middle Eastern women are subject to purdah, which includes covering the face in public. **4.** Romance and love are important in the West; in the Middle East, traditional marriages may be arranged by the parents and family ties are more important than love. **5.** Middle Eastern manners are more courtly and more concerned with hospitality. Western manners tend to be more informal.

Chapter 34

Section 1 Review

1. Oil has transformed Bahrain into a nation of wealth. No one in Bahrain pays income taxes. Medical care and schooling are free for all citizens. Luxury cars, televisions, and boats are common.

2. Cause: Oil-rich countries have imported foreign workers. Effect: Countries not rich in oil receive money from these wealthy lands.

Section 2 Review

1. Both Damascus and Kuwait City have grown rapidly in recent years. On the other hand, Damascus is described as a city "suffering from too many people in too little space." Kuwait City has had more controlled growth, with a general level of prosperity unseen in Damascus.

2. Answers will vary, but should reflect a knowledge of the profile of Damascus in the section. Since Damascus is described as city on the edge of the desert, students should assume that further growth will intensify the crowding in an already crowded city.

Section 3 Review

1. Many Middle Eastern women wear veils in public places today because there has been a resurgence of Islamic fundamentalism. This fundamentalism has led some women to return to the veil out of religious conviction and some out of fear of punishment.

2. Wearing veils is commonplace in Iran, a fundamentalist country. Many people in Iraq are also devout Muslims, but law in Iraq is not based on the Koran alone. Women do not have to wear the veil.

Case Study Review

1. Saudi Arabia used its oil wealth to build hospitals, schools, and roads.

2. King Fahd decided to make reforms in government because of unease among the Saudi population with total control by the Saud family.

Reviewing Chapter 34

I. Reviewing Vocabulary: **1.** a **2.** d **3.** b **4.** c

II. Understanding the Chapter: **1.** Oil changed the lives of people in oil rich countries by providing vast amounts of money for public developments. **2.** Workers returning from oil-rich countries bring changes to their countries. They bring home wealth that has been used to improve the lives of families. **3.** Education has provided many new opportunities for women, allowing them to work outside the household. **4.** The Saudi government has set up a council of citizens to advise the royal family and has given citizens a bill of rights.

III. Building Skills: **1.** The speaker means that Saudi Arabia cannot simply import foreign goods if there is no connection with their culture. **2.** The speaker seems to admire U.S. affluence, but she also suggests that family ties are not strong enough in the United States. **3.** The speaker suggests that Saudi culture is more family based and private and U.S. culture more oriented toward society.

Chapter 35

Section 1 Review

1. At Camp David in 1978, Israel and Egypt signed a peace treaty ending more than 30 years of warfare.

2. Answers will vary. Students should understand that each side believed that the territory belonged to it.

Case Study Review

1. Farmers solved the problems of farming in the desert by inventing the drip system of irrigation. They also found plants that did not soak up the salt of the desert.

2. Answers will vary, but students should realize that a national language can be a unifying force.

Section 2 Review

1. The Lebanese civil war grew out of religious differences between Christians and Muslims in the country. Tensions grew worse when the Palestine Liberation Organization moved its headquarters to Lebanon in 1975.

2. Islamic fundamentalism grew out of opposition to the westernization of many Middle Eastern cultures. Fundamentalists saw this as a threat to traditional Islam.

Section 3 Review

1. In general, Middle Eastern nations have tried to use wealth brought by oil to develop various industries and thereby further strengthen their economies.

2. Both oil-rich and oil-poor countries face a rapidly growing population, high defense spending, lack of skilled managers and workers, and poor farming conditions.

Reviewing Chapter 35

I. Reviewing Vocabulary: **1.** c **2.** a **3.** b **4.** d

II. Understanding the Chapter: **1.** The founding of Israel was a unifying factor for Arabs of the Middle East, who joined together to oppose the new state. **2.** The Lebanese civil war arose out of religious differences in the country between Christian and Muslims. **3.** The shah was toppled by increasing opposition to his westernization policies, by hatred of corruption and brutal control by the shah's secret police, and by the rise of Islamic fundamentalism. **4.** Countries have tried to deal with the lack of water by joint irrigation ventures, by removing the salt from saltwater, and by adjusting farming methods to conform to the arid climate.

III. Building Skills: **1.** fact **2.** opinion **3.** opinion **4.** fact

Chapter 36

Section 1 Review

1. Iraq invaded Kuwait to gain control of its huge oil reserves and because Saddam Hussein thought that other nations would not interfere.

2. Without Soviet arms and money, Middle Eastern nations were forced to cooperate with Western nations. They also began to explore possible solutions to the Arab-Israeli dispute.

Section 2 Review

1. The intifada was the result of 20 years of strict Israeli rule. The Palestinians were increasingly angry over their poor living conditions.

2. Answers will vary, but should express the idea that political violence does not solve problems.

Section 3 Review

1. "Arabsat" is a series of communications satellites that connect the Arab nations with other communications systems.

2. Jordan wants to build a dam on the Yarmuk River to provide badly needed water for the Jordan valley. However, Israel will not approve the project without the promise that it will get a fair share of the water.

Section 4 Review

1. Naguib Mahfouz is an Egyptian novelist who won the Nobel Prize for literature in 1988.

2. Islamic artists have produced some of the world's finest works of art. Since many Muslim societies ban art that shows human or animal life, much Islamic art is based on symbols or calligraphy.

Case Study Review

1. The Kurds are an Islamic people who live in northern Iraq and Iran and southwestern Turkey.

2. Answers will vary, but should reflect a realistic course of action.

Reviewing Chapter 36

I. Reviewing Vocabulary: **1.** c **2.** a **3.** b **4.** d

II. Understanding the Chapter: **1.** The OPEC oil embargo forced Western nations to begin measures for conservation of gasoline. **2.** The Iran-Iraq war was caused by a dispute over an oil-rich area. **3.** Calligraphy is an important part of Middle Eastern art because some Middle Eastern societies ban art that shows humans or animals. **4.** The Kurds, who live in a number of Middle Eastern countries, are seeking a country of their own. They are seen as a threat to Iraqi unity.

III. Building Skills: Answers to all four scenarios will vary, but should reflect a reasonable consequence of the action.

UNIT 5 REVIEW

I. **1.** (a) Since most of the region is very dry, water is the region's most important resource. (b) Most of agriculture in the region takes place around the fertile river valleys. Soil around the rivers is made fertile each year by flooding. As a result, most of the region's population live in these river valleys. Some of the oldest civilizations in history have arisen in Middle Eastern river valleys such as the Nile and the Tigris and Euphrates. **2.** (a) Most people in the Middle East speak the Arabic language and practice Islam. (b) Other common cultural characteristics are the use of traditional gowns and similar mannerisms. **3.** Students may identify any three of the following: the idea of written language, measuring time, calendars, medicine and science, and preserving bodies. **4.** (a) Turkey emerged from what remained of the Ottoman empire. (b) Great Britain and France took over the rest of the Middle East. (c) European interest grew in the Middle East because of the discovery of oil in the Arabian Peninsula **5.** Students should note the differences among village life, city life, and nomadic life in the Middle East. They should understand that village and nomadic life are more traditional than city life. **6.** (a) Students should describe the traditional role of women in marriage, divorce, and family life, and the issue of wearing veils while in public. (b) Some countries have lifted some of the restrictions on women going out in public without a veil. In addition, women have increased access to education and are becoming professionals. Women in some urban areas, partic-

ularly in Israel, live modern, Western-style lives.
7. (a) Arabs and Israelis both claim the land that was given to the state of Israel in 1948. Palestinians claim that the land had been theirs and was taken from them without their consent. Israelis claim it as their ancestral homeland. (b) Most of the wars have resulted in a gain of territory for Israel and increased bad feelings between the two. **8.** (a) OPEC (Organization of Petroleum Exporting Countries) is an alliance of major oil producing and exporting countries. Its goal is to work together to limit competition between them and to keep prices high. (b) OPEC was very successful in meeting this goal in the 1970s. In recent years, however, industrialized nations have been more successful in conserving fuel and finding fuel sources of their own. The reduced demand in oil has reduced OPEC's power.

II. 1. Answers will vary. Arabs spread Islam through conquest and trade. It was a religion that many in the conquered areas blended with their own religions. **2.** Answers will vary. Students may give Damascus and Kuwait City as examples. Descriptions of the place that benefits from oil should include high per capita income, state paid services, such as medical care and schooling, modern houses, office buildings, hospitals, and roads. Descriptions of the place that has not benefited from oil may include overcrowding, narrow, old roads and homes, a traditional suq or market, and traditional village life. Similarities might include devotion to the Islamic faith and a monarchy or autocratic style of government. **3.** Students should mention the role of oil in the Persian Gulf War. Many nations became involved in the war to protect oil fields in Kuwait from Iraqi control. If Iraq had retained control of Kuwait, it might have taken control over the oil fields that much of the industrialized world depends on. This may have thrown the global economy into a depression similar to the ones in the 1970s.

III. Answers will vary. Students should describe the breakup of the Ottoman empire, British colonization and occupation, traditional life in the Middle East, the economic effects of oil, the political effects of Israel, the wars against Israel, the recent peace talks, the Persian Gulf War, and the rise of fundamentalism. Opinions will likely vary on what life would be like without the discovery of oil and without the state of Israel.

IV. 1. (a) 2.1 billion barrels (b) about 500 million barrels **2.** The Middle East and North and South America produced the most oil. **3.** Possible answer: The Middle East is extremely important as an oil producer to many countries throughout the world.

Global Issues: The Growth of World Cities

1. It is cheaper to provide such services to people in a smaller, more concentrated area than a larger, more spread-out area. **2.** Possible answer: A farmer would find the city more crowded and would have to find a different way of making a living. A farmer would also find a variety of entertainment and increased educational opportunities.

UNIT 6
Previewing the Unit

1. 196 years **2.** 1500s **3.** Peter the Great **4.** World War II **5.** World War II

Exploring Regional Issues

1. (a) per capita income in U.S. dollars (b) $14,300 **2.** $9,735 lower **3.** These two countries have low per capita incomes compared to the other countries of Europe.

Chapter 37
Section 1 Review

1. Europe's four major geographic areas are the Northwest Mountain region, the North European plain, the Central Uplands, and the Alpine Mountains. **2.** Ports in Eastern Europe and the Heartland are less busy because many of them are frozen over during the winter. Also, Western Europe has developed important trade links with the Americas, Asia, and Africa, whereas Eastern Europe and the Heartland are less dependent on international trade.

Section 2 Review

1. The steppe is a better farming area. **2.** Western Europe has a far longer growing season. The Heartland has one of the world's greatest forest resources in the taiga. Water power is used extensively to generate electricity in both Western Europe and the Heartland.

Section 3 Review

1. Western Europe is the most densely populated part of Europe. **2.** Answers will vary. Some may focus on economic problems; other may focus on ethnic differences of minority groups.

Case Study Review

1. Answers will vary. Some possibilities are Speyer's cathedral, the cathedral at Cologne, the city of Cologne, castles built in the Middle Ages. **2.** The Rhine is important for both historical and economic reasons. It contains many important historic sites. It also is an important means of transportation for Germany.

Reviewing Chapter 37

I. Reviewing Vocabulary: **1.** b **2.** c **3.** d **4.** a
II. Understanding the Chapter: **1.** Navigable rivers are important to the economies because many of them are important means for moving manufactured goods and agricultural products to ports on the coast. **2.** Europe's "backbone and ribs" are the Alps and a series of mountains that run perpendicular to it. **3.** Western Europe is more densely populated than the Eurasian Heartland. **4.** The steppe has rich deep, fertile soil. The taiga is thick forest.
III. Building Skills: **1.** Cold winters are the cause of

the unusable ports. **2.** Mild weather allows grapes to be grown in the region. **3.** Differences between Serbs, Croats, and Muslims are the cause of ethnic violence in Bosnia.

Chapter 38

Section 1 Review

1. The freedoms and rights that the citizens had due to democracy made government in ancient Greece unique. The Greeks established the first democratic governments. **2.** Other ancient societies had governments in which the people had no say.

Section 2 Review

1. The Crusades were military campaigns to free Jerusalem and the Holy Land from Muslim control. **2.** Feudalism developed as a response to the weaknesses of governments during the early Middle Ages.

Section 3 Review

1. England was the most important European country to develop a constitutional monarchy. **2.** Increased travel and trade helped Europe to develop commercial economies and caused Europeans to look beyond their borders for raw materials and markets.

Section 4 Review

1. Germany remained divided because the emperor had little power over Germany's 300 different states. **2.** Germany and Poland were both divided. On the other hand, Germany was divided into different states while Poland was controlled by other countries.

Section 5 Review

1. The Industrial Revolution brought about a factory system. Many workers worked long hours in factories for little pay. **2.** Answers will vary but should refer to the insecurities and breakdowns of authority during times of revolution.

Case Study Review

1. The "groans and other sad sounds" were the sounds of machines bringing up the coal. **2.** Answers will vary. One possibility: During the Industrial Revolution, many women found employment in textile mills. However, wages were very low, hours were long, and conditions very dangerous.

Reviewing Chapter 38

I. Reviewing Vocabulary: **1.** b **2.** c **3.** d **4.** a

II. Understanding the Chapter: **1.** Many Greek city-states had democratic governments. Other ancient societies had autocratic governments. **2.** The Romans contributed the ideas that all people were equal before the law and that all citizens accused of a crime were innocent until proven guilty. **3.** Europeans sought a new route to Asia because the old routes were controlled by

Muslims and the Italian city-states. **4.** The English government was a constitutional monarchy; the French government was an absolute monarchy. **5.** By increasing productivity, the Industrial Revolution allowed the production of goods at a far cheaper price than they had been previously.

III. Building Skills: **1.** Pericles meant that the many citizens of Greece had an important role in government. **2.** Pico's view was an expression of the Renaissance view that humans had the power to control their destinies. **3.** It says that even after a long day of work in the mines, she still had to do work at home.

Chapter 39

Section 1 Review

1. A crisis began in the Balkans in 1914 that led to World War I. **2.** He meant that peace was ending and a bloody war was about to begin.

Section 2 Review

1. The causes of World War II included the rise to power of aggressive totalitarian states in Germany, Italy, and Japan. **2.** The Nazis capitalized on anger and despair over the depression to attract support.

Section 3 Review

1. The "iron curtain" was an imaginary line following the borders between the Communist countries of Eastern Europe with the non-Communist countries of Western Europe. **2.** The prosperity of Western Europe was in stark contrast to the failure of Communist economies to be productive.

Case Study Review

1. The Soviet Union controlled the territory around Berlin at the end of World War II. **2.** The Berlin Airlift was a direct result of the beginning of the Cold War between Communist and non-Communist countries.

Reviewing Chapter 39

I. Reviewing Vocabulary: **1.** b **2.** c **3.** d **4.** a

II. Understanding the Chapter: **1.** The alliance system led the countries of Europe to divide into armed camps and led to the outbreak of World War I. **2.** Germany was treated harshly after World War I and forced to pay reparations to the Allies. **3.** The Nazis rejected the treaties that had ended World War I and began a campaign against Germany's Jews. **4.** World War II weakened Europe and shifted the balance of power to the Soviet Union and the United States. **5.** Churchill meant that Europe was divided into two hostile camps.

III. Building Skills: **1.** The Great Depression caused despairing Germans to turn to Hitler. **2.** The Nazis' rise to power caused the destruction of Germany's democracy. **3.** The growing tensions between the Soviet Union and the Allies caused the Soviets to blockade West Berlin.

Chapter 40

Section 1 Review
1. A welfare state is one in which the government assumes responsibility for the welfare of its citizens. 2. Answers will vary. In support: Many people need assistance that only the government can provide. In opposition: The government can't do everything; people must do it for themselves.

Section 2 Review
1. The Louvre is a museum in Paris. 2. The British system is a constitutional monarchy and the United States a republic. The two systems are similar because they are both democracies.

Section 3 Review
1. The people of Central Europe face a serious pollution problem. Many rivers are polluted and forests have died. 2. The Berlin Wall was an important symbol because it represented a divided Germany. When it came down, the Germans were in a position to reunify the country.

Section 4 Review
1. The Mediterranean Sea is the "highway" that ties Southern Europe together. 2. Italy has the largest population. Spain has the largest area.

Case Study Review
1. Italy has made tremendous economic progress since World War II. 2. Northern and southern Italy are similar in language and religion. They are different because the north is an industrial area and the south is a rural area.

Reviewing Chapter 40
I. Reviewing Vocabulary: 1. c 2. d 3. a 4. b

II. Understanding the Chapter: 1. The Swedish welfare state has become expensive to maintain and has strained the economy. 2. Paris is the embodiment of French culture with many important cultural attractions. 3. The House of Commons is part of Parliament, the legislative body of Britain. 4. Eastern Europe's most serious environmental problem is pollution of air and water. Careless development of industry caused the problem.

III. Building Skills: 1. The monarch has little actual power in Britain. However, most English people respect the monarchy and want to preserve its traditions. 2. The Berlin Wall symbolized a Europe divided between a Communist east and a non-Communist west. 3. Tourists visit Italy to see the buildings of the Roman Empire. Another attraction is the Vatican, the world center of the Roman Catholic Church.

Literature Connections
1. He was trying to save the property of his

neighbor. 2. Possible answer: The man expressed the hatred most Germans felt toward Jews.

Chapter 41

Section 1 Review
1. Because of violence between Hindus and Muslims, two nations were formed, a Hindu-dominated India and a Muslim-dominated Pakistan. 2. Answers will vary. One possible answer: The forces of nationalism were too strong for the forces of colonialism.

Section 2 Review
1. The two Germanies reunited because of a spirit of nationalism, combined with the collapse of communism in the east. 2. East Germany made the transition from communism without violence. In Romania, there was widespread violence.

Section 3 Review
1. Since the end of World War II, countries in Western Europe have taken steps toward greater economic cooperation. 2. The European Union helps build prosperity by removing tariffs and other barriers to trade.

Case Study Review
1. Under Havel's leadership, the government passed laws that guarantee basic rights and liberties. 2. Answers will vary, but should express the idea that Slovak nationalism was stronger than economic factors.

Reviewing Chapter 41
I. Reviewing Vocabulary: 1. a 2. d 3. c 4. b

II. Understanding the Chapter: 1. World War II weakened Europe. It also strengthened the sense of nationalism among the people of the colonial world. 2. The year 1989 saw the toppling of Communist governments throughout East Europe. 3. The EU was an attempt to strengthen the economies of the nations of Western Europe by eliminating tariff barriers between countries. 4. Czech and Slovak nationalism led to distrust between the two major ethnic groups, prompting the breakup.

III. Building Skills: 1. East Germany had a larger proportion of workers in agriculture. 2. In West Germany, the majority of workers were employed in commerce, transportation, and communications. 3. West Germany had more workers in construction. (The percentage is the same, but the working population of West Germany is larger.) 4. Germany has 38.3 million workers. 77.5% of the workers lived in West Germany, while 22.5% of the workers lived in East Germany.

Chapter 42

Section 1 Review
1. Kievan Russia adopted Orthodox Christianity. 2. The Mongols destroyed everything in their path.

The Mongols placed high taxes on the people and cruelly punished anyone who refused to obey.

Section 2 Review

1. Russian serfs could not move, marry, or learn to read without their landlord's permission. They could be drafted into the army and had to pay very heavy taxes. **2.** Answers will vary. However, they should refer to the fact that both rulers waged many wars in which many peasants and ordinary people died.

Section 3 Review

1. Alexander's greatest reform was freeing the serfs in 1861. **2.** Russia's massive defeats in the early part of World War I undermined morale and confidence in the tsar.

Section 4 Review

1. Stalin tried to modernize Russia's industries in an effort to make the Soviet Union an industrial power. **2.** Answers will vary, but should relate to the content of the section, including his forced collectivization and the Great Purge.

Case Study Review

1. Gorbachev tried to establish real elections and at the same time preserve communism. **2.** The reforms, once begun, could not be controlled. They led to a rising tide of opposition to communism.

Reviewing Chapter 42

I. Reviewing Vocabulary: **1.** d **2.** a **3.** b **4.** c

II. Understanding the Chapter: **1.** Peter's goal was to westernize Russia. He brought Western experts to Russia. He established schools and new industries. He built St. Petersburg as a "window to the west." **2.** The Bolsheviks overthrew the Provisional Government in a bloody civil war. **3.** Stalin used terror and the Great Purge to modernize the Soviet Union. **4.** During the Great Purge, Stalin had the secret police arrest millions of people. Among those arrested were most of the Communist party's leaders and the top generals.

III. Building Skills: **1.** Both Peter and Stalin wanted to modernize their country. **2.** Under both systems, Russia had autocratic rule. **3.** Under Khrushchev, the standard of living improved in the Soviet Union. Under Brezhnev, the economy weakened in the Soviet Union.

Chapter 43

Section 1 Review

1. Moscow and St. Petersburg are Russia's two largest cities. **2.** Under communism, the state discouraged religion, so religious practice was difficult.

Section 2 Review

1. Russia used force to suppress nationalism in Belarus. **2.** A variety of languages spoken in a country can be an obstacle to unity.

Section 3 Review

1. In 1915, the Ottoman Empire committed genocide against the Armenians. The Turks murdered more than 1.5 million Armenians. **2.** Answers will vary. Three possibilities: Why are you fighting? When will this war end? Why don't you allow the various parts to split off?

Section 4 Review

1. Because its water supply has been diverted, the Aral Sea is drying up. Winds have blown the salty sands across the countryside, ruining the farmland. **2.** Answers will vary, but should relate to the widespread water and air pollution in Central Asia.

Case Study Review

1. Crimea is a part of the Ukraine. Yet two thirds of Crimea's population is Russian. **2.** With the breakup of the Soviet Union, the Russians of Crimea suddenly found themselves in a "foreign" country, Ukraine.

Reviewing Chapter 43

I. Reviewing Vocabulary: **1.** d **2.** a **3.** b **4.** c

II. Understanding the Chapter: **1.** Industrialization changed Russia from a rural to an urban country. **2.** Nagorno Karabakh, an area populated by Armenian Christians, is the source of the dispute between Azerbaijan and Armenia. **3.** The water sources of the Aral Sea have been diverted, causing the sea to dry up. Salty sand has blown over farmland, ruining it. **4.** Two thirds of the people of Crimea are Russian. However, the peninsula is a part of Ukraine.

III. Building Skills: **1.** opinion; Religion is a strong force among the Russian people. **2.** fact **3.** fact

Chapter 44

Section 1 Review

1. The Comintern was an organization to promote Communist revolutions. **2.** Answers will vary. Most students will realize that many people in the West were horrified by the Nazi-Soviet pact.

Section 2 Review

1. The Cuban missile crisis of 1962 was a confrontation between the Soviet Union and the United States caused by the Soviet attempt to place nuclear missiles in Cuba. **2.** The Cuban missile crisis was so dangerous because the United States and the Soviet Union came close to war.

Section 3 Review

1. The new republics wanted to keep nuclear weapons as a protection against the other new republics. **2.** Answers will vary. One possibility is confrontation between the republics formed by the breakup of the Soviet Union.

Case Study Review

1. In 1986, there was a nuclear explosion at Chernobyl. **2.** The Kola Peninsula is poisoned by huge plants that make nickel from ore.

Reviewing Chapter 44

I. Reviewing Vocabulary: **1.** b **2.** a **3.** d **4.** c

II. Understanding the Chapter: **1.** Soviet foreign policy was different because the goal was to destroy the capitalist system in other countries. **2.** World War II resulted in the deaths of 20 million Soviet citizens, the destruction of cities, and the destruction of factories. **3.** It was important for the new nations to give up their nuclear weapons because of the threat of nuclear confrontation. **4.** Soviet policies had a destructive effect on Russia's environment.

III. Building Skills: **1.** Kazakstan and Uzbekistan **2.** Russia and Kazakstan **3.** Azerbaijan, Georgia, Russia, Kazakstan, Uzbekistan, Turkmenistan **4.** the Volga and Ural rivers

UNIT 6 REVIEW

I. 1. Ancient Greece is the birthplace of democracy. Over thousands of years, democratic ideals gradually spread through Western Europe, first among philosophical thinkers, then to governments through revolution. **2.** (a) It changed the way people worked and made things in society. It began in England. (b) Because of newly developed machines, products were produced faster and more cheaply. This led to a higher standard of living for most people but at the cost of poor working conditions. **3.** (a) Alliances made between Britain, France, and Russia on one side, and Germany and Austria-Hungary on the other side escalated already existing tensions and crises. (b) An assassination in the Balkans started the war. **4.** (a) The Cold War was a period of hostility between the United States and the Soviet Union. (b) It began after the end of World War II, when the Allied powers disagreed on the fate of Eastern Europe. (c) The United States and the Soviet Union carved up "spheres of influence" with Eastern Europe under Soviet control and Western Europe allied with the United States. **5.** (a) The Berlin Wall came down in 1989. (b) Shortly after the Wall came down, East and West Germany united into one country, the Soviet Union broke apart, and communism fell in most of Eastern Europe. The fall of the Berlin Wall signaled the end of the Cold War. **6.** (a) Russian people were very poor and dissatisfied with the feudal system and the autocratic government of the tsars. (b) Revolutionaries wanted to make Russia a socialist country in which the government owns and runs the economy and all people share wealth equally. **7.** Answers will vary, but students are likely to mention ethnic fighting in the former Yugoslavia and the fighting by ethnic Armenians in Azerbaijan. **8.** Students may mention any three of the following: ethnic problems, nuclear weapons, environmental problems, crime, and economic problems.

II. 1. People live where the land is most hospitable to human life. The land in Western Europe is friendlier than in Eastern Europe and the Heartland. Reasons why Western Europe is more densely populated than other regions include access to the ocean and warm water ports, fertile, relatively flat land, and wide navigable rivers. **2.** During World War II, the Nazis tried to wipe out the entire Jewish population of Europe. The Nazis tried to make Jews scapegoats for all of their problems after World War I. Never before had a country so carefully planned and systematically implemented the destruction of an entire people on such a large scale.

III. Answers will vary. Students should trace the history of Russia, the Heartland, and the Soviet Union in the 1900s. Students should mention the causes of the Russian Revolution, the rise of communism and the Soviet Union, the treatment of Soviet people under Stalin, the Soviet Union during World War II, the Cold War from the Soviet perspective, the recent breakup of the Soviet Union, and the newly won independence of the Ukraine.

IV. 1. (a) agriculture, services, industry, construction, and other jobs (b) Germany, Italy, Ukraine, United Kingdom **2.** (a) United Kingdom (b) United Kingdom **3.** Possible answer: Ukraine has the greatest percentage of its work force in agriculture.

Global Issues: The UN Works to Preserve the Peace

1. The UN provides a forum for the countries of the world to settle disputes peacefully. **2.** Two reasons the UN might succeed are continued cooperation and the continued use of coalitions. Two reasons the UN might not succeed are a breakdown of cooperation and a breakdown of coalition forces.

Reproducible Masters

Introduction

Critical Thinking Activity Worksheet

1. in 1900, 86.4 percent; in 1990, 57 percent **2.** It increased by 0.5 percent. **3.** It will increase by 19.1 percent. **4.** by one billion **5.** Possible answer: During the twentieth century, the number of people moving to cities has consistently increased.

Introduction Test

1. d **2.** a **3.** e **4.** b **5.** c **6.** c **7.** a **8.** d **9.** a **10.** b

Essay In democracies, citizens participate in government and have the power to shape it through voting or other means. An example of a democracy is the United States. In monarchies, a king or queen heads the government and holds all power. A number of countries today have constitutional monarchies that combine features of democracy and monarchy. Great Britain is a constitutional monarchy. In a dictatorship, a leader or group holds power by force. Citizens have few rights and are forbidden to express their opinions. Iraq is a dictatorship.

UNIT 1

Exploring Regional Issues Worksheet

1. (a) the 0-4 year-olds (b) the 75+ year-olds 2. (a) All three African countries have large young populations and small older ones. (b) The population of the United States is more evenly distributed.

Critical Thinking Activity Worksheets

Chapter 1

1. broadleaf trees that lose their leaves in the fall 2. tropical rain forest 3. on the northern and southern coasts of Africa 4. desert and no vegetation regions 5. the desert and no vegetation regions

Chapter 2

1. (a) 622 (b) 650–700 2. Mayan civilization 3. Songhai empire 4. Muslims invade Ghana; city of Zimbabwe is founded.

Chapter 3

1. b 2. g 3. i 4. d 5. c 6. h 7. f 8. j 9. a 10. e Proverbs will vary, but should contain a moral or subject.

Chapter 4

1. Africa 2. squeezing it 3. (a) Lending Nations (b) dollars, money 4. Possible answer: The cartoonist believes the lending nations are unfairly pressuring the nations of Africa. 5. Answers will vary, but should show an understanding of the subject of the cartoon.

Chapter 5

1. Africa at the beginning of a new day 2. the colors of the African landscape 3. birds and insects 4. "Glad of a warm sheet" in the cold of dawn 5. The author has very warm feelings about Africa. 6. Letters should demonstrate students' understanding of the poem.

Chapter 6

1. to all people who live in it, black and white 2. land, liberty, and peace 3. all South Africans regardless of color, race, sex, and belief 4. all South Africans living in brotherhood, enjoying equal rights and opportunities 5. to work together, sparing nothing of their strength and courage

Chapter 7

1. the world's refugees by region 2. Africa has the most; Latin America has the fewest. 3. Middle East: 5,448,000; East Asia and the Pacific: 444,000 4. East Asia and the Pacific: 3%; Europe and North America: 16%; Latin America: 0.01%; Middle East: 33.5%; South and Central Asia: 11% 5. The political or economic situations in Africa and the Middle East are less stable than those in East Asia and Latin America.

Chapter Tests

Chapter 1

1. c 2. a 3. d 4. e 5. b 6. a 7. d 8. b 9. b 10. c

Essay Students should mention the different climate regions of Africa, including the desert, savanna, tropical rain forest, and Mediterranean region, as well as the different landforms, including mountains, Rift Valley, lakes, and rivers. Students should describe how life differs in each of these different climates and land types. Specific examples could include life in the rain forest vs. life in the desert, or life in the mountains vs. life in the savanna.

Chapter 2

1. c 2. b 3. d 4. e 5. a 6. c 7. b 8. b 9. a 10. c

Essay Students could mention and discuss any one of the following empires and civilizations: Egypt, Kush and Axum, Ghana, Mali, Songhai, Benin, Zimbabwe. The discussions should include the rise and fall of each empire as well as a description of life in each empire. Students should mention how the arrival of Europeans contributed to the downfall of the great African empires.

Chapter 3

1. b 2. e 3. a 4. c 5. d 6. b 7. c 8. c 9. a 10. c

Essay In this essay, students should describe the role of the family in African life. Students should mention the shared responsibility of the extended family and the role of clan and tribe in African society. Students should mention the role of chief and of tribal elders in making the rules and decisions in African society. Students should describe tribal religions and cultural practices such as initiation ceremonies. Students should mention the economies of traditional African societies, including subsistence agriculture and livestock herding.

Chapter 4

1. e 2. c 3. d 4. b 5. a 6. d 7. b 8. a 9. d 10. a

Essay Students should discuss the division of Africa by European powers. In this discussion, students should mention the economic motivations of Europeans. Students should also mention the role of the Berlin Conference in dividing up the continent. A discussion of the positive and negative effects of imperialism should include the following: effects on traditional African society, family, and political systems; economic exploitation; working conditions; the building of roads and schools; and improved medical care. Specific examples could include the Zulus. Students should discuss the rise of African nationalism which led to independence movements.

Chapter 5

1. b 2. e 3. c 4. a 5. d 6. a 7. c 8. d 9. b 10. c

Essay Students should discuss oral vs. written literature in Africa. In their discussion of written literature, students should mention the common themes of celebrating African culture and exploring the problems of modern Africa. In their discussion of oral literature, students should mention the importance of storytelling in African life. Students should describe the visual arts from Africa and discuss their influence on modern Western art.

Chapter 6

1. e 2. a 3. d 4. b 5. c 6. b 7. a 8. b 9. d 10. c

Essay Students should discuss the problem of building democracy among the variety of ethnic groups in most African countries, and the effect that colonial rule had on drawing national borders in Africa. Students should discuss the following economic challenges and problems: developing agriculture, diversifying economies, drought and famine, rising populations, and debt payments. Students should mention recent agricultural developments in technology as a way to grow more food to feed a rising African population.

Chapter 7

1. b 2. d 3. a 4. c 5. e 6. b 7. c 8. c 9. a 10. d

Essay Students should discuss any two of the following issues: health, education, refugees, drought and famine, desertification, and endangered species. For each issue, students should write about the source of the problem and what is being done to alleviate the problem. For example, health problems are caused by disease and malnutrition. People are learning better methods of hygiene and improved methods of farming to counter these problems.

UNIT 1 TEST

1. nomad 2. imperialism 3. nationalism 4. plateaus 5. barter 6. scribe 7. secede 8. urbanization 9. c 10. d 11. a 12. b 13. a 14. b 15. d 16. c 17. a 18. d 19. Students should cite geographic reasons such as waterfalls and lack of natural harbors as reasons for difficulties. They should discuss the efforts of European explorers and missionaries in reaching the interior and should describe how imperialism affected African culture. 20. Possible answers: (a) cause: urbanization; effect: more women in the workforce
(b) cause: need for trained workforce; effect: increased literacy rates (c) cause: lack of land in the rural areas; effect: crowded cities (d) cause: demonstrations by the people; effect: more freedom

UNIT 2

Exploring Regional Issues Worksheet

1. (a) Malaysia (b) Malaysia 2. (a) Japan, Singapore (b) All 3. (a) Malaysia (b) Bhutan, Myanmar, Nepal NOTE: Answers are based on information that appears in the chart; when students add information about Laos and New Zealand, answers may change.

Critical Thinking Activity Worksheets

Chapter 8

1. Buddhism, Christianity, Hinduism, Islam, Sikhism, Jainism, and tribal religions 2. India, Pakistan, Bangladesh, Bhutan, Nepal, and Sri Lanka 3. Hinduism 4. Pakistan and Bangladesh 5. Possible answer: This region is likely to have had the most contact with other cultures because it shares borders with other countries. It is therefore more diverse.

Chapter 9

1. 321 B.C. 2. 28 years 3. 500 B.C. 4. 1947 5. India won independence and Mohandas Gandhi was assassinated.

Chapter 10

1. (a) 6,842,232 (b) 2,961,561 2. 2,775,211 3. 47 percent 4. 55 percent are male; 45 percent are female.

Chapter 11

1. Women in Higher Education in India 2. years 3. women enrolled per hundred men enrolled 4. about 17 5. about 41 6. The number of women per hundred men has increased. The larger bars indicate the increase in the number of women students. 7. Possible answer: Traditionally, educating women was not a priority. Educating men was seen as more important.

Chapter 12

Check students' graphs for accuracy.

Chapter 13

1. kampung 2. consensus 3. rice 4. religion 5. gamelan 6. puppets 7. gong 8. family life 9. Jakarta 10. Singapore

Chapter 14

Possible causes: lack of farmland; hope for better jobs; need to send money home; better opportunities for education, entertainment and culture

Possible effects: growth of ethnic neighborhoods in some cities, money sent back to villages, increased job opportunities; growth of slums and shantytowns, spread of health problems related to overcrowding, poverty

Chapter 15

1. Average Rainfall for Selected Cities in Australia 2. cities and months 3. rainfall in millimeters 4. Sydney, Perth, Alice Springs, Darwin 5. Perth 6. Darwin 7. desert; there is little rainfall all year

Chapter Tests

Chapter 8

1. d 2. a 3. e 4. c 5. b 6. c 7. a 8. c 9. a 10. d

Essay The peoples of South and Southeast Asia have many different cultural backgrounds. In India alone, there are more than 845 languages and dialects. There are hundreds of religious and ethnic groups. People of diverse origins have different ideas about government, economy, religion, and culture. These traditions have merged and formed unique cultures.

Chapter 9

1. a 2. d 3. e 4. b 5. c 6. d 7. b 8. b 9. c 10. a

Essay The INC was formed in order to push the British government to allow more Indians to serve in the government. After World War I, the

INC started to make many more demands. It also led an investigation of the massacre of more than 400 Indians who were demonstrating against British rule. Mohandas Gandhi became the leader of the INC in 1920. He urged nonviolent protest against the government. He and the INC pushed Britain for independence for India. In 1947, Britain granted India independence.

Chapter 10

1. d 2. c 3. e 4. b 5. a 6. d 7. a 8. d 9. b 10. c

Essay India is the second most populated country in the world. With a quickly growing population, India is having a difficult time ensuring the well-being of its citizens. In order to control population growth, the Indian government has instituted policies to encourage couples to have fewer children. The environment is another problem India is facing. Extensive erosion caused by logging is affecting farming patterns. The cities do not have safe drinking water and they are polluted by sewage. The flood of migrants into the cities of India is creating overpopulation problems. Although India has begun to open new schools, education in India is also severely lacking, especially in the villages.

Chapter 11

1. b 2. a 3. e 4. d 5. c 6. b 7. d 8. a 9. d 10. c

Essay India's policy of non-alignment meant that during the Cold War, it did not side with either the United States or the Soviet Union. India hoped that non-alignment would allow it to have good relations with both nations. However, this policy angered both the Soviet Union and the United States. The United States was angered when India voted to let China join the United Nations. India felt threatened in 1954, when the United States signed a treaty with Pakistan.

Chapter 12

1. d 2. e 3. c 4. a 5. b 6. a 7. b 8. a 9. b 10. c

Essay Vietnam was ruled by China for about 1,000 years. The Vietnamese were influenced by Chinese religion, language, art, and poetry. In 939 A.D., the Vietnamese broke away and formed the kingdom of Dai Viet.

The Pagan kingdom was built by peoples from Tibet and China. Buddhism was the kingdom's primary religion. The writing system of the Angkor kingdom was influenced by an Indian language. The kingdom also adopted Hinduism, an Indian religion. They built canals and were productive farmers.

Chapter 13

1. b 2. d 3. a 4. c 5. e 6. a 7. d 8. c 9. d 10. b

Essay The basis for most of the arts in Southeast Asia is religion. Many of the arts combine elements of different religions. The Indonesian gamelan orchestra is made up of gongs, xylophones, and other percussion instruments.

Gamelan music is used for dance and religious ceremonies. Southeast Asian dances use ornate costumes and tell stories, often from Hindu legends. Literature was historically an oral tradition passed down through the generations; many of these stories were based on religious epics. Recently, modern writers have begun to write these stories down. Many Southeast Asian religious temples are prominent features of the skylines of Southeast Asian cities and villages.

Chapter 14

1. a 2. b 3. e 4. d 5. c 6. c 7. b 8. b 9. c 10. a

Essay Lack of industry and undeveloped economies in the nations of Southeast Asia were two problems. Additionally, many of the people who knew how to run the factories had left. Some Southeast Asian countries adopted communism. Communist countries such as Cambodia, Laos, and Vietnam set up an economy in which the state owned the factories. States such as Thailand and the Philippines set up market economies. In a market economy, private companies own and run the businesses.

Chapter 15

1. a 2. d 3. c 4. b 5. e 6. a 7. d 8. b 9. c 10. a

Essay Australia is almost one third desert. It is almost as large as the United States, but has a relatively small population. Most of the rain falls on the coast and thus most of the cities and farms are located there. New Zealand is very different from Australia: It is green and mountainous. However, as in Australia, most people live in cities near the coasts. Unlike Australia, New Zealand has few deposits of natural resources, and so it relies on other sources of energy, such as hydroelectricity and geothermal energy.

UNIT 2 TEST

1. delta 2. caste 3. non-alignment 4. animism 5. consensus 6. capitalism 7. atolls 8. monsoons 9. b 10. a 11. c 12. c 13. d 14. a 15. a 16. d 17. b 18. c 19. Students should discuss Hinduism, Buddhism, and Islam. Hinduism developed in India out of the culture and traditions of the ancient Aryans. Students should refer to the caste system and reincarnation. Buddhism was founded by a Hindu named Siddhartha Gautama who experienced enlightenment and became known as Buddha. It is practiced in large portions of Southeast Asia. Students should refer to the four noble truths and the goal of nirvana. Islam spread to South and Southeast Asia from the Middle East. It is practiced in Pakistan, Bangladesh, and Indonesia. Students should refer to belief in one god, the belief that all people are equal before Allah, and the Koran. 20. Students should mention that trade brought foreigners to the region. Students should discuss the impact of European education and World War II on Southeast Asian independence movements.

UNIT 3

Exploring Regional Issues Worksheet

1. Check students' maps for accuracy. **2.** Most of the cities are on coastal plains. (b) over 520 people per square mile **3.** (a) The coastal plains have the highest population density. (b) The mountains have the lowest population density. (c) It is more difficult to live in the mountains.

Critical Thinking Activity Worksheets

Chapter 16

1. East Asia's landforms **2.** (a) a barren or desolate area (b) a mountainous or hilly section of a country (c) a flat or gently rolling area of land with few changes in elevation (d) a large area of flat land higher than the surrounding land **3.** the Gobi and the Taklimakan **4.** Honshu; a highland

Chapter 17

1. France, Britain, Germany, Russia, Japan **2.** Japan **3.** because the United States did not have a sphere of influence in China **4.** They were angered; some Chinese organized rebellions.

Chapter 18

1. 1641 **2.** (a) 1853 (b) Matthew Perry and the U.S. Navy **3.** The Meiji Restoration occurred after the Tokugawa shogunate. **4.** The Japanese took control of Korea.

Chapter 19

Possible answers: Japanese universities are very competitive; parents in Japan push their children to study hard; Japanese students attend school six days a week.

Chapter 20

1. (a) the domination by one country of the political, economic, or cultural life of another country or region (b) a loosely organized system of government in which local lords governed their own lands, but owed military service and other support to a greater lord (c) to persist in the face of obstacles or discouragement (d) without stopping **2.** Mao Zedong **3.** imperialism, feudalism **4.** Possible answer: He wanted the Chinese people to revolt against feudalism and imperialism. **5.** Possible answer: Yes. Mao wanted to restore enthusiasm for the revolution. He wanted the Chinese people to believe in and support communism.

Chapter 21

1. at a Japanese port **2.** imports **3.** imports **4.** Possible answer: The cartoonist believes that Japan unfairly restricts imports.

Chapter 22

1. The United States imports more than it exports. **2.** (a) $47,891 million (b) $102,246 million (c) trade deficit **3.** $119,963 million

Chapter Tests

Chapter 16

1. c **2.** d **3.** a **4.** e **5.** b **6.** c **7.** c **8.** a **9.** d **10.** d

Essay All three languages use symbols in their written form. The Koreans and Japanese borrowed their written language from the Chinese. Both the Koreans and Japanese have adapted the symbols in various ways to fit their language. The Koreans also use an alphabet with 24 letters called *han'gul*.

Chapter 17

1. b **2.** d **3.** c **4.** e **5.** a **6.** a **7.** b **8.** b **9.** d **10.** b

Essay Led by Sun Yat-sen and Chiang Kai-shek, the Nationalists wanted to modernize China. The Communists were led by Mao Zedong. These two groups fought together against the warlords, but in 1927 the Nationalists began fighting against the Communists. In 1936, the Nationalists and Communists allied again to fight the Japanese. After World War II, the two groups fought one another again. In 1949, the Communists won and the Nationalists retreated to Taiwan.

Chapter 18

1. e **2.** d **3.** a **4.** c **5.** b **6.** c **7.** a **8.** a **9.** b **10.** d

Essay In A.D. 552, Chinese monks introduced Buddhism, which was merged with the native Shinto religion. The Japanese adopted elements of Chinese culture such as styles of dress, art, and music. The Japanese also adapted Chinese characters to the Japanese language.

Chapter 19

1. b **2.** d **3.** e **4.** c **5.** a **6.** b **7.** b **8.** a **9.** c **10.** a

Essay Possible answer: In China, marriages were traditionally arranged by parents when the children were very young. When the Communists took over, they banned child marriages. In Japan, traditionally the father ruled the family and the wife took a subservient role. In modern Japan, women may vote and work outside the home. For centuries, Korea used the Confucian methods of teaching, with males receiving the benefits of education. Today both males and females attend school.

Chapter 20

1. c **2.** a **3.** d **4.** e **5.** b **6.** c **7.** c **8.** a **9.** d **10.** b

Essay When the Communists came to power, they tried to change the "four olds"–old ideas, old habits, old customs, and old culture. They set limits on family size, and allowed women to choose a husband, in contrast to arranged marriages. They destroyed traditional landowners and divided the land among the poor. They expanded education and industry. The Communist government directed the arts and literature in China to serve the Communist state and reflect Communist teachings.

Chapter 21

1. c **2.** b **3.** e **4.** d **5.** a **6.** a **7.** a **8.** b **9.** c **10.** d

Essay After World War II, Japan rebuilt its destroyed industries. It has become the world's second largest economy. Reasons for this "economic miracle" include Japanese workers' strong work ethic and their ability to work in teams; close links between business and government, ensuring careful planning; and the manufacture of inexpensive, high quality goods.

Chapter 22

1. e **2.** c **3.** a **4.** b **5.** d **6.** b **7.** b **8.** d **9.** a **10.** b

Essay During World War II, the United States and China were allies. After the Communists took control of China in 1949, relations changed. During the 1950s and 1960s, the United States banned all trade with China. This effectively isolated China from the rest of the West. In 1969, the Soviets and China fought a brief border war. This ended the Soviet-Chinese friendship. The Chinese then became eager to increase ties with the West. In the early 1970s, diplomatic relations were restored between China and the United States. By the 1980s, trade boomed between China and the United States.

UNIT 3 TEST

1. typhoons **2.** dynasties **3.** vassal **4.** samurai **5.** collective farms **6.** coalition **7.** self-sufficiency **8.** trade surplus **9.** a **10.** c **11.** a **12.** d **13.** c **14.** c **15.** a **16.** c **17.** a **18.** a **19.** Students should discuss the geographical features of Korea: mountains running north to south, plains along the coasts. Students should mention that the south has a longer growing season while the north has most of the mineral resources. Both speak the same language and share the same culture. Students should discuss the post-war split of Korea, including United States and Soviet occupation of South Korea and North Korea respectively. Students should mention the role that the Korean War played in the Cold War and the distrust it caused between North Korea and South Korea.
20. Students should discuss the rise of the Communist party in China in the 1920s under Mao Zedong. They should mention Mao's goals of building a Marxist society and modernizing. Students may mention the Long March as an example of this relationship. Students should discuss the changes the Communists made in Chinese society once they came to power, including collective farming, improvements in industry, restrictions on political freedom, the campaign against the traditional family, the population policies, and the focus on educating boys and girls. Students should describe the Great Leap Forward and the Cultural Revolution and the effect these policies had on China.

UNIT 4

Exploring Regional Issues Worksheet

1. (a) about 18 percent (b) 25.4 percent **2.** San José (b) San José **3.** San José

Critical Thinking Activity Worksheet

Chapter 23

1. Elevation levels in Latin America **2.** The highest region in Mexico is in the center of the country. **3.** (a) The highest region in South America is located along the west coast of the continent. (b) the Andes Mountains **4.** 0–1000 feet **5.** Both have mountains running north to south, but South America's mountains are much higher.

Chapter 24

1. 1501 **2.** the Mayan civilization **3.** the Aztec civilization **4.** Muslims and Jews were expelled from Spain. **5.** Mayan civilization began to decline.

Chapter 25

1. a Spanish conquistador or conqueror **2.** an Indian prince **3.** He is stabbing the Indian prince. **4.** Possible answer: The artist is showing the brutality and cruelty with which the Spanish treated the Native Americans in Latin America.

Chapter 26

1. (a) Mexico City, São Paulo, Rio de Janeiro, Buenos Aires (b) Mexico City **2.** (a) Calcutta (b) Buenos Aires (c) Calcutta would be more crowded because there are more people living in a smaller area. **3.** (a) Mexico City–1992: 41,408, 2000: 53,395; São Paulo–1992: 42,956, 2000: 56,217; Rio de Janeiro–1992: 46,188, 2000: 54,496; Buenos Aires–1992: 21,950, 2000: 24,133, (b) Rio de Janeiro (c) São Paulo

Chapter 27

1. area of the tropical rain forest in three continents in 1980 and 1990 **2.** continents/regions of the world **3.** hectares of forest are (in thousands) **4.** in 1980: 920,000 thousand hectares; in 1990: 840,000 thousand hectares **5.** in 1980: 310,000 thousand hectares; in 1990: 280,000 thousand hectares **6.** Latin America **7.** Latin America **8.** Possible answer: Deforestation affects world climate and eliminates natural resources that are not available elsewhere.

Chapter 28

1. García Márquez was accepting the Nobel Prize for Literature. **2.** He makes reference to the United States and other nations trying to control Latin American nations' economies and governments. **3.** He says that Western nations respect Latin America's originality in literature, but not in their attempts at social change. **4.** (a) García Márquez believes its source is colonialism. (b) European leaders think it is the result of a Soviet conspiracy. **5.** García Márquez's dream is for a peaceful world where Latin Americans can choose their own destiny.

Chapter 29

Pro Arguments: Possible answers: The project would create jobs and income for Quebec; the project would create needed electricity and power;

the project would help Canada's economy through exports to the United States Con Arguments: Possible Answers: The project will hurt the environment; the land belongs to the Cree; the project violates the James Bay and Northern Quebec Agreement.

Chapter Tests

Chapter 23
1. c **2.** b **3.** a **4.** e **5.** d **6.** a **7.** c **8.** d **9.** b **10.** a

Essay Students might discuss how geography has led to regionalism in Latin America. They might use the Aymarás of the altiplano as an example of how climate and geography affect how people live.

Chapter 24
1. c **2.** a **3.** e **4.** b **5.** d **6.** b **7.** a **8.** d **9.** a **10.** b

Essay Students should identify the three major early civilizations in Latin America as the Mayas, the Aztecs, and the Incas. Similarities among the civilizations include the importance of farming, and the development of complex governments and religions. In discussing differences, students might refer to location and specific accomplishments.

Chapter 25
1. d **2.** a **3.** c **4.** e **5.** b **6.** d **7.** c **8.** a **9.** b **10.** d

Essay Students' answers should mention that Latin Americans wanted control over their own affairs, that most nations fought for independence, but that Brazil won its freedom peacefully. Challenges after independence included building new governments and economies.

Chapter 26
1. c **2.** a **3.** e **4.** d **5.** b **6.** a **7.** b **8.** c **9.** c **10.** d

Essay Students should discuss the effects of urbanization on traditional family life and on the types of work people do. They might also discuss how urbanization affects ties to religion.

Chapter 27
1. e **2.** b **3.** c **4.** a **5.** d **6.** c **7.** a **8.** d **9.** c **10.** b

Essay Fidel Castro rose to power by defeating the dictator Fulgencio Batista in 1956. Castro promised to take land away from the rich and give it to the poor. While he has made great strides in providing housing, medical care, and education for Cuba's citizens, Castro has ruled as a dictator and the country on the whole is very poor. Cuba's relationship with the United States is strained because Cuba is a Communist country.

Chapter 28
1. c **2.** a **3.** d **4.** e **5.** b **6.** b **7.** a **8.** b **9.** d **10.** c

Essay The United States has often interfered in the affairs of Latin American countries. Students might discuss the Panama Canal or the Spanish-American War as possible examples.

Chapter 29
1. b **2.** d **3.** e **4.** c **5.** a **6.** c **7.** c **8.** d **9.** b **10.** a

Essay Students should discuss the historical basis for the current relationship between the English and the French. They should mention Quebec's attempts to secede from Canada. They might also mention that Canada has two official languages, English and French.

UNIT 4 TEST
1. irrigation **2.** commonwealth **3.** culture **4.** bilingualism **5.** viceroy **6.** exiles **7.** squatter **8.** tariffs **9.** b **10.** c **11.** b **12.** b **13.** c **14.** a **15.** b **16.** c **17.** Possible answers: (a) cause: to escape poverty, seek better jobs, education, better living conditions; effect: pollution, poor working conditions, unemployment, traffic, poor living conditions, barrios, shantytowns, and squatters, the rise of the "mega-city" and the middle class (b) cause: location of Latin America near the U.S.; effect: Latin Americans' resentment over U.S. meddling in their affairs and recent changes in U.S. foreign policy. **18.** Students should describe the European conquest of the Aztec and Incan civilizations. They should discuss the effect of weapons and disease on Latin American natives. Students should discuss the reasons Latin Americans fought for independence, including the corruption and rigidity of colonial government and the hostility between the classes. Finally, students should describe the struggle for independence by Bolívar and San Martín.

UNIT 5

Exploring Regional Issues
1. (a) 15% (b) 19% **2.** (a) United States (b) Saudi Arabia **3.** (a) Canada (b) Kuwait

Critical Thinking Activity Worksheets

Chapter 30
1. The map shows the different ways in which Egyptians use their land. **2.** Cairo **3.** The major river running north-south is the Nile River. **4.** Students might name any three of the following: citrus, corn, cotton, rice, sugarcane, wheat **5.** The Nile River valley is the source of Egyptian agriculture. **6.** The river irrigates the surrounding land and the floods bring nutrients to the soil, making it more fertile. **7.** Most of Egypt can be classified as "wasteland."

Chapter 31
1. Menes **2.** the Phoenicians **3.** Alexander the Great **4.** (a) in the Tigris and Euphrates river valleys (b) after **5.** Indus valley civilization was emerging.

Chapter 32
1. Cause: Europeans develop superior weapons; new trade routes to Asia; Industrial Revolution; rise of nationalism. **2.** Effect: Egypt builds modern

fleet; Suez Canal built; Egypt gains control of Sudan. **3.** Cause: European nations compete for control of Ottoman territory. Effect: French and British take control of Ottoman territory; Ottomans lose more power. **4.** Cause: British and French promised Arabs independence from Ottomans. **5.** Effect: World interest in Middle East increases; increased wealth to region; Suez Canal gains in importance. **6.** Cause: Iranian nationalists rebel against British control. Effect: Reza Shah introduces reforms; reforms cause trouble with traditionalists. **7.** Cause: Egyptian government corrupt and under British influence. Effect: Egyptian government takes over major industries; builds Aswan Dam. **8.** Effect: Arab nations declare war on Israel; Israel wins more territory.

Chapter 33

1. headman: the leader of a village **2.** suq: a large market in the Middle East **3.** tradition: behavior handed down from generation to generation **4.** purdah: the practice of keeping women from public view **5.** hospitality: generous treatment of guests **6.** Ramadan: the holiest month in the Islamic calendar. Students' pictures will vary.

Chapter 34

1. Women in the work force, 1970 and 1990 **2.** former Soviet Union **3.** North Africa and the Middle East **4.** It rose. **5.** North Africa and the Middle East **6.** It is lower than the rest of the world. **7.** The percentage will continue to grow.

Chapter 35

1. The "we" refers to the Jewish nation of Israel, as a whole. **2.** Students should recognize that the final lines of the poem indicate hope for the future. **3.** The narrator means that many people have died and probably will continue to die in fighting for the separate causes. **4.** Some students might say that the author is sympathetic to the Jewish side in the confrontation. Others might say that he is referring to the peace process in his poem. **5.** Answers will vary.

Chapter 36

1. The two charts show crude oil reserves. **2.** (a) Algeria, Iran, Iraq, Kuwait, Libya, Qatar, Saudi Arabia, United Arab Emirates (b) Algeria, Gabon, Libya, Nigeria **3.** (a) 66 percent (b) 8 percent **4.** Answers will vary. Some possibilities are: The OPEC nations control almost three quarters of the world's crude oil reserves. Almost two thirds of the world's crude oil reserves are located in the Middle East.

Chapter Tests

Chapter 30

1. a **2.** d **3.** e **4.** b **5.** c **6.** c **7.** a **8.** d **9.** d **10.** c

Essay The two bonds are the Arabic language and the religion of Islam. Arabic is spoken in most parts of the region and though the spoken form may vary, the written form is uniform. Most of the people of the Middle East are Muslims, people who practice Islam.

Chapter 31

1. c **2.** a **3.** d **4.** b **5.** e **6.** c **7.** d **8.** a **9.** a **10.** b

Essay The Hebrews moved across the Jordan River into the land of Canaan about 3,000 years ago. The central tenet of Judaism is the belief in one God. Christianity developed 2,000 years ago based on the teachings of Jesus. He stressed love for God and good will toward other people. Islam grew out of the teachings of Muhammad, who was born about A.D. 570 in Mecca. Muslims believe that the Koran is the basis for law.

Chapter 32

1. a **2.** c **3.** b **4.** e **5.** d **6.** b **7.** a **8.** d **9.** d **10.** c

Essay Reforms included westernization of dress and names, greater rights for women, establishing a secular legal process that was not one based on the Koran. Traditionalists were opposed to these reforms, and saw them as the result of negative influence by the Western powers.

Chapter 33

1. d **2.** a **3.** e **4.** c **5.** b **6.** b **7.** c **8.** c **9.** b **10.** d

Essay Hospitality is an important tradition. Coffee drinking is a ceremony that is based on traditions of hospitality. Loyalty to family is another tradition. Gathering at the suq, or marketplace, is an important part of traditional village and city life.

Chapter 34

1. b **2.** e **3.** d **4.** a **5.** c **6.** d **7.** b **8.** a **9.** b **10.** b

Essay Students should agree that the statement is true. Positive aspects of oil wealth include large public works programs, better education, and health care for Middle Easterners. Negative aspects may include poor treatment of foreigners who work menial jobs and reliance on a finite supply of oil and natural resources.

Chapter 35

1. c **2.** b **3.** e **4.** a **5.** d **6.** c **7.** b **8.** c **9.** a **10.** d

Essay Some important aspects of fundamentalism include moving religion back to its central role in Islamic life, creating governments based on the Koran, cracking down on disorder, returning Palestine to Arab rule, and having women return to the home to raise their children. Fundamentalist movements and nations generally have strained relations with the West because Western influences are seen as damaging by fundamentalists.

Chapter 36

1. d **2.** e **3.** c **4.** a **5.** b **6.** d **7.** c **8.** c **9.** d **10.** a

Essay In discussing the methods of cooperation, students may make note of combined efforts to protect the environment, provide water to needy Middle Eastern nations, and help make communications from the Middle East more accessible to the rest of the world.

UNIT 5 TEST

1. nomads **2.** hieroglyphics **3.** pilgrimage **4.** protectorate **5.** fundamentalists **6.** embargo **7.** sanction **8.** intifada **9.** a **10.** b **11.** a **12.** d **13.** d **14.** c **15.** b **16.** d **17.** Students should mention that the discovery of oil made the Middle East an economic player for the first time since before European colonization. They should describe the changes in oil rich countries such as Bahrain and Kuwait due to the increase in income from oil. They might also mention the disparity of living standard between nations that have oil and those that do not. **18.** Islam was founded by Muhammad in Mecca (now Saudi Arabia) around A.D. 600, after a vision from Gabriel told him to preach the word of God. Major teachings include the belief in one God, that all people are equal before God, the Five Pillars of Islam, and the Koran. Students should discuss the influence of religion on everyday life, on women, and on the laws of many Middle Eastern nations. Students should discuss the trend toward fundamentalism and the effect this has had on the politics of the region.

UNIT 6

Exploring Regional Issues Worksheet

1. Per capita income is the average amount of money made per person. **2.** (a) France (b) Western Europe **3.** (a) Tajikistan (b) Possible answer: Per capita incomes in Europe and Eurasia vary a great deal.

Critical Thinking Activity Worksheets

Chapter 37

1. Iceland **2.** Finland, Latvia, Lithuania, Belarus **3.** The Uplands; the Northwest Mountain region; Central Europe **4.** Possible answer: People tend to live in areas that are relatively flat and have pleasant climates.

Chapter 38

1. Jacques Cartier **2.** Portugal **3.** 1519–1522 **4.** Mississippi River and present-day southeastern U.S. **5.** Spain **6.** North America and South America **7.** Answers will vary. Students' paragraphs may contain the following ideas: explorers sailed from Western Europe, particularly Spain and Portugal; explorers initially went to look for a new trade route to Asia; explorers found the Americas and began to explore North and South America.

Chapter 39

1. Mussolini **2.** India **3.** NATO was founded. **4.** Cuban missile crisis occurs.

Chapter 40

1. taxes in five countries as a percentage of GDP **2.** United States **3.** Finland **4.** Sweden **5.** almost two times **6.** 46.9% **7.** Denmark and Sweden **8.** Possible answer: Northern European countries have a much higher tax burden than the United States.

Chapter 41

1. the citizens of Czechoslovakia **2.** how the country flourished, how happy everyone was, how the government was trusted, and how bright the future was **3.** Industry is producing useless goods, necessary products are lacking, the state exploits its workers, the economy is obsolete, the physical and moral environment is contaminated. **4.** People have become selfish and cynical. **5.** People became used to saying something different from what they thought. They learned not to believe in anything and to ignore each other. **6.** freedom and democracy; participation in government

Chapter 42

1. "Message to Siberia" **2.** to members of a failed uprising against the tsar **3.** hope **4.** optimism, hope **5.** "heavy-hanging" **6.** freedom will come **7.** He feels it will eventually succeed. **8.** Answers will vary.

Chapter 43

1. native and Russian populations in the Eurasian Heartland **2.** Russia has the largest; Estonia has the smallest. **3.** Armenia **4.** Kazakstan **5.** Armenia **6.** Tajikistan, Armenia

Chapter 44

1. leaders of the United States and the Soviet Union **2.** playing chess **3.** missiles and warheads **4.** atomic energy **5.** the stalemate of the Cold War **6.** They look somber and grim; they do not like or trust each other. **7.** Possible answer: The Cold War was a dangerous game that threatened the safety of many people. It was a game that no one could win.

Chapter Tests

Chapter 37

1. c **2.** e **3.** d **4.** a **5.** b **6.** a **7.** d **8.** c **9.** d **10.** b

Essay Europe's rivers have for centuries served as highways for trade, travel, and the exchange of ideas. Along the Rhine River, in Germany, lay castles, churches, and towns that have played major roles in the history of Germany and Europe. Carrying more cargo than any river in the world, the Rhine plays a major role in Europe's economy.

Chapter 38

1. a **2.** e **3.** d **4.** c **5.** b **6.** b **7.** c **8.** c **9.** a **10.** d

Essay The Industrial Revolution began in Britain in the late 1700s. It consisted of a series of changes in the way in which people worked and manufactured goods. The Industrial Revolution made Great Britain the wealthiest nation in the world. As the revolution spread to other nations, they too gained wealth. The benefits of the Industrial Revolution include the growth of cities and the improvement of people's lives over time. Drawbacks include unsafe working conditions, child labor in factories, and poor living conditions in overcrowded cities.

Chapter 39

1. c 2. a 3. d 4. e 5. b 6. d 7. c 8. b 9. a 10. d

Essay Students should mention the Treaty of Versailles and the worldwide economic depression as contributing causes of World War II and the rise of dictators. The event that signaled the start of war was Germany's invasion of Poland on September 1, 1939.

Chapter 40

1. d 2. c 3. e 4. b 5. a 6. b 7. a 8. d 9. d 10. c

Essay Northern Europe is an urban region. Most people live in modern cities. Those who live in rural regions live a traditional life. In all but two countries, the major religion is Lutheranism. In Western Europe, the main groups are English, French, and Dutch. In Central Europe, most people are German speakers, Slavic speakers, or Magyars. Most people in this region are Roman Catholic. Southern Europe contains a variety of people, including Slavs, Italians, Greeks, and Spaniards. Most people in Italy, Spain, and Portugal are Roman Catholic. Large areas of the Balkans are Eastern Orthodox. There are also Muslims in the region. In all of the regions, most countries either are democratic or are undergoing reforms to become democratic.

Chapter 41

1. b 2. d 3. c 4. a 5. c 6. c 7. a 8. d 9. b 10. c

Essay The fall of communism freed the people of Eastern Europe from Soviet domination. It also ended the Cold War. Students might discuss Poland, where Communists lost elections, and East Germany, which was reunited with West Germany.

Chapter 42

1. c 2. d 3. b 4. e 5. a 6. a 7. a 8. b 9. d 10. c

Essay Students should recognize that the following factors were key in the creation of the USSR: autocratic rule by tsars, the development of socialism, the rise of the Bolsheviks, and the establishment of a communist dictatorship. They should mention that most people in the USSR had a relatively low standard of living. In discussing the breakup of the USSR, students should mention Gorbachev, the failing economy, and the role of various ethnic groups.

Chapter 43

1. b 2. e 3. d 4. a 5. c 6. b 7. d 8. a 9. b 10. c

Essay Students might mention the conflict between Azerbaijanis and Armenians in the Caucasus and the tension in the Crimea between Russians and Ukrainians.

Chapter 44

1. d 2. a 3. c 4. e 5. b 6. c 7. a 8. a 9. d 10. b

Essay Students could discuss nuclear weapons, ethnic tensions, the rise in crime, economic problems, and environmental problems.

UNIT 6 TEST

1. autocracy 2. nationalism 3. tundra 4. exports 5. revolution 6. feudalism 7. genocide 8. capitalism 9. c 10. d 11. b 12. d 13. a 14. c 15. a 16. d 17. Students should discuss such events as the division of Germany and the creation of U.S. and Soviet spheres of influence. They should also mention the Marshall Plan and NATO, the Berlin Wall, the Bay of Pigs and Cuban Missile Crisis, and the nuclear arms race. 18. Students should discuss the impact of Soviet domination on the people of Eastern Europe. They should describe the failed measures that Gorbachev took to strengthen communism in Eastern Europe and at home. They should describe the downfall of the Communist governments in various Eastern European nations, including Poland and Germany. Finally, students should describe the economic and social problems in the Soviet Union and its resulting demise in 1990.

Name _____   Date _____

On Assignment... Formulating Questions

Your assignment for this chapter is to think of at least five questions to ask about the regions of the world. Use the diagram below to help you formulate, or think of, questions about the world's regions. First, think of categories in which to ask questions. To help you get started, two categories, geography and people, have been suggested. Think of at least two more categories. Then, for each category think of at least two questions. For example, in the category of people, you might ask, "What culture groups are there in the world?" After you have completed the diagram, choose the best questions and list them below.

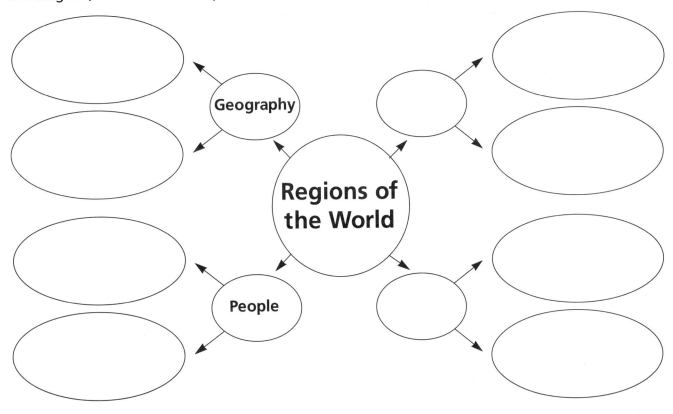

Choose the best questions and list them below.

1. _____

2. _____

3. _____

4. _____

5. _____

Name _____   Date _____

Critical Thinking...Analyzing a Pie Graph

As you read in the Introduction, *movement* is one of the five themes of geography. In recent times, more and more people from rural areas have been moving to cities. The pie graphs below show this trend. People usually move to cities to find work and other opportunities, such as a better education. However, around the world, cities suffer from the effects of overcrowding, pollution, and rapid growth. Study the graphs and answer the questions below.

MOVEMENT TO CITIES

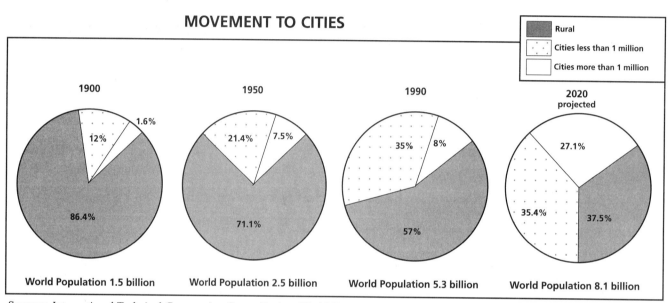

Sources: *International Technical Cooperation Centre Review*, *World Facts and Figures*, UN Population Reference Bureau

1. What percentage of people lived in rural areas in 1900? In 1990? _____

   _____

2. By how much did the percentage of people living in cities with more than 1 million

   people increase from 1950 to 1990? _____

3. According to the graphs, by how much will the population of cities with more than 1

   million people increase from 1990 to 2020? _____

4. By how much did the world's population increase from 1900 to 1950? _____

   _____

5. A generalization is a broad statement based on facts. What generalization can you make about the movement of people to cities based on the pie graphs?

   _____

Introduction Test   *The World and Its Cultures*

Name _____ Date _____

I. Matching Decide which definition in the right column best explains a term in the left column. Then write the letter of that definition in the space next to the term.

_____ 1. cultural diffusion

_____ 2. culture

_____ 3. global village

_____ 4. extended family

_____ 5. nuclear family

a. the way of life of a group of people, including their ideas, customs, skills, and arts

b. a family consisting of three or four generations living in one household

c. a family consisting only of a father, mother, and children

d. the spread of new ideas and new ways of doing things from one society to others

e. a world where diverse peoples communicate, share experiences, and depend on one another for resources

II. Multiple Choice Choose the answer that best completes the sentence or answers the question. Then write the letter of your choice in the space provided.

_____ 6. The United States is a country of cultural diversity because
   a. there is only one dominant culture living there.
   b. it is difficult to find people of different cultures in the United States.
   c. it is a country of many different cultures.
   d. culture there is different from culture in other countries.

_____ 7. The term "interdependent" refers to
   a. the state of being dependent on one another for support and survival.
   b. how much money someone makes.
   c. the state of being near one another.
   d. the sharing of a common language.

_____ 8. Economic systems determine
   a. what goods should be produced.
   b. how much should be produced.
   c. how much goods are worth.
   d. all of the above.

_____ 9. The five basic themes of geography are
   a. location, place, interaction, movement, and region.
   b. culture, diffusion, values, diversity, and family.
   c. who, what, where, when, and why.
   d. north, south, east, west, and hemisphere.

_____ 10. The natural features of a place include
   a. its longitude and latitude.
   b. its climate, land, and water.
   c. food and language.
   d. the number of immigrants who live there.

III. Essay Write your answer to the following question in paragraph form on a separate sheet of paper.

In this chapter, you read about different types of governments: democracies, monarchies, and dictatorships. Describe the features of each of these governments. Then identify one country that has each type of government.

Name _____ Date _____

Exploring Regional Issues...Reading a Population Pyramid

A population pyramid is a type of bar graph. Population pyramids help us to see the age break-down of a population. On page 12 of your text, you studied several population pyramids. Below is data and a space for you to draw a population pyramid for the African country of Zaire. Portions of the pyramid have been filled in as examples. Complete the pyramid and answer the questions below.

POPULATION PYRAMID FOR ZAIRE, 1995

AGE	Percentage of MALES	FEMALES
75+	0.03	0.04
70-74	0.03	0.5
65-69	.5	0.7
60-64	.8	0.9
55-59	1.0	1.1
50-54	1.3	1.4
45-49	1.6	1.7
40-44	2.0	2.1
35-39	2.5	2.5
30-34	3.0	3.0
25-29	3.6	3.6
20-24	4.4	4.3
15-19	5.5	5.2
10-14	6.0	6.2
5-9	8.0	7.7
0-4	9.3	9.0

NOTE: Figures may not add up to 100% due to rounding.

Source: Bos, Eduard, et al. *World Population Projections, 1992-93 Edition.* Baltimore: Johns Hopkins University Press for The World Bank, 1992.

1. (a) Which age group in Zaire is the largest? _____
   (b) Which is the smallest? _____

2. Compare the population pyramid for Zaire with those on page 12 in your text.
   (a) How are the pyramids for Zaire, Kenya, and Nigeria similar to or different from each other?

   _____

   _____

   (b) How do the pyramids for the African countries compare with the United States?

   _____

   _____

Name _____   Date _____

On Assignment...Creating Posters

Your assignment is to design posters for a United Nations' exhibit on Africa. Before you begin designing your poster, find at least three examples of advertisements in newspapers and magazines. Below, list what impresses you about each advertisement.

1. I liked/disliked the advertisement about _____ because _____

_____

2. I liked/disliked the advertisement about _____ because _____

_____

3. I liked/disliked the advertisement about _____ because _____

_____

Another important step in creating an effective advertisement is identifying who the audience for the advertisement is. In other words, who will be viewing your posters? What do you think they want to know about Africa? Will they want to know about the geography, the climate, the people, or the problems Africa faces? Perhaps your posters could combine some of these items.

Who will your audience be? _____

As you read Chapter 1, jot down ideas based on the On Assignment hint boxes or based on your own original ideas. Think of at least three ideas for your posters and list them below.

Idea number 1: _____

Idea number 2: _____

Idea number 3: _____

For each idea, think of images that you can use on your posters. Write these down below.

Images for idea number 1: _____

Images for idea number 2: _____

Images for idea number 3: _____

Now, begin sketching your posters on the back of this worksheet. Then write short paragraphs explaining what aspects of Africa's geography, climate, or culture your posters show.

Name _____   Date _____

On Assignment...Creating a Storyboard

Your task is to create a storyboard about African history. The On Assignment hint boxes in the chapter suggest that your scenes be on the following topics: Egyptian civilization, Mansa Musa's caravan, the gold and salt trade, the city of Timbuktu, or the slave trade. You may use these ideas or come up with ideas of your own. The questions below will help you create your storyboard panels.

1. List and describe three facts you learned about African history.

_____

_____

2. What did you find interesting about those facts? _____

_____

3. How would you present those facts in pictures and video images? _____

_____

Use the boxes below to sketch your scenes.

4. What might a narrator say as the pictures and images appear on the screen? If you choose to use actors and actresses to convey information, what would the characters say to one another?

_____

_____

_____

Name _____ Date _____

On Assignment...Creating a Collage

Your task is to create a collage showing various aspects of life in Africa. Review Chapter 3 and take notes on the aspects of traditional African life you wish to highlight in your collage. Below is a chart to help you organize what you want to show and how you might show it. Try to think of at least five aspects of African culture to show in the collage. An example is given.

IDEAS FOR A COLLAGE ON TRADITIONAL AFRICAN CULTURE

AFRICAN TRADITION	HOW TO SHOW TRADITION
Show a griot (traditional African storyteller)	Find a picture of a storyteller or of animals that are usually the subject of African stories. Find plastic spiders to glue to the collage. Create animals using yarn and old buttons.
1.	
2.	
3.	
4.	
5.	

Name _____ Date _____

On Assignment...Writing Diary Entries

Travelers often keep diaries to describe what they have seen and done on their trips. Many writers keep diaries to record their thoughts, feelings, and ideas. Your assignment is to create several diary entries about your impressions of imperialism and nationalism in Africa.

The page below is divided into three parts. Each part contains a possible opening line for a diary entry describing a different period in African history. Use the opening line or create one of your own to write your diary entries.

IMPERIALISM IN AFRICA

Date: _____

The Berlin Conference is finally over. The countries attending the conference have

decided to _____

_____

_____

_____

_____

AFRICANS FIGHT BACK

Date: _____

As Shaka predicted, whites are overrunning Southern Africa. The Zulus are _____

_____

_____

_____

_____

INDEPENDENCE IN AFRICA

Date: _____

Today the country of _____ won its independence. There is a great deal of

celebrating. Witnessing these events, I feel _____

_____

_____

_____

_____

_____

Global Studies. Copyright © **Globe Fearon Educational Publisher.** *All rights reserved.*

Name _____ Date _____

On Assignment...Creating a Fact Sheet

Your assignment for this chapter is to create a country fact sheet for three or four African countries. The hint boxes in the chapter suggest categories for your fact sheet. Use those suggestions or come up with your own. Use the chart below to organize information for your fact sheet.

FACT SHEET FOR AFRICA
Categories

COUNTRY	LOCATION	1._____	2._____	3._____	4._____	5._____
1.						
2.						
3.						
4.						

Name _____ **Date** _____

On Assignment...Creating a Mural

Your assignment is to create a mural showing Africa today. A mural is a very large wall painting. A mural often shows a series of historical events, activities, and people. To get ideas for your mural, scan the pictures in your text. You may also wish to use pictures from books that are in your school or local library. Below is an organizer that provides space for you to sketch ideas about some events in the chapter. After you are satisfied with your sketches, transfer them to a large sheet of paper.

History of Democracy   Effects of Imperialism   One-Party Rule   Military Rule

Socialism   Free Enterprise   Economic Diversification   End of Apartheid in South Africa

Name _____ Date _____

On Assignment...Creating African Stories

Your assignment is to create an African story. Review the On Assignment hint boxes in Chapter 7 for ideas about topics for stories. Use these ideas or think of some of your own. Once you have chosen a topic, use the diagram below to brainstorm ideas for a beginning, middle, and end for your story. Remember, the purpose of brainstorming is to write down any ideas that come to you. Don't worry about how the ideas sound. Just write them down and sort them out later. Let your creative juices flow!

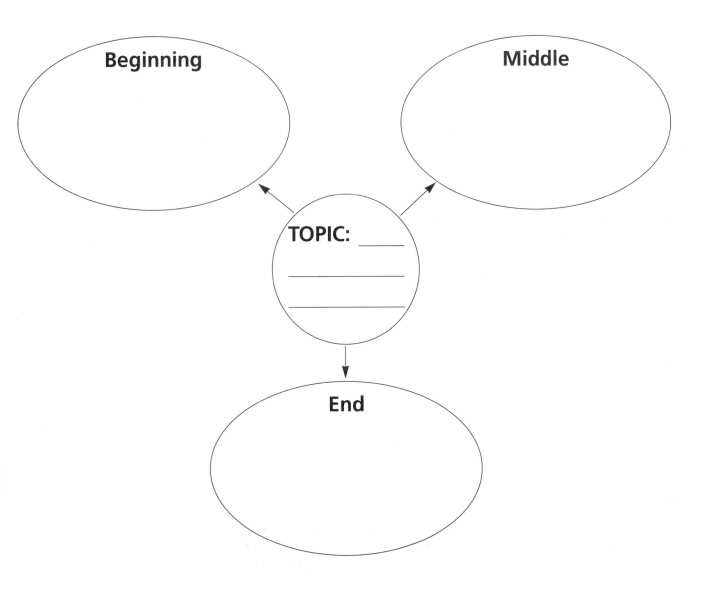

Name _____ **Date** _____

Critical Thinking...Interpreting a Map

The map below shows the **vegetation regions** of Africa. Vegetation is the type of plants and trees that grow in an area. As you study the map, keep in mind that vegetation is related to climate. The type of climate in a region is a major factor in determining the types of plant life that can grow there. Also note that vegetation has had an effect on population distribution, or where people live, in Africa. Study the map and answer the questions that follow.

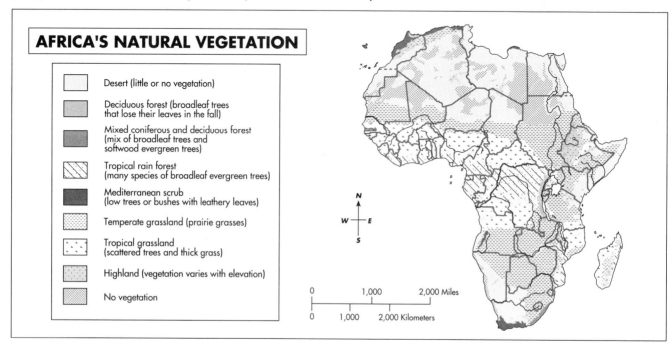

1. What type of trees grow in the deciduous forest? _____

   _____

2. What type of vegetation is in the region near the equator? _____

   _____

3. Where is the Mediterranean scrub vegetation region located? _____

   _____

4. What two types of vegetation regions are in the Sahara? _____

   _____

5. Based on the information in this map, which vegetation regions do you think are sparsely

   populated? _____

Name _____ Date _____

Critical Thinking...Making a Time Line

The sequence in which things happen in history is important. An event may come before another, come after another, or events may occur at the same time. A *time line* portrays events in *chronological,* or time, order.

Below is a list of events that occurred in Africa and elsewhere from A.D. 600 to 1600. Place these events on the time line below and answer the questions that follow.

AFRICA

1322	Mansa Musa journeys to Mecca.
1000	Ghana reaches height of its power.
600	The Ghana empire is established.
1450	The empire of Songhai is established.
1100	The city of Zimbabwe is founded.
1076	Muslims invade Ghana.
1441	Europeans arrive in Africa.
650–700	Islam spreads to North Africa.
1493	Songhai reaches the height of its power.
1300	Mali reaches the height of its power.
1591	The Songhai empire collapses.

ELSEWHERE

368	The Ming dynasty begins in China.
1096	The First Crusade begins.
1325	The Aztec empire in Latin America is founded.
700	The Mayan civilization in Latin America develops.
1431	Joan of Arc is burned at the stake.
800	Charlemagne is crowned emperor in France.
1492	Muslims are expelled from Spain.
622	The religion of Islam is founded in the Middle East.
1271	Marco Polo travels to China.
1215	The Magna Carta is signed.

600	850	1100	1350	1600

1. (a) In which year did Islam begin? _____

   (b) When did Islam spread to Africa? _____
2. Which Latin American civilization was in power at the same time as the Ghana empire?

   _____
3. Which African empire was the last to collapse? _____
4. What was happening in Africa when the First Crusade began? _____

   _____

   _____

   _____

Name _____ **Date** _____

Critical Thinking...Interpreting Proverbs

A proverb is a short saying that expresses some well-known fact or common experience. In many African cultures, proverbs are used to teach a lesson or carry a moral. Ten African proverbs are listed below. Match each proverb to its subject or moral. Then, write two of your own proverbs. After each proverb you write, explain its subject or moral.

AFRICAN PROVERB

_____ **1.** He is good who comes without being called.

_____ **2.** A locked house door should be opened only by its owner.

_____ **3.** A person who chews slowly can be sure he will swallow well.

_____ **4.** A big goat doesn't snort for no reason.

_____ **5.** A chattering bird builds no nest.

_____ **6.** Sticks in a bundle are unbreakable.

_____ **7.** Lies buzz like flies, but truth has the brilliance of sunshine.

_____ **8.** Two serpents, jealousy and envy, must be lulled, for they are unconquerable.

_____ **9.** The beetle in its hole is a sultan.

_____ **10.** Annoy your doctor and sickness will come laughing.

SUBJECT OR MORAL

a. the head of the household

b. Be responsible.

c. Stay focused and on task.

d. listening to the warnings of animals

e. Respect professionals.

f. Honesty is the best policy.

g. Keep your nose out of other people's business.

h. the power of numbers and people sticking together

i. Think carefully before you act.

j. the evils of jealousy

Your proverb #1: _____

Subject or moral: _____

Your proverb #2: _____

Subject or moral: _____

Name _____ Date _____

Critical Thinking...Interpreting a Political Cartoon

In Chapter 4, you read about how African nations gained independence from European colonial powers. As African nations struggled to develop their economies, they found they needed to borrow money from the wealthy industrialized nations of the West. Many countries soon were deep in debt.

Cartoonists use their artwork to express their opinions about events and issues. The political cartoon below was published in the early 1990s. It appeared in an Egyptian magazine. Study this cartoon and answer the questions that follow.

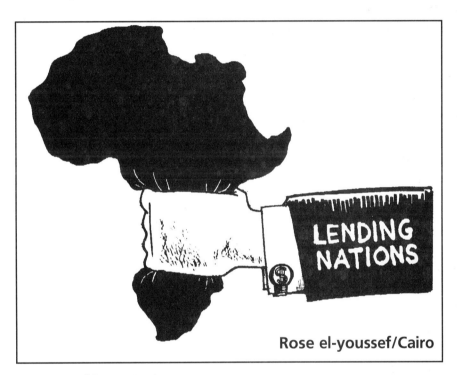

Rose el-youssef/Cairo

Source: *World Press Review*

1. What continent is shown on the map? _____

2. What is the hand doing to the continent? _____

3. (a) What label appears on the arm? _____

   (b) What does the cufflink on the arm represent? _____

4. Based on this drawing, how do you think the cartoonist feels about lending and debt?

   _____

   _____

5. What would be a good title for this cartoon? _____

Name _____   Date _____

Critical Thinking...Interpreting Poetry

A poem often represents what is in the heart and mind of its writer. Below is a poem written by an African poet named Susan Lwanga. In this poem, the author expresses her emotions about the African land at dawn. Read the poem carefully and answer the questions that follow.

DAYBREAK by Susan Lwanga

O dawn
Where do you hide your paints at night
That cool breath, that scent
With which you sweeten the early air?

O dawn
What language do you use
To instruct the birds to sing
Their early songs
And insects to sound
The rhythm of an African heartbeat?

O dawn
Where do you find the good will

To speed the early traffic on its way
Rouse the cold drunkard
And send your askaris* and barking dogs
To chase thieves to their dens?

O dawn
Whose cold breath makes young boys and girls
Glad of a warm sheet,
Enflames the dreams of unmarried ones,
And brings familiar noises
To gladden the hearts of the married.

*askaris — native policemen or watchmen of eastern Africa

1. What is the subject of this poem? _____

2. To what does the word "paints" in line two refer? _____

3. With what animals does the author represent the sounds and rhythms of Africa? _____
_____

4. How does the author describe young boys and girls? _____

5. What do you think the author feels about her African homeland? _____
_____

6. Complete the letter below to the author, describing your feelings about her poem.

   Dear Ms. Lwanga,
   I just read your poem. _____

   _____

   _____

   _____

   Sincerely,

Name _____ Date _____

Critical Thinking...Using Primary Sources

In 1955, the African National Congress joined with three other South African organizations to issue the Freedom Charter. This document called for a multiracial democracy in South Africa in which all groups would have equal rights. Below is the preamble (introduction) to the Freedom Charter.

This type of source is known as a **primary source.** *Primary* means "first" or "original." Primary sources provide a firsthand look at the intentions of their writers. Read the preamble to the Freedom Charter and answer the questions that follow.

THE FREEDOM CHARTER

We, the people of South Africa, declare for all our country and the world to know:
That South Africa belongs to all who live in it, black and white, and that no government can justly claim authority unless it is based on the will of the people;

That our people have been robbed of their birthright to land, liberty and peace by a form of government founded on injustice and inequality;

That our country will never be prosperous or free until all our people live in brotherhood, enjoying equal rights and opportunities;

That only a democratic state, based on the will of the people, can secure to all their birthright without distinction of colour, race, sex or belief;

And therefore, we the people of South Africa, black and white, together equals, countrymen and brothers adopt this Freedom Charter. And we pledge ourselves to strive together, sparing nothing of our strength and courage, until the democratic changes here set out have been won.

1. To whom does the document say South Africa belongs? _____

2. According to this document, what is the birthright of South African people? _____

   _____

3. According to this document, what classifications of people should be allowed to secure their

   birthright? _____

4. According to this document, what is required for South Africa to be free and prosperous?

   _____

5. What do the people of South Africa pledge to do to win democratic changes for their country?

   _____

Name _____   Date _____

Critical Thinking...Analyzing a Bar Graph

Graphs organize statistical information in an easy-to-read diagram. The graph on this page is called a **bar graph** because it uses bars to show amounts.

You begin reading any graph by identifying the information on it. Next, compare this information. What differences in size or amount can you spot? Can you see any patterns in the data? To practice these skills, study the graph below. Then answer the questions that follow.

THE WORLD'S REFUGEES, 1994

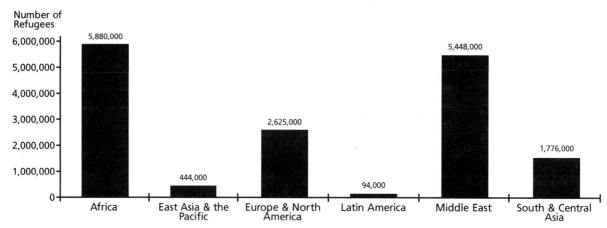

Source: *The World Almanac and Book of Facts, 1996*

1. What is the subject of this chart? _____

2. Which world region has the most refugees? The fewest? _____

3. How many of the world's refugees are from the Middle East? _____

   From East Asia and the Pacific? _____

4. The total number of refugees in 1994 was 16,267,000. You can calculate the percentage of refugees from each region by dividing the number of refugees from a region by the total number of refugees for 1994. For example, there were 5,880,000 refugees in Africa in 1994. If you divide 5,880,000 by 16,267,000, you will find that 36 percent of the world's refugees are from Africa. Calculate the number of refugees from each of the other world regions.

   _____

   _____

5. What conclusion can you reach concerning the large number of refugees from Africa and the Middle East versus the small number from East Asia and Latin America?

   _____

   _____

Chapter 1 Test   *The Land and People of Africa*

Name _____   Date _____

I. Matching Decide which definition in the right column best explains a term in the left column. Then write the letter of that definition in the space next to the term.

_____ **1.** delta

_____ **2.** plateau

_____ **3.** savanna

_____ **4.** landlocked

_____ **5.** fault

a. a large area of flat land higher than the surrounding land

b. a crack in the earth's crust caused by movements in that crust

c. broad areas of soil deposits near the mouth of a river

d. a grassy plain with scattered trees and bushes

e. having no outlet to the sea

II. Multiple Choice Choose the answer that best completes the sentence or answers the question. Then write the letter of your choice in the space provided.

_____ **6.** The Great Rift Valley was formed by
  a. movements in the earth's crust.
  b. hydroelectric power.
  c. a volcano.
  d. rapidly moving rivers.

_____ **7.** Africa's rivers are less useful for transportation than rivers in Europe or Asia because
  a. they flood too often.
  b. they are used for electric power instead.
  c. they do not empty into the ocean.
  d. they are too shallow in some places and too fast moving in other places.

_____ **8.** The desert is expanding southward in which of the following regions of Africa?
  a. North Africa
  b. West Africa
  c. Southern Africa
  d. Central Africa

_____ **9.** The largest climate zone in Africa is found in the
  a. desert.
  b. savanna.
  c. rain forest.
  d. mountains.

_____ **10.** The people of Africa
  a. live primarily in large towns and cities.
  b. speak similar languages.
  c. are very diverse.
  d. are of one ethnic group.

III. Essay Write your answer to the following question in paragraph form on a separate sheet of paper.

The geography of any region has an important impact on the people that live there. How do the geography and climate of the African continent affect the lives of African people? Use specific examples to describe how people live in different climate and landform regions.

Name _____ Date _____

I. **Matching** Decide which definition in the right column best explains a term in the left column. Then write the letter of that definition in the space next to the term.

_____ **1.** scribe

_____ **2.** mummy

_____ **3.** caravan

_____ **4.** rapids

_____ **5.** monument

a. something that is built to honor a person or event

b. a dead body treated with chemicals and wrapped so that it does not decay

c. the class of people in ancient Egypt whose job was to write

d. a group of travelers who band together for safety

e. a place where a river falls sharply and flows very quickly

II. **Multiple Choice** Choose the answer that best completes the sentence or answers the question. Then write the letter of your choice in the space provided.

_____ **6.** Ancient Egyptian civilization was formed around the

    a. Sahara.
    b. Sinai Peninsula.
    c. Nile River.
    d. Mediterranean Sea.

_____ **7.** The city of Zimbabwe was known for

    a. great centers of learning.
    b. great stone buildings.
    c. building great pyramids as monuments to its kings.
    d. trade with Asia.

_____ **8.** The two most important products traded by Western African empires were

    a. ivory and slaves.
    b. gold and salt.
    c. iron and wood.
    d. copper and bronze.

_____ **9.** The kingdom of Kush grew and prospered after

    a. Kushites began producing iron tools and weapons.
    b. Kushites won their independence from Egypt.
    c. it conquered the kingdom of Axum.
    d. Kushites converted to Christianity.

_____ **10.** Europeans were able to convince African rulers along the coast to capture Africans for the slave trade by

    a. threatening to invade their empires.
    b. promising a better life for those brought across the Atlantic.
    c. offering them weapons, gold, and European products.
    d. threatening to send the rulers themselves to slavery if they did not capture others.

III. **Essay** Write your answer to the following question in paragraph form on a separate sheet of paper.

Many great civilizations and empires have existed during Africa's history. Describe at least three great civilizations or empires of African history. How did each develop? How did each fall? What was life like at the height of each empire? Did the arrival of Europeans affect these African empires? If so, how?

Name _____ Date _____

I. Matching Decide which definition in the right column best explains a term in the left column. Then write the letter of that definition in the space next to the term.

_____ **1.** proverb

_____ **2.** nomad

_____ **3.** griot

_____ **4.** clan

_____ **5.** age set

a. an African storyteller

b. short saying that expresses some well-known fact or common experience

c. a group made of many extended families

d. a group made up of boys or girls who are the same age

e. person who moves from place to place in search of food

II. Multiple Choice Choose the answer that best completes the sentence or answers the question. Then write the letter of your choice in the space provided.

_____ **6.** In traditional African societies, the family includes

    a. parents and children only.

    b. parents, children, aunts and uncles, cousins, and grandparents.

    c. many extended families living together in a village.

    d. a father and many mothers.

_____ **7.** The most important job of women in traditional African societies is

    a. fetching water from the well.

    b. tending the fields and harvesting crops.

    c. caring for and feeding the children.

    d. keeping the home clean.

_____ **8.** Followers of most traditional religions do NOT believe in

    a. ancestor spirits.

    b. the idea of God as creator of the world.

    c. the idea of only one God.

    d. people with special powers such as medicine men and women.

_____ **9.** In African villages, the Council of Elders

    a. consisted of older people from different families of the clan.

    b. consisted of kings and chiefs.

    c. ruled by tyranny.

    d. consisted of the clan's greatest warriors.

_____ **10.** The majority of Africans make their living

    a. as craftspeople.

    b. as laborers on large farms.

    c. by growing food for their own families on small farms.

    d. as merchants.

III. Essay Write your answer to the following question in paragraph form on a separate sheet of paper.

    Describe the life of a typical traditional family in Africa. What is the family life like? What are some typical religious and cultural practices? How does the family earn a living? What is the village like? Who makes the rules and decisions for the village?

Chapter 4 Test *Modern History of Africa*

Name _____   Date _____

I. Matching
Decide which definition in the right column best explains a term in the left column. Then write the letter of that definition in the space next to the term.

_____ 1. nationalism
_____ 2. imperialism
_____ 3. legacy
_____ 4. protectorate
_____ 5 missionary

a. a person who is sent to do religious work in a territory or foreign country

b. country with its own government whose policies are controlled or directed by an outside power

c. a policy of conquering and taking over foreign territory

d. something handed down from the past

e. a strong devotion to and pride in one's country

II. Multiple Choice
Choose the answer that best completes the sentence or answers the question. Then write the letter of your choice in the space provided.

_____ 6. Which of the following was NOT a reason for imperialism?

    a. the belief that westerners were superior to other people
    b. the Industrial Revolution
    c. national pride
    d. the desire to learn more about other people and cultures

_____ 7. One effect of European imperialism on Africa was

    a. economic prosperity for African villages.
    b. weakened traditional life.
    c. allegiance to the tribal chiefs.
    d. the growth of African industry.

_____ 8. The first African nation to win independence was

    a. Ghana.
    b. Nigeria.
    c. South Africa.
    d. Zaire.

_____ 9. The strongest push for African independence came from

    a. veterans of World War I.
    b. tribal chiefs.
    c. oppressed farmers and workers.
    d. Africans who had been educated in Europe and the United States.

_____ 10. Newly independent African nations faced difficulties for all of the following reasons EXCEPT

    a. many Africans did not support independence.
    b. boundaries had been drawn without regard for ethnic and cultural differences among African tribes.
    c. Africans had little experience running European-style governments and economies.
    d. imperialism had destroyed many elements of traditional African culture.

III. Essay
Write your answer to the following question in paragraph form on a separate sheet of paper.

Discuss the causes of European imperialism and the effects it had on Africa. How did Europeans gain control of Africa? What were the effects of imperialism on Africans? Describe at least one specific example of European treatment of Africans. What factors led to the demand for independence among Africans?

Chapter 5 Test   *Changing Patterns of Life in Africa*

Name _____ Date _____

I. Matching Decide which definition in the right column best explains a term in the left column. Then write the letter of that definition in the space next to the term.

_____ **1.** literate
_____ **2.** barter
_____ **3.** fundamentalism
_____ **4.** Koran
_____ **5.** urbanization

a. the Muslim holy book
b. able to read and write
c. a movement or point of view that opposes modern ideas and favors a return to strict religious values
d. the movement of people from the countryside to the cities
e. to trade goods or services without exchanging money

II. Multiple Choice Choose the answer that best completes the sentence or answers the question. Then write the letter of your choice in the space provided.

_____ **6.** Islamic fundamentalism is strongest in
   a. North Africa.
   b. South Africa.
   c. East Africa.
   d. West Africa.

_____ **7.** The role of African women has changed most
   a. in rural areas.
   b. in Islamic families.
   c. in cities.
   d. in Christian families.

_____ **8.** The most urbanized region of Africa is
   a. West Central Africa.
   b. Southern Africa.
   c. East Africa.
   d. North Africa.

_____ **9.** African nations are finding it difficult to educate their citizens because
   a. African parents do not want their children to go to school.
   b. there are not enough teachers, schools, or materials.
   c. governments are not committed to the idea of education.
   d. educated Africans often cannot find good jobs.

_____ **10.** Which of the following is NOT an effect of the rapid urbanization of Africa?
   a. food production has gone down
   b. high unemployment
   c. increase of ethnic tensions
   d. breakdown of traditional family ties.

III. Essay Write your answer to the following question in paragraph form on a separate sheet of paper.

   Discuss the role that literature, art, and music play in African life. What are some of the common themes of African literature, art, and music? How have African art and music influenced Western art and music?

Economic and Political Trends

Name _____ **Date** _____

I. **Matching** Decide which definition in the right column best explains a term in the left column. Then write the letter of that definition in the space next to the term.

_____ **1.** secede

_____ **2.** coup

_____ **3.** federal system

_____ **4.** subsidy

_____ **5.** multinational

a. a takeover of government

b. assistance that a government provides to consumers or industries

c. having operations in many countries

d. a system in which the central government shares power with lower-level governments

e. to withdraw from a larger nation

II. **Multiple Choice** Choose the answer that best completes the sentence or answers the question. Then write the letter of your choice in the space provided.

_____ **6.** The greatest obstacle to democracy in many newly independent African nations is

   a. the reluctance of colonial powers to leave their colonies.
   b. the difficulty of building national unity among the different ethnic groups.
   c. corruption in local governments.
   d. military takeovers.

_____ **7.** The economic policy of most African nations today is

   a. a blend of African socialism and free enterprise.
   b. socialism.
   c. free enterprise.
   d. controlled by the government.

_____ **8.** The racial group that suffered most under South African apartheid was

   a. white.
   b. black.
   c. colored.
   d. Asian.

_____ **9.** Which of the following is NOT an argument used by Africans who are unhappy with the recent shift toward free enterprise?

   a. Governments are no longer working to protect poor people.
   b. Rich people will gain too much influence.
   c. Multinational corporations will gain too much influence.
   d. Private businesses are often slow to respond to changes in the economic or political climate.

_____ **10.** The goal of the African National Congress in South Africa was

   a. to rid South Africa of all native Europeans.
   b. to use violence and terrorism to promote African rights.
   c. to work peacefully for a multiracial South Africa.
   d. to maintain racial divisions in South Africa.

III. **Essay** Write your answer to the following question in paragraph form on a separate sheet of paper.

   Describe and discuss the political and economic challenges facing African countries today. What are the major political challenges facing Africans? What are the major economic problems facing Africans? What are African nations doing to meet these challenges?

Name _____ Date _____

I. **Matching** Decide which definition in the right column best explains a term in the left column. Then write the letter of that definition in the space next to the term.

_____ 1. hygiene
_____ 2. genocide
_____ 3. midwife
_____ 4. tribalism
_____ 5. refugee

a. a person who helps a woman during childbirth
b. personal cleanliness
c. the allegiance of many Africans to their tribes
d. the deliberate destruction of a racial group
e. a person who has been forced to flee for safety from his or her homeland

II. **Multiple Choice** Choose the answer that best completes the sentence or answers the question. Then write the letter of your choice in the space provided.

_____ 6. The main goal of the Organization of African Unity (OAU) is
　a. the political unity of African tribes.
　b. the economic revival of Africa.
　c. independence for black South Africa.
　d. the unity of oil-producing countries.

_____ 7. Which of the following African problems has NOT caused increased numbers of refugees?
　a. conflicts among rival tribes
　b. drought and famine
　c. industrialization
　d. civil war

_____ 8. Education in most African nations today
　a. is unavailable to most people.
　b. is viewed as a luxury.
　c. has resulted in a significant rise in literacy.
　d. has been unsuccessful in raising the literacy rate.

_____ 9. The region of Africa that is most seriously facing desertification is the
　a. Sahel savannas.
　b. Sahara.
　c. Ethiopian highlands.
　d. South African flatlands.

_____ 10. African governments have become interested in preservation of wild animals and the environment because
　a. the animals can be used as a source of food.
　b. tribal religions mandate the preservation of wild animals and the environment.
　c. the environment can be used as a source of firewood and pastureland.
　d. ecotourism brings in foreign money.

III. **Essay** Write your answer to the following question in paragraph form on a separate sheet of paper.

　Describe two social issues currently facing Africa's people. What is the source of each problem? What are African people doing to solve each problem?

Focus on Africa

Name _____ Date _____

I. **Fill in the Blank** Complete each sentence below by writing the correct term in the blank. You will not use all the terms.

plateaus	savannas	scribe	nomad	nationalism	imperialism
pan-Africanism	urbanization	barter	secede		

1. A person who moves from place to place in search of food and grazing lands is called a _____ .

2. During the 1800s, European nations conquered and took over most of Africa, following a practice that is called _____ .

3. _____ , a strong devotion to and pride in one's country, was responsible for imperialism as well as for independence movements in Africa.

4. Much of Africa's landscape is made up of a series of _____ , large areas of flat land that are higher than the surrounding land.

5. In many traditional African communities, people _____ or trade goods and services without exchanging money.

6. In ancient Egypt, a _____ was one of the few people trained to read and write.

7. In 1967, the Ibos of Biafra tried to _____ , or withdraw, from the nation of Nigeria.

8. The trend of many people moving to the cities is called _____ .

II. **Multiple Choice** Choose the answer that best completes the sentence or answers the question. Then write the letter of your choice in the space provided.

____ 9. The Nile River has always been important to the people of Egypt because it
   a. allows travelers to sail from North Africa to South Africa.
   b. protects Egypt from invaders from the east and the west.
   c. provides water for crops that are farmed along its banks.
   d. is the site of many of Egypt's famous pyramids.

____ 10. The kingdoms of West Africa, including Ghana, Mali, and Songhai, grew wealthy mainly due to
   a. farming.   c. tourism.
   b. mining.   d. trade.

____ 11. One effect of the Atlantic slave trade on West Africa was
   a. an enormous decrease in population.
   b. an enormous increase in population.
   c. a decrease in the number of guns.
   d. an increase in the development of African manufacturing.

____ 12. At the Berlin Conference, European nations decided to
   a. free African nations.
   b. divide Africa into colonies.
   c. go to war with Africa.
   d. support King Menelik of Ethiopia.

13. During the 1900s, traditional African art strongly influenced
   a. French abstract artists.
   b. European imperialists.
   c. American movie makers.
   d. oral literature.

14. The election of Nelson Mandela as president of South Africa highlighted the end of
   a. the African National Congress.
   b. the system of apartheid.
   c. European intervention in Africa.
   d. democracy in the region.

15. A number of African countries have turned from socialist economies to
   a. communism.
   b. one-party rule.
   c. military rule.
   d. free enterprise.

III. Analyzing a Map Answer questions 16–18 based on the map above.

16. Which of the following nations won its independence first?
   a. Algeria
   b. Mozambique
   c. Zaire
   d. Botswana

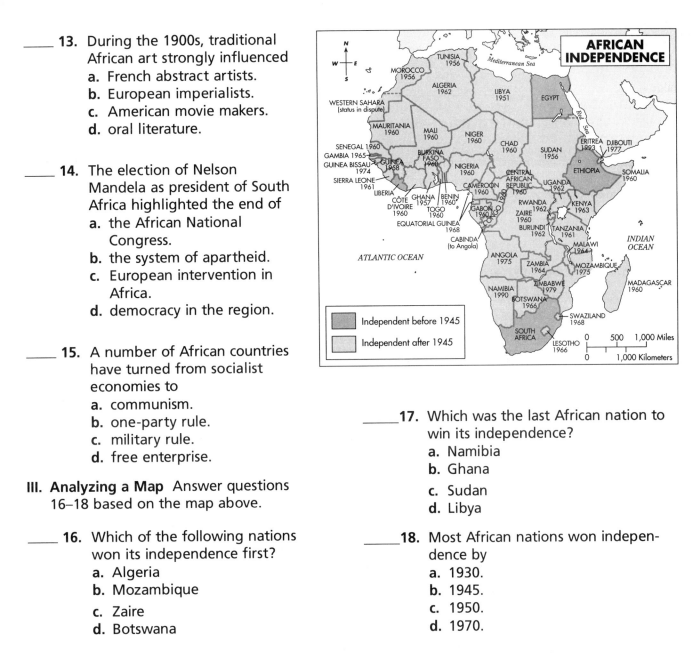

17. Which was the last African nation to win its independence?
   a. Namibia
   b. Ghana
   c. Sudan
   d. Libya

18. Most African nations won independence by
   a. 1930.
   b. 1945.
   c. 1950.
   d. 1970.

IV. Essay Answer the following questions in paragraph form on a separate sheet of paper.

19. For hundreds of years Europeans traded with Africans and set up trading posts along the coast. It took a long time for Europeans to explore Africa's interior fully. Identify and explain at least two reasons European explorers had difficulty reaching the African interior. How did they eventually overcome their difficulties? What effect did European exploration have on the people and cultures of the African interior?

20. Explain the causes and effects of two of the following trends in Africa: (a) the changing role of women in Africa, (b) increased emphasis on education in Africa, (c) urbanization, (d) a move toward democratic governments.

Name _____ Date _____

Exploring Regional Issues...Analyzing a Chart

Study the chart below. The information is from the *1996 Almanac and Book of Facts*. Use the most recent edition of the *Almanac and Book of Facts,* or a similar book, to fill in information for Laos and New Zealand. After you have completed the table, answer the questions below.

EXPORTS, IMPORTS, AND MAJOR TRADING PARTNERS OF SELECTED COUNTRIES OF SOUTH AND SOUTHEAST ASIA

Country	Exports		Imports		Trading Partners
	Earned (U.S. dollars)	Products	Spent (U.S. dollars)	Products	
Bhutan	$66 million	timber, handicrafts, cement, fruit, gypsum, precious stones, spices, electricity	$125 million	fuels, machinery, grain, vehicles, fabric	India
Malaysia	$50.2 billion	natural rubber, palm oil, tin, timber, petroleum, electronics, textiles	$44.8 billion	food, crude oil, capital equipment, chemicals, consumer goods	Japan, Singapore, United States, Western Europe, Taiwan
Myanmar (Burma)	$613.4 million	rice, teak, oil seeds, metals, rubber, gems	$1.02 billion	machinery, transportation equipment, chemicals, food products	Japan, EU**, China, Singapore, Thailand, India, Hong Kong, Malaysia
Nepal	$369 million	clothing, carpets, grain, leather goods	$789 million	petroleum products, fertilizer, machinery	India, Japan, United States, Europe

** European Union

Source: *The World Almanac and Book of Facts 1996,* Mahwah, NJ: Funk & Wagnalls, Corp., 1995.

1. (a) Which country on the chart earns the most in exports? _____

   (b) Which spends the most for imports? _____

2. (a) What trading partners do Malaysia and Myanmar have in common?

   _____

   (b) Which countries in the chart have trading partners in South and Southeast Asia?

   _____

3. (a) Which countries have trade surpluses? _____

   (b) Which have trade deficits? _____

Name _____ Date _____

On Assignment...Making a Brochure

A brochure is a small booklet that contains information about a particular subject. Your job is to create a four-page brochure to attract tourists to South and Southeast Asia. Below is a chart to help you organize your ideas.

IDEAS FOR BROCHURE

	PICTURES	WORDS
page 1 (cover)		
page 2		
page 3		
page 4		

Name _____   **Date** _____

On Assignment...Creating a Mural

Your assignment is to create a mural that shows events in the history of South Asia. A mural is a very large wall painting, often one that shows a series of events. To find ideas for your mural, scan the pictures in your text. You may also wish to use picture books from your school or local library.

Below is an organizer that provides space for you to sketch ideas about events in the chapter. Events in the chapter are listed under the space. After you are satisfied with your sketches, transfer them to a large sheet of paper.

[blank box]

Indus Valley/Aryans   Religion   Early Empires   Islamic Empires
                           in India   in India   in India

[blank box]

Europeans in South Asia   British in India   Independence in South Asia

Name _____   Date _____

On Assignment...Writing Letters

Travelers often write letters to family and friends describing what they have seen and done on their trips. Your assignment is to write two letters describing your travels to South Asia. First, decide which places you have visited. The On Assignment hint boxes suggest several possibilities. Use these suggestions or think of some ideas of your own. List at least four places below.

1. _____   3. _____

2. _____   4. _____

Next, choose one thing to say in your letters about each of these places. Use information from your text and from other library or classroom resources.

1. _____

2. _____

3. _____

4. _____

Begin to write your first letter on the lines below. After you complete both letters, write a one-page summary of your impressions of South Asia.

Dear _____ ,

I can't believe I'm really in_____! Today, I saw _____

_____

_____

_____

_____

_____

_____

_____

_____

_____

_____

_____

Name _____   **Date** _____

On Assignment...Creating an Illustrated Time Line

Your task is to create a time line with illustrations. On the chart below, list ten events from the chapter, the date each event occurred, and the importance of the event. If you wish to list more events, use the back of this worksheet.

EVENT	DATE	WHY THE EVENT WAS IMPORTANT
1.		
2.		
3.		
4.		
5.		
6.		
7.		
8.		
9.		
10.		

Choose three of the events to illustrate. In the boxes below, make three sketches or use words to describe a picture you would use to represent each event.

144

Name _____ Date _____

On Assignment...Creating a Mini-History

Your assignment is to create a mini-history of Southeast Asia for third graders. Begin by brainstorming ideas for possible chapters to include in your book. Use the cluster map below to help you organize your ideas.

History of Southeast Asia

Choose the best ideas and list three chapters for your mini-history below.

Chapter 1: _____

Chapter 2: _____

Chapter 3: _____

On the mini-pages below, think about how you will organize your book. Which pages will have pictures? Which pages will have writing?

| 1 (Cover) | 2 | 3 | 4 | 5 | 6 | 7 |

| 8 | 9 | 10 | 11 | 12 (Back Cover) |

Name _____ **Date** _____

On Assignment...Giving a Presentation

Your assignment is to make a three-minute presentation about Southeast Asia's culture. The first step in preparing your presentation is to choose one aspect of the culture of Southeast Asia. Use the questions and the cluster map below to help you brainstorm and then narrow down ideas for your talk.

1. What did I find most interesting about Southeast Asian culture? _____

2. Which topic might be interesting to my audience? _____

3. About which topics do I think I can find information in my text and in the library?

   _____

4. Which pictures or maps will I show during my presentation? _____

   _____

   _____

Culture of Southeast Asia

Choose one topic and use your text and the library to research it. If you think that your topic is too broad, narrow it down by drawing a cluster map in your notebook.

My topic will be: _____

Name _____   Date _____

On Assignment...Creating a Board Game

Games can be a fun way to learn. Your assignment is to create a board game that contains information about Southeast Asia and the world. The only requirement for your game is that players must answer questions about Southeast Asia. The rest of the rules and the form of the game are up to you. To begin creating your game, answer the questions below.

1. What kind of game pieces will players use to represent themselves? _____

   _____

2. How will players advance around the board? For example, players might throw dice, spin a

   dial, or simply answer questions about Southeast Asia to advance their pieces. _____

   _____

3. How will someone win the game? Will the first player around the board be the winner? Will

   players score points as they play? How will players win points? _____

   _____

4. What will happen if players land on special "bad" spaces or "good" spaces on the board?

   _____

   _____

Next, use the space below to sketch the board. The board should include at least 15 spaces through which the players will move their pieces. To help you think of a design, remember games that you have played and the ways in which these boards are designed. Think about "good" and "bad" spaces.

Finally, organize the questions you have written on index cards. Practice playing your game to make sure it works.

   147

Name _____ Date _____

On Assignment...Creating Posters

Your assignment is to design two posters to increase tourism to Australia, New Zealand, and Oceania. Before you begin designing your posters, find at least three examples of advertisements in newspapers and magazines. Below, list what impresses you about each advertisement.

1. I liked/disliked the advertisement about _____ because _____

_____

2. I liked/disliked the advertisement about _____ because _____

_____

3. I liked/disliked the advertisement about _____ because _____

_____

Another important step in creating an effective advertisement is identifying who the audience for the advertisement is. In other words, to whom do you want to sell your product? For example, you might decide that your posters will be directed at young people who want to visit the beaches of Oceania. On the other hand, you might decide that your posters will appeal to people who want to camp in Australia's outback.

Who will your audience be? _____

As you read Chapter 15, jot down ideas based on the On Assignment hint boxes or based on your own original ideas. Think of at least three ideas for your poster and list them below.

Idea number 1: _____

Idea number 2: _____

Idea number 3: _____

For each idea, think of images that you can use on your posters. Write these down below:

Images for idea number 1: _____

Images for idea number 2: _____

Images for idea number 3: _____

Now, choose two ideas and, on the back of this worksheet, begin to sketch your posters. Then write a paragraph that explains how your posters will attract tourists to the region.

Name _____ Date _____

Critical Thinking...Interpreting a Map

The map below shows the major religions of South Asia. It shows the countries and regions where each religion has the largest number of followers. Study the map and answer the questions that follow.

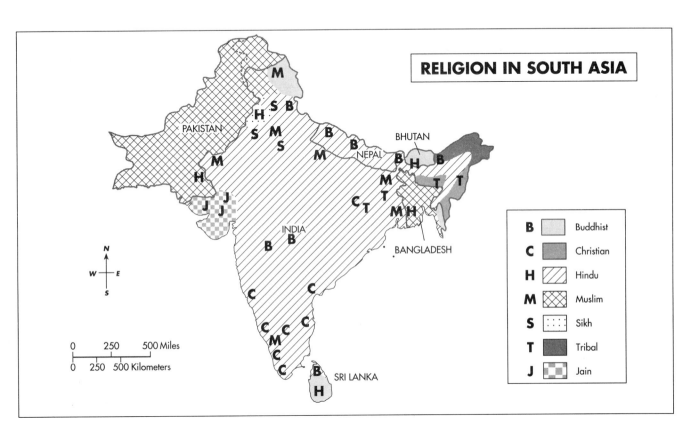

1. Which religions are shown on the map? _____

2. Which nations are shown on the map? _____

3. Which religion in India has the largest number of followers? _____

4. Which countries are mostly Muslim? _____

5. The northern region of South Asia is the most diverse. Based on what you have read about

   geography, why do you think this is so? _____

   _____

   _____

Name _____   **Date** _____

Critical Thinking...Making a Time Line

The sequence in which things occur in history is often important. An event may come before or after another, or events may occur at the same time. A *time line* portrays events in *chronological,* or time, order. Below is a list of events that occurred in South Asia. Place these events on the time line below and answer the questions that follow.

1948	Mohandas Gandhi is assassinated.
1200	The Delhi sultanate is founded in northern India.
1500 B.C.	Aryans conquer the peoples of the Indus valley.
500 B.C.	Buddhism is founded by Siddhartha Gautama.
1885	The Indian National Congress (INC) is formed.
1857	The Sepoy Rebellion occurs.
321 B.C.	The Maurya Empire is formed.
600s	Islam is begun by Muhammad in Saudi Arabia.
1920	Mohandas Gandhi becomes the leader of the Indian National Congress (INC).
1947	India is granted independence from Britain.
1498	The Portuguese discover a water route to India.

B.C.   A.D.
1500   1000   500   0   500   1000   1500   2000

|———————|—————————|—————————|—————————|—————————|—————————|—————————|

1. When was the Maurya Empire formed? _____

2. How many years after the Sepoy Rebellion was the Indian National Congress founded? _____

3. In what year was Buddhism founded? _____

4. In what year did India gain its independence? _____

_____

5. What was happening in India in the late 1940s? _____

_____

_____

Name _____ Date _____

Critical Thinking...Understanding a Table

The table below shows the enrollment of male and female children in primary school in Indian states. Study the table and then answer the questions that follow.

PRIMARY SCHOOL ENROLLMENT IN INDIA

State	Number of Males	Number of Females	State	Number of Males	Number of Females
Andhra Pradesh	3,141,226	2,821,509	Manipur	116,612	92,066
Assam	1,158,806	843,628	Meghalaya	104,732	95,413
Bihar	4,661,879	1,886,668	Nagaland	97,460	77,913
Gujarat	2,619,470	1,785,218	Orissa	1,632,604	1,112,104
Haryana	760,019	393,767	Punjab	1,145,694	936,070
Himachal Pradesh	206,571	223,432	Rajasthan	2,132,994	672,309
Jammu & Kashmir	350,682	196,888	Sikkim	24,715	17,071
Karnataka	2,462,459	1,879,092	Tamil Nadu	3,489,913	2,844,117
Kerala	1,707,195	1,921,540	Tripura	168,866	123,680
Madhya Pradesh	3,532,218	1,719,580	Uttar Pradesh	6,842,232	2,961,561
Maharashtra	4,770,331	3,623,128	West Bengal	4,057,313	2,403,260

Source: *The Social and Economic Atlas of India*, New York: Oxford University Press, 1987.

1. (a) How many primary school students in Uttar Pradesh are male? _____

   (b) How many are female? _____

2. How many more male students than female students attend primary school in Bihar? _____

_____

3. This table provides the number of students attending primary school in each Indian state. Using this data, you could figure out the percentage of males and females attending primary school in an Indian state. To do so, add the number of male and female students together. Divide the number of male students by that total to find out the percentage of male primary students. Divide the number of female students by the total to find out the percentage of females. For example, in Andhra Pradesh there are 5,962,735 primary school students (3,141,226 + 2,821,509). If you divide the number of males (3,141,226) by the total number of primary school students (5,962,735) you find out that 53 percent of the primary school students are male.

   Now, find out what percentage of the students in Andhra Pradesh are female.

_____

4. What percentage of the students in Tamil Nadu are male? _____

   What percentage are female? _____

Name _____ Date _____

Critical Thinking...Analyzing a Bar Graph

The graph on this page is called a **bar graph** because it uses bars to show amounts. It compares the proportions of women and men enrolled in college in India. Each bar represents one school year. The numbers show the number of women enrolled in college compared to one hundred men. For example, the bar that represents 1950–1951 shows that there were about 13 women for every 100 men enrolled in college. Study the bar graph and then answer the questions that follow.

WOMEN IN HIGHER EDUCATION IN INDIA

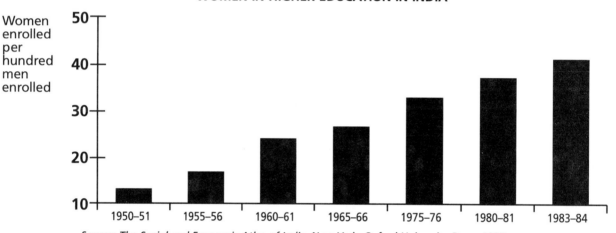

Source: *The Social and Economic Atlas of India*, New York: Oxford University Press, 1987.

1. What is the title of this bar graph? _____

2. The horizontal axis is the line on the graph that runs from right to left. What information is on the horizontal axis? _____

3. The vertical axis is the line that runs up and down. What information is on the vertical axis? _____

4. In 1955–56, how many women were enrolled in higher education per one hundred men? _____

5. In 1983–84, how many women were enrolled in higher education per one hundred men? _____

6. Is the number of women enrolled in college increasing or decreasing in proportion to the number of men enrolled? Explain how you found your answer. _____ _____

7. Why do you think so many more men than women are enrolled? _____ _____ _____

Name _____ Date _____

Critical Thinking...Creating a Pie Graph

Charts and graphs are important tools for organizing statistical information in an easy-to-read diagram. The graph you will be constructing is called a **pie graph** because it uses parts of a circle, or pie, to show amounts or percentages. Other graphs use different symbols to show amounts. **Line graphs** use indicator lines. **Bar graphs** use bars.

Below are the percentages of followers of different religions in four Southeast Asian countries. Look at the figures, then fill in the pie charts to represent the numbers given. Don't worry about being exact, just approximate the numbers. You may want to use different colors or create patterns for each piece of the pie to make your pie graph easier to read.

Philippines
83%   Roman Catholic
 9%   Protestant
 5%   Muslim
 3%   Buddhist and others

Thailand
94%   Buddhist
 4%   Muslim
 2%   Other

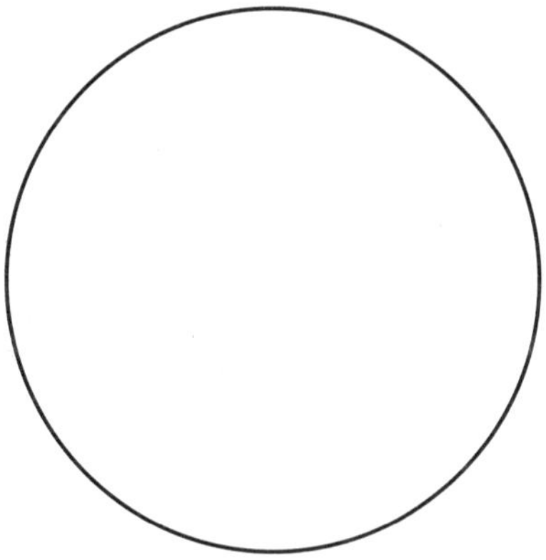

Philippines 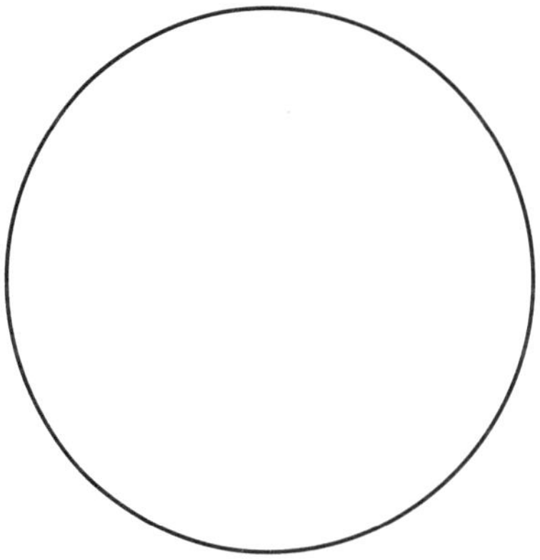   **Thailand**

Singapore
42%   Buddhist
18%   Christian
16%   Muslim
 5%   Hindu
19%   Other

Indonesia
87%   Muslim
 9%   Christian
 2%   Hindu
 2%   Buddhist

Singapore 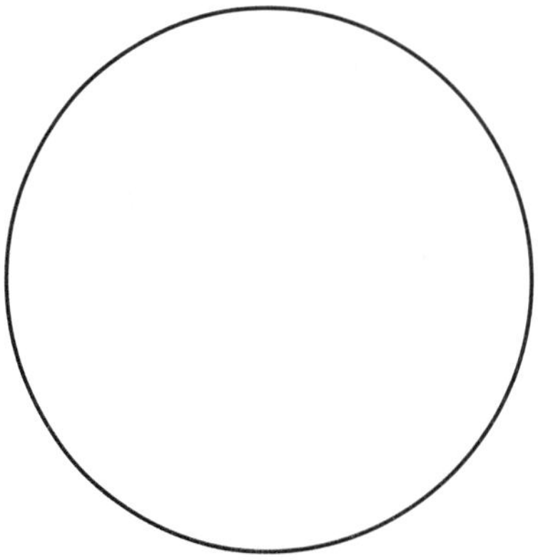   **Indonesia**

Source: *Grolier Global Studies Library: Japan and the Pacific Rim*, Dushkin Publishing Grp/Brown and Benchmark Publishing, 1995.

153

Name _____   Date _____

Critical Thinking...Building Vocabulary

The box below contains terms, places, and concepts that were used in Chapter 13. Read the questions carefully. Then, in the space provided, write the word that best answers the question.

gong	family life
puppets	religion
rice	kampung
Jakarta	consensus
gamelan	Singapore

1. A _____ is a name for a village in Southeast Asia; these villages are often poor.

2. Village government in Southeast Asia is often based on _____, an agreement reached by a group as a whole or by a majority.

3. The main crop that Southeast Asian farmers grow is _____.

4. _____ is a primary influence on Southeast Asian literature, dance, music, and art.

5. The Indonesian _____ orchestra is over 1,000 year old and is made up of gongs, xylophones, and percussion instruments.

6. The *wayang kulit* is a shadow play, often one based on Hindu epics. It uses _____ to tell a story.

7. A _____ is a round musical instrument that is struck; it is used in Southeast Asian ceremonies and festivals.

8. _____ is very important to Southeast Asians. Even if someone moves away, he or she usually moves in with relatives.

9. Indonesia's largest city, _____, is filled with shantytowns and is home to many poor people.

10. _____ is the most modern city in Southeast Asia.

Name _____ Date _____

Critical Thinking...Determining Cause and Effect

Understanding cause and effect is an important part of understanding history. To identify cause and effect, keep these tips in mind. A *cause* produces a result, or effect. An *effect* is the result of the cause. To discover the cause of an event, ask yourself: "Why did this event happen?" To discover the effects of an event, ask yourself: "What happened as a result of this event?"

The diagram below will help you organize the causes and effects of people moving to the cities in Southeast Asia. Add boxes if you need them. Also, don't worry if you can't fill up all the boxes. This chart is a tool for taking notes.

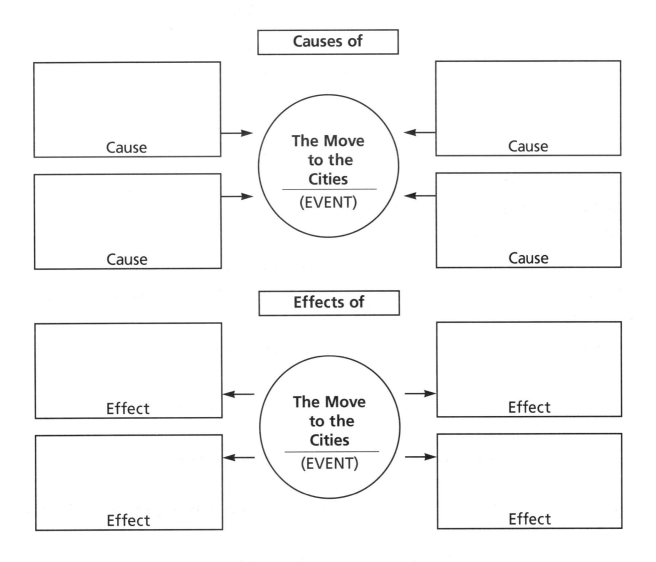

Name _____ Date _____

Critical Thinking...Analyzing a Bar Graph

Graphs organize statistical information in an easy-to-read diagram. The graph on this page is called a **bar graph** because it uses bars to show amounts.

Begin reading a graph by identifying what information is shown. Next, think about this information. What differences in size or amount can you see? Are there any patterns in the data? To practice these skills, study the graph below. Then answer the questions that follow.

AVERAGE RAINFALL FOR SELECTED CITIES IN AUSTRALIA

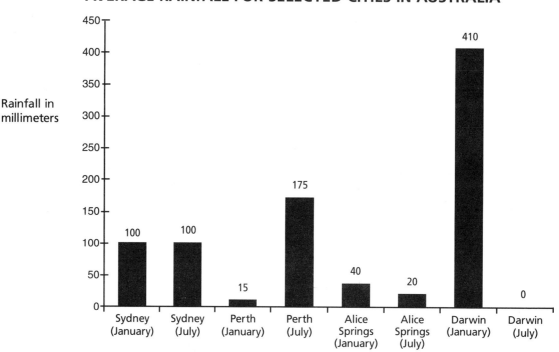

Source: *Australian Bureau of Meteorology, Climate of Australia* (1989), and *Climate Averages, Australia* (1989).

1. What is the title of this bar graph? _____

2. The horizontal axis is the line on the graph that runs from right to left. What information is on the horizontal axis? _____

3. The vertical axis is the line that runs up and down. What information is on the vertical axis?

_____

4. Which cities are shown on the graph? _____

5. Which city has the least rainfall in January? _____

6. Which city has the least rainfall in July? _____

7. In which climate region do you think Alice Springs is located? Why? _____

_____

Name _____   Date _____

I. Matching Decide which definition in the right column best explains a term in the left column. Then write the letter of that definition in the space next to the term.

_____ **1.** subcontinent

_____ **2.** dialect

_____ **3.** hydroelectricity

_____ **4.** cyclone

_____ **5.** plateau

a. a regional form of a language that has its own words, expressions, and pronunciations

b. a flat area that is higher than the land that surrounds it

c. a dangerous windstorm; often one that brings rain

d. a large landmass that juts out from a continent

e. the power that comes from the force of rushing water

II. Multiple Choice Choose the answer that best completes the sentence or answers the question. Then write the letter of your choice in the space provided.

_____ **6.** Southeast Asia is divided into two main areas, which are called
   a. the north and south.
   b. east and west.
   c. the mainland and the islands.
   d. the Indian Ocean and the South China Sea.

_____ **7.** The majority of the people living in South Asia are
   a. farmers.
   b. lawyers.
   c. tailors.
   d. teachers.

_____ **8.** The climate of the Indian sub-continent
   a. is always hot.
   b. is always very cold.
   c. varies from bitterly cold to steaming hot.
   d. is dry all year.

_____ **9.** Which of the following shows how monsoons help the people of South and Southeast Asia?
   a. Monsoons bring about 80 percent of the region's annual rainfall, allowing crops to grow.
   b. Monsoons bring heavy winds, allowing the use of windmills to harness electricity.
   c. Monsoons bring hot, sunny summers that draw tourists to the region.
   d. Monsoons bring heavy snowfall and a good ski season.

_____ **10.** What are the three main geographic regions of the Indian subcontinent?
   a. Muslim, Hindu, and Christian
   b. Burma, Thailand, and Cambodia
   c. monsoon, cyclone, and dialect
   d. the northern mountains, the northern plains, and the Deccan Plateau

III. Essay Write your answer to the following question in paragraph form on a separate piece of paper.

The people of South and Southeast Asia have been described as *diverse.* What does this mean? In what ways are they diverse? Explain your answer.

Name _____ Date _____

I. **Matching** Decide which definition in the right column best explains a term in the left column. Then write the letter of that definition in the space next to the term.

_____ 1. mosque

_____ 2. civil disobedience

_____ 3. nirvana

_____ 4. meditate

_____ 5. descendant

a. a place of worship for Muslims

b. to think deeply

c. a person who can trace his or her heritage to an individual or group

d. a person's refusal to follow laws that he or she believes are unjust

e. a state in which a person has achieved perfect happiness because he or she wants nothing

II. **Multiple Choice** Choose the answer that best completes the sentence or answers the question. Then write the letter of your choice in the space provided.

_____ 6. Which of the following was NOT a part of the Aryan culture?
   a. the caste system
   b. a love of war, horse-drawn chariots, music, and dance
   c. the worship of many gods and a belief in reincarnation
   d. the worship of Mohandas Gandhi

_____ 7. Which of the following is a religion that began in South Asia?
   a. Christianity
   b. Hinduism
   c. Aryanism
   d. Islam

_____ 8. The British East India Company
   a. was actually a secret French army.
   b. helped Britain take control of India.
   c. was made up of Sepoy soldiers.
   d. was a group of British missionaries.

_____ 9. Which of the following is NOT true about the Maurya Empire of India?
   a. It was the first great empire in India, formed in about 321 B.C.
   b. It had a well-organized government.
   c. Its rulers organized the first rebellion against British rule in India.
   d. Asoka was probably the most famous emperor of the Maurya Empire.

_____ 10. The Sepoy Rebellion was
   a. the rebellion of Indian soldiers against the British in 1857.
   b. the rebellion against Gandhi in 1948.
   c. the rebellion against the Mogol Empire in the 1700s.
   d. a rebellion of Theravada Buddhists against the Mahayana Buddhists.

III. **Essay** Write your answer to the following question in paragraph form on a separate piece of paper.

The Indian National Congress (INC) was formed in 1885 to fight for the rights of India's people. Gradually, however, its goals began to change. Write an essay in which you describe how the INC's goals changed. Also, be sure to discuss the leader of INC, Mohandas Gandhi, and the methods he used to achieve these goals.

Name _____   Date _____

I. Matching Decide which definition in the right column best explains a term in the left column. Then write the letter of that definition in the space next to the term.

_____ **1.** raga

_____ **2.** epic

_____ **3.** stupa

_____ **4.** bustee

_____ **5.** epidemic

a. an outbreak of disease

b. a poor area of a city where people live in shacks

c. a long poem that tells the story of a hero

d. one of the ancient melody patterns of Indian music

e. a dome-shaped burial mound that serves as a Buddhist holy site

II. Multiple Choice Choose the answer that best completes the sentence or answers the question. Then write the letter of your choice in the space provided.

_____ **6.** Which of the following was NOT a reason for many villagers in India moving to the cities?
   a. to get an education
   b. they lacked farmland
   c. to learn a trade other than farming
   d. to escape the Bhopal chemical plant

_____ **7.** Much of the Indian tradition of art, literature, music, and drama is based on
   a. religion.
   b. bustees.
   c. Chinese culture.
   d. epidemics.

_____ **8.** Which of the following is NOT a characteristic of Indian cities?
   a. bustees
   b. overpopulation
   c. poor sanitary conditions
   d. an excellent public school system

_____ **9.** Indian dance
   a. is very simple.
   b. has more than 140 poses and can take a minimum of ten years to learn.
   c. is called the Taj Mahal.
   d. is called Shah Jahan.

_____ **10.** The Indians who are most likely to be educated are
   a. poor farmers.
   b. poor city dwellers.
   c. wealthy city dwellers.
   d. women.

III. Essay Write your answer to the following question in paragraph form on a separate piece of paper.

India has experienced many changes since independence. Many of these changes have created new challenges that India will need to face in the future. Write an essay in which you describe at least three problems that India may face. What steps is the Indian government taking to deal with these potential problems?

Name _____ Date _____

I. Matching Decide which definition in the right column best explains a term in the left column. Then write the letter of that definition in the space next to the term.

_____ **1.** pact

_____ **2.** coup

_____ **3.** communism

_____ **4.** militant

_____ **5.** martial law

a. a revolt, often by military leaders, against a nation's government

b. an agreement

c. temporary rule by the military

d. a person who believes in using violence to promote a cause

e. an economic system in which the government owns and controls most property and industry

II. Multiple Choice Choose the answer that best completes the sentence or answers the question. Then write the letter of your choice in the space provided.

_____ **6.** Why was the choice of Indira Gandhi as prime minister a surprise to many?

    a. Indira Gandhi was very young.

    b. Indira Gandhi was a woman.

    c. Indira Gandhi was a Muslim.

    d. Indira Gandhi was from Pakistan.

_____ **7.** In 1971, East Pakistan

    a. became part of India.

    b. became part of China.

    c. became the nation of Sri Lanka.

    d. became the nation of Bangladesh.

_____ **8.** The island nation off the southeast coast of India that was once called Ceylon is now called

    a. Sri Lanka.

    b. East Pakistan.

    c. West Pakistan.

    d. Bangladesh.

_____ **9.** Which of the following is NOT true of the Indian government?

    a. It has a parliamentary structure similar to Britain's.

    b. A prime minister is the most powerful government official.

    c. The National Congress party controlled parliament for its first 20 years.

    d. The general of the army is also the leader of the government.

_____ **10.** Which of the following is NOT a problem that Indian farmers face?

    a. extensive destruction caused by plant diseases and rats

    b. large debts

    c. large deposits of iron and coal

    d. not enough water or fertilizer for their crops

III. Essay Write your answer to the following question in paragraph form on a separate sheet of paper.

    After World War II, India decided on a policy of non-alignment. What does *non-alignment* mean? How did non-alignment affect India's relationship with the United States and the Soviet Union?

Name _____ Date _____

I. Matching

Decide which definition in the right column best explains a term in the left column. Then write the letter of that definition in the space next to the term.

_____ 1. animism
_____ 2. canal
_____ 3. colony
_____ 4. revolt
_____ 5. guerrilla
            warfare

a. an uprising
b. hit-and-run attacks by small bands of fighters against a larger power
c. a land that is controlled by another country
d. the belief that spirits live in the natural world in such things as rocks, trees, and streams
e. a ditch made by humans to carry water

II. Multiple Choice

Choose the answer that best completes the sentence or answers the question. Then write the letter of your choice in the space provided.

_____ 6. Which of the following was an effect of Western rule of Southeast Asia?

a. The Western nations took the best land and paid little or nothing for it.
b. The Western nations made their colonies very rich by giving fair prices in trade.
c. The colonies rebelled, under the leadership of King Mongkut, and forced Westerners out in the early 1900s.
d. The Western nations destroyed roads, schools, and hospitals.

_____ 7. During World War II, much of Southeast Asia

a. was destroyed by the Philippine army.
b. was controlled by the Japanese.
c. was controlled by the Soviet Union.
d. was colonized by Western nations for the first time.

_____ 8. Which of the following nations controlled Vietnam from the late 1800s until 1954?

a. France
b. the United States
c. Japan
d. Britain

_____ 9. What products attracted Europeans to Southeast Asia in the 1500s?

a. factories
b. spices and raw materials
c. animism
d. canals

_____ 10. Which of the following was NOT a reason for migration to Southeast Asia?

a. riches, such as jewels, gold, and spices
b. nearness to China and India
c. the effects of the Cold War
d. trade goods

III. Essay

Write your answer to the following question in paragraph form on a separate sheet of paper.

    Many kingdoms existed in the early civilizations of Southeast Asia. Among them were the kingdoms of Vietnam, the Pagan kingdom, the Angkor kingdom, the Thai kingdom, and the kingdoms of Indonesia. Write an essay in which you describe the culture and history of at least two of these ancient civilizations. Be sure to include the influences that China and India had on these cultures.

Name _____ **Date** _____

I. Matching Decide which definition in the right column best explains a term in the left column. Then write the letter of that definition in the space next to the term.

_____ 1. kampung
_____ 2. consensus
_____ 3. gong
_____ 4. incense
_____ 5. gilded

a. a round musical instrument that is struck
b. a village
c. material that makes a scent when burned
d. an agreement reached by a group as a whole or by a majority
e. covered with a thin layer of gold

II. Multiple Choice Choose the answer that best completes the sentence or answers the question. Then write the letter of your choice in the space provided.

_____ 6. Most Southeast Asians work as
   a. farmers.
   b. technicians.
   c. teachers.
   d. artists.

_____ 7. Many villagers who move to the cities
   a. become very wealthy.
   b. are kampungs.
   c. attend high school and college.
   d. are forced to live in slums because they lack the education to find high-paying jobs.

_____ 8. Which of the following was NOT an important influence on the arts in Southeast Asia?
   a. religion
   b. Chinese culture
   c. U.S. culture
   d. Indian culture

_____ 9. A reason that Southeast Asian people move to the cities is that
   a. the government forces them to move.
   b. they are very well educated in the villages.
   c. they need to find kampungs.
   d. there is not enough land for them to farm in their villages.

_____ 10. The most important crop to Southeast Asian farmers is
   a. corn.
   b. rice.
   c. oranges.
   d. wheat.

III. Essay Write your answer to the following question in paragraph form on a separate sheet of paper.

The arts in Southeast Asia have fascinated visitors for centuries. Write an essay in which you describe some elements and influences of Southeast Asian drama, dance, music, literature, and art.

Chapter 14 Test *Southeast Asia in the World Today*

Name _____   Date _____

I. Matching
Decide which definition in the right column best explains a term in the left column. Then write the letter of that definition in the space next to the term.

_____ 1. capitalism

_____ 2. investors

_____ 3. insecticide

_____ 4. market economy

_____ 5. rigid

a. an economic system in which businesses are owned privately

b. people who put money into businesses in hopes of making a profit

c. stiff; tightly controlled

d. a system in which prices are based on what people are willing to pay and companies make goods based on what people want to buy

e. a chemical that kills insects

II. Multiple Choice
Choose the answer that best completes the sentence or answers the question. Then write the letter of your choice in the space provided.

_____ 6. Which of the following was NOT related to the Green Revolution?
   a. Farmers used chemicals to produce more crops.
   b. Food production increased.
   c. The Communists took control of farming methods.
   d. Chemicals from insecticides entered the water supply.

_____ 7. As the ruler of the Philippines from 1965 to 1986, Ferdinand Marcos
   a. was a Communist.
   b. ruled the country with an iron hand, gave his friends jobs in the government, and looted the country for himself.
   c. was a fair and honest leader.
   d. tried to take control of Vietnam.

_____ 8. The country of Singapore is
   a. very poor.
   b. one of Southeast Asia's success stories.
   c. Communist.
   d. controlled by the Chinese.

_____ 9. The governments of Southeast Asian countries
   a. are all democratic governments.
   b. are all Communist governments.
   c. include monarchies, democracies, and Communist governments.
   d. are all ruled by kings and queens.

_____ 10. Which of the following is NOT true about the Association of Southeast Asian Nations (ASEAN)?
   a. It is an organization of Communist countries.
   b. It is friendly to democratic countries like the United States.
   c. One of its goals is to increase trade among its member nations.
   d. It includes such countries as Thailand, Malaysia, Singapore, Brunei, and the Philippines.

III. Essay
Write your answer to the following question in paragraph form on a separate sheet of paper.

When the colonies of Southeast Asia became countries after World War II, they faced a number of challenges. Write an essay in which you explain some of the challenges that these countries faced. How did these countries deal with their problems?

Name _____   Date _____

I. Matching Decide which definition in the right column best explains a term in the left column. Then write the letter of that definition in the space next to the term.

_____ 1. atoll

_____ 2. squatter

_____ 3. outback

_____ 4. geothermal energy

_____ 5. geyser

a. a small coral island with a body of water at its center; most often found in the South Pacific

b. energy produced from heat within the earth

c. the dry lands of Australia where there are few settlers

d. someone who settles on land without the right to do so

e. a natural spring of hot water that shoots steam or hot water into the air from time to time

II. Multiple Choice Choose the answer that best completes the sentence or answers the question. Then write the letter of your choice in the space provided.

_____ 6. Which of the following is NOT one of the three groups of islands that make up Oceania?

a. Australia
b. Polynesia
c. Micronesia
d. Melanesia

_____ 7. Which of the following is NOT true of the early relations between the British and Maoris in New Zealand?

a. The British took land from the Maoris illegally.
b. There were many wars between the British and Maoris.
c. The Maoris sold land to the British in exchange for protection and government.
d. Relations were very peaceful between the British and Maoris.

_____ 8. Australia was first used by Britain as a

a. location for factories.
b. penal colony.
c. farming colony.
d. naval base.

_____ 9. The Aborigines

a. were the Europeans who settled in New Zealand.
b. were the Europeans who settled in Australia.
c. were the first people to live in Australia.
d. are wealthy farmers in New Zealand.

_____ 10. Because it has very few deposits of natural resources such as oil, which of the following does New Zealand use to produce energy?

a. hydroelectricity
b. atolls
c. solar energy
d. windmills

III. Essay Write your answer to the following question in paragraph form on a separate sheet of paper.

The geography of both Australia and New Zealand has had a powerful impact on how people live in these two countries. Write an essay in which you explain how the land, climate, and natural resources of these two countries have affected the lives of the people who live there. How are New Zealand and Australia similar? How are they different?

Name _____ Date _____

I. Fill in the Blank Complete each sentence below by writing the correct term in the blank. You will not use all the terms.

non-alignment	coup	caste	animism	atolls
delta	squatter	consensus	capitalism	monsoons

1. Most cities in Southeast Asia are found around a _____ , a triangle of land that forms where a river meets the sea.

2. The system that separates Hindus by class and job is called the _____ system; its social groups are based on birth.

3. After World War II, India's prime minister decided on a foreign policy of

   _____ , siding with neither the United States nor the Soviet Union.

4. Many Indonesian Muslims mix Islam with a traditional belief called _____ , which states that spirits live in the natural world in such things as rocks, trees, and streams.

5. Government in Southeast Asian villages is often based on _____ , an agreement reached by a group as a whole or by a majority.

6. Vietnam is a Communist nation struggling to incorporate _____ , an economic system in which businesses are owned privately, to help its economy.

7. Most of the "low" islands of Oceania are coral reefs, or _____ , which are surrounded by bodies of water called lagoons.

8. Seasonal winds called _____ blow across the South Asian subcontinent, bringing with them wet or dry weather.

II. Multiple Choice Choose the answer that best completes the sentence or answers the question. Then write the letter of your choice in the space provided.

_____ 9. The most densely populated area of South Asia is found near the
   a. northern Himalayas and Hindu Kush mountains.
   b. river valleys of the northern plain.
   c. deserts of the Deccan Plateau.
   d. low mountains of the Deccan Plateau.

_____ 10. The two major world religions that developed in South Asia are
   a. Buddhism and Hinduism.
   b. Hinduism and Islam.
   c. Islam and Christianity.
   d. Buddhism and Islam.

_____ 11. As leader of the Indian National Congress, Mohandas K. Gandhi wanted India to achieve independence from Great Britain through
   a. revolution.
   b. guerrilla warfare.
   c. nonviolence and noncooperation.
   d. the court system.

_____ 12. The highest standard of living in Oceania is on
   a. the mainland.
   b. the "low" islands.
   c. the "high" islands.
   d. Australia.

165

COUNTRIES OF SOUTH ASIA

COUNTRY	CAPITAL CITY	AREA (square miles)	POPULATION (millions of people)	POPULATION DOUBLING TIME (years)
Bangladesh	Dhaka	50,260	113.9	29
Bhutan	Thimphu	18,150	1.4	30
India	New Delhi	1,147,950	897.4	34
Maldives	Malé	120	0.2	20
Nepal	Kathmandu	52,820	20.4	28
Pakistan	Islamabad	297,640	122.4	23
Sri Lanka	Colombo	24,950	17.8	49

Source: World Population Data Sheet of the Population Reference Bureau, Inc.

____ 13. The major political and economic trend in Southeast Asia today is toward
  a. more government control of businesses.
  b. tighter military control.
  c. absolute monarchs who have total control.
  d. private ownership of businesses and less rigid Communist rule.

____ 14. East Pakistan split off from West Pakistan to become the nation of Bangladesh because East Pakistan
  a. had religious differences with West Pakistan.
  b. had ethnic differences with West Pakistan.
  c. wanted more territory
  d. felt that West Pakistan had too much power.

____ 15. The first Europeans to settle in Australia were
  a. convicts sent to a penal colony.
  b. farmers looking for better land.
  c. people looking for religious freedom.
  d. explorers seeking their fortunes.

III. Analyzing a Chart Answer questions 16–18 based on the chart above. The chart shows data from 1996.

____ 16. What is the capital city of Bangladesh?
  a. Colombo   c. Islamabad
  b. Kathmandu d. Dhaka

____ 17. Which country in South Asia has the largest population?
  a. New Delhi c. Pakistan
  b. India   d. Bangladesh

____ 18. In what year will the population of India be double what it was in 1996?
  a. 2064   c. 2030
  b. 2034   d. 2000

IV. Essay Answer the following questions in paragraph form on a separate sheet of paper.

19. Describe the three major religions found in South and Southeast Asia today. How did each religion develop or come to the region?

20. Discuss why so many outsiders came to Southeast Asia. How and why was Southeast Asia influenced by foreigners throughout its history?

Name _____ Date _____

Exploring Regional Issues...Analyzing Maps

Below are two maps of Japan. The one on the left is a landform map. The one on the right is a population density map. Study the two maps and answer the questions.

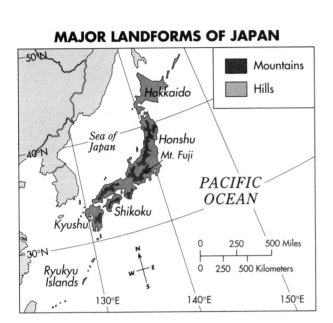

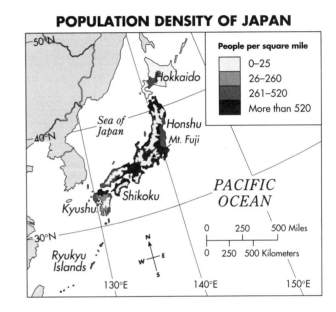

1. Use an atlas to locate the Japanese cities listed below. Then label the cities on the two maps. (a) Tokyo, (b) Yokohama, (c) Hiroshima, (d) Kitakyushu, (e) Sapporo.

2. (a) On which landforms are the cities you labeled located? _____

   _____

   (b) What are the population densities of the regions in which the cities are located?

   _____

3. (a) Which landforms have the highest population density? _____

   _____

   (b) Which have the lowest population density? _____

   _____

   (c) Why do you think this is so? _____

   _____

Name _____ **Date** _____

On Assignment...Creating a Mural

   Your assignment is to create a mural that shows the landforms, rivers, resources, climates, and people of East Asia. A mural is a very large wall painting that shows scenes and people. To find ideas for your mural, scan the pictures in your text. You may also wish to use picture books from your school or local library that feature China, Japan, and Korea. Below is an organizer that provides space for you to list ideas and to sketch some of them. Use the back of this worksheet if you need more space to list or sketch. Transfer your best ideas to a large sheet of paper.

TOPIC	CHINA	JAPAN	KOREA
Landforms			
Rivers			
Resources			
Climates			
People			

China: The Longest History

Name _____ Date _____

On Assignment...Writing and Performing a Skit

Your task is to write a skit about Chinese history. Your skit should include three scenes. The On Assignment hint boxes in the chapter suggest topics for each scene. You may use these ideas or ideas of your own. Below is a series of questions to help you organize your scenes. After you have decided on a topic, begin to write dialogue for the scenes.

SCENE ONE
Ideas for topics: _____

_____

1. Where will the scene take place? _____
2. What characters will you include in the scene? _____

_____

3. If you plan to perform this scene, what props, scenery, or costumes will you need?

_____

_____

SCENE TWO
Ideas for topics: _____

_____

1. Where will the scene take place? _____
2. What characters will you include in the scene? _____

_____

3. If you plan to perform this scene, what props, scenery, or costumes will you need?

_____

_____

SCENE THREE
Ideas for topics: _____

_____

1. Where will the scene take place? _____
2. What characters will you include in the scene? _____

_____

3. If you plan to perform this scene, what props, scenery, or costumes will you need?

_____

_____

Name _____ **Date** _____

On Assignment...Writing a Journal

    Many writers keep journals to record their thoughts, feelings, and ideas. Your assignment is to create journal entries telling about your imaginary travels through history to Japan and Korea. The page below is divided into five parts. Each part contains a possible opening line for a journal entry describing travels to one of the empires. Use the opening line or create one of your own to write your journal entries.

FEUDAL JAPAN

Date: _____

Today the Mongol ships were destroyed by the kamikaze. Yet Japan still faces so many problems.

The worst problem is _____

_____

_____

THE ARRIVAL OF COMMODORE PERRY

Date: _____

Commodore Perry has made some incredible demands. I think _____

_____

_____

KING KOJONG'S FUNERAL

Date: _____

Today Korea was turned upside down. I saw _____

_____

_____

THE KOREAN WAR

Date: _____

The war has divided many families. I feel _____

_____

_____

KOREAN CULTURE

Date: _____

How can I explain Korean names to my American friends? I can start by _____

_____

_____

     Global Studies. Copyright © **Globe Fearon Educational Publisher.** *All rights reserved.*

Name _____ **Date** _____

On Assignment...Conducting an Interview

Your assignment is to write questions for an interview about changing patterns of life in China, Japan, and Korea. Review the On Assignment hint boxes in Chapter 19 for ideas about questions to write. Use these ideas or think of some of your own. Working with a partner, use the diagram below to brainstorm at least three questions for Section 1. Then copy the diagram into your notebook and use it to think of three questions for the other sections in the chapter and for the case study.

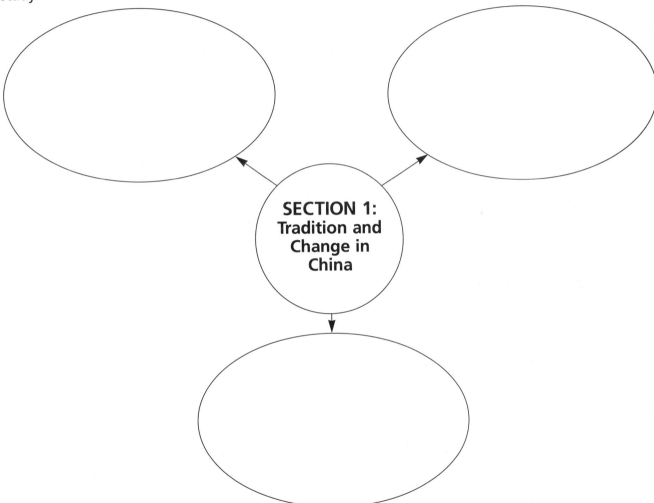

SECTION 1:
Tradition and Change in China

After you have written questions for all the sections, list them on a sheet of paper and review them. Have you asked questions about important issues in the region? Are questions phrased in a clear, direct way? Check the spelling and grammar of your questions. Revise any questions you do not like and add new questions. Then, use your text and library resources to create answers to your questions. Practice your interview with your partner until you feel comfortable. Perform your interview for the class.

Name _____ **Date** _____

On Assignment...Creating Posters

Your assignment is to create a poster about China today. Before you begin to create your poster, find at least three examples of advertisements in newspapers and magazines. Below list what impresses you about each advertisement.

1. I liked/disliked the advertisement about _____ because _____

_____

2. I liked/disliked the advertisement about _____ because _____

_____

3. I liked/disliked the advertisement about _____ because _____

_____

Another important step in creating an effective advertisement is identifying who the audience is for the advertisement. In other words, to whom are you directing your message? For example, you might decide that your poster will be directed at young people who are fighting for democratic change. Or you might decide to design a poster for Chinese parents about population control in China.

Who will your audience be? _____

As you read Chapter 20, jot down ideas based on the On Assignment hint boxes or based on your own original ideas. Think of at least three ideas for your poster and list them below.

Idea number 1: _____

Idea number 2: _____

Idea number 3: _____

For each idea, think of images that you can use on your poster. Write these down below:

Images for idea number 1: _____

Images for idea number 2: _____

Images for idea number 3: _____

Now, choose your ideas and on the back of this worksheet, begin sketching your posters. Choose the best of your sketches and create a slogan—catchy words or phrases—to add to the poster.

Once you have completed your poster, write a paragraph that explains your poster's message.

Name _____ Date _____

On Assignment...Writing a Letter

Travelers often write letters to family and friends describing what they see and do on their trips. Your assignment is to write letters describing your travels through Japan and Korea. First, decide what you have seen in these countries. The On Assignment hint boxes suggest several possibilities. Use these suggestions or create your own. List at least four possibilities below.

1. _____   3. _____

2. _____   4. _____

Next, decide one thing you would say about where you have been. Use information from your text and information you find in other library or classroom resources.

1. _____

2. _____

3. _____

4. _____

Begin to write your first letter on the lines below.

Dear _____ ,

I can't believe I'm really in_____! Today, I saw _____

_____

_____

_____

_____

_____

_____

_____

_____

_____

_____

_____

_____

Name _____ Date _____

On Assignment...Writing an Editorial

Your assignment for this chapter is to write an editorial expressing your opinion about an issue relating to East Asia and the world today. Find an editorial in your local newspaper. Read the editorial and identify the topic the editor has written about, the editor's opinion about the topic, and the facts the editor has used to back up his or her opinion. Write the information in the spaces below.

Topic: _____

Editor's opinion: _____

_____

Facts used to support opinion: _____

_____

_____

Review the notes that you took while reading this chapter. The broad topic for your editorial is East Asia's relationship with the world. However, it will help to narrow that topic and focus on one issue. For example, you might choose to write about China's actions since the Cold War. On the lines below, describe how you will narrow the topic:

My editorial will focus on: _____

_____

Once you have chosen an issue, you need to decide what your opinion of that issue is. Write your opinion below.

I believe that: _____

_____

_____

What facts will you use to support your opinion? Write supporting facts below.

Facts: _____

_____

_____

_____

_____

Now write your editorial on a separate sheet of paper.

Name _____   **Date** _____

Critical Thinking...Interpreting a Map

The map below shows the location of landforms in East Asia. It divides them into four categories: desert, highland, plain, and plateau. Study the map and then answer the questions that follow. You may need to refer to your text.

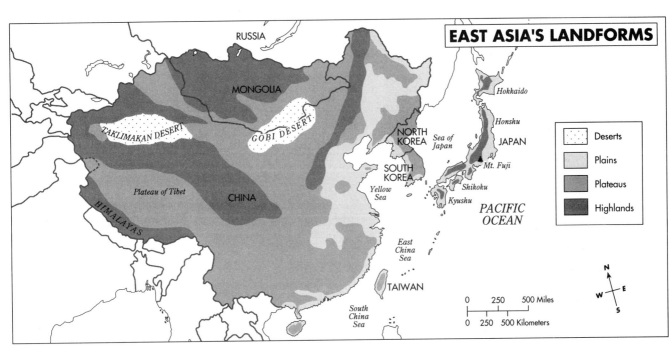

1. What information does the map show? _____

   _____

2. Write the definition of each type of landform below. You will find the definition of *plateau* in your text. Use a dictionary to define the other terms.

   (a) desert: _____

   (b) highland: _____

   (c) plain: _____

   (d) plateau: _____

3. What are the names of the two deserts in East Asia? _____

4. On what island is Mt. Fuji? What type of landform is Mt. Fuji? _____

   _____

175

Name _____   Date _____

Critical Thinking...Reading and Analyzing a Map

During the late 1800s, a number of foreign nations demanded special trading rights in China. They divided China into spheres of influence—areas in which a particular country would be dominant. Study the map below and then answer the questions that follow. You may need to refer to your text.

1. Which countries gained spheres of influence in China? _____

_____

2. Which Asian country had a sphere of influence in China? _____

3. Why did the United States ask the other countries to agree to the Open Door policy?

_____

_____

4. How did the Chinese react to the foreign occupation of China? _____

_____

Name _____ Date _____

Critical Thinking...Making a Time Line

The sequence in which things happen in history is often important. An event may come before another or after another, or events may occur at the same time. A *time line* portrays events in *chronological*, or time, order. Below is a list of events that occurred in East Asia from about 1600 to about 1950. Place these events on the time line and answer the questions that follow.

1603–1867	The Tokugawa shogunate rules Japan.
1929	The Great Depression begins.
1945	The U.S. drops atomic bombs on Hiroshima and Nagasaki, ending World War II.
1910	The Yi dynasty ends in Korea.
1853	Matthew C. Perry and the U.S. Navy open up Japan for trade.
1939	World War II starts.
1945–1951	The U.S. occupies Japan.
1910	Japan takes control of Korea.
1868	The Meiji Restoration of power to the emperor begins.
1953	The Korean War ends.
1950	North Korea attacks South Korea, starting the Korean War.
1941	Japan attacks Pearl Harbor, and the U.S. enters World War II.
1948	Korea is split into North and South.
1641	Japan stops foreign trade.
1904–1905	The Russo-Japanese War takes place.

```
1600          1700                    1800                 1900      1950
|--------------|------------------------|-------------------|---------|
```

1. In which year did Japan stop foreign trade?_____

2. (a) In which year did Japan open up to foreign trade?_____

   (b) Who opened up Japan to foreign trade?_____

   _____

3. Was the Meiji Restoration before or after the Tokugawa shogunate ruled Japan?

   _____

4. Why did the Yi dynasty end in Korea in 1910? _____

   _____

Name _____ Date _____

Critical Thinking...Determining Cause and Effect

Understanding cause and effect is an important part of understanding history. To identify cause and effect, keep these tips in mind. A *cause* produces a result, or effect. An *effect* is the result of a cause. To discover the cause of an event, ask yourself: "Why did this event happen?" To discover the effects of an event, ask yourself: "What happened as a result of this event?"

Look at the chart below. In the center is an effect: *Japanese students study for many hours every day.* The boxes around the effect are for you to fill in short-term and long-term causes. Don't worry if you can't fill all the boxes, or if you need more. The boxes are just there to help you organize your notes.

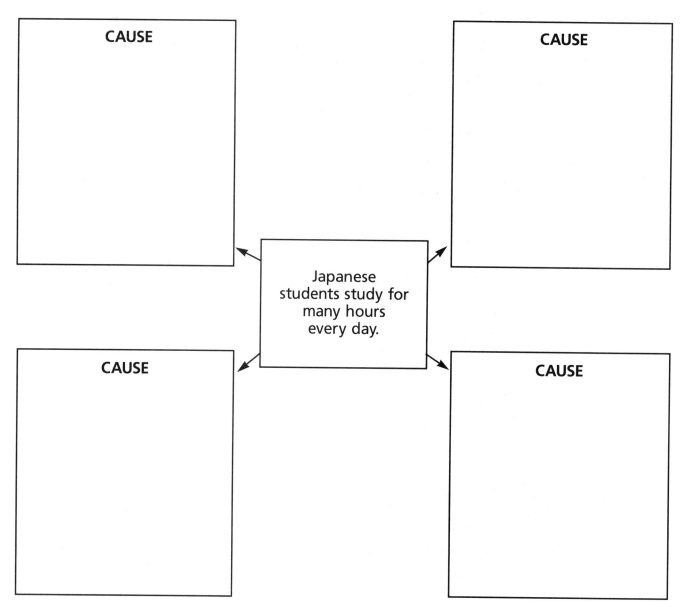

Global Studies. Copyright **© Globe Fearon Educational Publisher.** *All rights reserved.*

Name _____ Date _____

Critical Thinking...Using Primary Sources

Mao Zedong (1893–1976) was one of the most important leaders of the Communist party in China. Below is an excerpt from a speech by Mao to the Chinese people. This excerpt is called a *primary source. Primary* means "first or original." Speeches are primary sources because they provide information from someone who witnessed an event. Read the speech carefully and then answer the questions that follow. You may need to refer to your text for help.

Today, two big mountains lie like a dead weight on the Chinese people. One is imperialism, the other is feudalism. The Chinese Communist Party has long made up its mind to dig them up. We must persevere and work unceasingly, and we, too, will touch God's heart. Our God is none other than the masses of the Chinese people. If they stand up and dig together with us, why can't these mountains be cleared away?

1. Use a dictionary to define the following words.

    (a) imperialism: _____

    (b) feudalism: _____

    (c) persevere: _____

    (d) unceasingly: _____

2. Who is the author of the speech? _____

3. What are the "two big mountains" that the author mentions? _____

4. What do you think the author wants the people to do when he urges the Chinese people to

    "stand up and dig together"? _____

    _____

    _____

5. Do you think that Mao's words are consistent with the ideas about revolution you read about

    in the chapter? Explain your answer. _____

    _____

    _____

    _____

Name _____ Date _____

Critical Thinking...Interpreting a Political Cartoon

In Chapter 21, you read about Japan's economic miracle. Japan's economic recovery was due in part to its ability to export more goods than it imported. Today, Japanese products are sold worldwide. However, countries that try to sell products to Japan sometimes encounter difficulties, such as import quotas and taxes. Also, many Japanese citizens will buy only Japanese-made products.

The political cartoon below expresses a point of view about Japanese trade. As always when studying a cartoon or drawing, read all labels carefully to understand the message that the cartoonist is trying to convey. Look for symbols that express the cartoonist's feelings about an issue. Study the drawing below and answer the questions that follow.

Illustration by Arcadio, Costa Rica, Cartoonists & Writers Syndicate

1. Where is the ship docked? _____

2. What does the ship contain? _____

3. What label appears on the door near the ship? _____

4. In two or three sentences, explain the cartoonist's point of view about Japanese trade.

_____

_____

_____

Name _____   Date _____

Critical Thinking...Analyzing a Table

The table below contains data about U.S. trade with several other nations. To read and understand the data in a table, you must first note the title of the table. What does the title of this table tell you? Next, study the headings of each column. There are four columns in this table. What information does each column contain? Study the table and answer the questions below.

U.S. TRADE WITH SELECTED COUNTRIES AND AREAS, 1993
(in millions of dollars)

Country	Trade Balance	Exports from the U.S.	Imports to the U.S.
Japan	-54,355	47,891	102,246
China	-22,777	8,762	31,539
Canada	-10,772	100,444	111,216
Germany	-9,630	18,932	28,562
Taiwan	8,934	16,167	25,101
Italy	-6,752	6,464	13,216
Nigeria	-4,407	894	5,301
Korea	-2,336	14,782	17,118
Totals	-119,963	214,336	334,299

Source: Office of Trade and Economic Analysis, U.S. Department of Commerce

1. The U.S. trade balance with a country is the difference between the value of exports to that country from the United States and imports to the United States from that country. The trade balance figure is calculated by subtracting the value of imports from the value of exports. For example, $47,891 minus $102,246 equals -$54,355. What does the fact that the

   trade balance is negative tell you? _____

   _____

2. (a) What was the value of the goods that the United States exported to Japan in 1993?

   _____

   (b) What was the value of the goods that the United States imported from Japan?

   _____

   (c) Review the definitions of trade deficit and trade surplus in your text. Does the difference between imports and exports shown in this table result in a trade deficit or a trade surplus for the United States? Explain.

   _____

3. What was the total amount of the U.S. trade deficit for the countries listed in this table?

   _____

181

Name _____ Date _____

I. Matching
Decide which definition in the right column best explains a term in the left column. Then write the letter of that definition in the space next to the term.

_____ 1. dialect

_____ 2. delta

_____ 3. monsoon

_____ 4. hydroelectric power

_____ 5. exile

a. a seasonal wind that brings wet or dry weather

b. a person living outside his or her homeland for political reasons

c. a way of speaking found in a particular region

d. a broad area of soil deposits near the mouth of a river

e. electricity created by water

II. Multiple Choice
Choose the answer that best completes the sentence or answers the question. Then write the letter of your choice in the space provided.

_____ 6. With a population of about 1.2 billion people,
   a. China is one of the smallest countries in the world.
   b. Japan is one of the smallest countries in the world.
   c. China is the largest country in the world.
   d. Japan is the largest country in the world.

_____ 7. Tibet is located on a plateau, which is
   a. a large desert.
   b. a delta.
   c. a large area of flat land, higher than the surrounding land.
   d. an island.

_____ 8. Taiwan is
   a. an island off the coast of China that has its own government.
   b. the capital city of South Korea.
   c. part of the Korean peninsula.
   d. the name of China's largest river.

_____ 9. Three Gorges is
   a. a mountain range in Japan.
   b. an island off the coast of China.
   c. a large river in Korea.
   d. a dam being built on the Chang River in China.

_____ 10. The geography of East Asia is characterized by
   a. mountains.
   b. fertile plains.
   c. large plateaus.
   d. all of the above.

III. Essay
Write your answer to the following question in paragraph form on a separate sheet of paper.

How are the writing systems used in China, Japan, and Korea similar? How are they different?

Name _____ Date _____

I. Matching Decide which definition in the right column best explains a term in the left column. Then write the letter of that definition in the space next to the term.

_____ **1.** mandate

_____ **2.** dynasty

_____ **3.** republic

_____ **4.** tribute system

_____ **5.** warlord

a. a local ruler and military leader

b. permission to rule

c. a government led by officials who are elected by the people they govern

d. a family of rulers

e. an arrangement by which China collected payments from nearby nations

II. Multiple Choice Choose the answer that best completes the sentence or answers the question. Then write the letter of your choice in the space provided.

_____ **6.** The Mongols, who during their rule of China brought in outsiders to control the government and ignored Chinese traditions,

    a. were considered foreigners by the Chinese.

    b. ruled China for thousands of years.

    c. brought the ideas of Confucius to China.

    d. were part of the Shang dynasty.

_____ **7.** The Opium War began

    a. as a result of the Boxer Rebellion.

    b. when Chinese officials dumped thousands of chests of British opium into a river.

    c. when the Chinese refused to buy British opium.

    d. as a result of the Taiping Rebellion.

_____ **8.** The Shang dynasty, which lasted from 1700 B.C. until about 1000 B.C., is known for all of the following EXCEPT

    a. oracle bones.

    b. a Communist government.

    c. a written language.

    d. use of the wheel.

_____ **9.** The U.S. request in 1899 to have equal trading rights within China's borders was known as

    a. the "Mandate of Heaven."

    b. the Boxer Rebellion.

    c. the tribute system.

    d. the Open Door policy.

_____ **10.** The "Mandate of Heaven"

    a. allowed Korea to control China.

    b. allowed Chinese rulers to hold power until they abused their power and were overthrown.

    c. allowed Confucius to rule China.

    d. was an arrangement by which China collected payments from nearby nations.

III. Essay Write your answer to the following question in paragraph form on a separate sheet of paper.

The Nationalists and Communists fought for control of China between 1912 and 1949. Write an essay in which you describe both of these groups. Be sure to include information about each group's leaders and goals. Which group won control of China in 1949?

Chapter 18 Test *The History of Japan and Korea*

Name _____ Date _____

I. Matching Decide which definition in the right column best explains a term in the left column. Then write the letter of that definition in the space next to the term.

_____ **1.** feudalism

_____ **2.** truce

_____ **3.** shogun

_____ **4.** regent

_____ **5.** demilitarized zone

a. a military leader who ruled in the name of the Japanese emperor

b. an area of land in which armed troops are not permitted

c. someone who rules in the place of a child

d. a halt to the fighting in a war

e. a social system based on ties of loyalty and service

II. Multiple Choice Choose the answer that best completes the sentence or answers the question. Then write the letter of your choice in the space provided.

_____ **6.** Japan's best natural defense against invasion has been

   a. its samurai.
   b. its large mountains.
   c. the seas that surround the island.
   d. the emperor.

_____ **7.** The groups of families that controlled small areas of land in Japan were called

   a. clans.
   b. Shinto.
   c. the shogun.
   d. regents.

_____ **8.** After World War II, Korea was split into North and South, with the South becoming a democracy and the North ruled by

   a. the Communists.
   b. a shogun
   c. the Japanese.
   d. clans.

_____ **9.** The Meiji Restoration refers to

   a. the period after World War II when the Japanese rebuilt Japan.
   b. the period in the late 1800s when power was restored to the emperor.
   c. the rebuilding of Korea after the Mongols invaded in 1231.
   d. the period when the first Asians sailed to the island of Japan.

_____ **10.** In 1910 when Japan took over Korea,

   a. Korean citizens were given many more freedoms.
   b. Korean farmers became very wealthy.
   c. the United States defended Korea and prevented the Japanese from taking control.
   d. Japan tried to stamp out the Korean way of life.

III. Essay Write your answer to the following question in paragraph form on a separate sheet of paper.

Very early in its development, Japan was influenced strongly by Chinese ideas and culture. What are some of the Chinese ideas and practices that the Japanese adopted?

184   *Global Studies. Copyright* **© Globe Fearon Educational Publisher.** *All rights reserved.*

Changing Patterns of Life in East Asia

Name _____ Date _____

I. Matching Decide which definition in the right column best explains a term in the left column. Then write the letter of that definition in the space next to the term.

_____ 1. dissent

_____ 2. cooperative farming

_____ 3. meditate

_____ 4. divine

_____ 5. shaman

a. a priest or priestess who conducts ceremonies involving the worship of nature

b. opposition to a government's policies

c. godlike

d. a farm in which families join their lands and work together, sharing the output

e. to think deeply

II. Multiple Choice Choose the answer that best completes the sentence or answers the question. Then write the letter of your choice in the space provided.

_____ 6. When the Communists took control in China they broke up the large estates and eventually made them into
   a. grazing lands for cattle.
   b. cooperative farms.
   c. religious communities.
   d. reincarnation.

_____ 7. In Korean society, women often had low status as a result of the traditional ideas of
   a. shamans.
   b. Confucius.
   c. reincarnation.
   d. Japan.

_____ 8. Japanese schools
   a. are competitive and demanding.
   b. meet only three days every week.
   c. do not require students to do homework.
   d. are easy and not at all stressful.

_____ 9. Since World War II, the status of women in Japan has
   a. prevented them from working outside the home.
   b. become worse than it was before World War II.
   c. improved.
   d. stayed the same.

_____ 10. After Mao Zedong relaxed the restrictions on freedom of speech, there was an outpouring of criticism of the Communist government, so the Communist government
   a. put back the restrictions on freedom of speech.
   b. let the people vote.
   c. started a democracy.
   d. did nothing.

III. Essay Write your answer to the following question in paragraph form on a separate sheet of paper.

China, Japan, and Korea have cultures that are based on thousands of years of tradition. For each country, write about one traditional influence and about how that tradition may have changed in the modern society.

Name _____ Date _____

I. **Matching** Decide which definition in the right column best explains a term in the left column. Then write the letter of that definition in the space next to the term.

_____ 1. commune

_____ 2. Red Guards

_____ 3. moderate

_____ 4. incentive

_____ 5. hunger strike

a. students, workers, and soldiers who rampaged through China in support of Mao's Cultural Revolution

b. a refusal to eat; sometimes used as a tactic to pressure a government to meet a list of demands

c. a large farm, with all land and property jointly owned and operated by the farmers

d. less extreme in ideas or behavior

e. a reward offered to encourage people to take a desired action

II. **Multiple Choice** Choose the answer that best completes the sentence or answers the question. Then write the letter of your choice in the space provided.

_____ 6. The goal of Mao Zedong's Cultural Revolution was to

a. create a democratic government.

b. make Deng Xiaoping the leader of China.

c. restore enthusiasm in the Communist revolution.

d. start a hunger strike.

_____ 7. The Red Guards were

a. Russians who fought against the Chinese Communists.

b. Chinese supporters of democracy.

c. supporters of Mao Zedong and the Communists.

d. farmers on the communes.

_____ 8. China's Communist government believed that the arts should

a. serve the Communist state.

b. be removed from China.

c. be left free to reflect whatever perspective the artist wishes.

d. point out the problems with the Chinese Communist government.

_____ 9. Which part of the following was NOT a part of the Great Leap Forward?

a. People worked longer hours in the factories and fields.

b. Communes replaced large privately owned farms.

c. Communist leaders tried to encourage change in China.

d. The United States sent money and food supplies to China.

_____ 10. Which of the following was NOT a reason that many Communists called Deng Xiaoping a capitalist?

a. He tried to make China a major industrial power.

b. He started the Great Leap Forward.

c. He allowed people to start private businesses.

d. He encouraged incentives for people who worked hard.

III. **Essay** Write your answer to the following question in paragraph form on a separate sheet of paper.

After the Communists took control of China in 1949, they launched a campaign against many Chinese traditions. Write an essay in which you describe how the Communists changed traditional Chinese life.

186   *Global Studies. Copyright* **© Globe Fearon Educational Publisher.** *All rights reserved.*

Chapter 21 Test   *Japan and Korea Today*

Name _____   Date _____

I. **Matching** Decide which definition in the right column best explains a term in the left column. Then write the letter of that definition in the space next to the term.

_____ 1. zaibatsu
_____ 2. Diet
_____ 3. Cold War
_____ 4. self-sufficient
_____ 5. parliamen-
　　　　　 tary rule

a. a system of government in which a nation's legislature choos-es the country's leader
b. Japan's two-house parliament
c. giant family businesses in Japan, which supposedly were broken up during the U.S. occupation
d. making do with one's own resources
e. a conflict between the Soviet Union and the United States in which each side made threats against the other and built up its military forces and weapons

II. **Multiple Choice** Choose the answer that best completes the sentence or answers the question. Then write the letter of your choice in the space provided.

_____ 6. Japan's Liberal Democratic Party (LDP)
a. ruled the Japanese parliament with little opposition until 1993.
b. first took control of the Japanese parliament in 1996.
c. has never been very powerful.
d. was banned in 1993.

_____ 7. From 1961 until 1993, South Korea was ruled by
a. military leaders.
b. Communists.
c. the United States.
d. North Korea.

_____ 8. North Korean leader Kim Il Sung
a. kept North Korea democratic until 1993.
b. ruled Communist North Korea for almost 50 years.
c. was assassinated by his son.
d. opened trade with the United States.

_____ 9. The major difference between North Korea and South Korea is that
a. North Korea is a democracy and South Korea is Communist.
b. North Korea controls the South Korean government.
c. North Korea is Communist and South Korea is democratic.
d. North Korea is a powerful indus-trial country and South Korea is a weak industrial country.

_____ 10. Which of the following was NOT a goal of the United States during its occupation of Japan following World War II?
a. to ensure that Japan would remain a peaceful country
b. to give Japan a democratic government
c. to teach the Japanese to govern themselves
d. to convince Japan to attack the Soviet Union

III. **Essay** Write your answer to the following question in paragraph form on a separate sheet of paper.

Since World War II, the Japanese have experienced what some call an "economic miracle." What is the economic miracle? What are some of the reasons that this economic miracle occurred?

Name _____ Date _____

I. Matching Decide which definition in the right column best explains a term in the left column. Then write the letter of that definition in the space next to the term.

_____ 1. nuclear umbrella

_____ 2. trade surplus

_____ 3. coexist

_____ 4. non-aligned nation

_____ 5. trade deficit

a. to live peacefully side by side with others

b. a nation that claimed not to prefer one side over another in the Cold War

c. the result when a nation sells more to other nations than it buys from other nations

d. the result when a nation buys more from other nations than it sells to other nations

e. the military protection provided to a nation by another nation that possesses nuclear weapons

II. Multiple Choice Choose the answer that best completes the sentence or answers the question. Then write the letter of your choice in the space provided.

_____ 6. During the early part of the Cold War, China was
   a. a major U.S. ally.
   b. isolated from the West.
   c. a "paper tiger."
   d. controlled by Japan.

_____ 7. When Mao Zedong called the capitalist countries "paper tigers," he meant that
   a. they were to be feared.
   b. they were weaker than they seemed.
   c. they were non-aligned.
   d. capitalism was superior to communism.

_____ 8. Russia and Japan never signed a formal peace treaty to end World War II because
   a. Russia still holds Japanese prisoners of war.
   b. they were allies during the war.
   c. Russia was a non-aligned nation.
   d. a dispute over the Kuriles has not been resolved.

_____ 9. Under the nuclear umbrella, the United States promises to protect Japan, and Japan
   a. allows the U. S. to maintain troops and bases in Japan.
   b. promises to change Article 9 of its constitution.
   c. promises to stay out of China.
   d. promises to supply the United States with nuclear material.

_____ 10. The issue of trade has caused friction between the United States and Japan because
   a. the Japanese are banned from selling goods in the United States.
   b. Japan sells much more to the U.S. than it buys from the U.S.
   c. Japan only sells goods to China.
   d. most Americans refuse to buy Japanese products.

III. Essay Write your answer to the following question in paragraph form on a separate sheet of paper.

   Relations between the United States and China have changed a great deal since the end of World War II. Describe the changes and give reasons for these changes.

UNIT 3 TEST   *Focus on East Asia*

Name _____   Date _____

I. Fill in the Blank   Complete each sentence below by writing the correct term in the blank. You will not use all the terms.

coalition	vassal	trade surplus	dynasties	samurai	republic
	commune	typhoons	self-sufficiency	collective farms	

1. Japan's islands are often exposed to _____ , fierce storms similar to hurricanes.

2. For most of China's history, its leaders came from powerful _____ , or families of rulers.

3. Under the Japanese feudal system, a person who served a more powerful lord was called a _____ .

4. Members of the traditional warrior class in Japan were known as _____ .

5. During the Great Leap Forward in Communist China, individual farms were replaced by _____ , one in which all land and property were jointly owned and operated by the farmers.

6. In the 1990s, Japan established a _____ government, one in which a combination of two or more parties act together to form a government.

7. North Korea's economic policy is one of _____ , or making do with one's own resources.

8. Since the 1970s, Japan has built a large _____ with the United States, selling more products to the U.S. than it buys.

II. Multiple Choice   Choose the answer that best completes the sentence or answers the question. Then write the letter of your choice in the space provided.

_____ 9. Japan's location along the Pacific Ring of Fire means
   a. earthquakes and volcanic eruptions are common.
   b. forest fires occur frequently.
   c. fires have protected Japan from invasion.
   d. Japanese natives observe religious ceremonies involving fire.

_____ 10. The Great Wall of China was built to
   a. provide a tourist attraction for foreigners visiting China.
   b. provide a transportation route from the east to the west.
   c. protect southern China from invaders.
   d. keep northern nomadic tribes from invading.

MAJOR JAPANESE EXPORTS AND IMPORTS

PRODUCT EXPORTED	EXPORTS (in thousands of U.S. dollars)	PERCENT OF TOTAL EXPORTS
Machinery	$125,108,690	37.7%
Electrical Equipment	56,217,640	18.0
Passenger Cars	44,712,595	14.2
Transport Equipment	31,310,506	10.0
Industrial Chemicals	17,195,281	5.5
Toys and Musical Instruments	16,243,823	5.2

Data covers the year 1991.

PRODUCT IMPORTED	IMPORTS (in thousands of U.S. dollars)	PERCENT OF TOTAL IMPORTS
Mineral Fuels	$54,756,348	23.1%
Food and Other Consumable Goods	34,698,137	14.7
Machinery	27,419,324	11.6
Crude Materials	24,644,751	10.4
Industrial Chemicals	16,909,947	7.1
Metals	15,078,356	6.4

Source: U.S. Department of Commerce; "Summary of Trade," Japan Tariff Association, January 1992.

_____ 11. After A.D. 1200, power and leadership in Japan were held by
   a. the warrior class.
   b. the emperor.
   c. landowners.
   d. bureaucrats.

_____ 12. After World War II, Korea split into two countries because of
   a. a religious war.
   b. a mutual agreement.
   c. a UN conference.
   d. a disagreement between Communists and non-Communists.

_____ 13. The moral code established by Confucius stresses
   a. respect for nature.
   b. equality between men and women.
   c. obedience to authority.
   d. giving up the desire for material possessions.

_____ 14. Which of the following was a goal of the Communists when they came to power in China in 1949?
   a. to increase family loyalty
   b. to promote population growth
   c. to return land to the people
   d. to promote religion

_____ 15. Japan has become a world economic leader by producing and exporting
   a. high-tech products.
   b. natural resources.
   c. agricultural products.
   d. traditional industrial products.

III. Analyzing a Chart Answer questions 16–18 based on the chart above.

_____ 16. What product is Japan's chief import?
   a. machinery
   b. electrical equipment
   c. mineral fuels
   d. metals

_____ 17. What product comprises more than 25 percent of Japan's total exports?
   a. machinery
   b. electrical equipment
   c. mineral fuels
   d. metals

_____ 18. What is the difference between Japan's imports and exports in machinery (in thousands of U.S. dollars)?
   a. $97,689,366
   b. $125,108,690
   c. $27,419,324
   d. $26.6

IV. Essay Answer the following questions in paragraph form on a separate sheet of paper.

19. Compare and contrast the countries of North Korea and South Korea. What are the similarities and differences in their geography, people, and goverments?

20. Describe the rise of communism in China. How did the Communists come to power? What changes did the Communists make in Chinese life?

Name _____   Date _____

Exploring Regional Issues...Reading a Line Graph

Latin America's cities are growing rapidly. Below is a graph showing the growth of La Paz, Bolivia, from 1960 to 1990. Study the graph, then add the information provided for the cities of San José, Costa Rica, and Mexico City, Mexico, to the graph. Use a different colored pencil or a different pattern for each city. Add the color or pattern of the line to the key next to the graph. When you have completed the graph, answer the questions below.

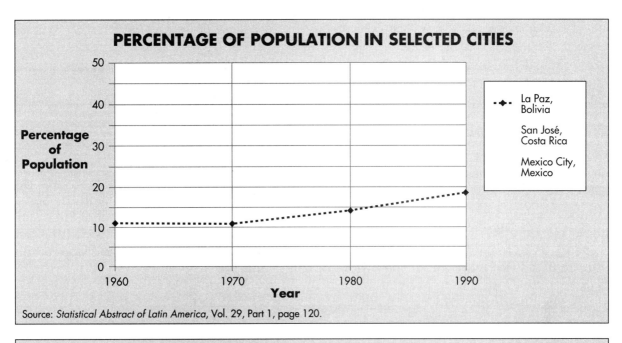

Source: *Statistical Abstract of Latin America*, Vol. 29, Part 1, page 120.

City	1960	1970	1980	1990
San José, Costa Rica	22.6	25.4	29.8	34.6
Mexico City, Mexico	13.0	16.6	19.8	21.9

1. (a) What percentage of Bolivia's population lived in La Paz in 1990? _____

   (b) What percentage of Costa Rica's population lived in San José in 1970? _____

2. (a) Which of the three cities had the greatest percentage of its country's population in 1960?

   _____

   (b) Which had the greatest percentage in 1990? _____

3. Which city's population has increased the most from 1960 to 1990? _____

Name _____ Date _____

On Assignment...Creating Posters

Your assignment is to design a poster for an advertising campaign with the theme "Visit Latin America—A Place of Beauty and Diversity." Before you begin designing your poster, find at least three examples of advertisements in newspapers and magazines. Below list what impresses you about each advertisement.

1. I liked/disliked the advertisement about _____ because _____

_____

2. I liked/disliked the advertisement about _____ because _____

_____

3. I liked/disliked the advertisement about _____ because _____

_____

Another important step in creating an effective advertisement is identifying who the audience for the advertisement is. In other words, to whom do you want to sell your product? For example, you might decide that your posters will be directed at young people who want to visit the beaches and dance clubs in Latin American cities. You might decide that your posters will appeal to people who want to learn more about the history of Latin America.

Who will your audience be? _____

As you read Chapter 23, jot down ideas based on the On Assignment hint boxes or based on your own original ideas. Think of at least three ideas for your poster and list them below.

Idea number 1: _____

Idea number 2: _____

Idea number 3: _____

For each idea, think of images that you can use on your posters. Write these down below:

Images for idea number 1: _____

Images for idea number 2: _____

Images for idea number 3: _____

Now, choose your favorite idea for your poster.

    Global Studies. Copyright **© Globe Fearon Educational Publisher.** *All rights reserved.*

Name _____ Date _____

On Assignment...Keeping a Journal

    Travelers often keep journals to describe what they have seen and done on their trips. Many writers keep journals to record their thoughts, feelings, and ideas. Your assignment is to create journal entries telling about your travels to the Mayan, Aztec, and Incan empires. If you are having trouble beginning the assignment, you might think about all the things you have done since you woke up this morning. Write a journal entry describing your day.

    The page below is divided into three parts. Each part contains a possible opening line for a journal entry describing travels to one of the three empires. Use the opening lines or create your own to write your journal entries.

THE MAYAN EMPIRE

Date: _____

Today we visited the city of Tikal. It was _____

_____

_____

_____

_____

THE AZTEC EMPIRE

Date: _____

When I met the emperor Montezuma, I thought _____

_____

_____

_____

_____

THE INCAN EMPIRE

Date: _____

The Incas are a fascinating people. I didn't realize that the Incan farmers could _____

_____

_____

_____

_____

Name _____ **Date** _____

On Assignment...Creating a Mini-History

Your assignment is to create a mini-history of Latin America for third graders. Begin by brainstorming ideas for possible chapters to include in your book. Use the cluster map below to help you organize your ideas.

Choose the best ideas and list three chapters for your mini-history below.

Chapter 1: _____

Chapter 2: _____

Chapter 3: _____

On the mini-pages below, organize the pages of your book. What pages will have pictures on them? What pages will have writing?

1	2

3	4

5	6

7	8

9	10

11	12

Name _____ Date _____

On Assignment...Creating a Storyboard

Your task is to create a storyboard about life in Latin America. The On Assignment hint boxes in the chapter suggest that the three scenes in your storyboard be on the following topics: cultural diversity, family life, and city life. You may use these ideas or come up with ideas of your own. The questions below will help you create your storyboard.

1. What is the most interesting fact you learned about the people of Latin America?

_____

_____

2. What did you find interesting about that fact? _____

_____

3. How would you present that fact in pictures and video images? _____

_____

Use the boxes below to sketch your scenes.

4. What might a narrator say as the pictures and images appear on the screen? If you choose to use actors and actresses to convey information, what would the characters say to one

another? _____

_____

_____

_____

Name _____ Date _____

On Assignment...Creating a Map

Your assignment for this chapter is to create a resource map for a Latin American country. In the space below write the name of the country you choose.

COUNTRY: _____

The chart below will help you organize information for your map. As you fill in the chart, think of symbols for each element included on your map. For example, you might want to use a star to show the capital city. Some of the information you will need can be found in your text. Other information can be found in almanacs or other reference books. You can find these books in your school or local library.

	INFORMATION	IDEA FOR SYMBOL
Capital city		
Population		
Area		
Type of government		
Chief resources and major industries		
Other information		

Name _____ Date _____

On Assignment...Creating an Illustrated Time Line

Your task is to create a time line with illustrations. On the chart below, list ten events from the chapter, the date each event occurred, and the importance of the event. If you wish to list more events, use the back of this worksheet.

EVENT	DATE	WHY THE EVENT WAS IMPORTANT
1.		
2.		
3.		
4.		
5.		
6.		
7.		
8.		
9.		
10.		

Choose three events to illustrate. In the boxes below, make three sketches or use words to describe a picture you would use to represent each event.

Name _____   Date _____

On Assignment...Making a Presentation

Your assignment is to give a three-minute presentation about Canada's geography and people. The first step in preparing your presentation is to choose one aspect of Canada's geography or people to talk about. Use the questions and the cluster map below to help you brainstorm and narrow down ideas for your talk.

1. What interests me most about Canada's geography and people? _____

2. Which topic might be interesting to my audience? _____

3. About which topics do I think I can find information in my text and in the library? _____
_____

4. What pictures or maps would I show during my presentation? _____
_____
_____

Canada: Geography and People

Choose one topic and begin researching it using your text and the library. If you think your topic is too broad, continue to narrow it down by drawing another cluster map in your notebook.

My topic will be: _____

Name _____ Date _____

Critical Thinking...Interpreting a Map

The map below shows the elevation levels in Latin America. Elevation is the height of a place above sea level. The higher the elevation, the higher the land is above sea level. Also, the higher the elevation, the colder the climate. Study the map and answer the questions that follow.

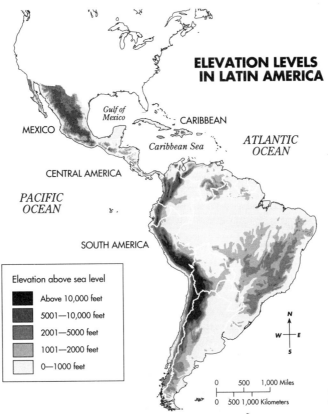

Source: *Latin America 1994,* The World Today Series.

1. What information does the map show? _____

2. Where is the highest region in Mexico? _____

3. (a) Where is the highest region in South America? _____
   (b) Compare this map with the one in your text on page 304. What landform represents the

   highest region in South America? _____

4. What is the elevation of northern Brazil? _____

5. Compare the elevations of Mexico and Central America to the elevations of South America.

   What similarities do you see? Differences? _____

   _____

Name _____ Date _____

Critical Thinking...Making a Time Line

   The sequence in which things happen in history is important. An event may come before another, come after another, or events may occur at the same time. A *time line* portrays events in *chronological,* or time, order. Below is a list of events that occurred in Latin America and elsewhere from about 1000–1600 A.D. Place these events on the time line below and answer the questions that follow.

LATIN AMERICA

1325 Aztecs build Tenochtitlán.

1000 The Mayan city of Tikal is abandoned.

1521 Cortés conquers the Aztec empire.

1501 Vespucci explores the coast of Brazil.

1438 The Incan empire is established in Peru.

1533 Pizarro conquers the Incas.

1492 Columbus sails to the Americas.

1100 Mayan civilization begins to decline.

1546 Mayas are conquered by the Spanish.

ELSEWHERE

1368 The Ming dynasty begins in China.

1096 The First Crusade begins.

1215 The Magna Carta is signed.

1522 Magellan circumnavigates (travels completely around) the globe.

1271 Marco Polo travels to China.

1431 Joan of Arc is burned at the stake.

1492 Muslims and Jews are expelled from Spain.

```
1000              1200              1400              1600
|-----------------|-----------------|-----------------|
```

1. In which year did Vespucci explore the coast of Brazil? _____

2. Which of the three Latin American empires was established first? _____

3. Which of the three Latin American empires was the first to be conquered by Europeans?

_____

4. What happened in Europe the same year that Columbus sailed to the Americas? _____

_____

5. What happened in Latin America about the time that the First Crusade began?

_____

_____

Name _____ Date _____

Critical Thinking...Interpreting a Drawing

Artists often use their artwork to express a point of view about an issue. The drawing below presents a point of view on the treatment of Native Americans by Spanish conquerors. As always when studying a drawing or cartoon, read all labels and captions to understand the message that the artist is trying to convey. Study the drawing below and answer the questions that follow, using what you have learned from the text.

Spanish conqueror and conquered Indian prince. Illustration © by the Royal Academy of Denmark.

1. Who is the character on horseback? _____

2. Who is the character lying down on the ground? _____

3. Describe what the character on horseback is doing. _____

_____

4. In your own words, describe what you think the artist is saying in this drawing. _____

_____

_____

_____

Name _____ Date _____

Critical Thinking...Analyzing a Table

The table below contains data for the ten largest cities in the world. To read and understand the data in a table, you must first note the title of the table. What does the title of this table tell you? Next, study the heads of each column. There are five columns in this table. What information does each column contain? Study the table for a few moments and read the questions below. The questions will help you analyze and interpret the data in the table.

THE TEN LARGEST CITIES IN THE WORLD

City, Country	1992 (millions)	1995 (millions)	2000 projected (millions)	Area (sq.mi.)
Tokyo-Yokohama, Japan	27,540	28,447	29,971	1,089
Mexico City, Mexico	21,615	23,913	27,872	522
São Paulo, Brazil	19,373	21,539	25,354	451
Seoul, South Korea	17,334	19,065	21,976	342
New York, U.S.A.	14,628	14,638	14,648	1,274
Osaka-Kobe-Kyoto, Japan	13,919	14,060	14,287	495
Bombay, India	12,450	13,532	15,357	95
Calcutta, India	12,137	12,885	14,088	209
Rio de Janeiro, Brazil	12,009	12,788	14,169	260
Buenos Aires, Argentina	11,743	12,232	12,911	535

Source: *Information Please Almanac, Atlas & Yearbook 1995*, Houghton Mifflin, Boston.

1. (a) Which Latin American cities appear on the chart? _____

   (b) Which Latin American city had the highest population in 1992? _____

2. Compare the 1995 populations of Calcutta and Buenos Aires. (a) Which city has a larger

   population? _____ (b) Which city is larger in area? _____

   (c) Which city is more crowded? How do you know? _____

3. The term *population density* refers to the number of people who live in a particular area. Population density tells how crowded an area is. To figure out population density, divide the population of a city by its area. For example, to find out the population density of Tokyo-Yokohama in 1995, divide 28,447,000 by 1,089. The answer is 26,122. That means that there is an average of 26,122 people per square mile.

   (a) Find the population density of the four Latin American cities in 1992 and 2000.

   _____

   _____

   (b) Which Latin American city had the highest population density in 1992? _____

   (c) Which Latin American city will have the highest population density in 2000? _____

   _____

Name _____ Date _____

Critical Thinking...Reading a Bar Graph

    Graphs organize statistical information in an easy-to-read diagram. The graph on this page is called a **bar graph** because it uses bars to show amounts. Other graphs use different symbols to show amounts. **Line graphs** use indicator lines. **Circle graphs** use parts of circles.

    You begin reading any graph by identifying the information on it. Next, compare the information. What differences in size or amount can you spot? Can you see any patterns in the data? To practice these skills, study the graph below. Then answer the questions that follow.

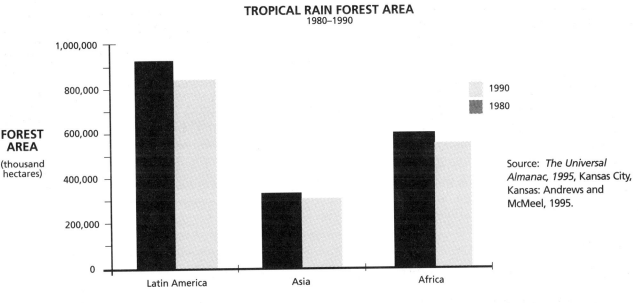

TROPICAL RAIN FOREST AREA
1980–1990

Source: *The Universal Almanac, 1995*, Kansas City, Kansas: Andrews and McMeel, 1995.

1. What is the subject of this graph? _____
2. The horizontal axis is the line on the graph that runs right to left. What information is on the horizontal axis? _____
3. The vertical axis is the line that runs up and down. What information is on the vertical axis?

   _____

4. How much forest area was there in Latin America in 1980? _____ In 1990?

   _____

5. How much forest area was there in Asia in 1980? _____ In 1990?

   _____

6. Which region has the largest amount of tropical rain forest? _____
7. The deforestation of the rain forest refers to cutting down and clearing away the trees that make up the forest. Which region had the largest amount of deforestation between 1980

   and 1990? _____
8. What is one effect of the deforestation of the rain forests? _____

Name _____ Date _____

Critical Thinking...Using a Primary Source

Gabriel García Márquez, a Colombian author, won the Nobel Prize for Literature in 1982. Below is an excerpt from the speech García Márquez delivered when accepting the prize. This excerpt is called a **primary source**. *Primary* means "first" or "original." Speeches are primary sources because they provide a firsthand look at what is in the mind of the writer. Read the speech carefully and answer the questions that follow.

Latin America neither wants, nor has any reason, to be a puppet without a will of its own.

Why do the Western nations respect our originality in literature but mistrust our originality in our attempts at social change? Why do they think the social justice sought by progressive [forward thinking] Europeans is not also the goal of Latin Americans? Why don't they understand that since the conditions are different, the methods must also be different?

No: the immeasurable [large amount of] violence and pain of our history are the result of age-old inequalities and untold bitterness, and not a conspiracy plotted 3,000 miles from our homes [in the Soviet Union]. But many European leaders and thinkers have thought so.

... Faced with this awesome reality, we the inventors of tales, who will believe anything, feel entitled to believe that it is not yet too late for people to try to create a perfect world. A world where no one will be able to decide for others how they die, where love will prove true and happiness be possible, and where the races condemned to one hundred years of solitude will have, at last and forever, a second opportunity on earth.

1. Why was García Márquez giving this speech? _____

2. Why does García Márquez describe Latin America as a "puppet"? _____

_____

3. How do Western nations view Latin America, according to García Márquez?_____

_____

4. (a) What does García Márquez think is the cause of Latin America's violence and pain?

_____

(b) According to García Márquez, what do European leaders think is the cause of this violence and pain?_____

5. What is García Márquez's dream for the future?_____

_____

_____

Name _____ Date _____

Critical Thinking...Debating an Issue

As you read in Case Study 29, people in Quebec, the rest of Canada, and the United States debated whether or not to construct the James Bay II hydroelectric project. Those who supported the project argued that it would be good for the economy of Canada. Those who opposed the project argued that the plant would not only be expensive to build, but it would also destroy Cree culture. Think about what position you might have taken on this issue. Then prepare an argument in support of or opposition to building the project by filling out the chart on this page. Whatever position you take, keep track of the arguments likely to be made by the opposing side.

Issue: Should the James Bay II project be constructed on ancient Cree territory?	
Possible Pro Arguments	**Possible Con Arguments**

Position _____

Argument:
Evidence:

Argument:
Evidence:

Argument:
Evidence:

Summary Argument: I support/oppose building the James Bay II project because

_____

_____

_____

_____

_____

_____

_____

The Land and People of Latin America

Name _____ Date _____

I. Matching Decide which definition in the right column best explains a term in the left column. Then write the letter of that definition in the space next to the term.

_____ 1. mestizo

_____ 2. volcano

_____ 3. tropics

_____ 4. peninsula

_____ 5. moderate

a. lands that are near the equator

b. a mountain from which hot melted rocks, ash, and gases sometimes flow

c. a person who is part Native American and part European

d. mild

e. a body of land that is surrounded on three sides by water

II. Multiple Choice Choose the answer that best completes the sentence or answers the question. Then write the letter of your choice in the space provided.

_____ 6. The grassy plains of South America between the eastern and western highlands are called
   a. llanos or pampas.
   b. the Andes.
   c. the Amazon.
   d. altiplanos.

_____ 7. Which of the following statements about the climate of Latin America is NOT true
   a. Lands that are south of the equator have seasons opposite to those in North America.
   b. Temperatures in the mountains may be cold while those in the valley may be warm.
   c. The climate in all of Latin America is very similar.
   d. Regions near the equator may be very hot while lands far away from the equator can be cold.

_____ 8. The fastest-growing group in Latin America is
   a. people with African backgrounds.
   b. people with European ancestors.
   c. Asian immigrants.
   d. people whose background is a mix of Native American, African, and European ancestry.

_____ 9. Haciendas are found in the
   a. Andes Mountains.
   b. savannas.
   c. Amazon rain forest.
   d. South American deserts.

_____ 10. All of the following products, which are consumed throughout the world, are native to Latin America EXCEPT
   a. tea.
   b. mahogany wood.
   c. coffee.
   d. oil.

III. Essay Write your answer to the following question in paragraph form on a separate sheet of paper.

The geography of any region has an impact on the people who live there. Describe how the landforms of Latin America have affected the lives of Latin American people. Use specific examples to describe how people live in the different climate regions and physical regions of Latin America.

Name _____   Date _____

I. **Matching** Decide which definition in the right column best explains a term in the left column. Then write the letter of that definition in the space next to the term.

_____ 1. nomads

_____ 2. pyramid

_____ 3. aqueduct

_____ 4. glacier

_____ 5. drought

a. a building that is square at its base, has triangular sides, and rises to a point

b. a huge sheet of ice

c. a group of people who have no permanent home but move from place to place in search of food and water

d. a long period without rain

e. pipe that carries water to places where it is needed

II. **Multiple Choice** Choose the answer that best completes the sentence or answers the question. Then write the letter of your choice in the space provided.

_____ 6. Europeans began exploring the Americas in search of

a. good land for farming.
b. riches to send back to Europe.
c. religious freedom.
d. a new way of life.

_____ 7. Mayan people built pyramids to serve as centers of

a. religion.
b. trade.
c. sports and athletic games.
d. learning.

_____ 8. At first, Montezuma thought the light-skinned strangers were

a. enemies of the Aztec people.
b. merchants who would be eager to trade products.
c. ghosts who had come to punish the Aztec people.
d. gods of legend who had come to reward the Aztec people.

_____ 9. Which of the following statements does NOT characterize Incan civilization?

a. The Incas lived in the Amazon rain forest.
b. The Incas were scientific farmers.
c. The Incas were great builders.
d. The Incas worshiped the sun.

_____ 10. The discovery of farming led to ALL of the following changes for Native Americans EXCEPT

a. growth of a nomadic way of life.
b. population increase.
c. growth of larger communities and towns.
d. an increase in the complexity of religion and government.

III. **Essay** Write your answer to the following question in paragraph form on a separate sheet of paper.

The three major ancient civilizations in Latin America grew and expanded in very different ways. Compare the three ancient civilizations of Latin America. How were they similar? How were they different? Which civilization would you have preferred to live in? Explain.

207

Breaking the Grip of the Crown

Name _____ Date _____

I. Matching Decide which definition in the right column best explains a term in the left column. Then write the letter of that definition in the space next to the term.

_____ 1. Creole

_____ 2. Middle Passage

_____ 3. viceroy

_____ 4. peon

_____ 5. mission

a. the journey of slave ships across the Atlantic Ocean

b. a religious settlement devoted to spreading Christianity

c. a person who governs a colony as a representative of the king or queen of Spain

d. a Latin American whose parents or ancestors were Spanish

e. a poor person who works all his or her life for rich landowners

II. Multiple Choice Choose the answer that best completes the sentence or answers the question. Then write the letter of your choice in the space provided.

_____ 6. During Latin America's colonial days, the Roman Catholic Church tried to
   a. convert Native Americans and Africans to Christianity.
   b. protect Native Americans from cruel treatment.
   c. teach the Spanish language and Spanish customs to Native Americans and Africans.
   d. all of the above.

_____ 7. Which of the following shows the social order of Latin American colonies, from highest to lowest class?
   a. Creoles, native Europeans, Native Americans, mestizos and mulattos
   b. native Europeans, mestizos and mulattos, Creoles, Native Americans
   c. native Europeans, Creoles, mestizos and mulattos, Native Americans
   d. mestizos and mulattos, Creoles, native Europeans, Native Americans

_____ 8. Simón Bolívar led the struggle for independence in
   a. the northern part of South America.
   b. the southern part of South America.
   c. Cuba.
   d. Mexico.

_____ 9. All of the following were reasons Latin Americans fought for independence EXCEPT
   a. The viceroy system of government was very rigid.
   b. Colonists wanted an end to slavery.
   c. Colonial governments were corrupt.
   d. People in lower social classes resented the power of the upper class.

_____ 10. U.S. investment in Central American countries resulted in
   a. high paying jobs for Central American people.
   b. economic prosperity for most people in Central America.
   c. greater power for Central American governments.
   d. U.S. domination of Central America for many years.

III. Essay Write your answer to the following question in paragraph form on a separate sheet of paper.

Describe the Latin American struggles for independence from the European powers. Why did Latin Americans want independence? How did they achieve independence? What challenges did Latin Americans face after independence?

Name _____ Date _____

I. Matching Decide which definition in the right column best explains a term in the left column. Then write the letter of that definition in the space next to the term.

_____ 1. urban

_____ 2. dialect

_____ 3. chaperon

_____ 4. liberation theology

_____ 5. squatter

a. a form of a language that belongs to a certain region

b. person who settles on land he or she does not own

c. characteristic of the city or city life

d. a belief that the Roman Catholic Church should take an active role in ending poverty in Latin America

e. an older person who accompanies a boy and girl on a date

II. Multiple Choice Choose the answer that best completes the sentence or answers the question. Then write the letter of your choice in the space provided.

_____ 6. Mega-city is a term used to describe a city where

   a. a large portion of a country's people live.
   b. a region where several large cities are located.
   c. a modern city.
   d. a computer game is used to build simulated cities.

_____ 7. The language of Brazil is

   a. Spanish.
   b. Portuguese.
   c. French.
   d. English.

_____ 8. According to liberation theology,

   a. church officials should run for public office.
   b. the church should not get involved in politics.
   c. the church must take an active role in changing society.
   d. politicians must practice their religion.

_____ 9. All of the following statements are true EXCEPT

   a. many Latin American cultures are a mix of European, African, and Native American cultures.
   b. Latin America is a diverse region.
   c. all Latin Americans speak Spanish, are Roman Catholic, and are poor.
   d. culture includes language, religious beliefs, and foods.

_____ 10. One issue that Latin American farmers face is that

   a. much of the best land is owned by landlords who demand high rents.
   b. farmers often use outdated farming methods.
   c. many farmers move to the cities in search of a better life.
   d. all of the above.

III. Essay Write your answer to the following question in paragraph form on a separate sheet of paper.

As in other parts of the world, many people in Latin America continue to move to cities from rural areas. As a result, Latin America is becoming more urban. Which aspects of Latin American culture do you think will be most affected by the growth of cities? Which traditions do you think will survive? Which might disappear? Explain your answers.

The Changing Face of Latin America

Name _____ **Date** _____

I. Matching Decide which definition in the right column best explains a term in the left column. Then write the letter of that definition in the space next to the term.

_____ 1. illiterate

_____ 2. exile

_____ 3. caudillo

_____ 4. land reform

_____ 5. civilian

a. a government policy that involves breaking up large estates and giving the land to peasants

b. a person who settles in another country because of political disagreements

c. a military strongman

d. citizen who does not belong to the military

e. unable to read and write

II. Multiple Choice Choose the answer that best completes the sentence or answers the question. Then write the letter of your choice in the space provided.

_____ 6. The first Latin American nation to carry out land reform was
   a. Cuba.
   b. Brazil.
   c. Mexico.
   d. Guatemala.

_____ 7. Land reform programs are very hard to enforce for ALL of the following reasons EXCEPT
   a. People prefer to live in cities than own farmland.
   b. People who own large amounts of land strongly resist reform.
   c. Effective land reform programs are very expensive.
   d. Land reform often endangers the rain forest.

_____ 8. The greatest threat to Latin American nations today is
   a. the destruction of the rain forest.
   b. civil war.
   c. military oppression.
   d. poverty.

_____ 9. After independence, power in many Latin American countries was in the hands of
   a. democratic governments.
   b. government bureaucrats.
   c. military strongmen.
   d. middle class workers.

_____ 10. In the Nicaraguan civil war, the United States supported
   a. the Sandanistas.
   b. the contras.
   c. the government.
   d. the peasants.

III. Essay Write your answer to the following question in paragraph form on a separate sheet of paper.

Describe Fidel Castro's rise to power in Cuba. How did he first come to power? Why did his message appeal to Cuban peasants? What effect has Castro's rule had on the Cuban people? What effect has his rule had on Cuban relations with the United States and the rest of the world?

Name _____ Date _____

I. Matching Decide which definition in the right column best explains a term in the left column. Then write the letter of that definition in the space next to the term.

_____ 1. tariff

_____ 2. commonwealth

_____ 3. extract

_____ 4. mural

_____ 5. gunboat diplomacy

a. a self-governing state with close ties to another more powerful state

b. a foreign policy that calls for threatening the use of force to achieve a country's goals

c. a tax on goods entering or leaving a country

d. to remove or take from

e. a large painting or photograph that is applied to a wall or ceiling

II. Multiple Choice Choose the answer that best completes the sentence or answers the question. Then write the letter of your choice in the space provided.

_____ 6. The Monroe Doctrine stated that
  a. the United States would not interfere in Latin American affairs.
  b. the United States would help defend Latin American countries against European nations.
  c. the United States would step in if Latin American countries could not pay their debts to other nations.
  d. the United States would build a canal through Panama.

_____ 7. The United States supported revolutions to overthrow socialist or Communist governments in ALL of the following countries EXCEPT
  a. Mexico.
  b. Chile.
  c. Nicaragua.
  d. Cuba.

_____ 8. Members of the Organization of American States work for
  a. increased trade with the United States and Canada.
  b. the peaceful settlements of disputes in the Americas.
  c. an end to the destruction of the rain forest.
  d. uniting all Latin American nations under one government.

_____ 9. Common themes among Latin American writers and artists include
  a. Latin American history.
  b. causes of the poor.
  c. the world as unstable and insecure.
  d. all of the above.

_____ 10. Today Puerto Rico is a
  a. state of the United States.
  b. completely independent from the United States.
  c. a commonwealth of the United States.
  d. a member of a federation with other Caribbean nations.

III. Essay Write your answer to the following question in paragraph form on a separate sheet of paper.

The relationship between Latin America and the United States has been characterized by anger, distrust, and bloodshed. What effect has U.S. policy had on Latin America since its independence? Why does Latin America resent the United States for interfering in its affairs? Use at least one example to show the relationship between these two regions.

211

Name _____ Date _____

I. Matching
Decide which definition in the right column best explains a term in the left column. Then write the letter of that definition in the space next to the term.

_____ 1. province

_____ 2. bilingualism

_____ 3. federal system

_____ 4. hydroelectricity

_____ 5. mosaic

a. a design made up of many small pieces of material
b. a territory governed as an administrative or political unit of a country
c. power that comes from the force of rushing water
d. the policy of recognizing two official languages
e. government power divided between a central government and local governments

II. Multiple Choice
Choose the answer that best completes the sentence or answers the question. Then write the letter of your choice in the space provided.

_____ 6. Which of the following statements does NOT characterize the land of Canada?
   a. It is one of the largest countries in the world.
   b. Geographic barriers isolate pockets of people from one another.
   c. It has few natural resources.
   d. Generally, winters are long and cold, while summers are short and cool.

_____ 7. The first Europeans who successfully set up colonies in Canada came from
   a. Spain.
   b. Scandinavia.
   c. France.
   d. England.

_____ 8. All of the following had an effect on the culture of Native Americans in Canada EXCEPT
   a. missionaries trying to convert Native Americans to Christianity.
   b. disease brought by Europeans.
   c. settlers eager for good farmland.
   d. slavery on plantations.

_____ 9. Most of the people of Canada
   a. live in rural areas.
   b. live close to the U.S. border.
   c. are scattered over the entire country.
   d. speak French.

_____ 10. Which of the following regions has tried to gain its independence from the rest of Canada?
   a. Quebec
   b. Ontario
   c. the Maritime Provinces
   d. the Prairie Provinces

III. Essay
Write your answer to the following question in paragraph form on a separate sheet of paper.

Describe in detail the relationship between English and French Canadians. What is the history of the relationship? How does each group feel about the other? What is the current status of the relationship?

212

Focus on Latin America and Canada

Name _____ Date _____

I. Fill in the Blank Complete each sentence below by writing the correct term in the blank. You will not use all the terms.

culture	mestizo	irrigation	viceroy	squatter	caudillo
commonwealth		tariffs	bilingualism	immune	exiles

1. A major Native American development in farming was _____, a system of human-made ditches that carry water from streams to fields.

2. Puerto Rico is a _____ of the United States, a self-governing state with close ties to another more powerful state.

3. _____ is the way of life of a group of people, including their ideas, customs, skills, and arts.

4. Canada's policy of _____ recognizes French and English as the country's two official languages.

5. Each Latin American colony was ruled by a _____, who governed the colony as a representative of the king or queen.

6. The United States supported an invasion of Guatemala in 1954 led by Guatemalan

   _____, people who live in another country because of political disagreements.

7. A _____ is a very poor person who goes to a city and lives on land he or she doesn't own.

8. Latin Americans are working together to improve their economies by lowering

   _____, or taxes on goods entering or leaving each country.

II. Multiple Choice Choose the answer that best completes the sentence or answers the question. Then write the letter of your choice in the space provided.

_____ 9. The relationship between Latin America and the United States is best characterized by
   a. mutual trust and respect.
   b. Latin American resentment over U.S. meddling in its affairs.
   c. Latin America having the upper hand.
   d. little involvement of either region in the other's affairs.

_____ 10. The greatest threat to a united Canada today is
   a. border disputes between Canada and the United States.
   b. Great Britain asserting its power over Canada.
   c. the rivalry between French speakers and English speakers.
   d. territorial disputes between Native Americans and Canadians.

ETHNIC GROUPS IN SOME LATIN AMERICAN COUNTRIES

Argentina
| 85% European | 15% Mestizo |

Brazil
| 55% European | 39% Mulatto | 6% African |

Guatemala
| 55% Native American | 45% Mestizo |

Guyana
| 51% Asian | 43% African | 6% Other |

Mexico
| 60% Mestizo | 30% Indian | 10% European |

Source: *World Almanac*, 1995.

_____ 11. Which of the following was NOT a result of the struggle for independence in Latin America?
   a. People who had been thrown off their land flocked to the cities.
   b. Latin America was unified into one large republic.
   c. Spain lost control of all its colonies except Cuba and Puerto Rico.
   d. The Creoles became the new ruling class.

_____ 12. The two European countries that claimed the most land in Latin America were
   a. Britain and France.
   b. Spain and Portugal.
   c. the United States and the Netherlands.
   d. Britain and Spain.

_____ 13. Which ancient Latin American civilization was known for its harsh treatment of the people it conquered?
   a. Guatemalan   c. Aztec
   b. Mayan   d. Incan

III. Analyzing a Chart Answer questions 14–16 based on the chart above.

_____ 14. Which country has the highest percentage of Europeans?
   a. Argentina   c. Guatemala
   b. Brazil   d. Mexico

_____ 15. Which country has a mixture of Europeans, mulattos and Africans?
   a. Argentina   c. Guatemala
   b. Brazil   d. Mexico

_____ 16. What percentage of Mexicans is of mixed European and Native American descent?
   a. 10 percent   c. 60 percent
   b. 30 percent   d. 100 percent

IV. Essay Answer the following questions in paragraph form on a separate sheet of paper.

17. Explain the causes and effects of the following issues in Latin America: (a) the movement of people from rural areas to cities and (b) Latin American and U.S. relations.

18. Discuss colonization and independence movements in Latin America. How and why did Europeans conquer Latin America? How did most of Latin America win its independence?

Name _____ Date _____

Exploring Regional Issues...Comparing Circle Graphs

Study the circle graph below. It shows crude oil production in the Western Hemisphere. Using the data provided, create a circle graph that shows crude oil production in the Middle East. When you have completed the circle graph, answer the questions that follow.

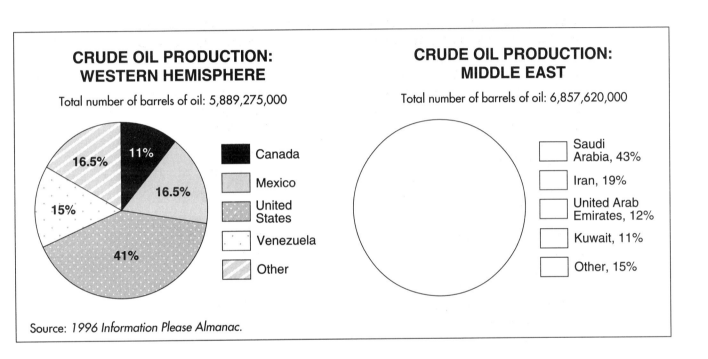

CRUDE OIL PRODUCTION: WESTERN HEMISPHERE

Total number of barrels of oil: 5,889,275,000

- 11%
- 16.5%
- 16.5%
- 15%
- 41%

- ■ Canada
- ☐ Mexico
- ☐ United States
- ☐ Venezuela
- ▨ Other

CRUDE OIL PRODUCTION: MIDDLE EAST

Total number of barrels of oil: 6,857,620,000

- ☐ Saudi Arabia, 43%
- ☐ Iran, 19%
- ☐ United Arab Emirates, 12%
- ☐ Kuwait, 11%
- ☐ Other, 15%

Source: *1996 Information Please Almanac.*

1. (a) What percentage of the oil produced in the Western Hemisphere does Venezuela produce? _____

   (b) What percentage of the oil produced in the Middle East does Iran produce? _____

2. (a) Which country listed in the Western Hemisphere produces the most oil? _____

   (b) Which country listed in the Middle East produces the most oil? _____

3. (a) Which country listed in the Western Hemisphere produces the least oil? _____

   (b) Which country listed in the Middle East produces the least oil? _____

Name _____ Date _____

On Assignment...Giving a Talk

Your assignment is to give a talk to people who will be visiting the Middle East. Your talk will focus on the land and the people of the region. To prepare for your talk, you must organize the notes you took while you read the chapter. Use the questions and the cluster map below to help you.

1. List three important facts about the land of the Middle East. _____

_____

_____

2. List two facts about the climate of the region. _____

_____

3. What languages do people in the region speak? _____

4. What are the cities of the region like? _____

5. Are there any pictures or maps I would like to show during my presentation? _____

_____

_____

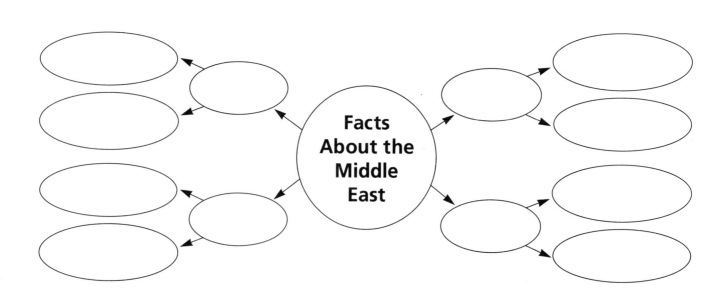

Organize the ideas in your cluster map into an outline from which you may write your talk.

Name _____ Date _____

On Assignment...Creating a Time Line

Your task is to create a time line of events in Middle Eastern history. Use the organizer below to help you list your ideas for each section of the chapter. If there is not enough space under a section, use the back of this worksheet or a separate sheet of paper. After you have listed all the events and dates, create a time line for the entire chapter on a long sheet of paper.

SECTION 1: CIVILIZATION BETWEEN THE RIVERS

Events	Dates
1.	
2.	
3.	
4.	

SECTION 2: CIVILIZATION IN EGYPT

Events	Dates
1.	
2.	
3.	
4.	

SECTION 3: JUDAISM AND CHRISTIANITY

Events	Dates
1.	
2.	
3.	
4.	

SECTION 4: THE GROWTH OF ISLAM

Events	Dates
1.	
2.	
3.	
4.	

SECTION 5: ISLAM AND THE WORLD

Events	Dates
1.	
2.	
3.	
4.	

Name _____ Date _____

On Assignment...Creating a Mural

Your assignment is to create a mural showing events in the Middle East from the late 1700s to World War II. A mural is a very large wall painting that often shows a series of historical events. To get ideas for your mural, scan the pictures in your text. You may also wish to use picture books from your school or local library. Below is an organizer that provides space for you to sketch ideas about events in the chapter. Some events from the chapter are listed beneath the box. After you are satisfied with your sketches, transfer them to a large sheet of paper.

Ottoman Empire   Egypt and   Young Turks   British and French in
                              Muhammad Ali   meet in secret   the Middle East

Oil is discovered in   Iran and the shah   Egypt and Nasser   Israel is founded
the Middle East

Global Studies. Copyright © **Globe Fearon Educational Publisher.** *All rights reserved.*

Name _____ Date _____

On Assignment...Writing Letters From the Middle East

Travelers often write letters to family and friends describing what they have seen and done on their trips. Your assignment is to write letters describing your travels through the Middle East. First, decide where you have been and who you have seen. The On Assignment hint boxes suggest several possibilities. Use these suggestions or come up with your own. List at least three situations below.

WHERE I WAS	WHO I VISITED
1.	
2.	
3.	

Next, decide one thing you would say about each of these places in your letters. Use information in your text and information you can find in other library or classroom resources.

1. _____

2. _____

3. _____

Begin to write your first letter on the lines below. Remember, after you complete your letters, write an introduction that ties the letters together.

Dear _____ ,

I can't believe I'm really in _____ ! Today, I saw _____

_____

_____

_____

_____

_____

_____

Name _____ Date _____

On Assignment...Creating A Radio Report

For this chapter, you have been asked to create a radio report about recent changes in the Middle East. Below is an outline listing major changes in the Middle East. Under each change, there is space for you to write at least three ways that it has affected the region. Make additional notes on the back of this worksheet. Use your outline and notes to create your radio report.

1. Changes brought about by the discovery of oil

   a. _____

   _____

   b. _____

   _____

   c. _____

   _____

2. Changes brought about by urban growth

   a. _____

   _____

   b. _____

   _____

   c. _____

   _____

3. Women in the Middle East: Changes and Traditions

   a. _____

   _____

   b. _____

   _____

   c. _____

   _____

Global Studies. Copyright **© Globe Fearon Educational Publisher.** *All rights reserved.*

Name _____ Date _____

On Assignment...Creating a Picture Book for Young Children

Your assignment is to create a picture book about the Middle East for young children. The topic of the picture book is how economics and politics have shaped the Middle East. Begin by brainstorming ideas for possible chapters to include in the book. Use the cluster map below to help you organize your ideas.

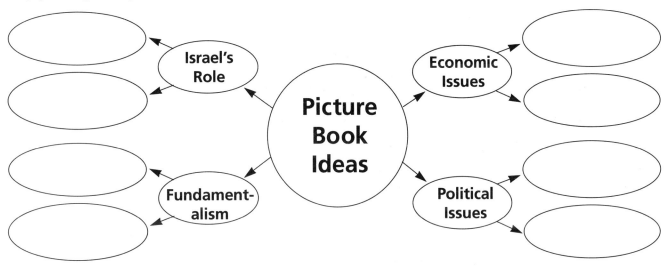

Choose the best ideas and list three chapters for your picture book below.

Chapter 1: _____

Chapter 2: _____

Chapter 3: _____

On the mini-pages below, think about how you will organize your book. What pages will have pictures on them? What pages will have writing?

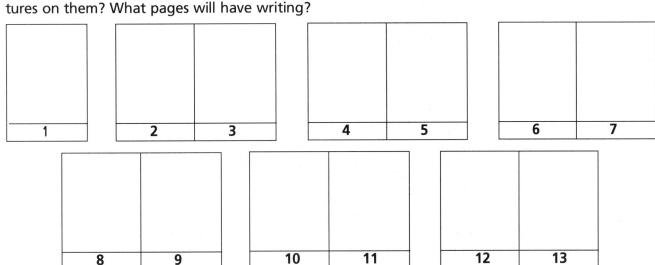

Name _____   Date _____

On Assignment...Writing a Feature Story

Your assignment is to write a feature story about a current issue in the Middle East. Review the On Assignment hint boxes in Chapter 36 for ideas about questions to ask. Use these ideas or think of some of your own. Work with a partner. Use the diagram below to brainstorm at least three questions for Section 1 in the chapter.

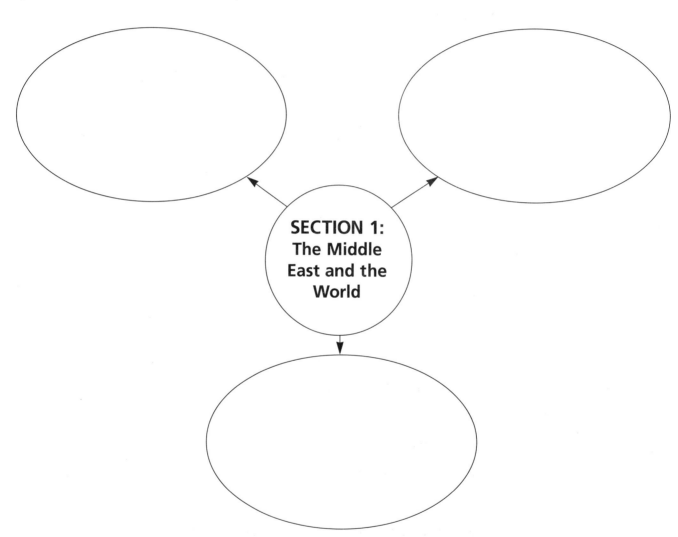

SECTION 1: The Middle East and the World

Copy a similar diagram into your notebook and write questions for sections 2, 3, and 4 and for the Case Study. After you have written questions for all the sections, choose one section from the chapter on which to focus. List the questions on a sheet of paper and review them. Have you asked questions about important issues in the region? Are questions phrased in a clear, direct way? Check the spelling and grammar of your questions. Revise any questions you do not like and add new questions. Then, use your text and library resources to create answers to your questions. Now, write your feature story. Include a headline and some pictures.

Name _____ Date _____

Critical Thinking...Interpreting a Map

The geography of the Middle East has had an important impact on its people. The map below shows the way the country of Egypt uses its land. Study the map and answer the questions that follow.

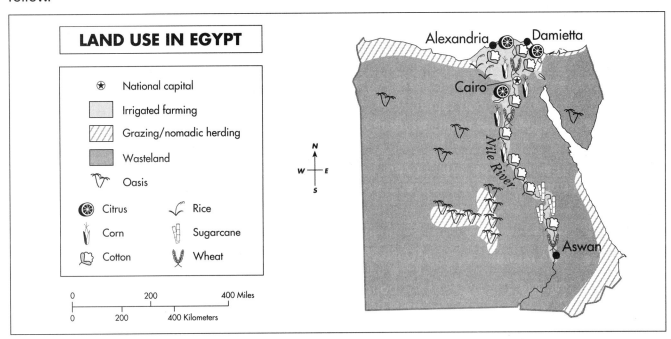

1. What information does the map provide? _____

2. What is the capital of Egypt? _____

3. What is the major river running north-south through Egypt? _____

4. Name three of the main agricultural products produced in Egypt. _____

_____

5. Where does most of the agricultural production in Egypt take place? _____

6. Why do you suppose that most of Egypt's agricultural production takes place where it does?

_____

_____

7. Which of the following is most common in Egypt: irrigated farming, rough

grazing/nomadic herding, or wasteland? _____

Name _____ Date _____

Critical Thinking...Understanding the Sequence of Events

The sequence in which things happen in history is often important. An event may come before another, come after another, or events may occur at the same time. A *time line* presents events in *chronological,* or time, order. Below is a list of events that occurred in the Middle East and around the world from about 5000 B.C. to about 300 B.C. Place these events on the time line below and answer the questions that follow.

MIDDLE EAST

1450 B.C.	Hittites produce iron.
3100 B.C.	Menes becomes the first pharaoh of Egypt.
334 B.C.	Alexander the Great conquers Persia.
1750 B.C.	Hammurabi's laws are enacted in Babylon.
5000 B.C.	Civilizations develop in the Tigris and Euphrates river valleys.
1100 B.C.	The Phoenicians develop an alphabet.
600 B.C.	Cyrus the Great expands the Persian Empire from India to Egypt.
2500 B.C.	Sargon I creates the world's first empire.

ELSEWHERE

450 B.C.	Athens in Greece reaches height of power.
3000 B.C.	Minoan civilization emerges on Crete.
1200 B.C.	Olmec civilization arises in Mexico.
2000 B.C.	The Shang becomes the first dynasty in China.
725 B.C.	Kingdom of Kush in Africa conquers Egypt.
2500 B.C.	Indus valley civilization begins in South Asia.
500 B.C.	Romans establish a republic.

5000 B.C.	4000 B.C.	3000 B.C.	2000 B.C.	1000 B.C.	500 B.C.	300 B.C.

1. Who was the first pharaoh of Egypt? _____

2. Which people developed an alphabet? _____

3. Who conquered Persia? _____

4. (a) Where in the Middle East did the first civilizations develop? _____
   (b) Did the Shang become China's first dynasty before or after the first civilizations developed
   in the Middle East? _____

5. When Sargon I established the world's first empire, what was happening in South Asia?

_____

Name _____ Date _____

Critical Thinking...Understanding Cause and Effect

Understanding cause and effect is an important part of understanding history. To identify cause and effect, keep these tips in mind. A **cause** produces a result, or an effect. An **effect** is the result of a cause. To discover the causes of an event, ask yourself: "Why did this event happen?" To discover the effects of an event, ask yourself: "What happened as a result of this event?" The chart lists events that you read about in Chapter 32. For each event, use the information in the chapter to fill in the cause, the effect, or both. The first entry is filled in as an example.

CAUSE	EVENT	EFFECT
Suleiman wants to rid Asia of Christian rule.	The Ottomans take Constantinople. **Date:** 1453	Ottomans rename the city Istanbul.
1.	Ottoman Empire falls into decline. **Date:** 1600s	Countries break away from the Ottoman Empire.
2. Muhammad Ali slaughters his opponents.	Muhammad Ali wins control of Egypt. **Date:** early 1800s	
3.	The Crimean War is fought. **Date:** _____	
4.	Arabs support Britain and France during World War II. **Date:** _____	Britain and France carve up Arab territory into mandates.
5. Scientists discover oil in Saudi Arabia.	Oil is discovered in the Middle East. **Date:** 1920s	
6.	Reza Khan becomes shah of Iran. **Date:** _____	
7.	Gamal Nasser rises to power in Egypt. **Date:** 1952	
8. Jews wanted to establish a homeland.	Israel declares its independence. **Date:** 1948	

Name _____ Date _____

Critical Thinking...Understanding Vocabulary

In this chapter, you read about Arab culture. Skim through the chapter, paying special attention to the terms or words in boldface type. Write a short definition of each word below. Then, in the space provided, illustrate two of the words.

1. headman _____

2. suq _____

3. tradition _____

4. purdah _____

5. hospitality _____

6. Ramadan _____

WORD: _____   WORD: _____

Global Studies. Copyright © **Globe Fearon Educational Publisher.** *All rights reserved.*

Name _____ Date _____

Critical Thinking...Analyzing a Bar Graph

Graphs organize statistical information in an easy-to-read diagram. The graph on this page is called a **bar graph** because it uses bars to show amounts.

You begin reading any graph by identifying the information on it. Next, compare this information. What differences in size or amount can you spot? Can you see any patterns in the data? To practice these skills, study the graph below. Then answer the questions that follow.

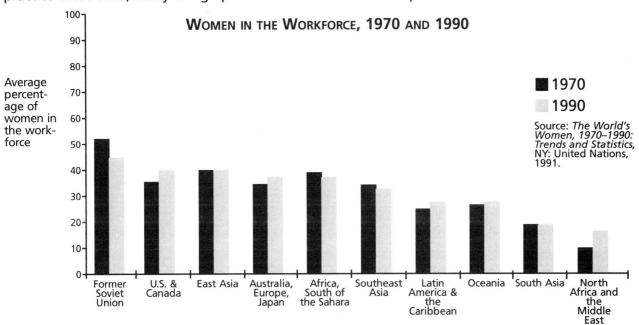

WOMEN IN THE WORKFORCE, 1970 AND 1990

1. What is the title of this graph? _____
2. Which region had the highest percentage of women in the workforce in both 1970 and 1990?

   _____
3. Which region had the lowest percentage of women in the workforce in both 1970 and 1990?

   _____
4. On average, did the number of women in the workforce in the world rise or fall between

   1970 and 1990? _____
5. Which region experienced the greatest increase in the percentage of women in the work-

   force between 1970 and 1990? _____
6. How does the number of women in the workforce in the Middle East and North Africa com-

   pare to the rest of the world? _____
7. Based on the information in this graph, what predictions would you make about women in

   the workforce in the Middle East and North Africa? _____

   _____

Name _____ **Date** _____

Critical Thinking...Interpreting a Poem

Poetry often represents what is in the heart and mind of its writer. Below is a poem written by a young Jewish poet named Gersham Ben-Avraham. The title of the poem is "Drive." It is about the fighting between Jewish and Arab settlers in the Middle East. Read the poem carefully, answering the questions that follow.

It may seem the point of no return
We passed some time ago
The wages of war duly earned
Though the price was hardly low
Time we have in uncertain measure
It waits not for you and I
The life we're given, a priceless treasure
The greatest loss is not to try
So look up, the stars still shine
And day still follows night
In the end we'll all be fine
As long as someone keeps up the fight

1. In the poem, Ben-Avraham refers to "we" several times. Who do you think "we" means?

   _____

2. Would you say that Ben-Avraham has hope for the future? Why or why not? _____

   _____

3. What does the author mean when he says, "....though the price was hardly low"? _____

   _____

4. In your own words, describe the main idea of the poem. _____

   _____

5. Imagine you are a Muslim living in the Middle East. How does this poem make you feel? Do

   you agree or disagree with the author? _____

   _____

   _____

   _____

Name _____ Date _____

Critical Thinking...Analyzing a Pie Graph

Graphs organize statistical information in an easy-to-read diagram. The graph on this page is called a **pie graph** because it uses parts of a circle, or pie, to show amounts or percentages.

You begin reading any graph by identifying the information on it. Next, compare this information. What differences in size or amount can you spot? Can you see any patterns in the data? To practice these skills, study the graphs below. Then answer the questions that follow.

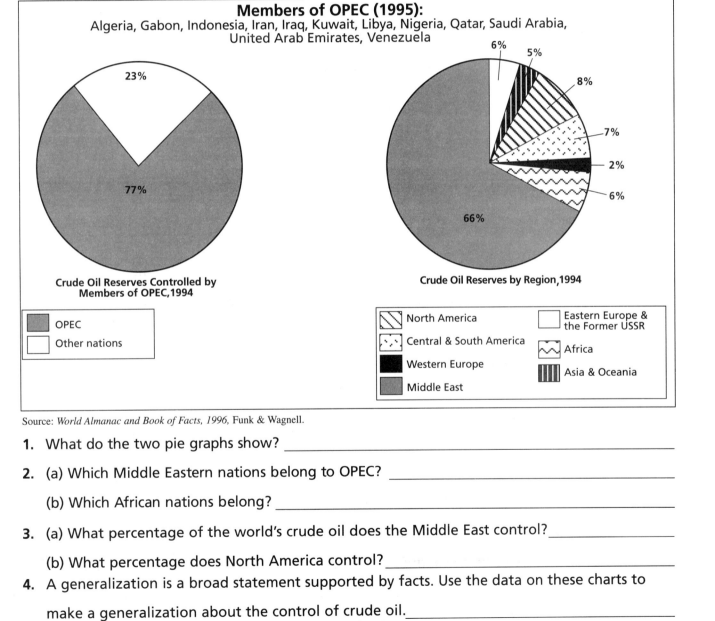

Members of OPEC (1995):
Algeria, Gabon, Indonesia, Iran, Iraq, Kuwait, Libya, Nigeria, Qatar, Saudi Arabia, United Arab Emirates, Venezuela

Crude Oil Reserves Controlled by
Members of OPEC,1994

OPEC
Other nations

Crude Oil Reserves by Region,1994

North America
Central & South America
Western Europe
Middle East
Eastern Europe & the Former USSR
Africa
Asia & Oceania

Source: *World Almanac and Book of Facts, 1996,* Funk & Wagnell.

1. What do the two pie graphs show? _____

2. (a) Which Middle Eastern nations belong to OPEC? _____

   (b) Which African nations belong? _____

3. (a) What percentage of the world's crude oil does the Middle East control? _____

   (b) What percentage does North America control? _____

4. A generalization is a broad statement supported by facts. Use the data on these charts to

   make a generalization about the control of crude oil. _____

_____

229

The Land and People of the Middle East

Name _____ Date _____

I. **Matching** Decide which definition in the right column best explains a term in the left column. Then write the letter of that definition in the space next to the term.

_____ 1. migrate
_____ 2. oasis
_____ 3. kibbutz
_____ 4. refugee
_____ 5. mosque

a. to move from one place to another
b. a person who is forced to leave his or her country
c. an Islamic house of worship
d. a place in the desert where water comes to the surface
e. a farm in Israel where the land is owned by everyone who farms it

II. **Multiple Choice** Choose the answer that best completes the sentence or answers the question. Then write the letter of your choice in the space provided.

_____ 6. The mountains of the Middle East are
   a. very hot and dry.
   b. fertile farming areas.
   c. important because their streams carry fertile soil to the valleys.
   d. home to many large ski areas.

_____ 7. Middle Eastern countries such as Saudi Arabia and Kuwait have become very wealthy through trade in
   a. oil.
   b. automobiles.
   c. cattle.
   d. diamonds.

_____ 8. The Arabic language
   a. is only spoken in Saudi Arabia.
   b. is only spoken in North Africa.
   c. has created divisions among Middle Easterners.
   d. is a cultural bond that links most of the people of the Middle East.

_____ 9. Which of the following is NOT true about the population of the Middle East?
   a. It is growing very quickly.
   b. Many people are moving from one place to another.
   c. People are moving from the country to cities.
   d. The population is declining.

_____ 10. The "ribbons of green" that cut through the Middle East, such as the one along the Tigris and the Euphrates, are
   a. large underground pools of oil.
   b. mountains.
   c. fertile river valleys.
   d. deserts.

III. **Essay** Write your answer to the following question in paragraph form on a separate sheet of paper.

   Although they live in many different countries, the people of the Middle East are tied together primarily by two cultural bonds. What are these two bonds? Describe how these bonds link Middle Easterners.

Global Studies. Copyright © **Globe Fearon Educational Publisher.** *All rights reserved.*

Chapter 31 Test   *The Rich Heritage of the Middle East*

Name _____   Date _____

I. Matching Decide which definition in the right column best explains a term in the left column. Then write the letter of that definition in the space next to the term.

_____ 1. pilgrimage

_____ 2. covenant

_____ 3. pharaoh

_____ 4. hieroglyphics

_____ 5. city-state

a. an agreement or contract

b. a form of writing in ancient Egypt that used characters that look like pictures

c. a journey that a believer makes to a religious site

d. a ruler of ancient Egypt

e. a large community that has its own government and controls the land around it

II. Multiple Choice Choose the answer that best completes the sentence or answers the question. Then write the letter of your choice in the space provided.

_____ 6. Mesopotamia grew and prospered primarily as a result of
a. the growth of Islam.
b. Hammurabi's laws.
c. advancements in farming techniques.
d. the strong rule of the pharaoh.

_____ 7. Which of the following was NOT a contribution of Sumerian society?
a. the calendar
b. the wheel
c. the sail
d. the Islamic religion

_____ 8. The Egyptian form of writing is called
a. hieroglyphics.
b. pyramids.
c. papyrus.
d. pharaoh.

_____ 9. Just as Mesopotamia developed around the Tigris and the Euphrates rivers, Egypt developed around
a. the Nile River.
b. the Fertile Crescent.
c. the Jordan River.
d. Alexander the Great.

_____ 10. The Islamic religion is based on
a. the teachings of the pharaoh.
b. the teachings of the prophet Muhammad.
c. the life of Alexander the Great.
d. the Tigris and Euphrates.

III. Essay Write your answer to the following question in paragraph form on a separate sheet of paper.

Three world religions have their roots in the Middle East: Judaism, Christianity, and Islam. Choose two of these religions and describe how each of them began and developed in the Middle East.

Name _____ **Date** _____

I. Matching
Decide which definition in the right column best explains a term in the left column. Then write the letter of that definition in the space next to the term.

_____ 1. Industrial Revolution

_____ 2. Holocaust

_____ 3. ethnic group

_____ 4. anti-Semitism

_____ 5. corrupt

a. the change from goods made by hand to goods made by machine

b. a large group of people with the same cultural background

c. the systematic slaughter of approximately six million Jews by the Nazis during World War II

d. dishonest

e. prejudice against Jews

II. Multiple Choice
Choose the answer that best completes the sentence or answers the question. Then write the letter of your choice in the space provided.

_____ 6. The city of Istanbul was the capital of
   a. Egypt.
   b. the Ottoman Empire.
   c. the Nile.
   d. Saudi Arabia.

_____ 7. Mustafa Kemal, Reza Shah Pahlavi, and Colonel Gamal Nasser were all
   a. Young Turks.
   b. Western politicians.
   c. leaders of the Ottoman Empire.
   d. Middle Eastern leaders who tried to bring reform to their countries.

_____ 8. The Young Turks
   a. built the Suez Canal.
   b. started the Industrial Revolution.
   c. were followers of Muhammad Ali.
   d. were a group of army officers who hoped to restore the glory of the Ottoman Empire.

_____ 9. Which of the following is NOT a reason for the decline of the Ottoman Empire?
   a. the Holocaust
   b. superior weapons of the Europeans
   c. new trade routes used by Europeans
   d. the Industrial Revolution

_____ 10. The discovery of oil in the Middle East increased the importance of the Suez Canal because
   a. the canal had to be destroyed to get to the oil.
   b. the Suez Canal was the largest pool of oil in the Middle East.
   c. the canal was important in transporting the oil.
   d. the canal was owned by Iraq.

III. Essay
Write your answer to the following question in paragraph form on a separate sheet of paper.

In Turkey, Iran, and Egypt during the 1900s, leaders took power and made reforms in their countries. What were some of the reforms that these leaders made? How did "traditionalists" react to these reforms?

Name _____   Date _____

I. Matching Decide which definition in the right column best explains a term in the left column. Then write the letter of that definition in the space next to the term.

_____ 1. tradition
_____ 2. Ramadan
_____ 3. headman
_____ 4. purdah
_____ 5. hospitality

a. the holiest month in the Islamic calendar
b. generous treatment of guests
c. the practice of keeping women hidden from view
d. behavior handed down from generation to generation
e. the leader of a village

II. Multiple Choice Choose the answer that best completes the sentence or answers the question. Then write the letter of your choice in the space provided.

_____ 6. Most cities in the Middle East
   a. have only been built during the last 50 years.
   b. have existed for thousands of years.
   c. are getting smaller.
   d. are located only in the deserts.

_____ 7. The nomadic people of the Middle East
   a. live in cities.
   b. live in villages.
   c. wander through the desert.
   d. use technology to find food in the desert.

_____ 8. The holiest book in the Islamic religion is
   a. Ramadan.
   b. suq.
   c. the Koran.
   d. purdah.

_____ 9. In traditional Middle Eastern marriages
   a. it is expected that couples will fall in love before they decide to marry.
   b. the most important concern is that the marriage be good for the families of the bride and groom.
   c. a woman may marry up to four men.
   d. couples date for a long time before they decide to get married.

_____ 10. If you were to eat at a Muslim family's table, you could be served all of the following EXCEPT
   a. lamb.
   b. rice.
   c. coffee.
   d. pork.

III. Essay Write your answer to the following question in paragraph form on a separate sheet of paper.

   Preserving tradition is very important to many Middle Eastern people. Describe some of the traditions that are important to people living in cities, villages, and the desert. Be sure to use specific examples.

233

Changing Patterns of Life

Name _____   **Date** _____

I. Matching Decide which definition in the right column best explains a term in the left column. Then write the letter of that definition in the space next to the term.

_____ **1.** morality

_____ **2.** emir

_____ **3.** fundamentalists

_____ **4.** literacy

_____ **5.** public works

a. the ability to read and write

b. specific rules about proper behavior

c. projects which are done for the good of all citizens, such as building hospitals

d. people who oppose modern ideas and favor a return to strict religious values

e. an Arab ruler

II. Multiple Choice Choose the answer that best completes the sentence or answers the question. Then write the letter of your choice in the space provided.

_____ **6.** The island nation of Bahrain has made most of its wealth through

    a. the sale of sugar cane.

    b. fishing.

    c. international trading in diamonds.

    d. the sale of oil.

_____ **7.** Most of the people who work in low-paying jobs in oil-rich countries are

    a. women.

    b. foreigners.

    c. uneducated.

    d. treated very well by their employers.

_____ **8.** Most of the people of the Middle East are

    a. very poor.

    b. wealthy from trading in oil.

    c. Christians.

    d. thinking of immigrating to the West for higher paying jobs.

_____ **9.** The growth of Middle Eastern cities as a result of the oil boom occurred

    a. during the early 1800s.

    b. in the middle of the 20th century.

    c. during the 1990s.

    d. during the early 1900s.

_____ **10.** The role of women in the Middle East

    a. is the same in every Middle Eastern nation.

    b. varies from country to country, depending on the influence of Islam.

    c. has not changed in the last 50 years.

    d. none of the above.

III. Essay Write your answer to the following question in paragraph form on a separate sheet of paper.

"The discovery of large deposits of oil under some Middle Eastern nations has both helped and hurt those nations." Do you agree or disagree with this statement? Explain in detail your point of view.

Global Studies. Copyright © **Globe Fearon Educational Publisher.** *All rights reserved.*

Name _____   Date _____

I. Matching

Decide which definition in the right column best explains a term in the left column. Then write the letter of that definition in the space next to the term.

_____ 1. peninsula   a. not having to do with religion

_____ 2. sabras   b. Jewish people who were born in Israel

_____ 3. Knesset   c. a body of land surrounded on three sides by water

_____ 4. secular   d. sent to other countries for sale

_____ 5. exported   e. the governing body of Israel

II. Multiple Choice

Choose the answer that best completes the sentence or answers the question. Then write the letter of your choice in the space provided.

_____ 6. Camp David

a. is a vacation place for Middle Eastern oil tycoons.

b. is the first city that was constructed after Israel was formed.

c. is the place where Jimmy Carter, Anwar Sadat, and Menachim Begin met to hold peace talks.

d. none of the above.

_____ 7. The main source of Israel's population growth after 1948 was

a. the baby boom.

b. immigration.

c. the fact that more people got married at younger ages.

d. an exodus of Arabs from Palestine.

_____ 8. The Six Day War

a. was a major blow to the Israelis.

b. established the nation of Israel.

c. was a major blow to the Arab nations of the Middle East.

d. had no "winners" or "losers."

_____ 9. After the Ayotollah Khomeini took power in Iran, the country

a. became the center of Islamic fundamentalism.

b. became more secular.

c. waged war on Kuwait.

d. became an ally of the United States.

_____ 10. Which of the following is NOT a major problem facing Middle Eastern nations?

a. rate of population growth

b. lack of food

c. distribution of wealth

d. trade embargoes

III. Essay

Write your answer to the following question in paragraph form on a separate sheet of paper.

As you have read, religion has always been an important force in the Middle East. Recently, fundamentalist groups have called for a return to traditional Islamic values. Discuss some of the issues that fundamentalists find important. How are relations with the West affected by the fundamentalist movements in the Middle East?

The Middle East in the World Today

Name _____ Date _____

I. Matching
Decide which definition in the right column best explains a term in the left column. Then write the letter of that definition in the space next to the term.

_____ 1. minaret

_____ 2. sanction

_____ 3. intifada

_____ 4. calligraphy

_____ 5. consumers

a. creative and beautiful handwriting

b. people who purchase and use products

c. an uprising against Israel by Palestinians

d. a large tower near a mosque from which Muslims are called to prayer

e. a decision to cut off trade with another country

II. Multiple Choice
Choose the answer that best completes the sentence or answers the question. Then write the letter of your choice in the space provided.

_____ 6. OPEC is
a. an organization that fights against Israel.
b. a terrorist organization.
c. a group trying to organize peace in the Middle East.
d. an organization of oil exporting nations.

_____ 7. The Arab oil embargo occurred
a. in 1965.
b. after World War II.
c. in 1973.
d. in 1993.

_____ 8. Nearly _____ Arabs were killed during the Iran-Iraq War.
a. ten thousand
b. one-hundred thousand
c. one million
d. ten million

_____ 9. Muammar al-Qaddafi, head of the Libyan government,
a. nationalized Libyan banks.
b. built new roads, airports, and schools for his nation.
c. supported Arab terrorist attacks against Israel.
d. all of the above.

_____ 10. Arabsat refers to
a. satellites that link Arab nations together.
b. Israel's nuclear arsenal.
c. an ancient Islamic practice.
d. a city in Saudi Arabia.

III. Essay
Write your answer to the following question in paragraph form on a separate sheet of paper.

As the 20th century draws to an end, Arab nations have begun to look less at the issues that divide their nations, and more toward a program of cooperation. Discuss some of the different methods of cooperation that exist among Middle Eastern nations.

Name _____   **Date** _____

I. Fill in the Blank Complete each sentence below by writing the correct term in the blank. You will not use all the terms.

protectorate	intifada	nomads	immigration	hieroglyphics
fundamentalists	nationalism	sanction	embargo	pilgrimage

1. Some Middle Easterners are _____, people who have no permanent home and travel from place to place in search of food and water.

2. The ancient Egyptian form of writing, called _____, used characters that looked like pictures.

3. The fifth pillar of Islam is a _____, a journey that a believer is expected to make to the religious site of Mecca.

4. In the early 1900s, Great Britain made Egypt a _____, a country that has its own government but is controlled by an outside power.

5. In many Middle Eastern countries, _____ oppose modern ideas and favor a return to the strict religious values of the past.

6. During the Yom Kippur War, Arab oil producing nations began an oil _____, restricting the export of oil to countries that sided with Israel.

7. When Iraq invaded Kuwait, the United Nations placed a trade _____ on Iraq, cutting off all trade until Iraq withdrew from Kuwait.

8. The series of protests and attacks that began in 1987 by Palestinians against Israeli rule in the West Bank and Gaza is known as the _____ .

II. Multiple Choice Choose the answer that best completes the sentence or answers the question. Then write the letter of your choice in the space provided.

_____ **9.** The trend toward Islamic fundamentalism in the Middle East has meant that
   a. life is more restricted for women.
   b. laws have become more secular.
   c. women now rule the family while men work outside the home.
   d. women have more opportunities outside the home.

_____ **10.** The Persian Gulf War was fought because
   a. Egypt invaded Israel.
   b. Iraq invaded Kuwait.
   c. Iraqi Kurds fought for a homeland.
   d. Christians and Muslims in Lebanon could not live together.

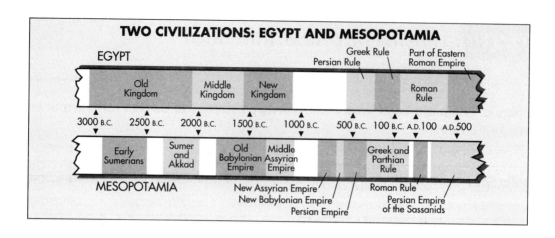

TWO CIVILIZATIONS: EGYPT AND MESOPOTAMIA

11. The most valuable and important natural resource in the Middle East is
    a. oil.
    b. water.
    c. gold.
    d. spices.

12. The source of the conflict between Arab countries and Israel is
    a. ethnic differences between Arabs and Israelis.
    b. religious differences between Arabs and Israelis.
    c. philosophical differences between communists and capitalists.
    d. Arab and Israeli claims to the same land.

13. The oldest civilizations in the Middle East grew around
    a. the foothills of mountains.
    b. oases in the desert.
    c. the coast of the Mediterranean Sea.
    d. fertile river valleys.

III. Analyzing a Time Line Answer questions 14—16 based on the timeline above.

14. In approximately what year did the New Kingdom of Egypt begin?
    a. 800 B.C.
    b. 1400 B.C.
    c. 1600 B.C.
    d. 3000 B.C.

15. Which Mesopotamian civilization ended in approximately 2500 B.C.?
    a. The Old Kingdom
    b. Early Sumaria
    c. Sumer and Akkad
    d. the Roman Empire

16. Which Mesopotamian empire began during the time of the Middle Kingdom in Egypt?
    a. Sumer and Akkad
    b. Early Sumaria
    c. the Middle Assyrian Empire
    d. the Old Babylonian Empire

IV. Essay Answer the following questions in paragraph form on a separate sheet of paper.

17. Discuss how the discovery of oil in the Middle East has affected the region. What economic changes occurred in Middle Eastern countries as a result of the discovery of oil?

18. Discuss the influence of Islam on the Middle East. When and how did Islam begin? What are the major beliefs of Islam? What impact has Islam had on the culture and governments of the region?

Name _____ Date _____

Exploring Regional Issues...Reading a Bar Graph

The bar graph below shows the per capita income of France. Use the data provided to add the per capita incomes of Ireland, Lithuania, Spain, and Tajikistan to the graph. When you have completed the bar graph, answer the questions below.

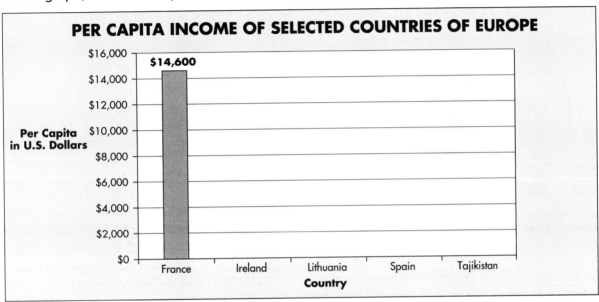

PER CAPITA INCOME OF SELECTED COUNTRIES OF EUROPE

Country	Per Capita Income
Ireland	$8,900
Lithuania	$3,000
Spain	$10,100
Tajikistan	$2,340

Source: *Information Please Almanac, World Almanac and Book of Facts, World Population Data Sheet of the Population Reference Bureau, Time.*

1. Look on page 500 in your text. Define the term *per capita income*.

   _____

2. (a) Which country on the graph above has the highest per capita income? _____

   (b) Look at the map on pages 602–603 in your text. In which region of Europe is this country

   located? _____

3. (a) Which country on the graph has the lowest per capita income? _____

   (b) Based on the information on the graph, what conclusion can you draw about per capita

   incomes in Europe and Eurasia? _____

239

Name _____ **Date** _____

On Assignment...Creating Posters

Your assignment is to create posters to promote tourism in Europe and the Eurasian Heartland. The theme of the advertising campaign is "Visit a Beautiful and Diverse Region." Before you begin to create your sketches, find at least three examples of advertisements in newspapers and magazines. Below, list what impresses you about each advertisement.

1. I liked/disliked the advertisement about _____ because _____

_____

2. I liked/disliked the advertisement about _____ because _____

_____

3. I liked/disliked the advertisement about _____ because _____

_____

Another important step in creating an effective advertisement is identifying who the audience for the advertisement is. In other words, to whom do you want to sell your product? For example, you might decide that your posters will be directed at young people who want to visit the seaside resorts of Europe and the Eurasian Heartland. Or you might decide to design posters that will appeal to people who want to visit the cities or learn more about the history of the region.

Who will your audience be? _____

As you read Chapter 37, jot down ideas based on the On Assignment hint boxes or based on your own original ideas. Think of at least three ideas for your posters and list them below.

Idea number 1: _____

Idea number 2: _____

Idea number 3: _____

For each idea, think of images that you can use on your posters. Write these down below.

Images for idea number 1: _____

Images for idea number 2: _____

Images for idea number 3: _____

Now, choose your two best ideas and on the back of this worksheet, begin sketching your posters. Choose the best of your sketches and create a slogan—catchy words or phrases—to add to the poster.

When you have completed your sketches, analyze them. Which one would attract more tourists to Europe or the Heartland? Choose one sketch and make a finished poster.

Name _____ Date _____

On Assignment...Creating a Storyboard

Your task is to create three storyboards about the history of Europe. The On Assignment hint boxes in the chapter suggest that your scenes be on the following topics: democracy in ancient Athens, art during the Renaissance, and the effects of the Industrial Revolution. You may use these ideas or ideas of your own. The questions below will help you create your storyboards.

1. Which period of European history did you find most interesting? Why? _____

_____

2. In which period of European history would you most like to have lived? Why? _____

_____

3. Imagine that you lived in that period of history. Describe the world around you. How do you

   dress? To whom do you talk? _____

_____

_____

4. If your sketches were turned into a movie, what might a narrator say to link the pictures and
   images? If you choose to use actors and actresses, what would the characters say to one

   another? _____

_____

_____

Use the boxes below to sketch your scenes. Use the lines below the boxes to take notes for your narration.

Name _____ Date _____

On Assignment...Writing Newspaper Articles

For this assignment, you have been asked to write two newspaper articles. Good newspaper articles contain answers to the "five Ws"—**W**ho, **W**hat, **W**here, **W**hen, and **W**hy. To help you identify the "five Ws," find a newspaper article on any topic and read it. Then answer the questions below.

1. **What** is the title of the article? _____

2. **Who** is the article about? _____

3. **What** is the article about? _____

4. **Where** did the action described in the article take place? _____

5. **When** did the action in the article take place? _____

6. **Why** did the action in the article take place? _____

Now it's time to think about topics for your articles. The On Assignment hint boxes suggested the following two topics: trench warfare during World War I and the Berlin airlift. You may use these topics or you may choose two others. In the chart below, write your two topics and information about the "five Ws" for each topic.

	TOPIC 1: _____	TOPIC 2: _____
Who: Who is the article about? (Your article may be about more than one person or about a group.)		
What: What is your article about?		
Where: Where did the action in your article take place?		
When: When did the action in your article take place?		
Why: Why did the action in the article take place?		

You are now ready to write your articles. You may wish to use reference books from your school or local library to help you add details. When you complete the articles, write a headline for each one below.

Headline for Article 1: _____

Headline for Article 2: _____

Name _____   **Date** _____

On Assignment...Writing a Letter

Travelers often write letters to family and friends describing what they see and do. Your assignment is to write letters that describe your travels through Europe. First, decide which places you will describe. The On Assignment hint boxes suggest several possibilities. Use these suggestions or ideas of your own. List below four places that you will describe.

1. _____   3. _____

2. _____   4. _____

Next, decide one thing you will say in your letters about each place. Use information from your text and from library or classroom resources.

1. Idea for place number 1: _____

2. Idea for place number 2: _____

3. Idea for place number 3: _____

4. Idea for place number 4: _____

Begin to write your first letter on the lines below. Remember, after you complete your letters, write a one-page summary of your impressions of Europe.

Dear _____ ,

I can't believe I'm really in _____! Today, I saw _____

_____

_____

_____

_____

_____

_____

_____

_____

_____

_____

Name _____ **Date** _____

On Assignment...Conducting an Interview

Your assignment is to write questions for an interview about Europe. Review the On Assignment hint boxes in Chapter 41 for ideas about questions to write. Use these ideas or ideas of your own. Working with a partner, use the diagram below to brainstorm at least three questions for each section in the chapter and for Case Study 41. Begin by asking questions about Section 1.

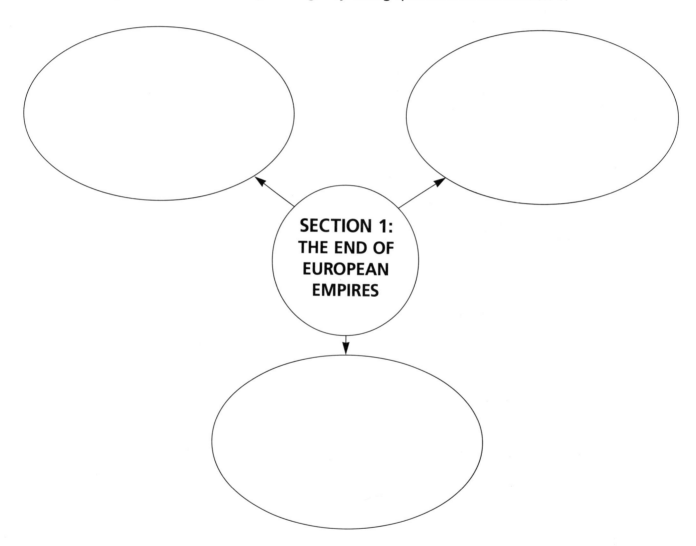

SECTION 1: THE END OF EUROPEAN EMPIRES

Copy a similar diagram into your notebook and write questions for Sections 2 and 3 and for Case Study 41. After you have written questions for all the sections, review them. Have you asked questions about important issues in Europe? Are your questions phrased in a clear, direct way? Check the spelling and grammar of your questions. Revise any questions that you do not like and add new questions. Then, use your text and library resources to create answers to your questions. Practice your interview with your partner until you feel comfortable. Present your interview to the class.

Name _____   **Date** _____

On Assignment...Writing a Journal Entry

Your assignment is to write journal entries for different periods in the history of Russia and the Eurasian Heartland. Journals describe daily experiences, thoughts, and feelings. The page below is divided into five parts. Each part contains a possible opening line for a journal entry for a person living in a particular period of history. Use these opening lines or create your own to write your journal entries.

KIEVAN RUSSIA

Date: _____

Last night, the Mongols invaded our town. It was _____

_____

_____

RUSSIA UNDER THE TSARS

Date: _____

Peter the Great has done a great deal to make Russia more modern. He has _____

_____

_____

REVOLUTIONARY RUSSIA

Date: _____

The demonstrations have brought Nicholas II's government to an end. I am feeling _____

_____

_____

COMMUNIST SOVIET UNION

Date: _____

Stalin has begun a reign of terror. He is _____

_____

_____

THE FALL OF COMMUNISM

Date: _____

Mikhail Gorbachev was not able to save the Soviet Union. No one knows what the future will

bring. I hope _____

_____

_____

Name _____   Date _____

On Assignment...Creating an Atlas

An atlas is a collection of maps. Your assignment for this chapter is to create an atlas that shows Russia and the Heartland. Use the chart below to help you organize information for one of your maps. Then copy the chart and use it for the other maps you will include in your atlas. Think of symbols you can use for each element you decide to include on your map. An example of a symbol would be to use a star to show a capital city. Some of the information can be found in your text. Other information can be found in almanacs or other reference books. You can find these books in your school or local library.

Title of Map: _____

	INFORMATION	IDEA FOR SYMBOL
Countries		
Cities		
Rivers		
Oceans and seas		
Mountain ranges		
Other information		

Name _____   Date _____

On Assignment...Writing an Editorial

Your assignment for this chapter is to write an editorial that expresses your opinion about Russia's relationship with its neighbors and with the rest of the world. Find an editorial in your local newspaper. Read the editorial and identify the topic, the editor's opinion about the topic, and the facts the editor has used to support this opinion. Write the information in the spaces below.

TOPIC: _____

Editor's opinion: _____

_____

Facts used to support opinion: _____

_____

_____

Review the notes you took while reading this chapter. The broad topic for your editorial is Russia's foreign policy. However, it will help to narrow that topic and focus on one issue. For example, you might choose to write about Russia's relationship with just one country or region. On the lines below, describe how you will narrow the topic.

My editorial will focus on: _____

_____

Once you have chosen an issue, you need to decide what your opinion is of that issue. Write your opinion below.

I believe that: _____

_____

_____

What facts will you use to support your opinion? Write supporting facts below.

Facts: _____

_____

_____

_____

_____

_____

Now write your editorial on a separate sheet of paper.

Name _____   Date _____

Critical Thinking...Interpreting a Map

Some parts of Europe are very densely populated. In other areas, there are very few people. The map below shows population distribution, or where people live, in Europe. Use this map to answer the questions that follow.

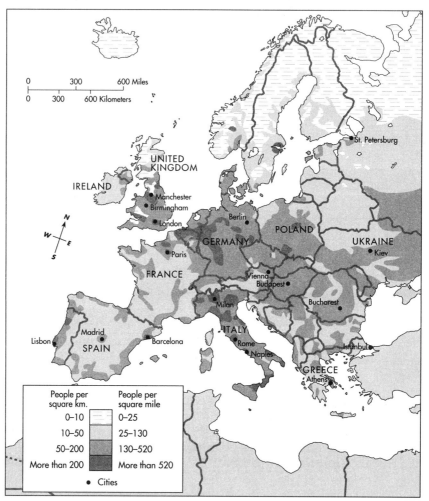

1. Which country has no more than 25 people per square mile? _____

2. List four countries that have no more than 130 people per square mile. _____

   _____

3. Which of the four regions of Europe is the most densely populated? The least densely

   populated? _____

4. How do you think climate and geography affect where people live in Europe? (Hint: Study

   the map in Chapter 37 of your text.) _____

Name _____   Date _____

Critical Thinking...Interpreting a Chart

During much of the Middle Ages, Europeans rarely traveled. Beginning in the late 1400s, however, Europeans began to explore the land and the seas. The reasons for this travel were mainly economic. Europeans were looking for new routes to Asia to increase trade for spices, silks, and other goods. The chart on this page shows some early explorers and the journeys that they took. Use the information in this chart to answer the questions that follow.

Explorer	Country Represented	Year of Exploration	Journey
Bartolomeu Dias	Portugal	1487–1488	First European to round the southern tip of Africa
Christopher Columbus	Spain	1492	First voyage to the Americas; explored the Caribbean (West Indies)
Vasco da Gama	Portugal	1497–1498	First to sail from Europe to India by sea
Vasco de Balboa	Spain	1513	First European to see the Pacific Ocean
Juan Ponce de Leon	Spain	1513	Explored Florida
Ferdinand Magellan	Spain	1519–1522	First to circumnavigate (sail completely around) the earth
Hernán Cortés	Spain	1519–1521	Conquered the Aztecs in Mexico
Francisco Pizarro	Spain	1531	Conquered the Inca empire in Peru
Jacques Cartier	France	1535	Sailed up the St. Lawrence River
Hernando de Soto	Spain	1539–1542	Explored the Mississippi River and present-day southeastern U.S.
Francisco de Coronado	Spain	1540–1542	Explored present-day southwestern U.S.
Henry Hudson	Netherlands	1609	Explored the Hudson River and eastern North America
Sir Francis Drake	England	1577–1580	Sailed around the world
Samuel de Champlain	France	1603	Explored the Great Lakes and eastern North America

1. Which explorer sailed up the St. Lawrence River? _____

2. For what country did Vasco da Gama sail? _____

3. When did Ferdinand Magellan make his journey? _____

4. What area did Hernando de Soto explore? _____

5. For what country did the majority of the explorers listed above sail? _____

6. On which two continents did most of the explorations listed above take place? _____

7. Imagine that you are a news writer in the early 1600s. Use the back of this sheet to write a paragraph that summarizes the past 120 years of exploration.

Name _____   **Date** _____

Critical Thinking...Making a Time Line

The sequence in which things happen is often important. An event may come before or after another event, or events may occur at the same time. A time line portrays events in chronological, or time, order. Below is a list of events that occurred in Europe and elsewhere in the 20th century. Place these events on the time line below and answer the questions that follow.

EUROPE

1917 Russian Revolution occurs.
1939 World War II begins.
1949 NATO is founded.
1929 The Great Depression begins.
1989 Communism falls in Eastern Europe.
1946 The Cold War begins.
1961 The Berlin Wall is built.
1922 Mussolini becomes dictator of Italy.
1914 World War I begins.
1933 The Nazi party comes to power in Germany.
1955 The Warsaw Pact is founded.

ELSEWHERE

1965 The Vietnam War begins.
1949 Communist rule of China begins.
1976 The Soweto uprising in South Africa begins.
1953 The Korean War breaks out.
1941 Japan attacks Pearl Harbor.
1979 U.S. hostages are taken in Iran.
1948 The state of Israel is founded.
1980 Zimbabwe gains independence in Africa.
1947 India gains independence.
1979 The Sandinistas take power in Nicaragua.
1962 The Cuban missile crisis occurs.

1900	1925	1950	1975	2000

1. Who came to power first, Mussolini or the Nazi party? _____

2. Which country gained independence first, India or Zimbabwe? _____

3. What happened in Europe the year Communist China was created? _____

_____

_____

4. What was happening in Cuba around the time that the Berlin Wall was built? _____

_____

_____

Name _____ Date _____

Critical Thinking...Reading a Bar Graph

Graphs organize statistical information in an easy-to-read diagram. The graph on this page is called a *bar graph* because it uses bars to show amounts. Other graphs use different symbols to show amounts. *Line graphs* use indicator lines. *Circle graphs* use parts of circles.

You begin reading any graph by identifying the information on it. Next, compare this information. What differences in size or amount can you spot? Can you see any patterns or changes over time or area? The bar graph below shows the percentage of the gross domestic product (GDP) that is collected in taxes by several countries. The GDP is the amount of goods and services produced within a country's borders. Study the information in this graph and answer the questions that follow.

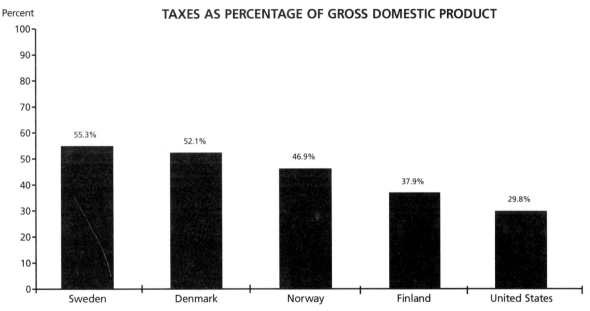

TAXES AS PERCENTAGE OF GROSS DOMESTIC PRODUCT

Source: *Statistical Abstract of the United States,* 1991

1. What information is shown on this graph? _____

2. Which country has the lowest tax burden (percentage of GDP)? _____

3. Which European country has the lowest tax burden? _____

4. Which country has the highest tax burden? _____

5. How many times higher is the tax burden in Sweden than in the United States? _____

6. Approximately what percentage of its GDP does Norway collect in taxes? _____

7. Which two countries collect more than half of their GDPs in taxes? _____

8. What conclusion can you reach based on the information on this graph? _____

_____

Name _____   Date _____

Critical Thinking...Using a Primary Source

Playwright Vaclav Havel of Czechoslovakia was one of the leaders of the Czech movement for human rights, which opposed the Communist regime. In December 1989, communism fell in Czechoslovakia and Havel became his country's president. In his first speech as president, Havel described the state of the country after 40 years of communism. Below is an excerpt from that speech. This type of source is known as a *primary source. Primary* means "first" or "original." Speeches are primary sources because they provide a firsthand look at what is in the mind of the speaker.

My Dear Fellow Citizens,

For forty years you heard from my predecessors [former leaders] . . . how our country flourished, how many million tons of steel we produced, how happy we all were, how we trusted our government, and what bright perspectives [futures] were unfolding in front of us. I assume you did not propose me for this office so that I, too, would lie to you.

Our country is not flourishing. . . . Entire branches of industry are producing goods which are of no interest to anyone, while we are lacking the things we need. A state which calls itself a workers' state humiliates [shames] and exploits [uses] workers. Our obsolete [outdated] economy is wasting the little energy we have available. . . . We have the most contaminated [poisoned] environment in Europe. . . .

But all this is still not the main problem. The worst thing is that we live in a contaminated moral environment. We fell morally ill because we became used to saying something different from what we thought. We learned not to believe in anything, to ignore each other, to care only about ourselves. . . .

We had all become used to the totalitarian system and accepted it as an unchangeable fact and thus helped to perpetuate it. . . .

Let us not be mistaken: the best government in the world, the best parliament, and the best president, cannot achieve much on their own. . . . Freedom and democracy include participation and therefore responsibility from us all.

1. Who is the audience for the speech? _____

2. List three lies that Havel says his predecessors told. _____

    _____

3. List three problems Havel says Czechoslovakia faced in 1989. _____

    _____

4. What does Havel mean by a "contaminated moral environment"? _____

    _____

5. According to Havel, how did Czechoslovakia's moral environment become contaminated?

    _____

6. What does Havel think is the solution to his country's problems? _____

    _____

    Global Studies. Copyright © **Globe Fearon Educational Publisher.** *All rights reserved.*

Name _____   Date _____

Critical Thinking...Interpreting Poetry

Poetry often represents what is in the heart and mind of its writer. Below is a poem written by a Russian poet named Alexander Pushkin in 1827. The poem is addressed to the participants of an unsuccessful 1825 uprising against the autocracy. Read the poem carefully and look up any words you do not know. Then answer the questions that follow.

Message to Siberia
by Alexander Pushkin

Deep in the Siberian mine,
Keep your patience proud;
The bitter toil shall not be lost,
The rebel thought unbowed.

The sister of misfortune, Hope,
In the under-darkness dumb
Speaks joyful courage to your heart:
The day desired will come,

And love and friendship pour to you
Across the darkened doors,
Even as round your galley beds
My free music pours.

The heavy-hanging chains will fall,
The walls will crumble at a word;
And Freedom greet you in the light,
And brothers give you back the sword.

1. What is the title of the poem? _____

2. To whom is the author talking in the poem? _____

3. What is described as the "sister of misfortune"? _____

4. What emotions does the author ask the participants in the uprising and other readers of the

   poem to feel? _____

5. In the last stanza, how does the author describe the chains? _____

6. What does the author suggest will happen when the chains fall? _____

7. What does the author think about the future of the revolutionary movement? _____

   _____

8. Complete the letter below to the author, describing your feelings about his poem.

   Dear Mr. Pushkin,

   I just read your poem. _____

   _____

   _____

   _____

   Sincerely,

Name _____ Date _____

Critical Thinking...Interpreting Statistics

Only a few of the many ethnic groups living in Russia and the Eurasian Heartland have their own country. When the Soviet Union collapsed, the 15 former Soviet republics gained independence. This placed many ethnic Russians within the borders of independent countries, and left other ethnic groups outside the borders of their native countries. The chart below shows the native ethnic and Russian populations in the Eurasian Heartland. Study the information in this chart and answer the questions below.

NATIVE AND RUSSIAN POPULATION IN EURASIAN HEARTLAND

Former Soviet Republics	Population (in thousands)	Percent Native	Percent Russian
Russia	147,022	81.5	na
Ukraine	51,452	72.7	22.1
Belarus	10,152	77.9	13.2
Uzbekistan	19,810	71.4	8.4
Kazakstan	16,464	39.7	37.8
Georgia	5,401	70.1	6.3
Azerbaijan	7,021	82.7	5.6
Lithuania	3,675	79.6	9.4
Moldova	4,335	64.5	13.0
Latvia	2,667	52.0	34.0
Kyrgyzstan	4,258	52.4	21.5
Tajikistan	5,093	62.3	7.6
Armenia	3,305	93.3	1.6
Turkmenistan	3,523	72.0	9.5
Estonia	1,565	61.5	30.3

Source: *The New Eurasia: A Guide to the Republics of the Former Soviet Union*, David T. Twining. Westport, CT: Praeger, 1993

1. What information is shown in this table? _____

2. Which former republic has the largest total population? The smallest? _____

_____

3. Which former republic has the largest percentage of native population? _____

4. Which former republic (other than Russia) has the largest percentage of ethnic Russians?

_____

5. Which region has the smallest percentage of ethnic Russians? _____

6. All of the former republics have other ethnic groups—in addition to the native group and Russians—living within their borders. Find the percent of other groups living in each former republic by adding up the "percent native" and "percent Russian" columns for each republic and subtracting that number from 100 percent. Which former republic has the largest "percent other"? The smallest? _____

_____

Name _____   Date _____

Critical Thinking...Interpreting a Political Cartoon

Cartoonists use their artwork to express a point of view about an issue. The cartoon below presents a point of view on relations between the Soviet Union and the United States during the Cold War. When you study a political cartoon, read all labels and captions to understand the artist's message. Study the cartoon, then use what you have learned from the text about the Cold War to answer the questions.

1. Who are the main figures in the cartoon? _____

2. What are the two men doing? _____

3. What are the players using for chess pieces? _____

4. What do the symbols above the "chess pieces" represent? _____

5. To what does the caption refer? _____

   _____

6. Describe the men's facial expressions. Why do they look this way? _____

   _____

7. Express in your own words what the cartoonist is saying. _____

   _____

   _____

Chapter 37 Test   *The Land and People of Europe and Eurasia*

Name _____   Date _____

I. Matching Decide which definition in the right column best explains a term in the left column. Then write the letter of that definition in the space next to the term.

_____ 1. tundra
_____ 2. taiga
_____ 3. steppe
_____ 4. plateau
_____ 5. peninsula

a. a flat area that is higher than the land that surrounds it
b. a body of land that is surrounded on three sides by water
c. a level, treeless region that has long winters
d. a large, treeless plain in the Heartland that is very fertile
e. a large forest of the Eurasian Heartland

II. Multiple Choice Choose the answer that best completes the sentence or answers the question. Then write the letter of your choice in the space provided.

_____ 6. The best warm-water ports in Europe are in
   a. Western Europe.
   b. Eastern Europe.
   c. Northern Europe.
   d. the Heartland.

_____ 7. The soil is most fertile for farming in
   a. the Northwest Mountain region.
   b. the Central Uplands.
   c. the Alpine Mountains.
   d. the North European Plain.

_____ 8. The largest city in Europe is
   a. Paris.
   b. Amsterdam.
   c. London.
   d. Athens.

_____ 9. The most densely populated regions in Europe and Eurasia are in
   a. Northern Europe.
   b. Eastern Europe.
   c. the Heartland.
   d. Western Europe.

_____ 10. The most important river in Germany is the
   a. Thames.
   b. Rhine.
   c. Volga.
   d. Danube.

III. Essay Write your answer to the following question in paragraph form on a separate sheet of paper.

   Explain why Europe's rivers are an important resource. What role have rivers played in European history? What role have rivers played in Europe's economy? Use examples of rivers in Europe to support your points.

256   *Global Studies. Copyright* © **Globe Fearon Educational Publisher.** *All rights reserved.*

Name _____ Date _____

I. Matching Decide which definition in the right column best explains a term in the left column. Then write the letter of that definition in the space next to the term.

_____ 1. republic

_____ 2. feudalism

_____ 3. absolute monarchy

_____ 4. constitutional monarchy

_____ 5. capitalism

a. a form of government in which citizens elect their leaders

b. a system in which people, not government, make economic decisions

c. a system in which a monarch's power is limited by law

d. a system in which one person has total rule

e. a system in which a person gave loyalty to a lord in return for protection

II. Multiple Choice Choose the answer that best completes the sentence or answers the question. Then write the letter of your choice in the space provided.

_____ 6. In Germany during the 1500s and 1600s, several wars were fought between
   a. rivals to the throne.
   b. Protestants and Catholics.
   c. peasants and nobles.
   d. the rich and the poor.

_____ 7. The Crusades were a series of campaigns by Europeans to
   a. gain territory in Asia.
   b. find a trade route to India.
   c. free Jerusalem from Muslim control.
   d. spread ideas about democracy through the world.

_____ 8. During the 1600s, power in England was held by
   a. the king alone.
   b. Parliament alone.
   c. the king and Parliament together.
   d. nobles.

_____ 9. Greece is important in European history because
   a. it was the birthplace of democracy.
   b. it created a huge empire.
   c. it established the first code of laws.
   d. it established the first republic in which citizens elect their leaders.

_____ 10. Enlightenment thinkers believed that
   a. the king's power should be absolute.
   b. change could come only through violent revolution.
   c. human society could not be studied in the same way as the natural world.
   d. they could use information they learned to improve the world.

III. Essay Write your answer to the following question in paragraph form on a separate sheet of paper.

What was the Industrial Revolution? What impact did it have on European history? What were some of the benefits and drawbacks of the Industrial Revolution in the 1800s? What impact has the Industrial Revolution in Europe had on our lives today?

Name _____ Date _____

I. Matching Decide which definition in the right column best explains a term in the left column. Then write the letter of that definition in the space next to the term.

_____ **1.** alliance

_____ **2.** fascism

_____ **3.** dictatorship

_____ **4.** Holocaust

_____ **5.** Cold War

a. a system of dictatorship that stresses extreme nationalism

b. the long period of hostility between Western and Communist countries that began after World War II

c. an agreement between two or more countries to help each other

d. rule by a person who has total power

e. the Nazi attempt to wipe out the Jews and other people in Europe

II. Multiple Choice Choose the answer that best completes the sentence or answers the question. Then write the letter of your choice in the space provided.

_____ **6.** The main cause of World War I was
   a. economic hardship.
   b. the German invasion of Poland.
   c. the Industrial Revolution.
   d. alliances and rivalries between European nations.

_____ **7.** During World War I, Germany was allied with
   a. Serbia.
   b. Russia.
   c. Austria-Hungary.
   d. France.

_____ **8.** World War II shifted the balance of world power to
   a. France and England.
   b. the U.S. and the Soviet Union.
   c. Germany.
   d. Asia.

_____ **9.** Adolf Hitler and the Nazi party took power in Germany by
   a. promising to restore the power and glory of Germany.
   b. treating all people equally.
   c. forming alliances with neighboring countries.
   d. taking responsibility for Germany's economic problems.

_____ **10.** During the Cold War, most Eastern European countries fell under the control of
   a. the United States.
   b. NATO.
   c. Asia.
   d. the Soviet Union.

III. Essay Write your answer to the following question in paragraph form on a separate sheet of paper.

Explain the underlying causes of World War II and the events that led to the outbreak of war. How did the peace settlement from World War I contribute to the start of World War II? What role did economics play? How were dictators able to come to power in Germany and Italy? What specific event signaled the start of World War II?

Patterns of Life in Europe

Name _____ Date _____

I. **Matching** Decide which definition in the right column best explains a term in the left column. Then write the letter of that definition in the space next to the term.

_____ **1.** emigrate

_____ **2.** pension

_____ **3.** bilingual

_____ **4.** hereditary

_____ **5.** export

a. to sell a country's products abroad

b. passed from one generation to another

c. a regular payment to retired people

d. to leave one country permanently and settle in another

e. speaking two languages

II. **Multiple Choice** Choose the answer that best completes the sentence or answers the question. Then write the letter of your choice in the space provided.

_____ **6.** All of the following characterize Sweden's welfare state EXCEPT

    a. Swedes pay very high taxes for their benefits.

    b. the Swedish economy has been very strong in the 1990s.

    c. the government pays a large part of its citizens' medical and dental bills.

    d. Swedes receive generous benefits from the government when they retire.

_____ **7.** Today Germany is

    a. united into one democratic country.

    b. united into one Communist country.

    c. divided into Communist East Germany and democratic West Germany.

    d. divided into democratic East Germany and Communist West Germany.

_____ **8.** British political power today is held by

    a. people with hereditary titles.

    b. the Queen.

    c. the Prince of Wales.

    d. Parliament.

_____ **9.** A large problem in Italy today is

    a. the lack of a modern economy.

    b. religious problems between Protestants and Catholics.

    c. civil wars.

    d. the economic differences between the northern and southern regions.

_____ **10.** The region of Europe with the highest standard of living is

    a. Southern Europe.

    b. Western Europe.

    c. Northern Europe.

    d. Central Europe.

III. **Essay** Write your answer to the following question in paragraph form on a separate sheet of paper.

Compare the people and cultures of each of the four regions of Europe. What are the major languages, religions, and systems of government of each? How is each region similar to the others? Different from the others?

Name _____ Date _____

I. Matching Decide which definition in the right column best explains a term in the left column. Then write the letter of that definition in the space next to the term.

_____ 1. civil disobedience

a. to end government control of factories, farms, and businesses and turn them over to individuals

_____ 2. stalemate

b. a form of protest that involves disobeying laws

_____ 3. tariff

c. a tax on a product one country sells to another

_____ 4. privatize

d. a situation in which two sides oppose each other but neither can win

II. Multiple Choice Choose the answer that best completes the sentence or answers the question. Then write the letter of your choice in the space provided.

_____ 5. In 1954, Vietnam gained its independence from
   a. Indochina.
   b England.
   c. France.
   d. Germany.

_____ 6. Mikhail Gorbachev believed that
   a. the Soviet Union would always be a Communist state.
   b. communism would be abolished in the Soviet Union.
   c. communism would have to change to survive.
   d. communism and democracy were similar.

_____ 7. Which of the following used civil disobedience as a technique to gain independence?
   a. Mohandas K. Gandhi in India.
   b. Ho Chi Minh in Vietnam.
   c. Muslims in Pakistan.
   d. the African colony of Rhodesia.

_____ 8. The first Eastern European country to elect a non-Communist government in the 1980s was
   a. Romania.
   b. East Germany.
   c. Czechoslovakia.
   d. Poland.

_____ 9. In 1957, six European countries formed an organization that is now called the European Union to
   a. build a high-speed train.
   b. promote economic cooperation in Western Europe.
   c. defend its members against the Soviet Union.
   d. help each other maintain their overseas colonies.

_____ 10. Czechoslovakia today
   a. has become an independent nation.
   b. remains under Communist rule.
   c. has split into two independent nations.
   d. has become part of an independent Yugoslavia.

III. Essay Write your answer to the following question in paragraph form on a separate sheet of paper.

Describe the impact of the fall of communism on Europe. What was the impact on the people of Eastern Europe? Describe how two Eastern European nations gained their independence from the Soviet Union.

Chapter 42 Test — The Heritage of Russia and the Eurasian Heartland

Name _____ Date _____

I. Matching Decide which definition in the right column best explains a term in the left column. Then write the letter of that definition in the space next to the term.

_____ **1.** revolution

_____ **2.** socialism

_____ **3.** provisional

_____ **4.** autocracy

_____ **5.** purge

a. to remove people who are considered undesirable

b. temporary

c. an attempt to overthrow a political system

d. the belief that the government should own a country's factories and farms and that people should share wealth equally

e. a form of government in which the ruler has almost complete power over the people

II. Multiple Choice Choose the answer that best completes the sentence or answers the question. Then write the letter of your choice in the space provided.

_____ **6.** The first tsar to try to get Russia to catch up with the West was
   a. Peter the Great.
   b. Catherine the Great.
   c. Ivan the Terrible.
   d. Alexander II.

_____ **7.** The Russian Revolution of 1917 occurred for ALL of the following reasons EXCEPT
   a. the majority of Russian people were very poor.
   b. revolutionaries wanted the government to stay out of economic affairs.
   c. earlier reforms did not go far enough.
   d. World War I was causing great hardship in Russia.

_____ **8.** Russia was invaded and conquered in the 1200s by the
   a. East Slavs.
   b. Mongols.
   c. Kievans.
   d. Byzantines.

_____ **9.** Joseph Stalin tried to modernize the Soviet economy by
   a. raising the standard of living for ordinary people.
   b. reforming the government.
   c. giving more freedom.
   d. seizing all land from the peasants and forcing them to work on large government farms.

_____ **10.** The Soviet Union was dissolved under the leadership of
   a. Nikita Khrushchev.
   b. Leonid Brezhnev.
   c. Mikhail Gorbachev.
   d. Vladimir Lenin.

III. Essay Write your answer to the following question in paragraph form on a separate sheet of paper.

Discuss the 75-year history of the Soviet Union. How and why was the country created? What was life like for ordinary people in the Soviet Union? How and why did the Soviet Union break up?

Name _____   Date _____

I. Matching Decide which definition in the right column best explains a term in the left column. Then write the letter of that definition in the space next to the term.

_____ **1.** nationalism

_____ **2.** genocide

_____ **3.** secede

_____ **4.** suppress

_____ **5.** divert

a. to put down by force

b. devotion to one's country

c. to channel in another direction

d. to break away from a country or another political unit

e. the destruction of a national or ethnic group

II. Multiple Choice Choose the answer that best completes the sentence or answers the question. Then write the letter of your choice in the space provided.

_____ **6.** Russia's capital and largest city is
   a. St. Petersberg.
   b. Moscow.
   c. Volga.
   d. Kremlin.

_____ **7.** Western Eurasians who are closely related to Romanians come from
   a. Belarus.
   b. Ukraine.
   c. Russia.
   d. Moldova.

_____ **8.** During World War I, the Turkish Ottoman Empire committed genocide against
   a. Armenians.
   b. Azerbaijanis.
   c. Georgians.
   d. Lithuanians.

_____ **9.** The religion of most of the people in Central Asia is
   a. Christianity.
   b. Islam.
   c. Buddhism.
   d. Judaism.

_____ **10.** In Russia and the Heartland, pollution and environmental problems are most serious in
   a. the Baltic states.
   b. the Caucasus.
   c. Central Asia.
   d. Western Eurasia.

III. Essay Write your answer to the following question in paragraph form on a separate sheet of paper.

   The collapse of the Soviet Union brought to the surface ethnic tensions all over Russia and the Heartland. Describe two specific examples of ethnic tension in the Eurasian Heartland. What is the source of this tension? What events occurred as a result of this tension?

Global Studies. Copyright © **Globe Fearon Educational Publisher.** *All rights reserved.*

Chapter 44 Test — *Russia and the Heartland in the World Today*

Name _____ Date _____

I. Matching Decide which definition in the right column best explains a term in the left column. Then write the letter of that definition in the space next to the term.

_____ 1. overthrow

_____ 2. foreign policy

_____ 3. black market

_____ 4. negotiation

_____ 5. barter

a. the way in which a country deals with other countries

b. the act of exchanging goods and services without using money

c. a place or system in which goods are sold illegally

d. to bring down from power by force

e. the act of dealing or bargaining with someone else

II. Multiple Choice Choose the answer that best completes the sentence or answers the question. Then write the letter of your choice in the space provided.

_____ 6. The Soviets built the Berlin Wall to
   a. celebrate their victory in World War II.
   b. keep U.S. officials out of East Berlin.
   c. stop East Germans from reaching West Berlin.
   d. keep criminals under control.

_____ 7. In 1962, the Soviets Union and the United States came close to waging nuclear war because
   a. the Soviets tried to place nuclear missiles in Cuba.
   b. the Soviet Union invaded Poland.
   c. the United States sold arms to Israel.
   d. U.S. officials were caught spying on the Soviets in Berlin.

_____ 8. The goal of the Soviet Union's foreign policy was to
   a. destroy the capitalist system in other countries.
   b. increase its territory.
   c. make peace with neighboring nations.
   d. increase economic activity.

_____ 9. Which of the following has NOT been a problem in the Eurasian Heartland since the breakup of the Soviet Union?
   a. economic difficulties
   b. ethnic tension
   c. nuclear weapons
   d. religious oppression

_____ 10. The worst nuclear disaster the world has seen occurred in 1986 at
   a. the Comintern.
   b. Chernobyl.
   c. the Kola Peninsula.
   d. Checkpoint Charlie.

III. Essay Write your answer to the following question in paragraph form on a separate sheet of paper.

Since the breakup of the Soviet Union, several major problems have plagued Russia and the Eurasian Heartland. Describe four of the major issues facing Russia and the Eurasian Heartland today. How did each of these problems arise? What do you think the Russian and Eurasian people can do to solve these problems?

Name _____ Date _____

I. Fill in the Blank Complete each sentence below by writing the correct term in the blank. You will not use all the terms.

tundra	feudalism	capitalism	fascism	nationalism
genocide	autocracy	revolution	stalemate	exports

1. Ivan the Terrible ruled over a form of government called an _____, in which the ruler has almost complete power over the people.

2. _____, or extreme devotion to one's country, is the cause of some of the ethnic fighting in Russia and the Eurasian Heartland.

3. The far northern region of the Eurasian Heartland is the _____, a level, treeless region with long winters.

4. Germany ranks with the United States and Japan in the amount it _____, or sells to other countries.

5. In the 1800s, Russians who were unhappy with the tzars wanted to stage a _____ to overthrow the existing political system.

6. During the Middle Ages, people lived under _____, a system in which a person gave loyalty to a lord in return for protection.

7. During World War I, the Ottoman Empire committed _____, or the destruction of a national or ethnic group, against Armenians.

8. The modern economic system of _____, in which people, not governments, make economic decisions, emerged in England after 1500.

II. Multiple Choice Choose the answer that best completes the sentence or answers the question. Then write the letter of your choice in the space provided.

_____ 9. Europe's rivers have played an important part in its history because they
a. provide a source of recreation.
b. serve as boundaries between nations.
c. have served as highways for trade.
d. have kept Europeans isolated from each other.

_____ 10. Which of the following was NOT a result of the Industrial Revolution?
a. rapid growth of cities
b. growth of large factories
c. better, cheaper products
d. increased amount of farming

_____ 11. Russia's revolutionaries believed in and fought for
a. fascism. c. capitalism.
b. communism. d. democracy.

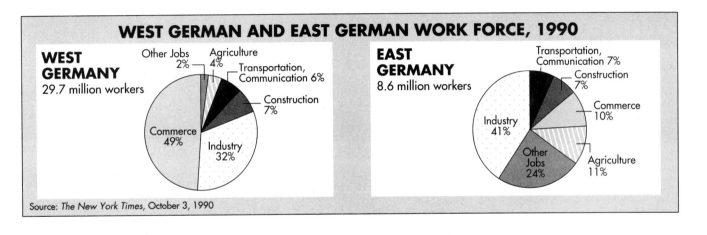

WEST GERMAN AND EAST GERMAN WORK FORCE, 1990

WEST GERMANY
29.7 million workers

- Other Jobs 2%
- Agriculture 4%
- Transportation, Communication 6%
- Construction 7%
- Industry 32%
- Commerce 49%

EAST GERMANY
8.6 million workers

- Transportation, Communication 7%
- Construction 7%
- Commerce 10%
- Agriculture 11%
- Other Jobs 24%
- Industry 41%

Source: *The New York Times*, October 3, 1990

_____ 12. After World War II, the alliance between the United States, the Soviet Union, Britain, and France fell apart because of
   a. tension over the fate of Poland.
   b. Britain's desire to maintain its empire.
   c. rivalry between France and Britain over territory won from Germany.
   d. philosophical differences between democracy and communism.

_____ 13. In 1962, the Soviet Union and the United States came close to waging nuclear war because
   a. the Soviets tried to place nuclear missiles in Cuba.
   b. the Soviet Union invaded Poland.
   c. the United States sold arms to Israel.
   d. U.S. officials were caught spying on the Soviets in Berlin.

III. Analyzing a Chart Answer questions 14–16 based on the chart above.

_____ 14. In 1990, how many workers were in East Germany and West Germany combined?
   a. 29.7 million
   b. 8.6 million
   c. 38.3 million
   d. 200 million

_____ 15. In what occupation was almost half of West Germany's work force employed in 1990?
   a. commerce
   b. industry
   c. agriculture
   d. construction

_____ 16. Which occupation has the same percentage of the work force employed in East Germany and West Germany?
   a. commerce
   b. industry
   c. agriculture
   d. construction

IV. Essay Answer the following questions in paragraph form on a separate sheet of paper.

17. What effect did the Cold War have on the relationships among Europe, the Soviet Union, and the United States from 1945 to 1990?

18. Discuss the breakup of the Soviet Union and the fall of communism in Eastern Europe in the late 1980s and early 1990s. How did the Soviet occupation of Eastern Europe lead to independence movements? What effect did the growth of independence movements have on the Soviet Union?

Name _____   **Date** _____

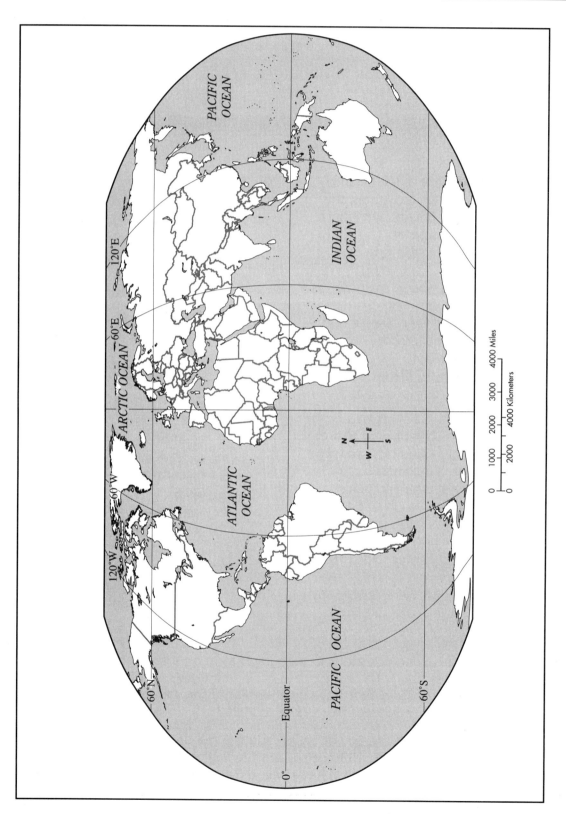

266   *Global Studies. Copyright* © **Globe Fearon Educational Publisher.** *All rights reserved.*

Name _____   **Date** _____

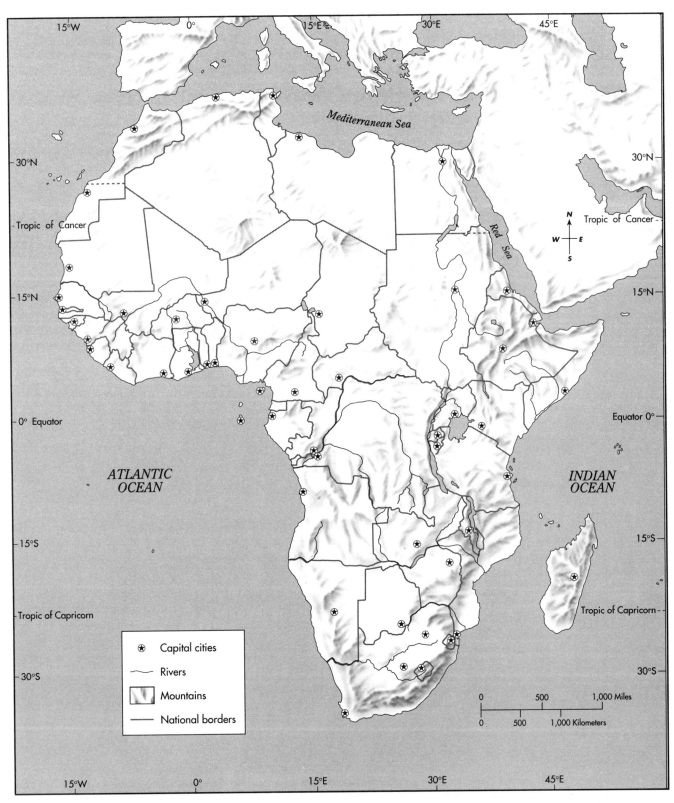

ATLANTIC
OCEAN

INDIAN
OCEAN

Mediterranean Sea

Red Sea

Tropic of Cancer

Tropic of Cancer

15°N

15°N

0° Equator

Equator 0°

15°S

15°S

Tropic of Capricorn

Tropic of Capricorn

30°S

30°S

30°N

30°N

⊛ Capital cities

—— Rivers

▨ Mountains

—— National borders

| 0 | | 500 | | 1,000 Miles |
| 0 | 500 | | 1,000 Kilometers | |

Outline Map 3   *North Africa*

Name _____   **Date** _____

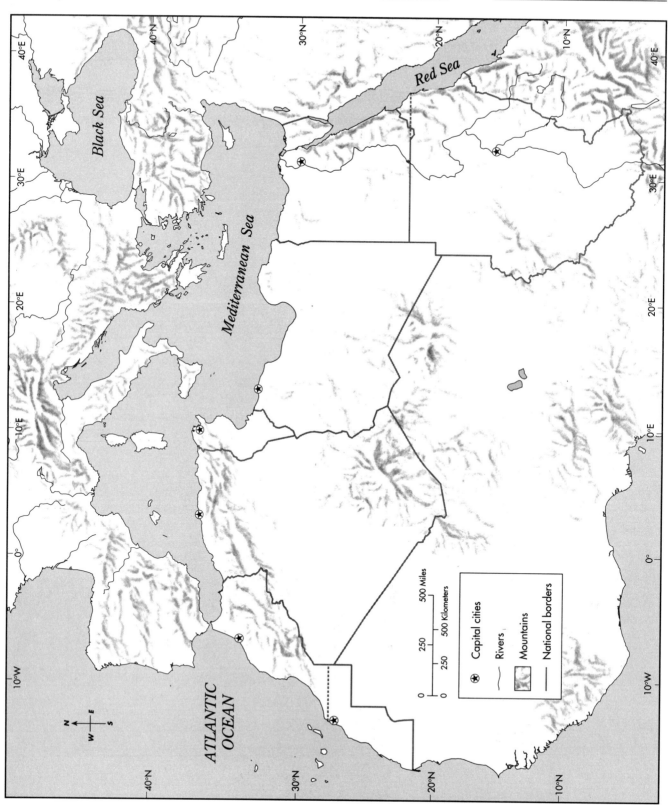

Black Sea

Red Sea

Mediterranean Sea

ATLANTIC OCEAN

500 Miles
500 Kilometers
250
250
0
0

◉ Capital cities
Rivers
Mountains
National borders

40°E 30°N 20°N 10°N 40°E
30°E
40°N
20°E 20°E
10°E 10°E
0° 0°
10°W 10°W
40°N 30°N 20°N 10°N

N
E
W
S

Global Studies. Copyright © **Globe Fearon Educational Publisher.** *All rights reserved.*

Name _____   **Date** _____

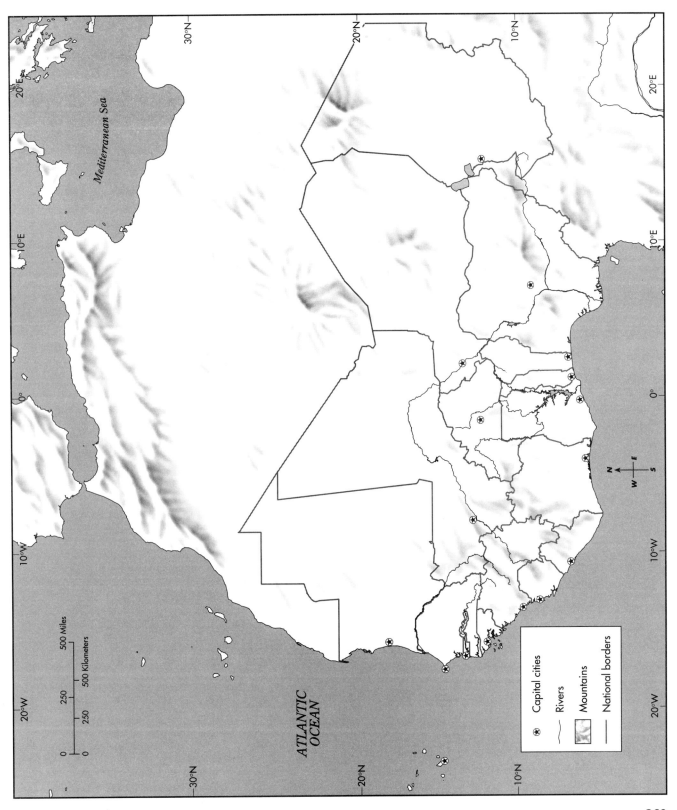

Mediterranean Sea

ATLANTIC
OCEAN

500 Miles

500 Kilometers

	Capital cities
	Rivers
	Mountains
	National borders

Name _____   **Date** _____

Legend	
⊛	Capital cities
⌒	Rivers
▨	Mountains
—	National borders

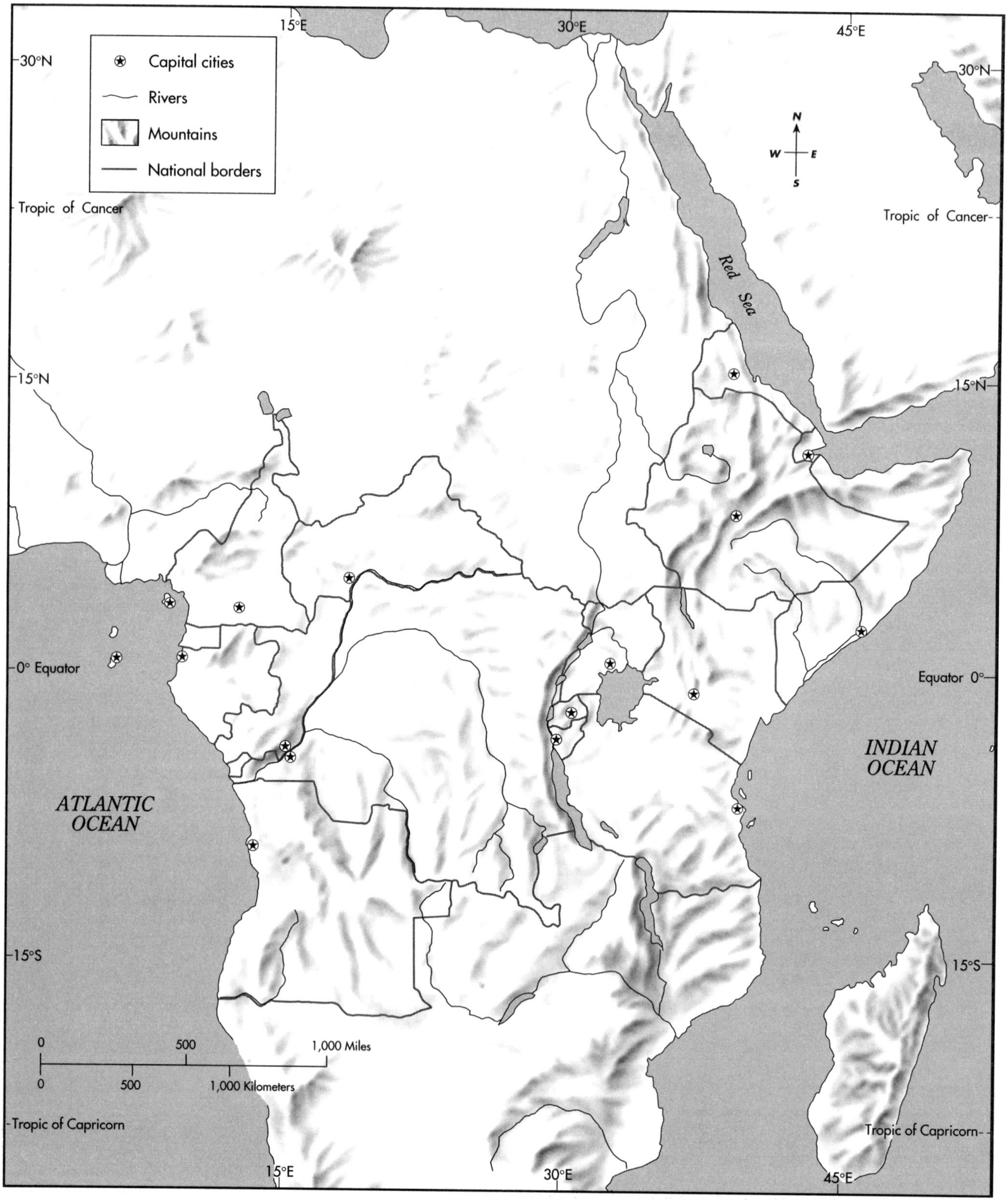

30°N

15°E   30°E   45°E

30°N

N
W   E
S

Tropic of Cancer

Tropic of Cancer

Red Sea

15°N

15°N

INDIAN
OCEAN

0° Equator

Equator 0°

ATLANTIC
OCEAN

15°S

15°S

Scale		
0	500	1,000 Miles
0	500	1,000 Kilometers

Tropic of Capricorn

Tropic of Capricorn

15°E   30°E   45°E

Name _____ **Date** _____

Equator 0°

INDIAN OCEAN

15°S

Tropic of Capricorn

30°S

45°E

30°E

15°E

	Capital cities
	Rivers
	Mountains
	National borders

N E S W

ATLANTIC OCEAN

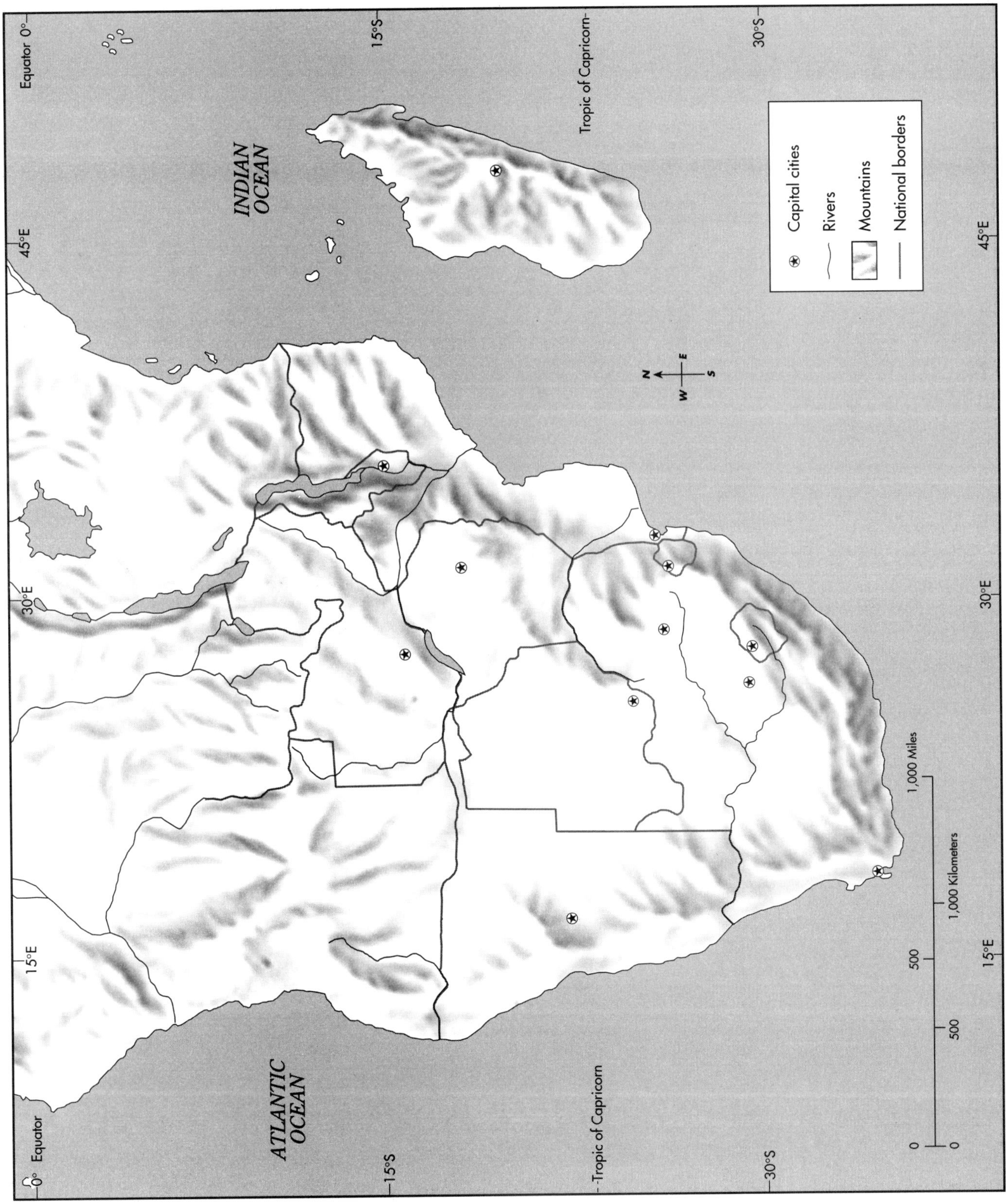

Equator 0°

15°S

Tropic of Capricorn

30°S

1,000 Miles

1,000 Kilometers

500

500

0

0

Outline Map 7   *South Asia*

Name _____   **Date** _____

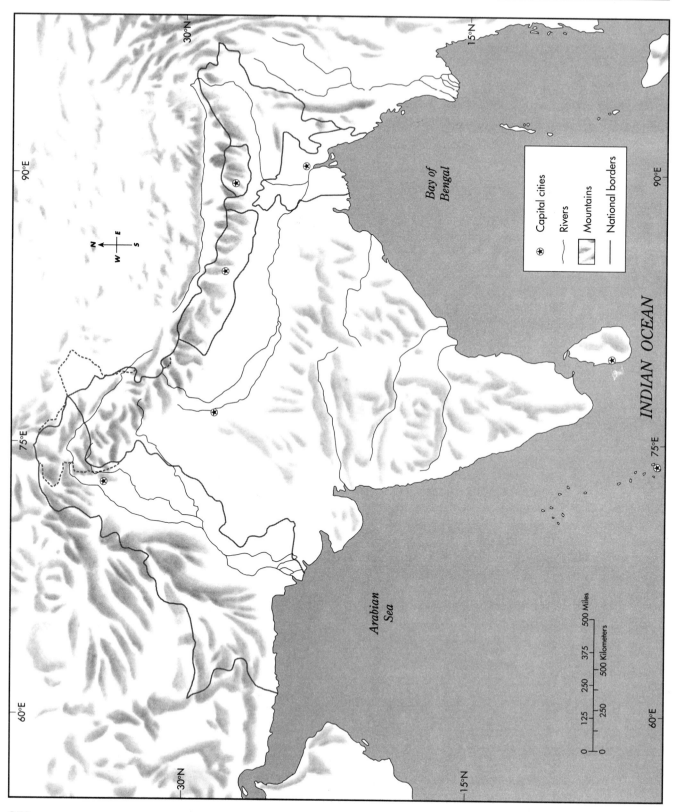

N
E
W
S

Bay of
Bengal

INDIAN OCEAN

Arabian
Sea

Capital cities

Rivers

Mountains

National borders

30°N

15°N

60°E

75°E

90°E

90°E

75°E

60°E

30°N

15°N

0	125	250	375	500 Miles
0	250	500 Kilometers		

Name _____   **Date** _____

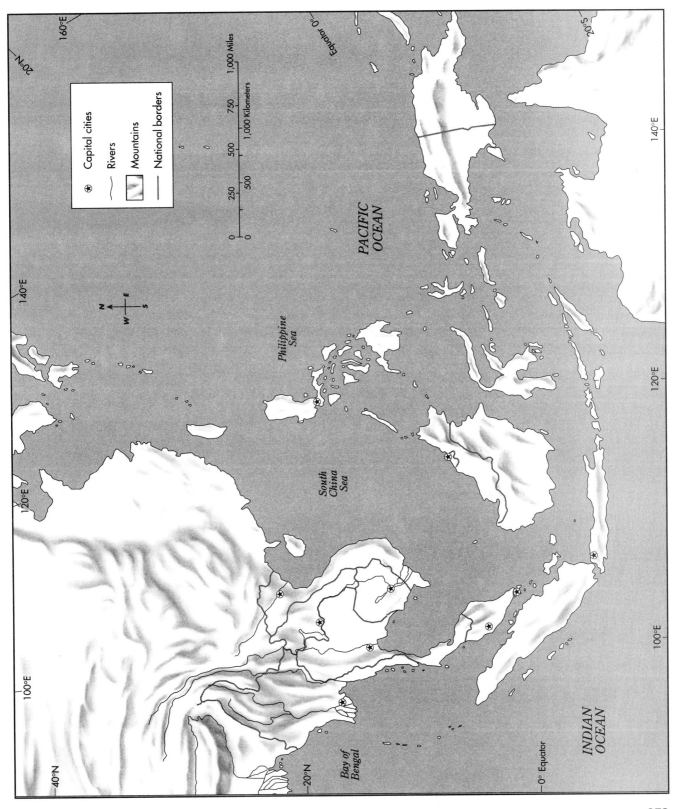

Name _____ **Date** _____

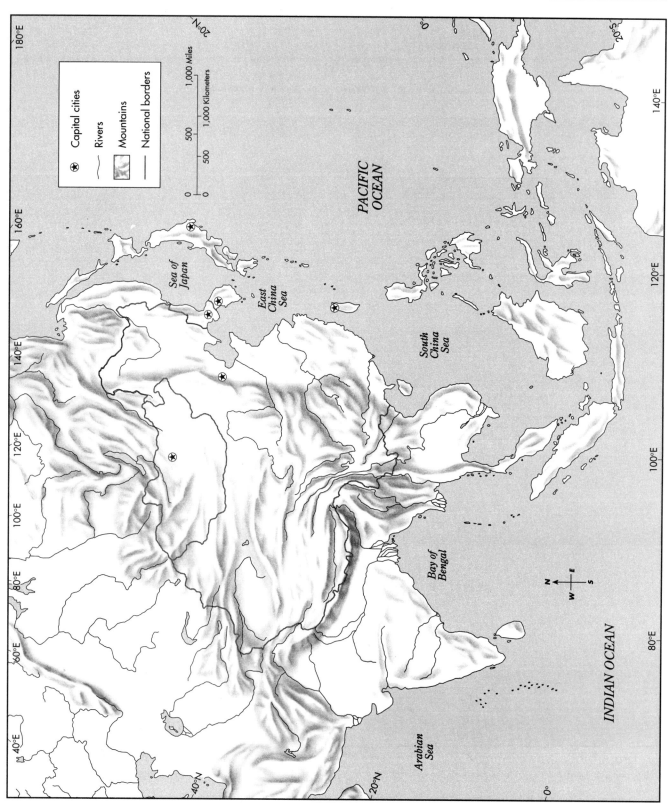

Name _____ **Date** _____

50°N
40°N
30°N
20°N

130°E
120°E
110°E
100°E
90°E
80°E
70°E

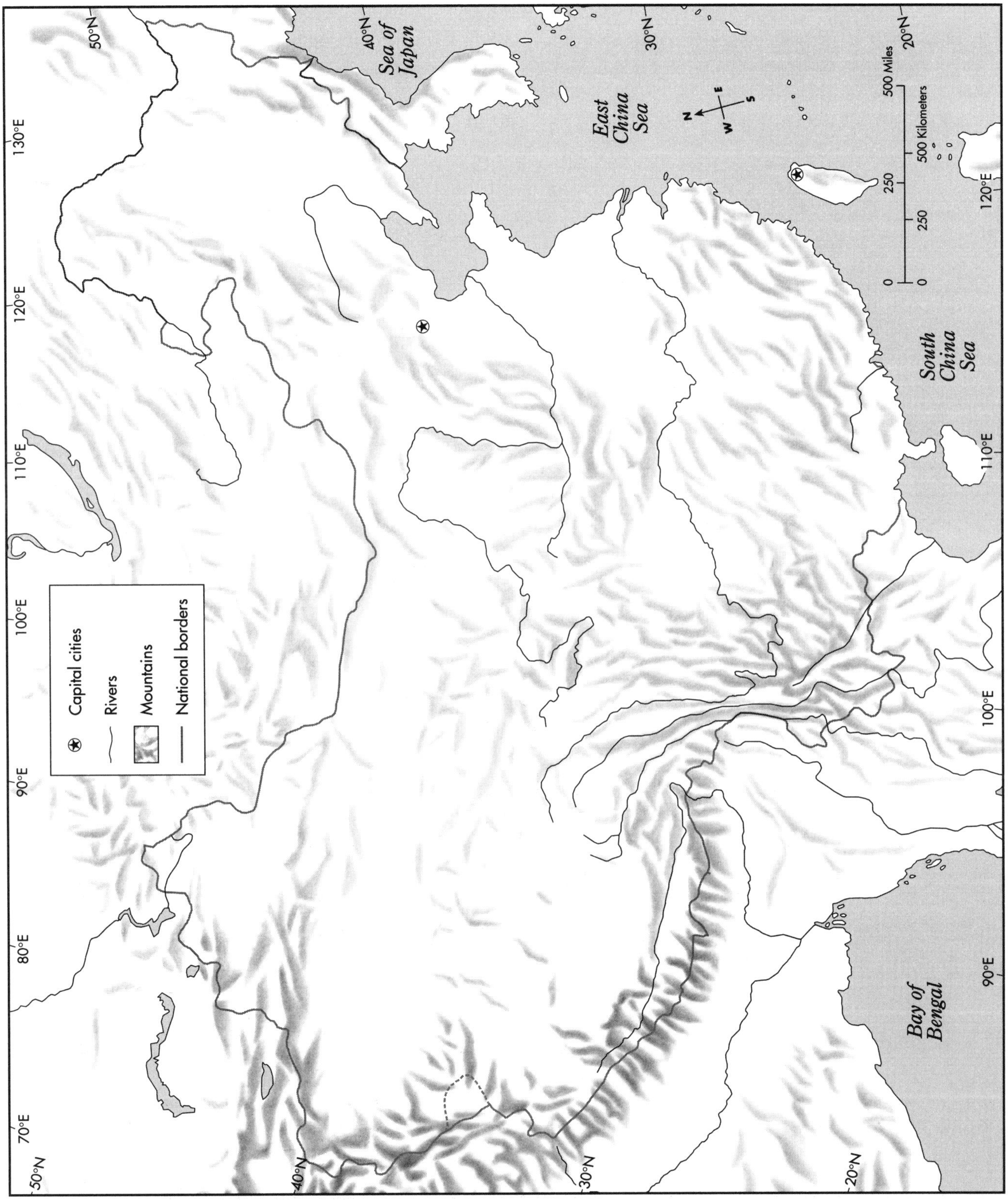

Sea of Japan

East China Sea

South China Sea

Bay of Bengal

N
E
S
W

500 Miles
500 Kilometers
250
250
0
0

Capital cities
Rivers
Mountains
National borders

50°N
40°N
30°N
20°N

120°E
110°E
100°E
90°E

Name _____   **Date** _____

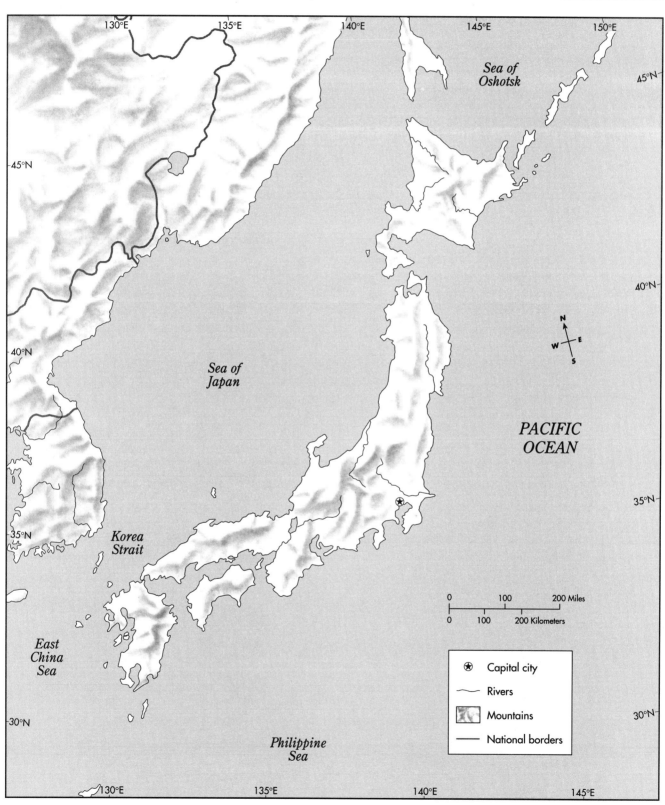

Sea of Okhotsk

Sea of Japan

PACIFIC OCEAN

Korea Strait

East China Sea

Philippine Sea

⊛	Capital city
◠	Rivers
▨	Mountains
—	National borders

0   100   200 Miles
0   100   200 Kilometers

Name _____   **Date** _____

Korea Bay

Yellow Sea

Sea of Japan

Korea Strait

East China Sea

Legend

★ Capital city

～ Rivers

▦ Mountains

— National borders

0 — 75 — 150 Miles
0 — 75 — 150 Kilometers

N W E S

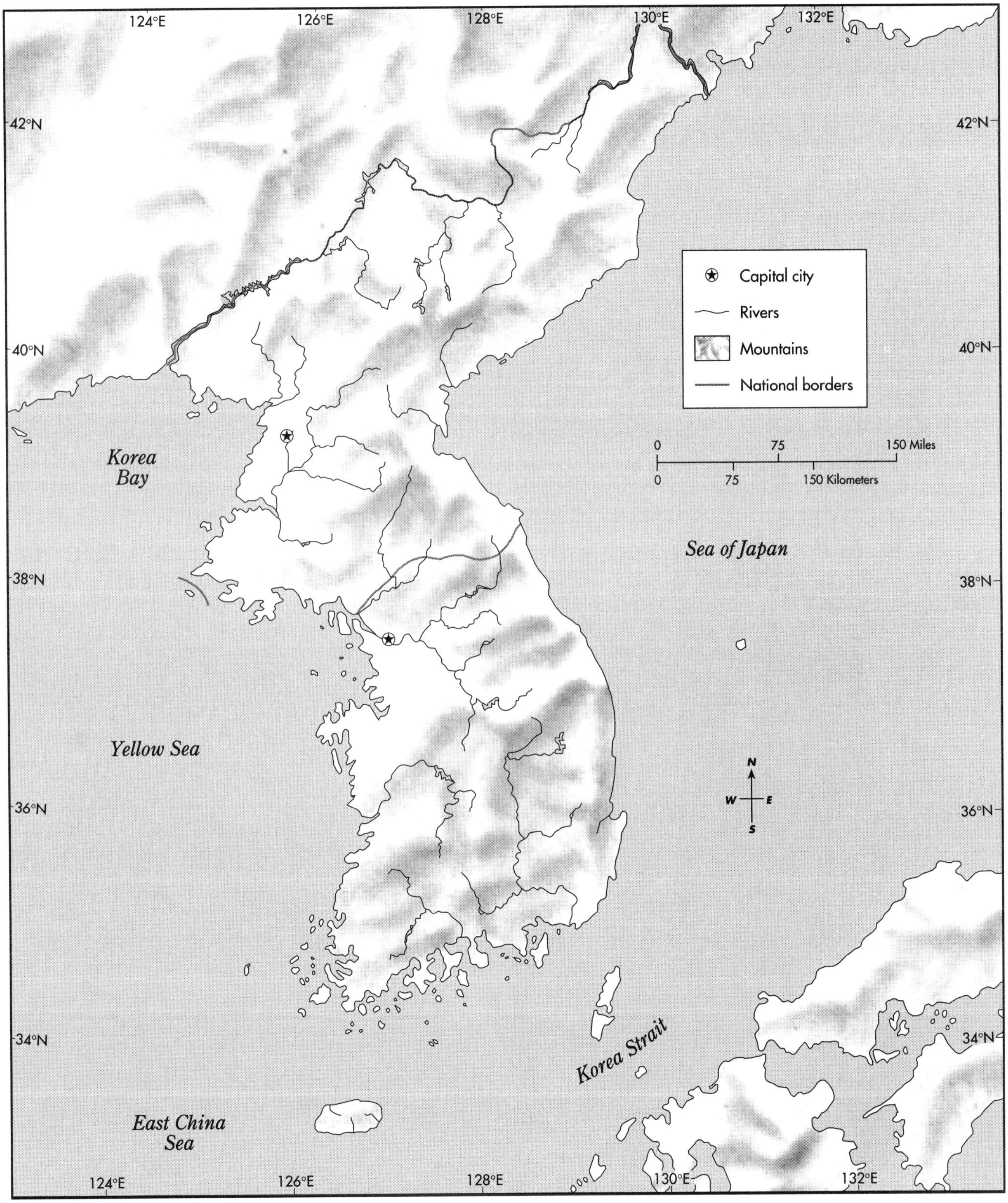

Name _____ **Date** _____

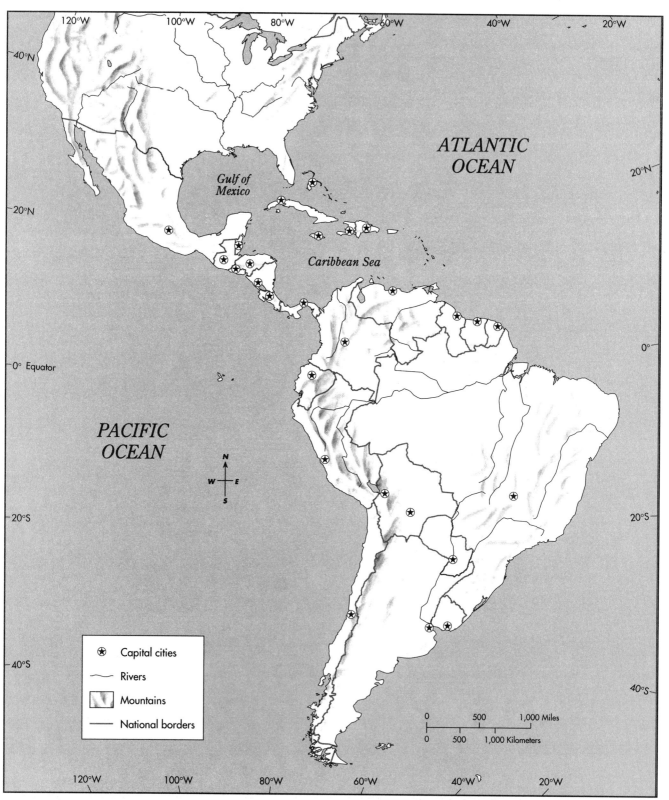

ATLANTIC
OCEAN

Gulf of
Mexico

Caribbean Sea

PACIFIC
OCEAN

N
W   E
S

⊛	Capital cities
—	Rivers
	Mountains
—	National borders

0   500   1,000 Miles

0   500   1,000 Kilometers

Name _____ **Date** _____

Caribbean Sea

ATLANTIC OCEAN

Equator 0°

PACIFIC OCEAN

80°W 60°W 40°W

0°

20°S

40°S

20°S

40°S

N
W — E
S

⊛	Capital cities
	Rivers
	Mountains
	National borders

0	500	1,000 Miles
0	500	1,000 Kilometers

80°W 60°W 40°W 20°W

Name _____ **Date** _____

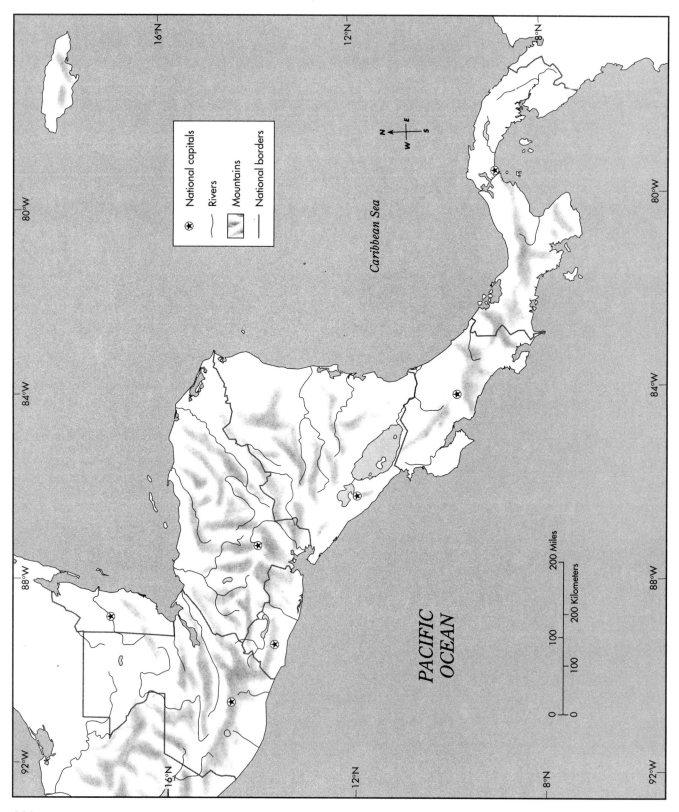

National capitals ⊛
Rivers
Mountains
National borders

Caribbean Sea

16°N
12°N
8°N

80°W
84°W
88°W
92°W

88°W
84°W
80°W

16°N
12°N
8°N

PACIFIC OCEAN

200 Miles
200 Kilometers
100
100
0
0

Name _____ Date _____

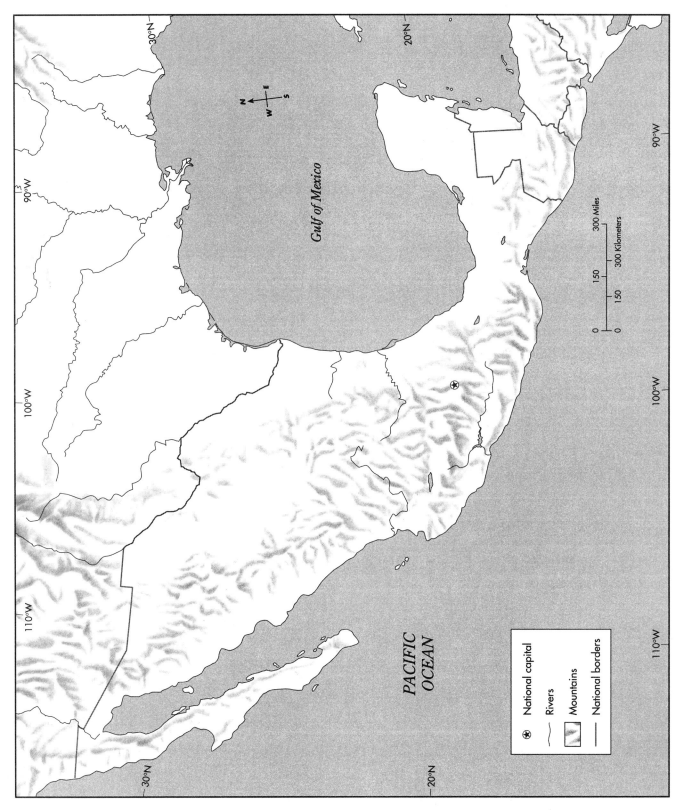

PACIFIC
OCEAN

Gulf of Mexico

National capital
Rivers
Mountains
National borders

Name _____   **Date** _____

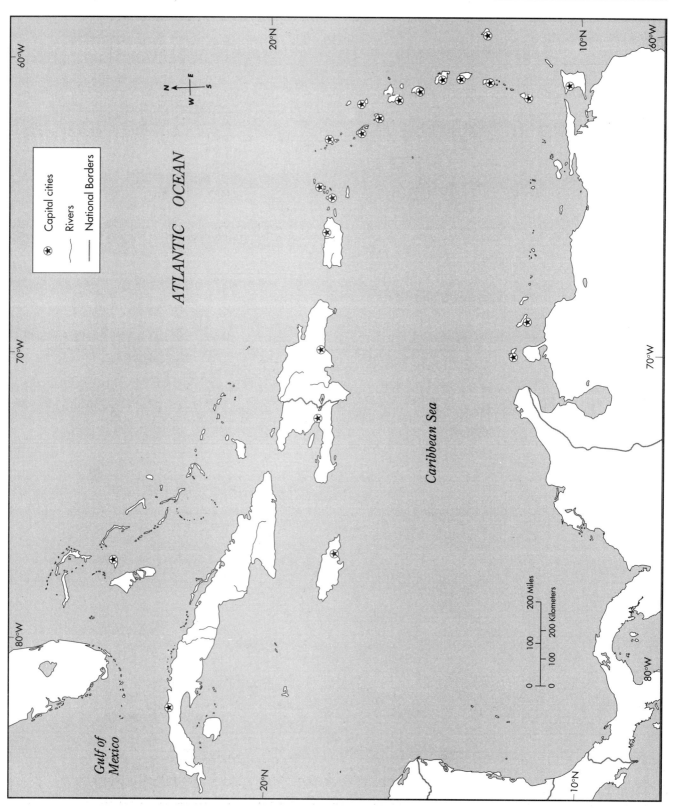

ATLANTIC OCEAN

Legend:
- ⊛ Capital cities
- Rivers
- National Borders

60°W
70°W
80°W
20°N
10°N

Caribbean Sea

Gulf of
Mexico

200 Miles
200 Kilometers
100
0

N
E
S
W

Name _____ **Date** _____

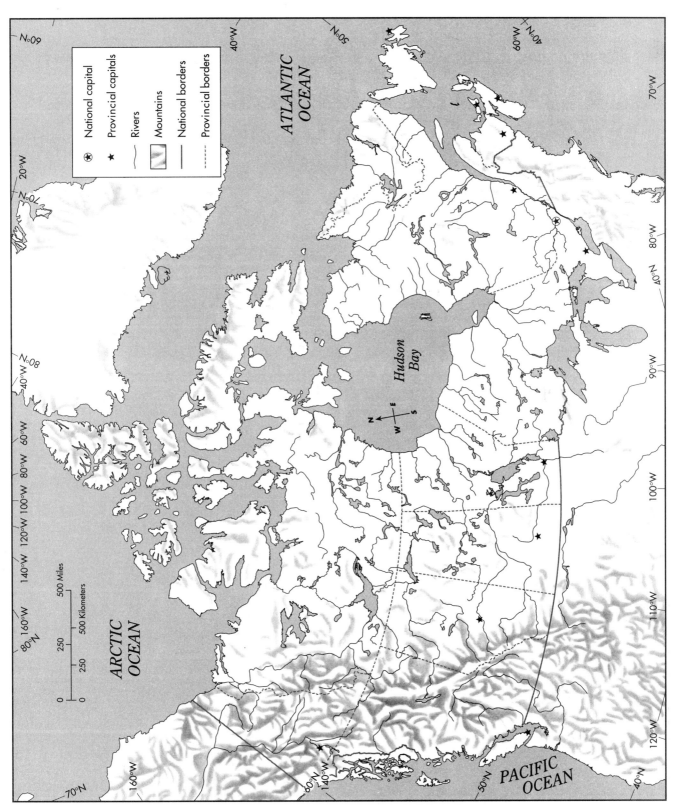

ATLANTIC
OCEAN

Hudson
Bay

ARCTIC
OCEAN

PACIFIC
OCEAN

Legend:
- National capital
- Provincial capitals
- Rivers
- Mountains
- National borders
- Provincial borders

500 Miles
500 Kilometers

Name _____ Date _____

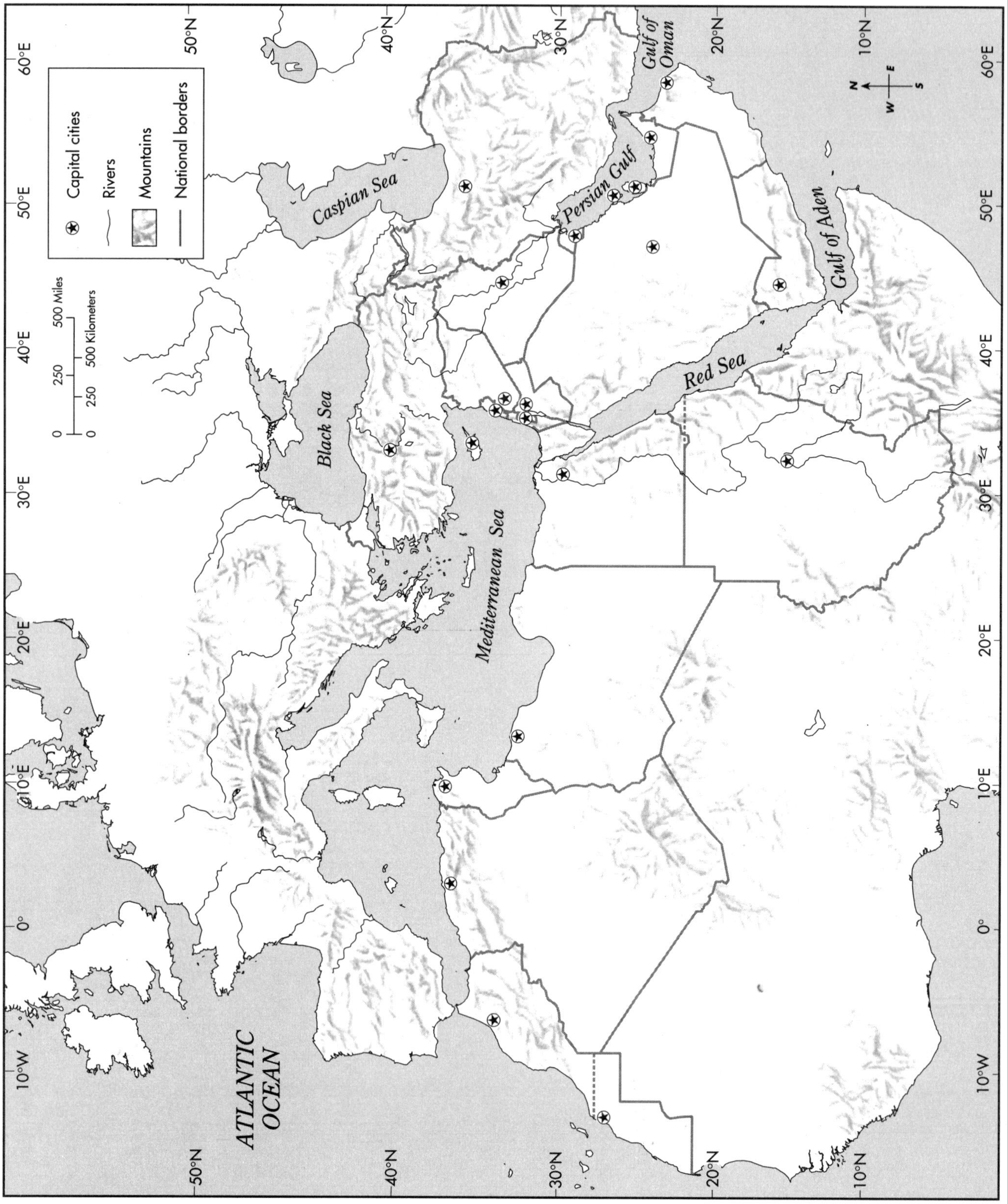

Capital cities

Rivers

Mountains

National borders

500 Miles

500 Kilometers

Caspian Sea

Black Sea

Mediterranean Sea

Persian Gulf

Gulf of Oman

Gulf of Aden

Red Sea

ATLANTIC OCEAN

Name _____ **Date** _____

Arabian
Sea

Gulf of Oman

Persian Gulf

Caspian Sea

Gulf of Aden

Red Sea

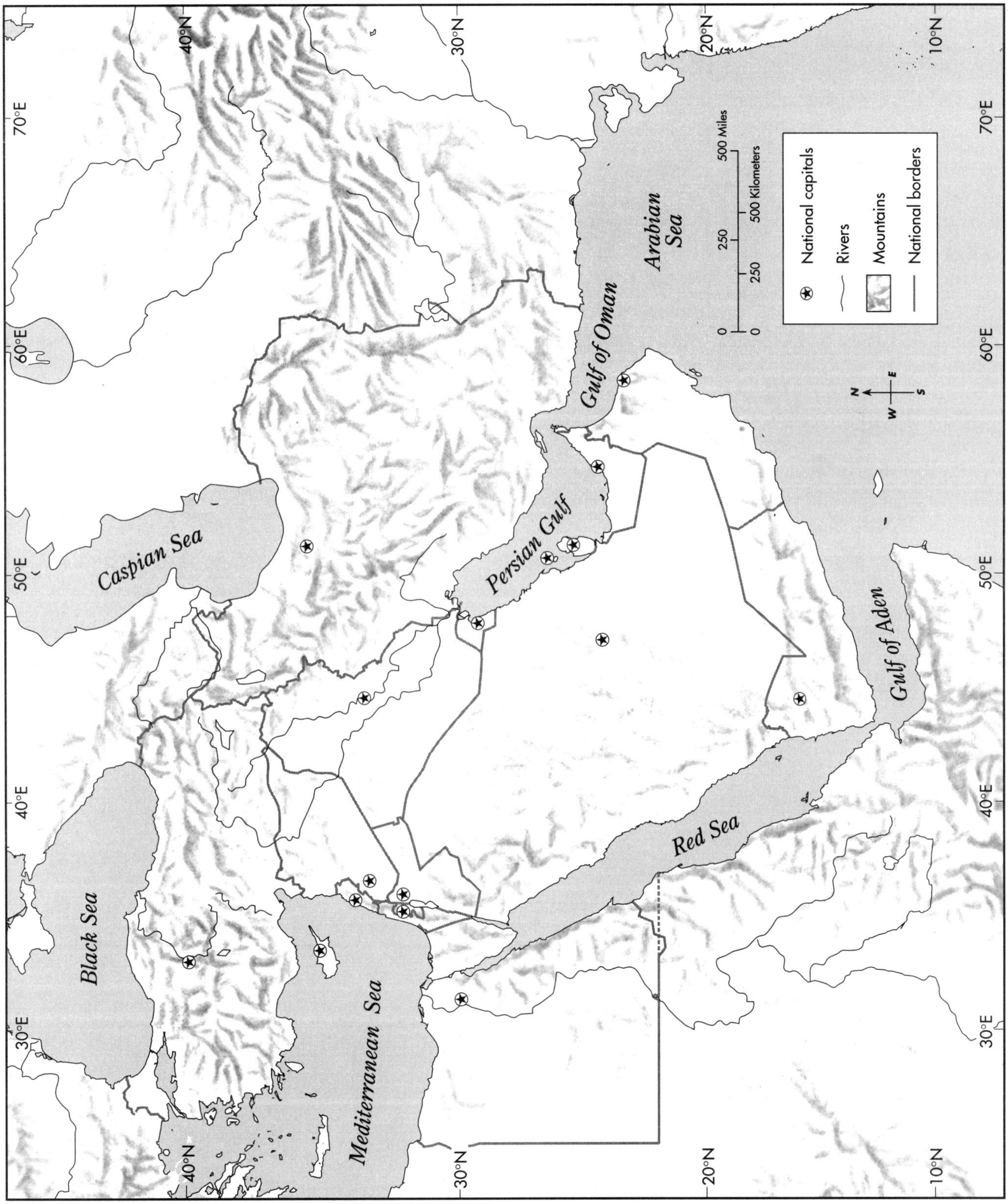

Black Sea

Mediterranean Sea

⊛	National capitals
	Rivers
	Mountains
	National borders

500 Miles

500 Kilometers

N
E
W S
S

70°E
60°E
50°E
40°E
30°E

40°N
30°N
20°N
10°N

Name _____   **Date** _____

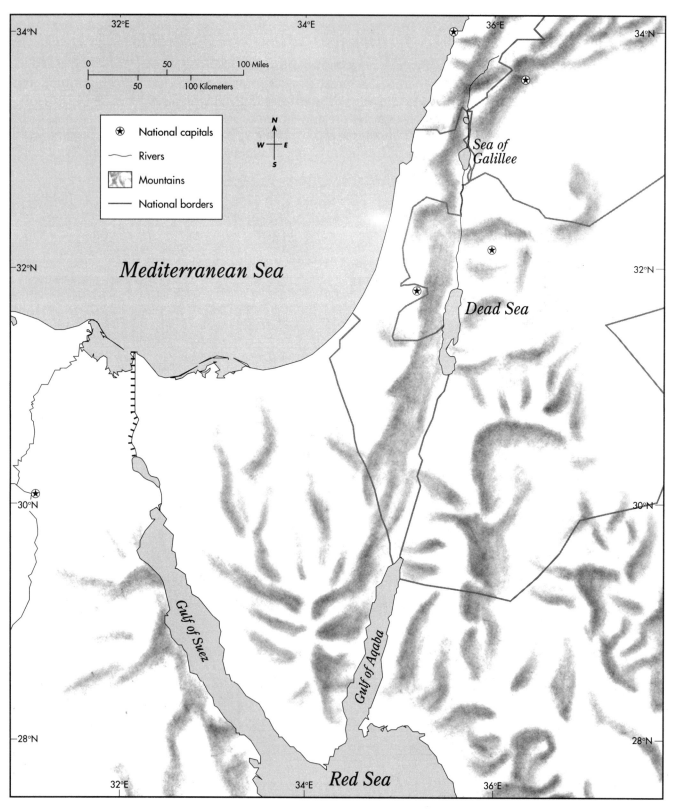

Name _____   **Date** _____

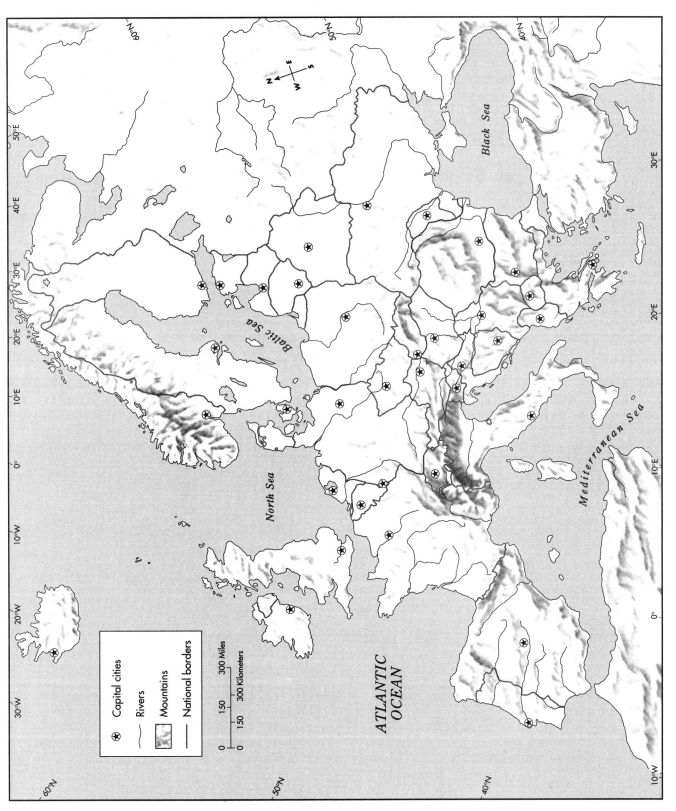

Name _____ Date _____

ARCTIC OCEAN

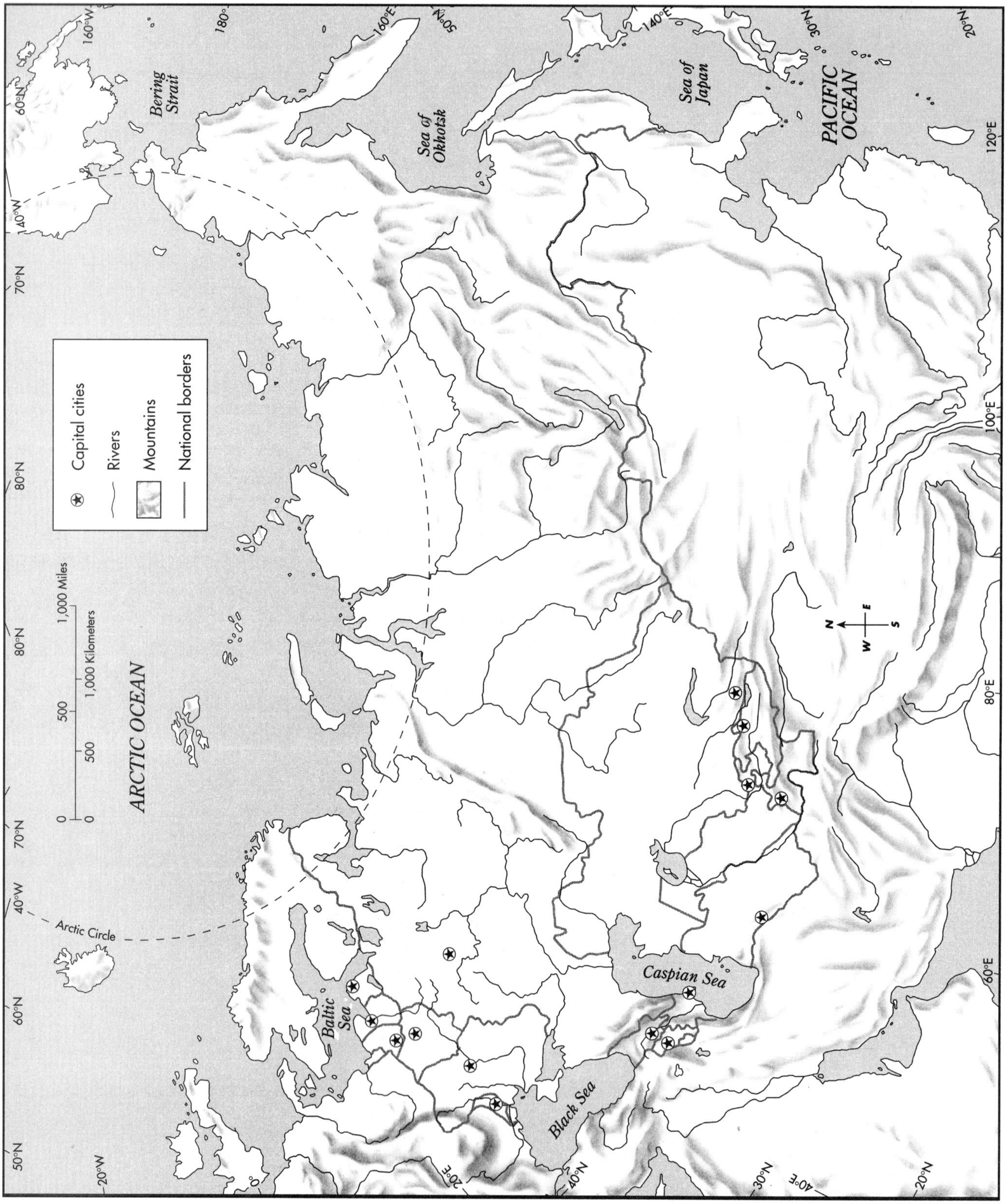

Bering Strait

Sea of Okhotsk

Sea of Japan

PACIFIC OCEAN

60°N
70°N
80°N

140°W
160°W
180°
160°E
140°E
90°E
120°E

50°N
60°N
70°N
80°N

Legend:
- ⊛ Capital cities
- Rivers
- Mountains
- National borders

1,000 Miles
1,000 Kilometers
500
500
0
0

Arctic Circle

40°W
20°W

Baltic Sea

Black Sea

Caspian Sea

30°E
40°E
60°E
80°E
100°E

20°N
30°N
40°N
50°N

288